Natural Remedies
for Healthy Living

Natural Remedies
for Healthy Living

Over 1000 Smart Solutions to Help You Live Better Today

THE READER'S DIGEST ASSOCIATION, INC.
New York / Montreal

Project Staff

PROJECT EDITOR Robert Ronald

SENIOR DESIGNER Andrée Payette

U.S. PROJECT EDITOR Barbara Booth

CONTRIBUTING EDITORS
Camilla Cornell, Jesse Corbeil

DESIGNER Olena Lytvyn

PROOFREADER Madeline Coleman

INDEXER Patricia Buchanan

TRANSLATOR Eric Bye

PRODUCTION COORDINATOR
Gillian Sylvain

MANAGER, BOOK EDITORIAL
Pamela Johnson

VICE PRESIDENT, BOOK EDITORIAL
Robert Goyette

The Reader's Digest Association, Inc.

**PRESIDENT AND
CHIEF EXECUTIVE OFFICER**
Mary G. Berner

**EXECUTIVE VICE PRESIDENT, RDA &
PRESIDENT, LIFESTYLE COMMUNITIES**
Suzanne Grimes

**EXECUTIVE VICE PRESIDENT, RDA &
PRESIDENT, READER'S DIGEST COMMUNITY**
Dan Lagani

**EXECUTIVE VICE PRESIDENT, RDA &
PRESIDENT, ALLRECIPES.COM**
Lisa Sharples

**EXECUTIVE VICE PRESIDENT, RDA &
PRESIDENT, EUROPE**
Dawn Zier

This book was first published as *Altes Wissen new entdeckt Die besten Tipps von einst fur den Alltag von heute* in 2009 by Reader's Digest—Germany, Switzerland, Austria
Verlag Das Beste GmbH—Stuttgart, Zürich, Vienna

Library and Archives Canada Cataloguing in Publication

    Traditional wisdom rediscovered: the best tips from yesteryear for daily living today / the editors of Reader's Digest.
—1st Canadian ed.
ISBN 978-1-60652-422-0
    1. House cleaning. 2. Hygiene.
I. Reader's Digest Association (Canada)

TX324.T73 2011	648' .5	C2010-907514-5

Address any comments about *Traditional Wisdom Rediscovered* to:

The Book Editors
Reader's Digest Association (Canada) ULC
1100 Rene-Levesque Blvd. West
Montreal, Quebec H3B 5H5 Canada

The Book Editors
The Reader's Digest Association, Inc.
Westchester One
44 S. Broadway
White Plains, NY 10601 U.S.A.

To order copies of *Traditional Wisdom Rediscovered* call 1-800-846-2100 in the United States and 1-800-465-0780 in Canada.

Visit us on the Web, in the United States at **rd.com**
and in Canada at **readersdigest.ca**

Printed in China

Yesterday's top tips
for today's busy lifestyles

Almost every day, new—and usually expensive—consumer products that promise to make our lives easier and simpler are introduced. But do we really need all these products? Despite their initial hoopla, few of them live up to expectations.

Our grandparents generation had abundant knowledge about how to solve everyday problems easily, inexpensively, and effectively, without running to the store—whether the problem was how to make cheese last longer, make your skin look younger, relieve toothache pain, or get your linens whiter. Wouldn't it be a shame if all that expertise was lost to future generations?

To prevent that from happening and to preserve yesterday's top tips for today's busy families, the editors at Reader's Digest gathered a wealth of traditional wisdom to create this book. *Traditional Wisdom Rediscovered* is a comprehensive collection of the best time-honored solutions from generations past. From your medicine cabinet to your freezer, your vegetable patch to your morning shower, here are clever suggestions and solutions that show you how to apply the good old ways from the good old days to improve the way we do things now.

It's not about harking back to a nostalgic past, but about presenting old-fashioned ideas in such a way that they can be easily used in today's world. It makes the wealth of our collective experience—built up over generations—accessible to people who need a helping hand today. Advice that is proven, timely, economical, and environmentally friendly.

And all these clever solutions, useful hints, practical tips, and helpful remedies from days gone by have been researched and tested for their practical applications in today's world. They offer alternatives to expensive products or the use of chemical additives and, more often than not, you'll find the ingredients right in your kitchen cabinets.

Organized into six main chapters that focus on health, beauty, home management, cooking, home decor, and the garden, this book is packed with more than 1,900 practical hints and tips our parents and grandparents trusted and relied upon. Every tip is guaranteed to help make life easier as well as less expensive. And each entry is presented alphabetically within in each chapter, making solutions a snap to find.

Traditional Wisdom Rediscovered steps back into the past to help you achieve a more rewarding way of living today—because the old ways still work best!

From the Editors of
Reader's Digest

contents

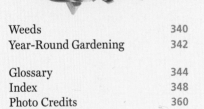

A Natural Approach to
Good Health

Today's medicine cabinets are filled with pills and potions made of chemical compounds that could have unhealthy side effects. But your grandmother knew that nature offers gentle remedies that can effectively treat minor ailments.

Acid Reflux

The searing pain of heartburn can happen after you gobble down a meal too quickly, or eat spicy, fatty, or acidic foods. It's a common complaint that's easy to combat, and if you play your cards right, you can avoid it altogether.

When stomach acid backs up into the esophagus, you feel the burning pain of acid reflux. At the first sign of heartburn, choose one of these effective home remedies.

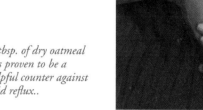

A tbsp. of dry oatmeal has proven to be a helpful counter against acid reflux..

HOME REMEDIES

▶ Try a little **baking soda.** It can be very effective at neutralizing the excess acid in your stomach (but do not use it if you have high blood pressure). Stir 1 tsp. (5 mL) into a glass of room temperature water and drink. It may not taste great, but you should feel better within minutes.

▶ Douse the flames with some **juniper berry tea.** A mixture of 1 tsp. (5 mL) of crushed berries in 1 cup (250 mL) of water provides noticeable improvement.

▶ Drink **ginger tea** to provide relief. Boil 1½ tsp. (7 mL) of fresh ginger or ½ tsp. (2 mL) of powdered ginger in 1 cup (250 mL) of water for about 10 minutes before drinking.

▶ Look for herbal relief. Mix ½ tsp. (2 mL) of **goldenseal extract** with 3 tbsp. (45 mL) water, and drink the mixture at the first sign of burning to soothe the membranes that line the upper gastrointestinal tract.

▶ Chew a **licorice tablet** before meals. Licorice protects your esophagus by encouraging the production of mucin, which provides a protective barrier against stomach acids.

▶ Season foods with **juniper berries** or **lovage,** where appropriate. They not only make food more digestible, they also soothe heartburn.

▶ Eat a piece of **dry white bread** or **toast** to neutralize stomach acids.

▶ Sleep with your **upper body slightly elevated** at night to keep acid from entering your esophagus.

PREVENTION

▶ Eat knowledgeably and avoid foods, drinks, and combinations that you know from experience give you heartburn. These may include such things as **fatty** or **acidic foods, chocolate** and **wine.**

▶ Avoid **alcohol, nicotine,** and **caffeine**—they allow the sphincter muscle of your stomach to slacken and thus facilitate heartburn.

▶ Eat slowly and always opt for **smaller, more frequent portions.**

▶ Go easy on **sweets.**

▶ **Eat early in the evening** to give your stomach about three hours for digestion. If you go to bed shortly after eating, the stomach acid can flow back into your esophagus.

▶ Consult a doctor if you're a frequent victim of heartburn.

Drink a glass of fresh carrot juice to soothe heartburn.

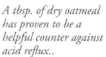

good to know

CAUSES OF ACID REFLUX

When the contents of your stomach flow back into your esophagus they cause a burning pain behind the breastbone and in the esophagus. A trapdoor of muscular tissue called the lower esophageal sphincter usually keeps stomach acid where it belongs. With heartburn, it allows acid to leak upward, a problem known as reflux.

Acne

Zits are the bane of many an adolescent's existence. But those pesky eruptions don't just occur during puberty. About four in every five adults between the ages of 20 and 30 suffer mild to moderate acne, and over half of all women, regardless of age, get pimples or blackheads.

The causes of acne vary: from hormonal changes that lead to elevated sebum production and plugged sebaceous glands, to sun exposure, medications, and oil-based cosmetics. Long before people had access to a wide range of drugstore pills and potions, they were treating breakouts with a range of masks and tinctures made from natural active ingredients. The most important thing to remember: don't squeeze blackheads and pimples, or you could be left with unsightly scars.

HOME REMEDIES

▶ Apply a healing mask. Mix together 3 tbsp. (45 mL) of **healing earth or fuller's earth** (available at health food stores) with an equal amount of water to produce a thick paste. Leave plenty of space around your eyes when applying it. After 30 minutes, rinse off the mask thoroughly with warm water. Use three times a week.

▶ Try this recipe: mix together 2 tbsp. (25 mL) of **yogurt** and one tbsp. (15 mL) of **honey** and spread on your face and neck. The yogurt has a cooling effect, and honey disinfects. Rinse with warm water after 30 minutes. Apply three times a week.

▶ Dilute **tea tree oil** or a **pot marigold (calendula) tincture** with water in a 1:4 proportion, and apply with a cotton swab to quickly heal pimples and blackheads.

▶ Squeeze **fresh plantain leaves** (the herb, not the banana) with a juice extractor or crush with a pestle, then dab the juice directly onto blackheads and pimples with a cotton swab.

▶ Drink about 1–2 cups (250–500 mL) of **stinging nettle tea** (available at health food stores) every day. It detoxifies blood and promotes skin healing.

▶ Take a **chamomile** facial twice a week to open your pores. Pour boiling water over chamomile flowers and position your face over the steam for 5 minutes.

TO CLEANSE THE SKIN

▶ Soap is too harsh for acne-prone skin, but **soap-free cleansers** with a pH of 5.5 (that matches the skin's acid-protection coating) can soothe and protect.

▶ Follow up by treating oily skin and acne-prone areas of your face with small amounts of **facial toner containing alcohol**.

one Peel a papaya, remove all the seeds, and puree the fruit.

two Stir 2–3 tbsp. (25–45 mL) of plain yogurt into the pureed fruit.

three Apply the puree to a compress, place it onto your face, and leave on for 30 minutes.

four Rinse off the blemish-fighting papaya mask with warm water.

A homemade mask cleanses your skin of grease and sebum, removes dead skin cells, and leaves skin toned and tightened.

Back Pain

Too much time spent slumped in front of a television and computer can put our musculoskeletal systems at risk. In our grandparents' time, good posture was considered a sign of moral superiority—hence the term "upright citizen." Today, it's still one of the best ways to prevent back pain.

If you want to do your back some good, as well as lose some weight, you need to be physically active. Strengthening your muscles takes pressure off your joints and tendons. If you think you need special back-conditioning exercises designed to improve flexibility and strenthen the muscles that help support your spine, join a gym to ensure that you have expert instruction and supervision—and so you don't risk injury.

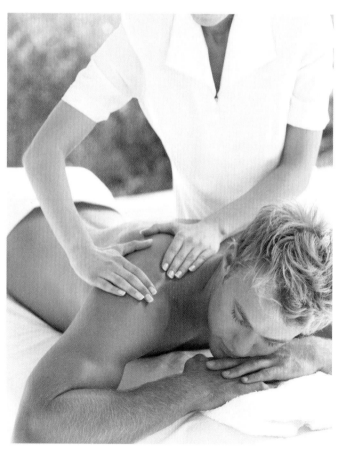

A gentle back massage relaxes muscles cramped by back pain. Use a massage oil containing lavender, rosemary, and ginger oils.

HOME REMEDIES

If you're experiencing acute back pain, a short period of bed rest is okay, but more than a couple of days will do you more harm than good. Then, as soon as possible, get moving again. Get some gentle exercise (e.g., bicycling or swimming) to improve circulation and prevent further problems.

▶ Apply heat to a sore back. Good choices include **hay flower wraps** warmed over steam; compresses with **rosemary** or **thyme tea**; warmed **cherry-pit** or **spelt bags**; **heat packs** (available in pharmacies); or **infrared light treatment**. *(Note: the benefits of cherry-pit bags were discovered during the manufacture of Kirsch liqueur. Workers found that if they put the leftover cherry pits in bags and warmed them, the soothing heat relieved their aches and pains.)*

▶ Relax tense muscles and promote circulation with **moor mud** and **sulfur baths**.

▶ Take hot oil baths with **rosemary** or **thyme extracts** to soothe pain, followed by massages with hand-warmed **tulipwood oil**.

▶ Bathe in a **natural hot spring**. It can be equally as good for your psyche as for your back.

▶ Rub your back with **spirits of lemon balm**. To prepare: steep 7 oz. (200 g) of fresh lemon balm leaves for ten days in 1 tightly sealed quart/liter of rubbing alcohol in a warm place. Strain and dilute with water in a 4:1 proportion.

▶ Fight pain with **St. John's wort oil**: ask a friend or significant other to gently massage your back using a small amount of oil.

▶ Try a **hot wheat pack**. Boil about 2 lb. (1 kg) of wheat grains until soft. Put the hot mix into a linen bag, and let it rest on your sore back for 15 minutes.

▶ Take a therapeutic seawater bath. Widely accepted in Europe since the 19th century, **thalassotherapy** is a treatment whose main components are algae, littoral deposits, and sea salt. It is available in health food stores and pharmacies.

▶ Place a **thick cushion** under your legs at night so that your thighs point straight up and your knees are bent at a right angle in order to take strain off your spinal column.

Pilates exercises help reduce acute back pain.

hot roll

one Fold a thick towel lengthwise and roll it up into a funnel. Wrap some more cloths around the funnel.

two Pour boiling water into the top of the funnel.

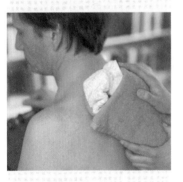

three Hold the hot roll wrapped in a dry cloth by the edges and have someone carefully massage your back with it.

PREVENTION

▸ Don't carry lopsided loads. Lift heavy weights only with **bent knees**, and always keep your back straight.

▸ **Keep your back warm.** Avoid exposing your back area to cold and draft.

▸ Replace **saggy mattresses** and don't pinch pennies when you buy a new one: it should be made from high-quality materials and should be neither too hard or too soft.

▸ Avoid sitting in **chairs without proper back support.** Replace old, worn-out chairs.

▸ Use a **wedge pillow** to encourage erect posture while sitting.

▸ If you have a sedentary occupation, change your **sitting position** frequently, and stand up and stretch every 30 minutes.

▸ Avoid high heels. Wear **comfortable shoes** as often as possible.

WHAT IS LUMBAGO?

Lumbago is actually a blanket term for pain in the lower back (or lumbar region) rather than a medical diagnosis. But it differs from "normal" back pain because it happens suddenly. A cold draft, jerky movement, or combination of bending and twisting can trigger an abrupt pain deep in your back muscles. However, a slipped disc also has similar symptoms; if you don't feel better after a few days, consult a doctor. Here are some remedies:

▸ Try a back massage with a **hot roll** (see box at right). As soon as the outer layer of the roll cools off, set it aside and begin the massage.

▸ Moist heat is particularly helpful for lumbago. To make a wrap, mix together 10 drops of **lavender oil**, 8 drops each of **chamomile oil** and **cedar oil**, plus 4 drops each of **juniper oil** and **clary sage oil** with 7 oz. (200 g) of **body lotion**. Dribble 2 tbsp. (25 mL) of the mixture onto a cloth soaked in hot water—and wrung out—and apply to the painful area. Spread a dry cloth over it and cover with a wool blanket. Repeat several times daily.

▸ A **verbena wrap** soothes all kinds of back pains, including lumbago. Stir together a handful of verbena with one egg yolk, 1 tbsp. (15 mL) of flour, and 2 tbsp. (25 mL) of warm water. Fold a cotton towel to fit the size of the painful area. Sprinkle with the verbena mixture, place it over a pot lid, and warm it over steam. Place a **hot spelt cushion** onto an exercise mat, spread the cotton cloth over it (with the verbena facing upward), and carefully lie down with your lower back on it. Cover up with a blanket and lie as long as possible on the hot underlay.

▸ **Large adhesive bandages** used with compounds like **capsaicin** that stimulate circulation can continue to warm the muscles for a long time.

Bladder and Kidney Problems

Liquids are extremely important when it comes to the proper functioning of the bladder and kidneys. They require plenty of water and other fluids in order to rid your body of harmful waste products and fend off bacteria. Lack of fluids may result in a bladder infection or kidney stones.

medicinal hay flower sitz bath

one Mix 2 handfuls of medicinal hay flowers with 4 quarts/liters of water and heat the mixture.

two Simmer for 30 minutes, strain, and add to a sitz bath.

BLADDER WEAKNESS AND INCONTINENCE

Do you map out the bathrooms in the mall before you get there? Or avoid sneezing or laughing because you're not sure you'll stay dry? You're most likely suffering from bladder weakness or incontinence. Both men and women suffer from this sometimes embarrassing condition, but the physical stresses of childbirth, combined with a decrease in estrogen at menopause, make women three times more susceptible.

Frequently, there's a psychological component to a weak bladder, so stress-reduction programs such as yoga or autogenic training may help.

The good news: the problem isn't new—even the ancient Egyptians developed remedies to deal with it. Read on for a variety of time-tested teas to strengthen your bladder muscles.

▶ **Blueberry tea** is a tried and true remedy for a weak bladder. Mix 2/3 oz. (20 g) of blueberry leaves with about 1 cup (250 mL) of water and drink three times a day.

▶ **St. John's wort** sweetened with **honey** can ease tension, which may in turn help with incontinence. Drink 1 cup twice a day for five weeks.

▶ For an effective three-week bladder cure, drink this tea three times a day: mix 1½ oz. (50 g) of **lady's mantle**, 1 oz. (30 g) of **fireweed**, and 2/3 oz. (20 g) of **fennel seeds**. Pour 1 cup (250 mL) of boiling water over 1 tsp. (5 mL) of this mixture and steep for 10 minutes before drinking.

▶ Never underestimate the healing power of heat. Our grandmothers were familiar with its soothing properties and regularly took **sitz baths with hay flowers** (see box at left), or placed a hot water bottle on their lower abdomen at bedtime. Both are simple, effective remedies that still work today.

PREVENT KIDNEY STONES

It's often been said that the pain of passing a kidney stone is comparable to that of giving birth. Stones might pass in a few hours, but sometimes it takes days. It's best to try to avoid developing kidney stones in the first place.

Dehydration is a key factor in kidney stone formation. Lack of fluids prevents mineral salts in urine from being dissolved, causing them to clump together as grit and slowly form kidney stones. To ensure your kidneys are well-irrigated and healthy, drink plenty of herbal and fruit teas, non-carbonated water, and diluted fruit juice.

Here are some pointers:

▶ If you have a tendency toward kidney problems, avoid **apple** and **grapefruit juices**, which can increase the risk of kidney stone formation.

▶ **Milk, beer, wine**, and **coffee**, contrary to popular belief, actually reduce the danger of kidney stones. But don't take that as an invitation to tipple—both alcohol and coffee have other harmful side effects.

▶ **Salt, sugar**, and **meat** can aggravate kidney stone formation. Consume them in moderation.

HOME REMEDIES

If grit or small stones have already formed in your kidney, home remedies may help flush them out.

▶ Flush out small stones with diuretic teas made from **birch leaves, goldenrod**, or **marshmallow root. Kombucha** (available at health food stores) has the same effect. This cold drink is fermented using what's known as the kombucha or tea mush-

To keep your bladder and kidneys healthy, drink about 2 quarts/liters of liquid a day.

Bladder Tea

This tea soothes pain, disinfects, and flushes out bacteria when you have a bladder infection. Mix together:

1½ oz. (50 g) bearberry leaves
½ oz. (15 g) green beans
½ oz. (15 g) horsetail
⅙ oz. (5 g) each of fennel, pot marigold blooms, and peppermint

Boil 1 tsp. (5 mL) of this mixture with 1 cup (250 mL) of cold water for 5 minutes. Steep for 10 minutes, strain and drink 1 cup three times daily.

room and contains live bacteria and yeast, similar to yogurt.

▶ Drink lots of water (2.5–3 quarts/liters per day). Sip flushing teas (such as **birch**, **goldenrod**, and **bearberry**) for three days after onset.

▶ If your kidney stones are causing pain, try a **potato wrap** made from boiled, mashed, and still-hot potatoes wrapped in cloth. Place it over the kidney area. The warmth will soothe your afflicted organs, as will exposure to infrared light or a hot bath.

▶ If you're experiencing **serious pain** in the kidney region and/or a buildup of urine, contact your doctor immediately.

TREATING A BLADDER INFECTION

About 50 percent of all women will experience a bladder infection at some point in their lives and many will have multiple infections. Women suffer from the problem more often than men because

their urethra is shorter, so bacteria can enter the bladder more easily. Often dehydration is a factor. Our grandmothers called on a host of home remedies to combat pain and the continual urge to urinate—but keep in mind, these remedies are most effective when applied early. If your bladder infection is not noticeably better after three days, consult a doctor.

▶ **Hot herbal tea** can help flush out the bacteria causing inflammation, and soothe pain.

▶ Acidic juices such as **cranberry, blueberry**, and **currant juice** lower the pH in your urine, making it harder for bacteria to multiply.

▶ A tbsp. (15 mL) of **pumpkin seeds** provides natural pain relief when you munch on them three times a day.

▶ Heat reduces the pain. Place a warm **spelt** or **cherry-pit bag** between your legs and/or over your bladder, or soak in a nice, hot bath.

Blood Pressure

Age, weight gain, lack of exercise, smoking, and alcohol abuse are just a few of the lifestyle factors that can subject your heart and circulatory system to tremendous strain. That, in turn, causes damage to your blood vessels, sending your blood pressure soaring. The good news: it's never too late to do something about it!

Regular exercise and gentle endurance sports such as bicycling, Nordic walking, and swimming can help both low and high blood pressure.

HIGH BLOOD PRESSURE

High blood pressure is one of the main risk factors for heart attack and stroke. Check your blood pressure regularly and seek medical treatment if it consistently measures high (140/90 and above).

Many plants contain ingredients that can effectively lower blood pressure, relax the muscles of your blood vessels, and have a calming effect on your nervous system. With a little help from nature, it's easy to bring slightly elevated blood pressure under control, or complement conventional medical therapy if your blood pressure is very high.

HOME REMEDIES

▶ Brew up. **Mistletoe**, **hawthorn**, and **arnica** have long been used to regulate blood pressure. These can be used individually for making tea, or as part of a tea blend.

▶ Try this recipe for **olive tea** from the Mediterranean: Pour about 1 cup (250 mL) of boiling water over 2 tsp. (10 mL) of dried, minced olive leaves, steep for 10 minutes, and strain. Press 3 garlic cloves and mix into the tea with 1 tsp. (5 mL) of honey.

▶ A daily glass of **fresh pineapple juice** or a serving of fresh pineapple can help get blood pressure under control. The fruit contains an enzyme called bromelain, which reduces plaque buildup on the walls of the blood vessels and opens them up again.

▶ Take a shot. In a clear bottle, pour **red wine** over 4 oz. (120 g) of minced **Salvia miltiorrhiza (red sage or Chinese sage) roots**. Let steep in a warm place for one month, then strain and pour into a dark bottle. Drink a shot glass (no more) morning and evening.

▶ Eat plenty of **bear's garlic,** one of the oldest medicinal herbs known to man. The tasty but odorless plant contains substances, like adenosine, that lower blood pressure. Use its leaves to give a boost to salads, in pesto, or on pasta.

▶ Chew a clove of garlic every day, or add to salads and other dishes. Raw **garlic** and **onions** keep your blood vessels elastic and lower blood pressure.

NUTRITION FOR HIGH BLOOD PRESSURE

▶ In April, May, and June chow down on fresh **asparagus**. This vegetable acts as a natural diuretic and can lower blood pressure by getting rid of elevated salt levels and water.

▶ Reduce salt consumption as much as possible as too much salt raises blood pressure. Season your food with **fresh herbs** instead.

▶ Avoid **alcohol**, **nicotine**, and **coffee**, as they increase blood pressure.

▶ Eat fresh ocean fish once a week, such as **mackerel** or **salmon**, which contain valuable fatty acids that lower blood pressure.

▶ Use **plant oils** for cooking and frying.

▶ Use **butter** or **margarine** sparingly, especially if you are predisposed to high blood pressure or lipid metabolic disorder.

▶ Cut out fat, but eat plenty of **fruit, vegetables,** and **whole-grain products.**

Nuts contain fatty acids that reduce blood pressure.

Regular exercise, such as hiking, improves low blood pressure.

LOW BLOOD PRESSURE

Fatigue and exhaustion are typical symptoms of excessively low blood pressure (systolic values under 100 mmHg for women and 110 mmHg for men). It is not a threat to your health, but can be an obstacle to well-being.

HOME REMEDIES

▶ Pump up the **fluids**. Dehydration reduces blood volume, which can lead to low blood pressure.

▶ Drink **black tea**. It's a stimulant, so don't let it steep for longer than 3-5 minutes.

▶ Knock back a shot glass of **rosemary wine** with a meal at midday and in the evening to get your blood vessels into shape in a jiffy. To make it, pour about 25 oz. (750 mL) of white wine over 2/3 oz. (20 g) of rosemary leaves. Strain and bottle after five days.

▶ Indulge your sweet tooth with **licorice**. But just one small piece a day, since the active ingredient in it, glycyrrhizin, can have undesirable side effects in large quantities.

▶ Sleep with your **upper body slightly elevated** to stimulate circulation and make it easier to rise and shine.

▶ Soak 30 **raisins** in water overnight. Raisins can do wonders for blood pressure. Eat the raisins in the morning, and then drink the raisin water.

▶ Alternate **hot and cold water** during your morning shower. This practice has long been a tradition in some parts of Europe. It forces your blood vessels to contract then expand, and helps blood pressure return to normal. Begin with warm water. After 2 minutes, turn the temperature to cold for 15 seconds, and repeat the procedure three times. Always end with cold water.

▶ Get moving. All physical activity increases blood pressure, so you can benefit from a regime of light exercise, as well as activities such as **walking, swimming** or **cycling**. However, you should first clear your exercise program with your doctor.

brush massage

one Massage may help those with hypertension to cope with stress. Start with a natural-bristle brush on the back of your right foot and brush your right leg up to the buttock in circular motions—first on the outside, then on the inside.

two Repeat on the left leg.

three Brush your buttocks, upper body, and arms.

four Finally, have someone massage your back in circular motions.

Breath

Halitosis is unpleasant. Luckily, much can be done to prevent it. If you've failed the breath test, and people back away when you stop to chat, rely on these remedies from the herb garden to quickly freshen your breath.

You usually can't tell if you have bad breath, and people are often reluctant to point it out. To quickly test your breath, hold your cupped hands in front of your mouth, exhale into them, and quickly move your hands to your nose to check the exhaled breath.

HOME REMEDIES

▶ Use mouthwash regularly after brushing your teeth: add a couple of drops of **chamomile**, **peppermint**, **sage**, or **lemon balm oil** to a glass of water and rinse your mouth with it.

▶ For morning breath, **rinse** your mouth with **cider vinegar** (1 tsp/5 mL in a glass of water) right after getting out of bed.

▶ For continuing bad breath, chew **parsley or mint leaves**—both will quickly freshen your breath.

anise mouthwash

one Bring 2 tbsp. (25 mL) of anise seeds to a boil in about 3½ oz. (100 mL) of water and let cool.

two Strain the mixture through a coffee filter and squeeze out the seeds.

three. Mix the remaining liquid with about ¼ cup (50 mL) of vodka and about ¼ cup (50 mL) of rose water and pour the solution into a dark bottle.

four After brushing your teeth, put a dash of the mouthwash into a glass of water and rinse your mouth thoroughly.

▶ If stomach problems have resulted in bad breath, try an old trusted home remedy. **Chewing a coffee bean** neutralizes the acid smell. Be sure to spit it out when you are done.

▶ Mix together **dill**, **anise**, and **fennel seeds** and occasionally chew a few of them.

▶ Both **apples** and **yogurt** taste very good, freshen your breath, and offer a healthy snack.

▶ When you are on the go, suck on **peppermint** or **eucalyptus candies**.

People who regularly gargle with lemon water avoid bad breath and a dry mouth.

PREVENTION

If digestive disorders or gum disease are the root cause of your halitosis, only a visit to the doctor will fix the problem. But if your dragon breath is caused by faulty hygiene or diet, it is best cured through consistent, gentle treatment.

In addition to brushing regularly, clean the spaces between your teeth with dental floss and a dental water jet.

▶ Eat and drink on a **regular schedule**—halitosis often occurs when your stomach is empty.

▶ People who eat **yogurt** regularly are less prone to halitosis than people who do not.

Burns and Scalds

Burns are the result of direct contact with a hot object, fire, or electrical current. Although scalds are produced by hot fluids or steam, treatment should be the same as for burns.

There are major distinctions between first-, second-, and third-degree burns. Only first-degree burns and scalds should be treated by home remedies. Otherwise, see a doctor immediately.

First-degree burns are characterized by reddened, painful skin, but the injury can be treated effectively with natural remedies (assuming you don't have an open wound).

WHEN TO SEE A DOCTOR

More serious burns (blisters start forming with second-degree burns), large burns (larger than a silver dollar on an adult), and burns on children or individuals older than 60 require immediate medical attention. Second- and third-degree burns that cause blistering and tissue damage are very serious; they have a high risk of becoming infected by germs that enter the body through the damaged skin.

HOME REMEDIES

▶ Make a simple compress by dabbing a little **St. John's wort oil** (from a pharmacy) onto a linen cloth folded several times and place this with the oily side on your skin for at least 30 minutes. Hold in place with a gauze bandage.

▶ Put 5–8 drops of **tea tree** or **lavender oil** onto a gauze bandage, apply to the burn, and let it work for several hours.

▶ Apply **pot marigold salve** to the burn. It can be a blessing to damaged skin.

▶ Cool the burn by applying salves containing **aloe vera** which encourages skin regeneration.

▶ Take **vitamin C** to build and maintain healthy new skin. **Fresh saue rkraut**—a traditional German burn remedy rich in vitamin C—can be applied directly to your burn.

▶ Rinse **white cabbage leaves** and remove the central vein. Roll the leaves with a rolling pin until soft, place them onto your burned skin, and secure with a gauze bandage. Change the bandage after several hours (replace twice a day).

▶ For healing without scars, pour 6 cups (1.5 liters) of water over 1 tbsp. (15 mL) of **flaxseeds**. Boil until scum forms on the surface, then strain and let cool. Soak a linen cloth in the broth, wring it out, and apply to the injury.

▶ Cool the burn by applying a **milk** compress for 15 minutes.

To cool your skin, reduce the pain, and clean the wound, hold the affected part under cold running water (not ice water).

good to know

OUTDATED RECOMMENDATION

You can't heed every home remedy from your grandmother's time. Some of them can actually be harmful. For example, never treat burns and scalds with butter, which can be a breeding ground for bacteria. Also, under no circumstances should you pierce or pop burn blisters—there's a danger of infection.

Colds

With winter come viruses that result in stuffy noses, sore throats, achy limbs, and fever. Antibiotics have proven powerless against these viral invaders. In fact, when it comes to cold symptoms, mother really does know best—most colds can be treated effectively with traditional home remedies.

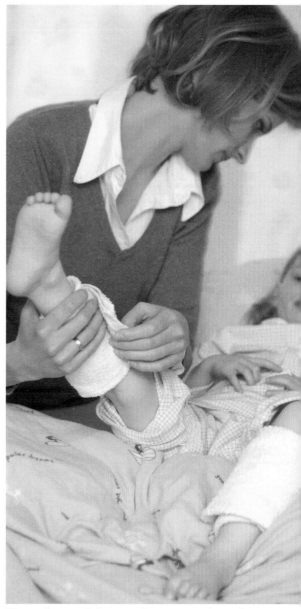

To treat fever, apply leg wraps for 5 minutes, then replace.

In the past, people often used the terms *cold* and *flu* interchangeably, but today doctors distinguish between the two. If your symptoms come on gradually and include sore throat, headache, achy limbs, coughing, a runny nose, elevated temperature, or slight fever, you probably have a cold. By contrast, flu comes on fast and hits hard, accompanied by a high fever, chills, and a serious feeling of illness. Even getting off the couch is a chore! Drinking fluids will flush out your system, prevent dehydration, and supply your body with vitamin C.

TO REDUCE FEVER

Fever is the body's response to illness and actually serves to fight infection. But a temperature higher than 103°F (39.5°C) will make you miserable. You could spend a bundle on the latest over-the-counter meds, but you may find the following tried-and-true traditional remedies equally effective.

▶ Apply **leg compresses** to reduce fever over time. Dip two linen cloths in cold water, wring them out, and wrap them tightly around the calves with a warm towel on top. Repeat as needed.

▶ Drink plenty of fluids: Good choices include **fruit juices** rich in vitamin C and antioxidants, such as orange juice, black currant and cranberry juice; or **non-carbonated mineral water** with a dash of fruit juice; or herbal or fruit teas, especially the vitamin-C-rich **rose hip tea**. Another classic: mix the juice of a lemon with 1 tsp. (5 mL) of honey in 1 cup (250 mL) of hot water.

▶ Have a cuppa. Often referred to in folk medicine as "fever teas," **linden** or **elder blossom tea** can help bring on sweating—the body's natural way of cooling itself—to help reduce a fever. To get the maximum benefit, sip a few cups, follow with a hot bath, and cozy up under a pile of blankets. When you begin to sweat, wait two hours, then dry off. Change your clothes and, if necessary, the bed linens. Drink some fluids and return to bed.

Chicken Soup

1 stewing chicken
1 large onion, quartered
salt and pepper
3 each, carrots and
celery stalks
1 kohlrabi (if available) or
  1 medium-sized cabbage
1 bunch of parsley

Simmer chicken, onion, salt, and pepper in 2 quarts/ liters of water for one hour. Add washed, cubed vegetables and boil for one hour longer. Remove chicken from the pot, debone, and cut meat into pieces. Pour soup through a strainer before returning chicken to the pot. Garnish soup with parsley and serve.

TO RELIEVE ACHES AND PAINS

Traditional wisdom has it that a hot water bottle can relieve pain, promote circulation, and help you to feel relaxed. Now scientists at University College London have discovered why: heat can physically shut down the normal pain response that triggers aches and pains. "It deactivates the pain at a molecular level in much the same way as pharmaceutical painkillers," says one senior researcher in physiology. Heat still brings only temporary relief, so frequent applications may be necessary.

▶ Evidence dating back to 4500 B.C. reveals that the ancients favored warm compresses of **peat, mud,** and **healing earth**. Now we have the luxury of a hot bath or a heating pad to ease pain.

▶ Apply a **mustard plaster**, a traditional congestion remedy. Crush a few tablespoons (25-45 mL) of mustard seeds or mustard powder, add the powder to a cup of flour, and mix with a little water to form a paste. Apply to the chest and leave on for 15 minutes.

TREATING A HEAD COLD

There's nothing as miserable as a head cold, and nothing soothes the misery better than a dose of "Jewish penicillin," otherwise known as chicken soup. As early as the 12th century, Jewish physician Moshe ben Maimonides touted the benefits of chicken soup for a cold. Since then, generations of mothers have followed his advice. Turns out they were right. Researchers from the Nebraska Medical Center found that chicken soup contains "a number of substances with beneficial medicinal activity," including an anti-inflammatory mechanism that may ease upper respiratory tract infections. See the box at left for a healing chicken soup recipe that has stood the test of time. Here are some other home remedies that soothe head colds.

▶ Aim an **infrared lamp** at your sinuses. In the past, people sometimes placed hot or warm, moist compresses with **healing earth**, **mashed potatoes**, or **flaxseeds** on the sinuses—an effective and economical remedy. Or simply warm a wet cloth in the microwave (not too hot!) and drape it across your face for 10 minutes at a time.

▶ To relieve nasal congestion, pour boiling water into a bowl, cover your head and the bowl with a towel, and inhale. For a little extra congestion-busting power, add six drops of **eucalyptus oil** or **chamomile** to the water.

▶ Spice it up. Foods that contain **chili peppers, hot mustard** or **horseradish** can remedy congestion. As a rule of thumb, if it makes your eyes water, it'll make your nose run.

▶ Try a nasal rinse. Irrigate your nose with a **saltwater solution** (from any pharmacy) to soothe stressed nasal mucous membranes.

▶ To make your own **nasal rinse,** dissolve 1 tsp. (5 mL) of salt in 2 cups (500 mL) of water. Use a nasal dropper to drop it in your nostrils and then blow your nose gently. Alternatively, make a horsetail-based nasal rinse (see box at right).

nasal rinse

one Put 2 tsp. (10 mL) of common horsetail (available at health food stores) in about ¾ quart (750 mL) of water, bring to a boil, strain, and cool.

two Put a little tincture in your cupped hand. Hold one nostril closed and inhale the tincture with the other. After 2 seconds let it run back out.

three Repeat process with the other nostril. Use the nasal rinse three times a day.

PREVENTION

A permanent cure for the cold does not exist, but you can reduce susceptibility significantly by boosting your immune system. For prevention:

▶ Get plenty of exercise in the fresh air and up your intake of **vitamin C** (fruits and vegetables).

▶ Eat lots of pungent **onion, garlic, radish,** or **horseradish**, which have an antibacterial effect and cleanse the blood.

▶ Take **echinacea** (purple coneflower), long used by North American aboriginal groups—recent studies support its ability to cut cold risk by as much as half.

▶ Avoid **stress**, **nicotine**, and **alcohol.**

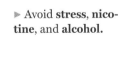

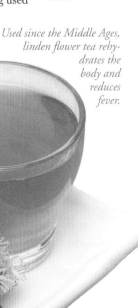

Used since the Middle Ages, linden flower tea rehydrates the body and reduces fever.

Constipation

Irregular bowel movements and hard, painful stools are uncomfortably common in today's world—but harsh laxatives shouldn't be necessary. Usually small changes in eating habits or natural cures can get things moving again.

A diet high in fiber that includes fruits, vegetables, and wholegrain products jump-starts digestion.

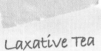

Laxative Tea

These medicinal herbs regulate digestion.

1½ oz. (50 g) senna leaves
½ oz. (15 g) fennel seeds, ground
½ oz. (15 g) elderflowers
⅓ oz. (10 g) chamomile flowers

Mix the ingredients together and pour 1 cup (250 mL) of boiling water over 1 tsp. (5 mL) of the mixture. Let steep for 5 minutes, then strain. Drink a freshly prepared cup three times a day.

When irregularity strikes, there's nothing better than the North American pioneer gold standard: 1 tbsp. (15 mL) of **castor oil** to dispel stubborn constipation. Here are a few additional home remedies that also work.

HOME REMEDIES

▶ Drink a glass of **prune** or **elderberry juice**, diluted **fruit vinegar**, or **warm water with honey** in the morning on an empty stomach.

▶ Dissolve 1 tsp. (5 mL) of **sea salt** in two cups (500 mL) of warm water and drink. This should soften the stool.

▶ Try a German cure. For centuries Germans have touted the curative effects of **sauerkraut**. In fact, this sausage-topper is rich in lactobacilli bacteria, which helps soften stool and keeps your intestinal flora healthy.

▶ Give yourself a daily **stomach massage** with a cold washcloth (in a clockwise direction) to stimulate your sluggish intestine.

▶ If your constipation fails to respond to any of these remedies, try a **warm water enema** (enema devices and instructions are available in pharmacies).

PREVENTION

▶ Consume only moderate amounts of **fats** and **sugars**, which slow down the intestines.

▶ Make room in your daily diet for additional digestion-regulating fibers, such as **wheat-** or **oat bran** and **flaxseeds.** Sprinkle them on your cereal.

▶ It is important to combine a diet high in fiber with **ample fluid intake**.

▶ Avoid the tannins contained in **dark chocolate, cacao, black tea,** and **red wine** as they disable your digestive muscles. Stay away from these foods if you have a tendency toward constipation.

▶ To get your sluggish intestine going, get some **exercise**; many times a bike ride, a regular walk, or an evening jog is all it takes.

▶ Take a **probiotic**. Good bacteria keeps things humming along nicely. **Yogurt** containing acidophilus may help, or opt for a supplement.

▶ **Relax and take your time.** Being pressed for time on the toilet doesn't help.

Prunes and other dried fruit relieve constipation naturally.

Depression

Our grandparents tended to face the blues with a stiff upper lip and little discussion, but they did have several effective home remedies to fall back on. Mild depression can often be treated successfully using these simple, natural techniques.

If your mother suggested a regimen of fresh air and sunshine to combat the blues, she was right on the money. Exposure to natural sunlight does indeed have an elevating effect on mood. But what if the winter sun rarely pokes through the clouds in your neck of the woods? Portable light boxes, which have recently become available, may sound like a gimmick—but they're actually very effective at combating the seasonal depression that flares up during dark winter months. The therapy seems to work best when used in every morning for about 30 minutes. If you're still feeling a little depressed, try some of these tips.

HOME REMEDIES

▶ Have a cup of tea. Teas made from **St. John's wort, hops, valerian,** or **powdered licorice** (from a pharmacy) help stabilize mood.

▶ Use essential oils to ease the blues: a tried-and-true mixture for the fragrant oil burner consists of 2 drops each of **rose** and **lemon balm oil** and 3 drops of **lavender oil**.

▶ Banish gloomy thoughts by slowly sipping **a glass of milk with fennel and honey** a half-hour before going to bed. Bring 2 tsp. (10 mL) of crushed fennel seeds and about 1 cup (250 mL) of milk to a boil, let it steep briefly, strain, and sweeten with honey.

▶ Smell yourself better. A scented sachet placed under your pillow may help you sleep better. Preferred scents include: **valerian, lavender, primrose, elder,** and **hops**.

a money-saving hint

Light boxes can be expensive, but check online for a good deal. Choose a model that produces at least 10,000 lux when set at a distance of about two feet (60 cm) from your head.

▶ Have a sweet. When is the last time someone told you to eat cookies? The fact is adding ½ tsp. (2 mL) each of **nutmeg** and **cinnamon** to any cookie recipe might lift your spirits.

BEHAVIOR TIPS

▶ Even light and color can have an impact on mood: a bright, friendly environment in **warm colors,** such as **yellow, red, or orange**, can lift your spirits.

▶ Evidence is piling up that **fish oil**, which contains a type of fatty acid called EPA, can help chase the blues away, especially when it is combined with pharmaceutical antidepressants.

▶ Cut back on pop and soft drinks that contain **caffeine.** Some research links caffeine, which suppresses serotonin production, to depression.

▶ Go away for a few days. A **break from your routine** and discovering someplace new will give you a boost.

good to know

ST. JOHN'S WORT

From the time of the ancient Greeks through to the Middle Ages, this plant was believed to have almost magical powers for healing. Modern research backs up that contention; short-term studies suggest it can be as effective as some antidepressants for treating mild depression. Keep in mind, however, that the hypericin contained in St. John's wort only releases its antidepressive effect after regular usage over an extended period. Take it in the form of tea, tablets, or drops at the same time every day and, since dosage standardization can be an issue, look for a preparation with at least 3 percent hyperforin and 0.2 percent hypericins. Note that St. John's wort can make your skin more sensitive to sunlight.

Diarrhea

Whether the cause of your discomfort is yesterday's lunch special or a nasty viral infection, "Montezuma's revenge" can be most unpleasant. But it's also terribly effective at expelling whatever it is that ails you. In the past, people tried to put a halt to diarrhea immediately, but now we generally allow it to run its course for a day or two, then deal with it using proven home remedies.

For the first 24 hours after diarrhea hits, drink plenty of clear fluids in order to replace the liquids and minerals you have lost. *Note: infants and small children with diarrhea should see a doctor. Adults should seek medical treatment if still running for the toilet after three days.*

good to know

OUTDATED RECOMMENDATION

People used to swear by cola and pretzels for diarrhea. In fact cola contains lots of sugar which can intensify diarrhea, and the carbonation leads to flatulence and tummy pains. As for pretzels, they do provide your body with salt, but they lack the all-important potassium.

FIRST AID

▶ Sip **non-carbonated mineral water** or **black tea,** flavored with sugar and a pinch of salt.

▶ Buy a package of special **glucose-electrolyte mixtures** from a pharmacy to offset salt loss. These solutions are especially important for children, expecting mothers, and older people, since major fluid loss is particularly dangerous for them.

▶ To make up a quick and inexpensive **electrolyte solution** of your own, mix 16 oz. (500 mL) of non-carbonated mineral water with 7 tsp. (35 mL) of sugar, 1 tsp. (5 mL) of table salt, and 16 oz. (500 mL) of orange juice or herbal or fruit tea (to provide potassium and flavoring). Drink throughout the day.

▶ Drink at least 1 cup (250 mL) of tea three times a day. Teas made from **oak bark** or **mulberry leaves** contain tannins that contract your blood vessels and have a soothing and antibacterial effect.

▶ Keep **activated charcoal tablets** on hand. Once the first line of defense for treating diarrhea, today they should not be used in the first 24 hours, since they trap harmful substances in your intestine. As a result, the pathogen will remain there longer. But

this may be a good choice if you contract diarrhea while you are traveling.

HOME REMEDIES

After a day or two, it's time to put a stop to your diarrhea and restore damaged intestinal flora. There are plenty of home remedies from the days of yore available for this purpose.

▶ Boil up a cup of **bloodroot tea** with ⅔ oz. (20 g) of bloodroot and 1 cup (250 mL) of water, and steep for 10 minutes. You can also buy bloodroot tincture and diarrhea pills with bloodroot in a health food store or pharmacy.

▶ Dissolve 1 tsp. (5 mL) of **powdered charcoal** or **healing earth** in a glass of water and drink it.

▶ Eat **yogurt** that contains "good bacteria" that chases out the "bad bacteria" that caused your diarrhea in the first place. Replacing it can help you feel better faster. Look for yogurt that contains **live bacterial culture** or **probiotics.** Look for a product with billions of bacteria in it. You need this many to effectively colonize your intestine.

▶ Eating 1–2 tsp. (15–25 mL) of dried **blueberries** is a time-honored Swedish cure for diarrhea. The

Because of the high percentage of cocoa and flavonoids it contains, dark chocolate eases diarrhea.

berries act as an astringent, contracting tissue, reducing inflammation in your intestine, and ultimately slowing diarrhea.

▶ Apply a little heat. Heat calms your intestine and makes you feel better. A **hot water bottle** or a **spelt** or **cherry-pit bag** should do the trick.

▶ Grandma's advice? Put 2 handfuls of crushed **pot marigold flowers** boiled in water into a cloth bag and place it on your stomach while warm. Test it with your fingertip first too make sure that it is not too hot.

▶ Calm your nerves. Nervous diarrhea can be treated with an aromatherapy massage. Mix 3–4 drops of **chamomile, sandalwood, juniper, or lavender oil** with 2 tsp. (10 mL) of cooking oil and massage your lower abdomen in a circle.

SLOWLY INTRODUCE A BLAND DIET

When diarrhea subsides, gradually return to a normal diet. Start with low-fiber foods such as **crackers, toast, rice, boiled potatoes,** and **chicken.** Often doctors will recommend a diet of **bananas, rice, applesauce,** and **toast,** called the BRAT diet (the name is an acronym for its components). These binding foods are suggested as the first to try after an episode of diarrhea. **Applesauce** contains pectin, and other nutrients your body needs. Because the apples are cooked, they are easier to digest. **Bananas** are eas-

Stick to low-fiber foods, like toast, when recovering from an acute case of diarrhea.

ily digested. In addition, they contain high levels of potassium, which helps replace the electrolytes you lose when you have diarrhea.

▶ Next treat yourself to a clear **vegetable broth** or a **potato-carrot soup** (see recipe below right) and dry toast.

▶ Try some **cooked carrots,** which are slso high in pectin—just cook and puree.

▶ Gradually broaden your menu with a little **fat** and easily digestible **protein**.

▶ Avoid **milk and dairy products** until the symptoms disappear. Some of the organisms that cause diarrhea can temporarily impair the ability to digest milk.

▶ During this time, also avoid **coffee** and **alcohol**.

The lactic acid bacteria contained in plain yogurt helps restore "good bacteria" in your stomach.

Potato-Carrot Soup

This soup delivers fluid and minerals without stressing your irritated intestinal mucous membrane.

1 cup (250 mL) water
2 medium potatoes
1 carrot
1 pinch salt

Bring the water to a boil. Add peeled and chopped veggies. Cook over low heat until tender, then puree and season with salt.

Earaches

Heat and medicinal plants are the traditional mainstays for treating earwax and earaches naturally. Home medicine also offers useful advice to combat annoying ringing or roaring in the ears, and alleviate discomfort.

While often the bane of childhood, earaches can strike anyone at anytime. Earaches often originate in the middle ear, which is the tiny space located behind the eardrum. A thin tunnel called the Eustachian tube, which runs from the middle ear to the back of the throat, allows fluid to drain. It's also a passage where the pressure inside your ear adjusts to meet external air pressure. A buildup of fluid caused by a cold can accumulate in the Eustachian tube, and cause significant pain.

EARACHES

If you're susceptible to earaches, don't leave the house in cold weather without a hat or scarf over your head, or at least a little cotton in your ears. When swimming, wear a bathing cap or don wax or silicon earplugs to avoid getting water in your ears. Consult a doctor immediately if your child has an earache, or an adult's earache does not respond to home treatment within a short time.

▶ Heat alleviates pain. Gently press a warmed **flaxseed pillow** against your painful ear, treat the ear with **infrared light**, or lay your head on a **hot water bottle** overnight.

good to know

OUTDATED METHODS
Don't use cotton swabs to clean your ears—they merely push the wax in deeper. Inserting a plastic syringe filled with fluid into your ear can injure your eardrum, so get a doctor to do it if you feel it's necessary. The same is true of using ear candles to cleanse your ear canal.

▶ Dribble **clove oil** onto a cotton ball and insert it in the entrance to your ear canal to relieve pain.

▶ Stir 3 tbsp. (45 mL) of **mustard powder** into warm water to form a thin paste, spread on a handkerchief and place behind your sore ear for 15 minutes.

▶ Try eardrops. For home-made eardrops, mix 3 drops of **tea tree oil** and 1 tbsp. (15 mL) of **olive** or **almond oil** and warm the mixture in a double boiler to body

Heat is the earache treatment of choice.

temperature. Tip your head to the side and use an eyedropper to dribble the drops into the affected ear.

▶ Drink 2–3 cups (500–750 mL) of **meadowsweet tea** per day. It alleviates pain.

▶ Place slices of **raw onion** behind your ear and hold them in place with a headband. It has long been known that onions have formidable anti-inflammatory properties. It's a quick (if smelly) traditional home remedy.

▶ Even more effective, but a bit more work, is a **chopped onion wrap** (see box at right). The heat has an additional role in soothing pain. Hold the wrap in place with a wool scarf or cap and leave it on your ear for 30 minutes. Apply three times a day.

EARWAX DROPS

The purpose of earwax is to protect your eardrums, keep the skin moist, and guard against dust and other particles. Normally the ear cleans itself, but sometimes wax builds up in your auditory canal and hardens into a plug. If water gets in, it will swell up and may partially or completely block your auditory canal. *Note: removal of a wax plug should be left to medical professionals—under no circumstances should you try to remove an earplug by inserting any kind of object into your ear.*

▶ Dribble a little slightly warmed **tea tree oil** or **glycerin** into your ear canal to soften the plug.

▶ Place a cotton ball moistened with **St. John's wort oil** in the entrance to the auditory canal.

► Mix a few drops of **olive oil** with a little **lemon juice** and **water**. Use a dropper to dribble the mixture into your ear, softening the plug. Eardrops from a pharmacy are also suitable for this purpose.

TINNITUS

If you have a constant roaring in your ears, but you're nowhere near the seaside, you may have *tinnitus*. The term refers to any ringing, rustling, humming, or roaring sound that originates in the head, rather than from an external source of noise. Sometimes tinnitus goes away on its own. But usually these annoying auditory hallucinations can't be cured—they can only be reduced. Causes for the condition range from infection to noise, stress, hearing loss, and circulatory disorders. But if tinnitus sets in, there are a number of things you can do about it.

► Make time for **relaxation exercises** and regular breaks in the daily routine.

► Improve blood circulation by **alternating hot and cold water in your morning shower** and consider starting a light exercise program.

► **Drink lots of fluids** to thin your blood and improve circulation to your inner ear.

► Enjoy a cup of **lemon balm tea** after a meal. It can have a positive effect on tinnitus.

Wear a hat in the wind and cold to prevent earaches.

► **Ginkgo extracts** promote circulation and can help some sufferers, but it takes several weeks for them to take effect.

► Avoid exposure to noise to prevent worsening your condition. Wear **earplugs or earmuffs** if your workplace is excessively noisy. On the other hand, total silence is also inadvisable—it makes the tinnitus all the more noticeable.

► Have a **subtle source of noise** at hand, particularly at night, such as a radio or sleep sounds CD. When you're outdoors, the rustling of the treetops or the splashing of a brook can mask the sounds in your head.

► If your tinnitus is accompanied by sudden difficulty hearing, it may be a **warning sign of deafness**; this requires immediate emergency medical attention.

onion wrap

one Cut 2 onions into thin rings and put them into a cloth bag.

two Warm the bag over some steam.

three Crush the onions with a rolling pin until the bag is soaked with juice.

four Place the bag over your aching ear and secure.

a money-saving *hint*

Instead of cloth handkerchiefs, which many no longer use, cut up old cotton or linen dishcloths and keep them available for ear or finger wraps.

Eyes

Your eyes may be the windows to your soul, but just like the windows in a house, they are exposed to numerous environmental factors that can affect your vision. It's easy to take care of your peepers with tried-and-true rinses and compresses, whether you have simple eyestrain, conjunctivitis, or a sty.

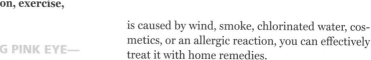

Your eyes are buffeted by countless irritants including wind, smoke, dust, sun, and even bacteria and viruses. The result can be eyestrain. To prevent eye ailments you should:

▶ Protect your eyes against direct sunlight, wind, or dust with **glasses.**

▶ **Reduce or avoid drafts** and keep humidity levels at 50–60%.

▶ Use an **adjustable reading lamp** with a wide emission angle for reading.

▶ Get **plenty of sleep** at night, and strengthen your body's defenses with **relaxation, exercise, and nutritious food**.

Refreshing Eye Compresses

¹/₃ oz. (10 g) cornflower
¹/₃ oz. (10 g) yellow sweet clover (yellow melilot)
²/₃ oz. (20 g) plantain (the herb, not the banana)

Pour about 10 oz. (300 mL) of boiling water over the herbs and strain after 10 minutes. Apply gauze pads soaked in the cooled solution onto your tired, closed eyes.

TREATING PINK EYE— CONJUNCTIVITIS

When the layer between your eyelid and eyeball, the conjunctiva, becomes inflamed, the result is itchy, red, and watery eyes. If the cause is a viral or bacterial infection, the ailment is highly contagious, so get yourself to a doctor. If, on the other hand, your conjunctivitis is caused by wind, smoke, chlorinated water, cosmetics, or an allergic reaction, you can effectively treat it with home remedies.

▶ Keep it clean. Carefully **remove the discharge** caused by the inflammation several times a day with a cotton ball soaked in distilled water.

▶ Give yourself an eyebath. After cleansing, soothe your inflamed eyes with **eyebright (euphrasia) compresses**. Finely chop 1–2 tsp. (5–10 mL) of the herb eyebright and pour 1 cup (250 mL) of boiling water over it (or use 1 tsp./5 mL of dried blooms). Let the mixture steep for 2 minutes before straining. When it's lukewarm, soak two sterile gauze pads in the liquid and apply to your eyes for several minutes.

SWOLLEN EYELIDS

Since swelling results from a buildup of tissue fluid in the eyelid, anything cold can help soothe the inflammation by contracting the blood vessels and stimulating circulation.

▶ Scoop a little **cold plain yogurt** onto a cloth to make a poultice and place it over your closed eyes for 15 minutes.

Squeezed-out black or green teabags cooled in the refrigerator work wonders for swollen eyelids.

▶ Apply slices of **cold cucumber** to your eyelids for 10 minutes.

▶ Apply a **cold pack** to your swollen eyelids. Crushed ice in a cloth works just as well, as does a **metal spoon cooled in the refrigerator** (not in the freezer!) and laid carefully onto your eyelids.

TIRED, STRAINED EYES

Long hours at the computer, poor lighting, lack of sleep—all of these can result in eye strain that shows up in the form of burning, itching, and watery eyes. For relief, rub your hands together until they're warm and place them gently over closed eyes. Look no further than your grandmother's cornucopia of natural remedies for more advice.

▶ Moisten a cloth with a calming tea made from boiled water and about ⅓ oz. (10 g) each of **rose blooms** and **thyme.** Apply to closed eyes for 5 minutes after mixture has cooled. It has a calming effect.

▶ Make a soothing pain-reducing eye wash from about 1 cup (250 mL) of water and a **fennel teabag**. Dilute the tea with an equal amount of water. When the solution is just lukewarm, rinse your eyes with it using an eyewash basin from the drugstore.

RED EYES

Windburn or even barbecuing over an open fire can leave you with red, burning eyes. You're not likely to get rid of the irritation by rubbing—in fact, you might just make it worse. But as your grandmother could probably tell you, a compress made from **daisy, eyebright, plantain,** or **garden rue** could be just the ticket. For hundreds of years, people have been using compresses made from these medicinal plants to soothe irritated eyes.

▶ You need go no further than the refrigerator to find another effective remedy for red eyes: just heat a little **milk** to lukewarm temperature, soak two gauze pads in it, and apply to your closed eyelids for 10 minutes.

▶ Apply **cucumber slices**. They not only help with swollen eyelids, but also with reddened eyes.

STY

The most common cause of that angry-looking pustule on the edge of your eyelid is bacteria. You should never squeeze a sty—you risk causing a severe infection. However, with a little help from heat and herbal compresses, you may be able to bring it to a head so that the pustule opens on its own.

▶ Use **infrared light** to hasten the ripening of a sty. You can speed the process by applying warm compresses soaked in an infusion made from **flaxseeds, fennel,** or **chamomile**—an effective and economical home remedy from long ago. Helpful hints: never reuse compresses and get plenty of rest.

▶ Soothe pain with a **yogurt cold pack.** Mix 3 tbsp. (45 mL) of yogurt, the juice of one lemon, and 1 tbsp. (15 mL) of milk. Spread the mixture on a cloth and apply to your closed eye for 20 minutes. Repeat.

Anyone who works at a computer should build ample rest breaks into their day—aim for at least 5-10 minutes per hour.

Fatigue

It's normal to feel tired after a long, strenuous work day. But if exhaustion is a constant companion, sapping your energy and your zest for life, it's time to do something about it.

Many people don't really wake up until after they drink their morning coffee. But unfortunately, coffee has only a short-term effect. Instead, do as your grandparents did—wake up, open your window wide, and breathe in the fresh air. Get your circulation going with a couple of deep knee bends, move your arms in a circle, and follow up with a healthy breakfast. If this approach doesn't energize you, here are a few other things to try.

cold arm shower

one Direct a cold stream of water at the outside of your arm, moving slowly from the fingers of your right hand up to the shoulder.

two Go back down with the water, this time on the inside of your arm.

three Do the same with the left arm.

HOME REMEDIES

▶ Alternate **hot and cold water** in your morning shower. A cold arm shower (see box at left) is also a real picker-upper—especially if low blood pressure is causing your chronic fatigue. If you don't have much time, you can take a **cold arm bath** in a few seconds: just dip your arms up to the elbows in a sink filled with cold water.

▶ Need a siesta after a big meal? Eat **smaller, more frequent meals**. After a big meal, high blood glucose levels can switch off the brain cells that keep you alert.

▶ If your fatigue is a result of ongoing physical or mental stress, **get moving** and take a walk. Exercise releases endorphins, the body's natural happy drugs, leaving you feel revitalized and happier.

▶ Drink 2–3 cups (500–750 mL) a day of **mistletoe, stinging nettle, ginger root,** or **hawthorn tea.** They're very stimulating.

▶ Try a little **ginseng**. As any Chinese grandmother will tell you, ginseng tea can reduce feelings of stress and anxiety and combat fatigue. Pour a cup of boiling water over 1½ tsp. (7 mL) of finely chopped ginseng, let steep for 10 minutes, and strain. Drink 2 cups (500 mL) a day.

▶ Drink an energy potion. A trusted home remedy is **molasses with cider vinegar**. In a cup, stir together 2 tsp. (10 mL) of blackstrap molasses and 4 tsp. (20 mL) of apple cider vinegar. Then fill the cup with honey and mix. Take 2 tsp. (10 mL) when you get up in the morning and before you go to bed, and 1 tsp. (5 mL) before both lunch and dinner.

▶ Brew a cup of tea made from **Iceland moss** (from the health food store). It can help fortify you when you're feeling pooped.

▶ Go herbal. For thousands of years, **rosemary** has been treasured for both its aroma and its medicinal effects. In 1603, its price shot sky-high because Londoners believed it could ward off the plague. That proved to be a myth, but when added to a cool, brief bath, rosemary can provide an effective remedy for fatigue and exhaustion. Alternatively, try **spruce needles** in your bathwater.

Regular visits to the sauna fortify and relax your body.

Make fresh fruit, rich in vitamins and minerals, part of your daily diet.

NUTRITION TO COMBAT FATIGUE

▶ Increase your iron level. If your diet is low in iron, your blood cells aren't able to carry their usual load of oxygen and your energy level plummets. Nosh on high-iron foods like **meat, liver, whole grains,** and **green leafy vegetables**.

▶ Iodine deficiency can also cause ongoing fatigue. You can counter it by eating **ocean fish** and sprinkling food with **iodized table salt**.

▶ Buy **wholegrain products**. Whole grains break down slowly in your body, releasing sugars into your bloodstream evenly. That means your body gets a constant energy supply and your blood sugar levels won't fluctuate dramatically, causing fatigue.

▶ Fresh **vegetables**, plus **milk and milk products,** contain a wide spectrum of vitamins and minerals crucial to well-being. They can boost your body's performance capacity, so include them in the menu plan every day.

▶ Enjoy a tasty and healthy vitamin and mineral bombshell. Try this: spread a slice of **wholegrain bread** with **cream cheese**, and add **avocado, alfalfa sprouts,** and **chives.**

▶ Avoid **coffee, cola**, and **champagne**. These drinks are often recommended as picker-uppers, but the boost doesn't last long and often has a boomerang effect.

▶ Stay away from sweets such as **chocolate** and **candy**. They contain what are referred to as simple sugars, which quickly elevate blood sugar levels and performance capability—but they crash just as quickly, sending you into an energy slump.

▶ Snack better. Instead of sweets or fast food, eat a container of **yogurt** or a piece of **fresh fruit.**

Feet

Too tight, too high, too pointed—bad footwear is one of the main causes of foot problems. Thankfully, there are many traditional remedies that help to heal the souls of our feet.

There's nothing better than a foot rub if you can find a friend or partner to give your aching feet a treat. But if there's no one around to rub your sore tootsies, here are easy, tried-and-true ways to relieve most foot ailments or discomforts.

vinegar bread

one Pour a little wine vinegar over a few slices of white bread in a bowl. Let stand for a few hours until it turns to mush.

two Spread the mush onto the painful area, cover with a cloth, and hold in place with a gauze bandage. Let it work overnight.

three Repeat the application as many times as needed.

CORNS

Calluses sometimes develop over time where a shoe pinches your skin or crowds your toes together. Once the callus thickens and forms a hard core, it has turned into a corn.

▶ Soften the callus with a footbath of **chamomile** or **tea tree oil** before a corn develops. Then rub it off carefully with a pumice stone or special corn file.

▶ To soften calluses and corns, rub them daily with a little **castor oil**.

▶ Place a fresh thin slice of **onion** on your corn and hold it in place with a gauze bandage until the core of the corn dissolves.

▶ Take the pressure off. Put a **piece of gauze** between your toes to reduce friction, rubbing, and to take pressure off the sore spot.

▶ Use a **corn patch** for stubborn cases. Pharmacies offer patches containing salicylic acid that soften the corn, so it can be pulled off along with the patch.

Every now and then, give your feet a break by going barefoot in the park.

BLISTERS

Ouch! Blisters occur when the two top layers of skin rub against one another until they separate, producing a hollow which fills with watery liquid.

▶ Prevent blisters from occurring by always wearing shoes with **socks** or **stockings**.

▶ Going for a hike? Opt for **two pairs of thin socks** instead of one pair of thick ones. The pairs of socks will rub against each other instead of rubbing against your foot.

▶ Before a long walk, rub some **petroleum jelly** into the sensitive skin of your feet.

ATHLETE'S FOOT

Athlete's foot is caused by hyphomycetes fungi, which thrive in moist, damp environments. You are at greatest risk of infection at the swimming pool or sauna. Wearing flip-flops, or donning socks and shoes made from natural materials, goes a long way to prevent this itchy, unpleasant ailment. But if you do catch it, try a few of these home remedies:

▶ Take **contrasting footbaths**—dip your feet in hot water for 5 minutes, followed by 10 seconds in cold water. This will effectively combat athlete's foot. **Chamomile** or **oak bark** can also help: boil 3 tbsp. (45 mL) of chamomile or oak bark for 30 minutes in 1 quart/liter of water, strain, and add to your footbath.

▶ Dribble a few drops of **tea tree oil** into your footbath or apply it directly onto the affected areas.

▶ **Sage**, which reduces sweating, is a good additive for footbaths. Add 5 tbsp. (75 mL) to 2 quarts/liters of water.

▶ Alternatively, apply **sage oil** straight to your affected skin with a cotton swab.

▶ To clear up athlete's foot more quickly, rub the itchy areas with a crushed **garlic clove** or fresh **bear's garlic oil**.

▶ To stop itching, apply a thick paste of **baking powder** mixed with warm water. Rinse after 3 minutes and dry your feet thoroughly.

▶ **Change socks daily** and wash in the hottest water possible.

FOOT PAIN

Walking or standing too long can leave you with aching, tired feet. An addiction to high heels or other fashionable, but uncomfortable, shoes, it will only add to the problem. Home remedies can produce quick relief.

▶ Try a relaxing warm footbath (at 100°F/38°C) with a few drops of **eucalyptus, rosemary, or juniper oil.**

▶ Make your own foot massage oil by slowly warming ¼ cup (50 mL) of **sesame** or **sunflower oil** in a double boiler and mixing in 5 drops of **lemon balm oil**. Gently massage thoroughly dry feet with the lukewarm oil mixture.

Gravel foot massages are used in Chinese medicine as a form of simple reflexology.

▶ Rubbing your feet with **ice cubes** brings them back to life. Wrap the ice in a clean cloth first.

▶ Use **rubbing alcohol** to massage painful legs and feet.

SWEATY FEET

Your feet are the natural habitat of millions of bacteria, which thrive on your sweat and skin cells. By-products produced by these bacteria are what give feet a stinky smell. Here's how to make sure people won't hold their noses when you take off your shoes.

▶ Wash your feet daily with **warm, soapy water** and dry well, especially between the toes, and change your socks at least once a day.

▶ Take a 10-minute footbath with **spruce needles**, **cider vinegar**, or **table salt** (½ cup/125 mL of each per 1 quart/liter of water) to nix sweaty feet.

▶ Make a **black tea** footbath—just pour a quart/liter of boiling water over four teabags, steep and then add cold water in a foot basin until the temperature is right.

a money-saving *hint*

Sweaty feet can make your shoes smelly too. Instead of treating them with expensive and often environmentally-harmful shoe sprays, sprinkle them with talcum powder or fill them with dried lavender flowers and let sit overnight.

Flatulence

Everyone has it. But passing gas in public can be embarrassing and, if you have excessive gas, you may well feel bloated and uncomfortable. Less-than-stellar nutrition, a lack of exercise, and stress can all leave you with an unpleasant feeling of abdominal pressure.

If it's any consolation, Hippocrates (the father of medicine) proclaimed that passing gas "is necessary to well-being." Ancient Roman emperor Claudius also declared that "Roman citizens shall be allowed to pass gas whenever necessary."

But even the ancients sometimes turned to nature to help their intestines bounce back and eliminate gas. A distressed intestine needs soothing. When your stomach is distended, it's wise to cut back on eating and try one of the following natural ways to reduce gas with medicinal plants or heat applied to your abdomen.

good to know

GAS IN BABIES AND SMALL CHILDREN

Who can miss the telltale signs of colic: your tiny baby's fists are clenched, face scrunched in an earth-shattering wail. Just about everyone, from your mother to the grocery store clerk, will probably have a solution to offer, but there are some gentle, time-honored remedies that may help. Even babies can benefit from the digestive properties of fennel tea. Mix 1 tsp. (5 mL) of tea into formula for bottle-fed babies. For breast-fed infants, use an eyedropper to administer the tea three times a day. Alternatively, place a warm hot water bottle on your child's stomach or gently massage its tummy in a circular motion to provide a little relief.

HOME REMEDIES

▶ Mix together ½ oz. (15 g) each of **caraway seed**, **fennel**, and **anise**. Pour about 1 cup (250 mL) of boiling water over 2 tsp. (10 mL) of the mixture. Let the tea steep for 10 minutes, strain, and drink unsweetened.

▶ Finely grind **caraway seed** and **coriander** and take ½ tsp. (2 mL) with a little water before every meal.

▶Use l**icorice root** to help with bloating: dissolve ⅔ oz. (20 g) of licorice (from a health food store) in about 1 cup (250 mL) of chamomile tea. Drink 1 cup per day.

▶ Let heat soothe discomfort. Heat a **cherry-pit** or **spelt cushion** to about 105°F (40°C) in the oven or microwave, and place it on your tummy.

Avoid high-fat foods when your intestine is irritated—stick to well-cooked veggies instead.

NUTRITION

▶ Season your food with spices that aid digestion, such as **caraway seeds, anise, marjoram,** and **ginger**—they can can reduce flatulence and bloating.

▶ Eat slowly, and **chew thoroughly**—you'll swallow less air and reduce gas.

▶ Want to play it safe? Avoid gassy foods—such as **beans** and **carbonated drinks.**

▶ Cook **legumes**, **leeks**, and **cabbage** thoroughly—the vegetables will be easier to digest.

▶ If you suffer from **food incompatibilities**, such as lactose intolerance, be aware that it could trigger a gas attack. Avoid the foods in question.

▶ Avoid candies and gum sweetened with **sorbitol, xylitol,** or **mannitol.** They are difficult to digest.

A mortar and pestle is an effective tool for preparing stomach-friendly spice mixtures.

Gallbladder

Your gallbladder acts as a kind of storage tank for bile—a substance your body needs to break down fatty food into digestible bits. But when there is too much cholesterol in the storage tank, gallstones begin to form in tiny hard globules that can grow to the size of an egg. A diet characterized by rich, high-fat foods is a big contributor, as are alcohol and nicotine.

Bile fluid contains high levels of cholesterol and the pigment bilirubin, both of which precipitate as crystals and form stones; these may be as fine as beach sand or as coarse as gravel. Gallstones can develop in both sexes, but they are most common in overweight, middle-aged women.

HOME REMEDIES

When your gallbladder goes on strike, it's a signal that your liver needs strengthening and the flow of bile must be restored.

▶ **Chicory tea** will help. Pour cold water over 1 tsp. (5 mL) of root and herb, boil for 3 minutes, and strain. Drink 2–3 cups (500–750 mL) daily.

▶ **Artichoke juice** can stimulate bile production. Mix 1 tbsp. (15 mL) of artichoke juice (from a health food store) with a little water and take three times a day after meals.

▶ Take the **dandelion cure**. The Iroquois ate bowls of boiled dandelions with plates of fatty meat to aid digestion. You can buy dandelion extract or capsules at a health food store. Alternatively, drink several cups of dandelion tea daily. Add 1 tsp. (5 mL) of the leaves to 1 cup (500 mL) of water, boil, and strain.

▶ Chew several **caraway seeds** every day or use them to flavor foods and aid digestion.

▶ Heat can ease the pain of a gallbladder attack: apply a small, warm **cherry-pit**, **flaxseed**, or **hay flower bag** to your liver area, cover with a cloth, and top with a wool blanket.

▶ **Turmeric** (**curcuma**) **tea** can help your inflamed gallbladder heal. Pour 1 cup (250 mL) of boiling water over ½ tsp. (2 mL) of powdered turmeric, let it steep for 5 minutes, strain and drink. Try to have at least 2–3 cups (500–750mL) per day.

▶ If it's packaged, don't eat it. Most of what your grandparents (or at least your great grandparents) ate was home-made and their gallbladders thanked them. **Processed** and **fast foods** generally contain plenty of the bad fats and oils that can lead to gallstones.

WHEN TO SEE A DOCTOR

Frequent, severe distension, a feeling of fullness in the upper abdomen, and pain in the liver area are early warning signs of gallbladder ailments. Gallstones can form with time, interfering with bile flow and causing a great deal of pain. Get yourself to the doctor early and nip painful gallstones in in the bud.

Herbal "Wine"

This may help with gall-stones:
- ⅔ oz. (20 g) lemon balm
- ⅔ oz. (20 g) dyer's green-weed
- ⅔ oz. (20 g) hops
- ⅔ oz. (20 g) agrimony
- ⅔ oz. (20 g) peppermint
- ⅔ oz. (20 g) wormwood
- 1 quart/liter apple juice

Mix together the herbs, pour the apple juice over them, and let steep for twelve hours. Heat the herbal "wine," steep for another 5 minutes, strain, and bottle. Take 1 tbsp. (15 mL) every hour eight times a day.

Hair Loss

Both women and men occasionally lose hair. Often, hormones or genes are to blame. If you want your hair to be your crowning glory, don't rely on expensive "wonder cures." Nature offers an array of effective remedies and applications that are much easier on the pocketbook.

Most hair problems respond well to home remedies. Hair loss may result from poor nutrition, stress, illness, or incorrect or harsh treatment. It may also be a side effect of medication.

HOME REMEDIES

Anything that stimulates circulation to your scalp will aid hair growth and help you avoid hair loss.

▶ Rub your head with an **onion**. It may sound quirky, but rubbing your scalp for 10 minutes with the surface of a freshly cut onion is a tried-and-true home remedy. The odorous vegetable contains plenty of sulfur, which aids in the formation of collagen, a substance that makes hair fuller and stronger. Follow up by washing your hair.

▶ Try a tonic that can guard against hair loss consisting of about 1½ oz. (50 g) each of **nasturtium** and **creeping thyme** plus 1 quart/liter of vodka. Let the ingredients stew in a closed container for ten days before straining. Massage the tonic vigorously into your scalp twice a day.

The sulfur contained in nasturtium fortifies hair and keeps it full and healthy.

▶ Another hair loss tonic consists of about 7 oz. (200 g) of **stinging nettle root**, 2 cups (500 mL) of **wine vinegar**, and 1 quart/liter of water. Boil the ingredients for 30 minutes, strain the liquid, and pour into a bottle after cooling. Use the tonic three times a week.

▶ Massage a few drops of pure **tea tree oil** into your scalp to stimulate hair growth.

▶ Use **rosemary oil** to activate your hair follicles to promote growth.

▶ Try contrasting **hot and cold water** while shampooing every morning and evening. End with cold water and towel the scalp dry.

PREVENTION

▶ To encourage blood circulation to your hair roots, **massage your scalp** with your fingertips for 5 minutes three times a day.

▶ **Avoid overstyling**. Washing with excessively hot water, extensive blow-drying, curling tongs, and curlers can damage your hair. Avoid **perms and hair dyes**.

▶ An unhealthy diet can contribute to hair loss. Nix some saturated fats and opt for foods high in hair-friendly vitamins and minerals, such as **iron, zinc, protein,** and **B vitamins**.

beer shampoo

one Wash your hair and rinse with warm water.

two Massage about 3½ oz. (100 mL) of beer into your scalp and let it sit for 15 minutes.

three Rinse hair with warm water and massage in another 3½ oz. (100 mL) of beer.

four Comb your hair and let the beer dry on your scalp. (It will soak in so well that no odor will remain.)

Hay Fever

People with pollen allergies have mixed emotions about springtime. Along with the awakening of nature come sneezing fits, red and watery eyes, and, in serious cases, even allergic asthma. The good news: you need look only as far as your cupboard to find plenty of time-tested home remedies for relief from sniffling and sneezing.

Allergy symptoms are signs that your immune system is on a rampage, reacting to normally harmless substances like pollen and ragweed. Here's how to wage war on the microscopic menaces that send your immune system into overdrive.

HOME REMEDIES

▶ **Black caraway** (or **black cumin**) **oils** have been used for centuries to promote health and fight disease. It can help to balance your twitchy immune system. Over the course of three months, take 2 capsules three times a day.

▶ Watch what you eat. Nutrition plays an important role, especially in the lead-up to hay fever season. **Vitamin C** (fresh fruit, lettuce, and vegetables) and **magnesium** (nuts, milk, and grain products) strengthen your immune system. It may also help to eliminate meat from your diet.

▶ Use a simple soother. A **nasal rinse with table salt** may help clear your congested nose and remove trapped irritants. Dissolve 1 tsp. (5 mL) of table salt in 1 cup (250 mL) of warm water. Put the salt solution into a container with a long, thin spout or a shallow bowl. Then lean over the sink and sniff in the liquid one nostril at a time, allowing it to drain out through your nose or mouth. Nasal rinses are best used before going to bed.

The types of pollen that most commonly cause allergic reactions are produced by plain-looking plants (trees, grasses, and weeds).

▶ **Cider vinegar** is a tried-and-true treatment for hay fever. Put 1 tsp. (5 mL) of cider vinegar into half a cup (125 mL) of water and sip the mixture slowly, preferably in the morning.

▶ Apply a **moist cloth** to your itching eyes for fast relief—use cold or warm water, whichever feels better.

BEHAVIOR TIPS

The following tips will keep your exposure to allergy causing pollen to a minimum.

▶ Keep your **windows closed** during the day: that inviting breeze is bad news for an allergy sufferer, potentially carrying a load of pollen.

▶ **Do not hang the wash outdoors to dry**. Pollen clings to moist surfaces.

▶ After outdoor activity, **change your clothes** as soon as possible.

▶ The **middle of the day** is peak pollen time, so stay indoors.

▶ **Vacuum rugs frequently**. Opt for a vacuum cleaner with an allergy filter, and regularly mop the floors.

▶ Avoid **blooming plants** and **cut flowers** in the house—regrettably they too spread pollen.

▶ **Wash your hair** before going to bed to avoid getting pollen on the pillow.

▶ **Don't smoke**. **Nicotine** increases susceptibility to allergies and heightens your discomfort.

▶ Take shelter inside before a **thunderstorm** and up to three hours afterward. Storms are preceded by high humidity which makes pollen grains swell, burst, and release their irritating starch.

▶ Wear **wraparound sunglasses** and/or a **cyclist's mask** when you go out to shield your face.

Headaches

Headaches are not an illness in themselves, but merely a symptom with a number of possible causes. In most cases, you shouldn't need to reach for the pain pills. Countless home remedies can provide gentle, quick, and lasting relief.

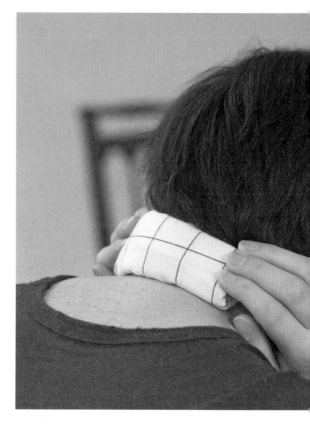

acupressure

one Use your index fingers to gently massage the easily perceptible depression just under the outer end of your eyebrows for 1 minute in a clockwise direction.

two Use your fingertip to massage the middle joint of your ring finger for 1 minute in a clockwise direction, on the side facing the pinky.

Headache triggers can include stress, overexertion, sensitivity to weather, low blood sugar, colds, tooth problems, and psychological issues. Tension headaches consist of a cramping of the neck and shoulder muscles, and respond well to acupressure treatments. Migraines occupy a special place among headaches; they take the form of pulsating pain on one side of the head, often accompanied by sensitivity to light and noise, nausea, vision abnormalities, and neurological problems. Possible triggers are foods such as alcohol (especially red wine), coffee, cheese, and the flavor enhancer monosodium glutamate (MSG), plus a lack of sleep, stress, and hormonal influences.

If unexplained headaches persist, consult your doctor.

HOME REMEDIES

▶ Rest for a few minutes on the sofa and place some **ice cubes wrapped in a cloth** on your forehead.

▶ Rub a few drops of **lemon balm**, **peppermint**, **clove**, or **rosemary essential oil** on your temples, forehead, and neck (not suitable for people with neurodermatitis or children under 2 years).

▶ After removing the white inner skin, place the inside of a **lemon peel** on your temples for a few minutes.

▶ Sprinkle freshly squeezed **plantain herb juice** on a cotton cloth and place the cloth on your forehead like a headband.

▶ For a hot, relaxing neck compress, wrap **flaxseeds**, **chopped onions** (both warmed in a double boiler or in a microwave), or **hot mashed potatoes** in a cotton cloth, and press onto your neck until the compress cools off.

▶ Go for the greens. Many migraine sufferers have a shortage of magnesium in their brains. **Dark green, leafy vegetables**, **nuts**, and **fruits** are good sources.

▶ **Posture** plays a large role in tension headaches—so put those shoulders back and stand up straight!

▶ Freshly-boiled tea made from **white willow bark** contains salicin, a natural relative of the acetylsalicylic acid used in many common pain medications. It's easy to prepare it the way your grandmother did: heat 1 tsp. (5 mL) of white willow bark in 1 cup (250 mL) of cold water and boil briefly. Let steep for 5 minutes, strain, and sip one cup at time, several times a day.

Neck compresses can soothe tension-related headaches.

▶ **Caffeine** makes pain medications 40 percent more efficient, so by all means indulge in small amounts to help hasten and increase relief.

▶ If a migraine strikes, head for a **quiet, dark room** for a little rest to help relieve the pain.

▶ If your headache is caused by nasal or sinus congestion, perhaps from a cold or hayfever, try a little bathwater aromatherapy. Put some **eucalyptus** or **peppermint oil** in your hot bathwater for an inhalation and relaxation.

PREVENTION

▶ If you are a frequent consumer of **aspirin or ibuprofen,** stop—these can cause "rebound headaches" that start just as soon as a dose of medication begins to wear off.

▶ Avoid any form of **nicotine**, which constricts your blood vessels.

▶ Go easy on **alcohol**. Its toxic metabolic products increase the danger of headache.

▶ **Red wine** and **chocolate** can trigger headaches in those with sensitivities.

▶ Drink a cup of **St. John's wort tea** to reduce stress, thus eliminating one major headache trigger.

▶ Get enough **sleep and rest**.

▶ **Exercise** (jogging, walking, swimming) encourages circulation and reduces stress.

▶ **Feverfew** doesn't just prevent fever, it reduces the frequency and intensity of migraines in those who take it regularly. Used for thousands of years by healers around the world, the herb can be grown in your garden, in a balcony pot, or picked up in supplement form from either the pharmacy or a health food store.

Espresso flavored with the juice from half a lemon can be a balm for headaches.

Juniper Berry Tea

about 1/10 oz. (3–4 g) juniper berries
1 cup (250 mL) water

Crush the juniper berries and pour boiling water over them. Let the tea steep for 5 minutes, strain, and sip 1 cup (250 mL) three times a day. (Caution: do not take during pregnancy or if you have kidney disease.)

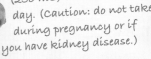

Heart and Circulatory System

It doesn't take much to keep your heart and circulatory system running smoothly. Simply eat a healthy diet with lots of vitamin-rich fresh foods and get regular exercise. But if a medical condition does arise, nature offers some time-honored, heart-healthy remedies.

The sulfur-containing substances in raw garlic protect the heart. Cooked garlic is significantly less effective.

Circulatory disorders can show up in the form of tingling in your fingers or toes, pale skin, and cold hands and feet. Your first line of defense should be a visit to your doctor's office. But cardiovascular disease is nothing new—a glimpse into grandmother's medicine cabinet turns up a few options to help you ward off heart disease and stroke.

HOME REMEDIES

▶ Get a gentle massage. Gentle **whole-body massages** encourage circulation, particularly when a few drops of **eucalyptus, pine needle,** or **rosemary oil** are added to massage oil.

▶ To promote blood flow, sip on tea made from equal parts dried **pot marigold blooms, daisies,** and **heartsease**: pour 1 cup (250 mL) of boiling water over 1 tsp. (5 mL) of the mixture. Strain after 5 minutes and drink slowly.

▶ Encourage blood flow to your skin by forcefully rubbing it in the shower with a **massage brush** or a coarse washcloth.

▶ Take **contrasting footbaths** to boost circulation, especially in your legs. Soak your feet in a basin of hot water at 100–108°F (38–42°C) for 5 minutes; then in a basin of cold water at 64–68°F (18–20°C). Repeat. Dry your feet thoroughly and rest for an hour. The remedy is particularly effective when practiced twice a week.

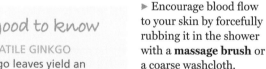

good to know

VERSATILE GINKGO
Ginkgo leaves yield an extract that contains a series of highly effective substances. Among other things, they encourage blood flow and prevent circulatory problems. Pharmacies sell commercial compounds in the form of teas, drops, and tablets.

▶ A **mustard bath** will increase your circulation, open your pores, and stimulate your sweat glands. Mix 7 oz. (200 g) of mustard powder with 2 quarts/liters of cold water. After a few minutes, strain the mustard water and pour it into a hot bath.

▶ Chinese physicians have long recommended drinking **green tea** for health. They have it absolutely right. Several clinical studies indicate the antioxidant-rich tea can reduce bad cholesterol and increase circulation.

▶ Health experts recommend 4,700 mg of blood pressure-lowering **potassium** per day. Good sources include **bananas, raisins,** and **currants.**

▶ Nix the **salt**. The more salt in your blood, the higher your blood volume. Why? Because sodium attracts and retains water. Spice up home-cooked meals with herbs instead, and stay away from packaged food.

▶ Munch on **celery**. Any grandmother will tell you that the crunchy vegetable is effective for controlling circulatory problems, and modern researchers concur. Four stalks a day should do it.

▶ Eat your **chocolate**. Yes, you read that right. Dark chocolate is not just good for the soul, it has a proven ability to lower blood pressure. Keep in mind, though, that just 1/5 oz. (6 grams) of chocolate (less than two Hershey's Kisses) will do the trick, and the darker the better.

WEAK HEART

If you feel exhausted at the slightest physical exertion, are constantly short of breath, and retaining fluid in your legs, a visit to the doctor is definitely in order. Still, you don't necessarily need to reach for a chemicals to pump up a weak heart.

▶ Here's a low-cost home remedy that is available to every household: freshly-squeezed **onion juice** mixed with a little **honey** strengthens the heart.

▶ **Peppermint milk** provides an economical and effective treatment for a weak heart. Pour boiling milk over some dried peppermint leaves and let it steep 5 minutes; strain and drink the milk in small sips.

▶ For six weeks, take 1 tbsp. (15 mL) each of **mistletoe** and **hawthorn juice** at midday and in the evening. The hawthorn shrub has been a stalwart of both European and Chinese herbal medicine since ancient times. In the 1800s, it became particularly renowned as a heart tonic, a contention that has since been backed up by clinical trials.

▶ Rub your feet with **rosemary oil**.

▶ Go nuts. **Nuts** have many healthy effects on the heart. They help lower the LDL (low-density lipoprotein or "bad" cholesterol) level in your blood—and high LDL is one of the primary causes of heart disease. In addition, nut consumption reduces your risk of developing blood clots that can cause a fatal heart attack, and improves the health of the lining of your arteries.

▶ Sprinkle lots of **cinnamon** on food. Cinnamon strengthens the cardiovascular system, shielding the heart from disorders, and acts as a blood-thinning agent, which increases circulation.

NERVOUS HEART AILMENTS

Anxious people have about a 25 percent higher risk of developing coronary heart disease than their calmer counterparts, and are almost twice as likely to die of a heart attack over about ten years, according to researchers at Tilburg University in the Netherlands. So chill out!

▶ Indulge in a daily cup of calming **valerian tea**, preferably in the evening: pour 1 cup (250 mL) of cold water over 2 tsp. (10 mL) of minced valerian root, let stand for a couple of hours, and strain. Warm up the tea and sip slowly.

▶ **Caraway** or **lemon balm tea** likewise soothes nervous heart ailments, and they're quick and easy to prepare from fresh ingredients or from teabags.

▶ Add **essential oils** (anise, lavender, wild mint, orange, rose) or use them in fragrant oil burners for a calming, relaxing effect.

▶ **Get more rest.** Mom always told you to get your sleep. Now medical science backs her up. Lack of sleep has been linked to high blood pressure, atherosclerosis, heart attack, and stroke. One theory: poor sleep causes inflammation, the body's response to injury, infection, irritation, or disease. That revs up your sympathetic nervous system, which is activated by fright or stress.

Fortifying Heart Tea

1¼ oz. (40 g) dried hawthorn blooms and leaves
½ oz. (15 g) arnica blooms
½ oz. (15 g) lemon balm leaves

Pour 1 cup (250 mL) of boiling water over 1 tbsp. (15 mL) of the herbal mixture. Wait 10 minutes and strain. Drink a cup three times a day.

Peppermint and milk make a powerful duo. The menthol in the peppermint stimulates your heart, and the B vitamins in the milk have a positive effect on your cardiovascular system.

Hemorrhoids

People may not like to talk about them, but when hemorrhoids hit, they need a remedy—and fast. Treated early, they can be controlled effectively with natural means.

Caused by excessive straining during a bowel movement, hemorrhoids are basically swollen veins in the anus, accompanied by itching and sometimes sharp pain. Hemorrhoids may be internal—that is, within the anal canal—or external, when they may be felt as little knobs or balls around the anal opening. Hemorrhoids are usually caused by constipation, and constipation also makes existing hemorrhoids worse.

HOME REMEDIES

▶ A **cold wash** after a bowel movement reduces itching and helps your blood vessels contract. Soak a linen cloth with cold water (54–60°F/12–16°C), wring it out, and wash the affected area, leaving a thin film of water on your skin. Do not dry it off, but put on your underwear and lie under the covers in bed until your skin warms up.

▶ Take a sitz bath. **Oak bark** and **horsetail** contain tannins that have an anti-inflammatory effect. Boil two handfuls of oak bark or horsetail in 2 quarts/liters of water for 15 minutes, then strain. Pour the broth, cooled to body temperature, into a small basin and sit in it for 5 minutes twice daily.

▶ An essential oil sitz bath also alleviates discomfort: put 2 drops each of **cypress** and **chamomile oil** and 1 drop of **peppermint oil** into a small basin filled with water at body temperature. Take a 5-minute sitz bath, then carefully dab the anal area dry and apply chamomile oil.

a money-saving *hint*

You don't need a special sitz-bath basin from a medical supply store—a large basin with a high rim will do the trick.

▶ Alleviate itching by placing a **cotton ball soaked in oil** between your buttocks to prevent friction.

▶ Salves containing **pot marigold** or **witch hazel** reduce inflammation and bleeding considerably.

▶ **Raspberries** can aid digestion and soften your stool to prevent further stress to your hemorrhoids. If you have a tendency toward hemorrhoids, it's a good idea to stock up on raspberries in season and freeze them in small portions.

▶ Dab on a little **zinc oxide** or **petroleum jelly** with a clean cotton ball. Tests prove that these everyday items are just as effective as pricier alternatives for soothing hemorrhoid pain.

PREVENTION

▶ A **diet high in fiber** produces softer stools, protecting against hemorrhoids.

▶ Adequate **fluid intake** prevents constipation. Drink at least six extra glasses of water daily to help soften stools.

▶ Gentle and regular **exercise** encourages regular bowel movements.

▶ Use **soft toilet paper** or moisten the paper with a little water before use.

▶ Be careful about **reading in the bathroom**—sitting too long on the toilet seat increases pressure on the rectum.

For a soothing sitz bath, mix equal amounts of chamomile and yellow sweet clover. Pour 1 cup (250 mL) of boiling water over 1 tbsp. (15 mL) of the mixture. Strain after 10 minutes and add to sitz bath.

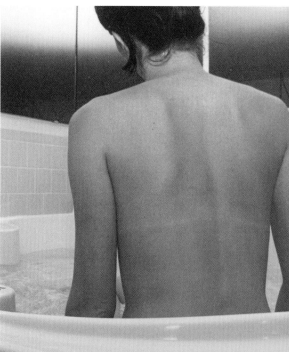

Insect Bites

Even the most beautiful summer day can have a dark side if you get stung by a bee, wasp, or mosquito. Since these pests have always plagued humankind, there are countless home remedies to relieve the pain and swelling and soothe the maddening itch.

Mosquito bites are usually a harmless nuisance; however, stings from bees, wasps, or hornets can be dangerous. A sting on the mouth or on the throat carries a risk of suffocation and, for people with allergies, a sting anywhere can be life-threatening. In either case, get to the emergency room immediately. Otherwise you can rely on the wealth of experience from home medicine.

HOME REMEDIES

▶ If you're stung by a bee, wasp, or hornet, remove the stinger and cool the swelling with **running water**, a **cold pack**, or **ice cubes** wrapped in a cloth.

▶ Cleanse the area. Stinging insects may have undesirable bacteria in their venom. Wash the sting well with **soap and water** or an **antiseptic.**

▶ Neutralize it with **lemon or onion juice.** To prevent swelling, place fresh slices of onion (a natural anti-inflammatory) or lemon (the acid neutralizes the venom) on the sting.

▶ **Tea tree oil** disinfects and reduces inflammation: put 1 drop on the site of the sting.

▶ Spread a thick paste of **baking powder and water** onto the site of the sting.

▶ Stir together 2 drops of **lemon essential oil** and 1 tsp. (5 mL) of **honey** and spread generously on the site of the sting to prevent inflammation.

▶ If you're away from home: **coltsfoot** and **plantain herb** can often be found growing at the edge of many highways; crush a leaf between your fingers and press it onto the site of the sting.

▶ After removing a tick, disinfect the bite site with a few drops of **tea tree oil**, **iodine**, or **alcohol.**

PREVENTION

▶ **Don't swat** bees or wasps.

▶ When outdoors, drink only from a **clear glass** or through a **straw** to avoid swallowing a wasp.

▶ After a picnic quickly **pack up the leftovers** so that the smell doesn't attract any insects.

▶ Keep away from **garbage cans**.

▶ Use discretion with **perfumes** and **hairsprays**—they frequently attract insects.

▶ Wear **long pants** and a **long-sleeved shirt** while hiking, if possible, and keep your skin covered up when in an area where insect bites are likely.

▶ Change out of **sweaty clothing**—sweat always attracts insects.

▶ **Don't walk barefoot** over summer lawns.

▶ Avoid **tall grass** or **underbrush** where ticks are present.

▶ Repel insects by adding five drops of **citronella oil** to 1 cup (250 mL) of water and dabbing on exposed skin.

good to know

TICK BITE

If you get bitten by a tick, it is crucial to quickly remove it, including the head. Grasp it with tweezers as close to the skin as possible and slowly pull it out. If the head remains buried, consult a doctor. Be particularly wary of a circular redness spreading around the site of the bite some days or weeks afterward—this can be the first indication of Lyme disease.

Essential oils such as lavender and tea tree oil are a big help with insect stings.

Joints

In the past, rheumatism was a catch-all term for any ailments involving the joints. Nowadays, we distinguish between rheumatoid arthritis, osteoarthritis, and gout—ailments that have very different causes, but which can all result in serious pain and reduced mobility.

Rheumatoid arthritis is an autoimmune disease that results in joint pain and deformity; osteoarthritis is a degenerative joint disease; and gout is a metabolic disease which can result in joint damage.

OSTEOARTHRITIS

▶ Apply cold (not hot!) **moor mud** or **healing earth poultices** to the affected joints once a day. This noticeably soothes discomfort.

▶ Rub in **St. John's wort** or **arnica oil** to combat joint inflammation and pain.

▶ A **mud** or **hay flower bath,** no hotter than body temperature (98.6°F/37°C), also eases arthritis pain.

▶ A cup of **stinging nettle tea** three times daily helps with pain and inflammation. Use 1 tbsp. (15 mL) of dried herb in 1 cup (250 mL) of water and let steep 10 minutes.

▶ Try **borage oil** capsules or salves containing **arnica**, **comfrey**, or **capsaicin** (the active ingredient in chili peppers). Your local health food store or pharmacy can provide you with a range of compounds containing natural ingredients to bring down inflammation.

▶ The roots of **devil's claw** contain substances that soothe pain and inflammation. Originally from Africa, it has long been used around the world to treat joint pain.

RHEUMATOID ARTHRITIS

With rheumatoid arthritis, whether you should opt for a hot or cold treatment depends on the phase of the malady. If your joints are inflamed, hot, and swollen, treat them with ice and cold packs made from mud, healing earth, or clay (from a health food store or pharmacy). When the condition is less acute, turn to heat to soothe discomfort and promote circulation.

Regular, gentle activities, such as brisk walking and light weight lifting, strengthen the joints.

▶ **Relax**. When your body is tensed up, you tend to hurt more. Relaxation techniques may ease pain.

▶ In addition to stinging nettle tea, teas made from **meadowsweet** or **heartsease** (1–2 tsp./5–10 mL per cup/250 mL) alleviate symptoms.

▶ A **celery infusion** can be a quick and effective remedy. Mince 1 heaping tbsp. (20 mL) of celery and pour 1 cup (250 mL) of water over it. Boil, steep briefly, and strain. Sweeten with honey and drink 2 cups (500 mL) a day. *Note: always prepare the infusion fresh and do not use if you have a kidney infection.*

▶ Grind **fern root** in a mortar, use a gauze bandage to make a pack, and place on the painful joint.

ARTHRITIS AND RHEUMATOID ARTHRITIS PREVENTION

▶ Ocean fish such as **mackerel, salmon,** and **herring** provide omega-3 fatty acids that ease swelling and pain. Don't like fish? Pick up supplements.

▶ Cross **eel** off your menu. It contains arachidon acids, which allow pain to occur in the body.

▶ **Vitamin C** has a positive influence on the course of the disease. It is particularly abundant in **citrus fruits, seabuckthorn, kiwis,** and **bell peppers.**

▶ **Vitamin E** (abundant in plant oils) intercepts so-called oxygen radicals, which form in greater quantities with acute inflammatory joint diseases.

▶ Avoid **coffee, alcohol,** and **nicotine.**

▶ Didn't your mother tell you to eat your veggies? And isn't she always right? Some studies indicate that rheumatoid arthritis can be positively impacted by a diet rich in **fruits, vegetables, salads, wholegrain,** and **reduced-fat milk products**—but you should consume little fat in the form of meat, hot dogs, fatty cheese, butter, and cream.

▶ **Slim down.** Being overweight can enhance damage to your joints.

▶ Take up **tai chi,** or Chinese shadowboxing. When practiced correctly, it relaxes all joints.

GOUT

Gout is a metabolic disease. When your kidneys become less effective at flushing away excess uric acid, the acid begins to crystallize in your joints, tendons, and muscles, leading to swelling, pain, and tenderness. To guard against gout, eat ocean fish twice a week (but not eel), reduce the amount of meat you eat (no organ meats and consommés), and nosh on lentils, peas, and red and white beans only in moderation. It's best to pass up alcohol and sweets entirely—both considerably slow your ability to excrete uric acid.

▶ Drink plenty of **water** and **herbal tea** to help your kidneys flush out uric acid.

Salves with horse chestnut extract can reduce the inflammation from arthritis.

▶ **Birch leaf tea** acts as a diuretic, helping to flush out uric acid. It also contains salicylate—the same pain-relieving compound found in aspirin. Pour 1 cup (250 mL) of boiling water over 2 tsp. (10 mL) of birch leaves, steep for 10 minutes, and strain. Drink 2 cups (500 mL) a day. *Note: do not use if you have reduced heart, kidney, or bladder function.*

▶ **Horsetail tea** (1 heaping tsp./7 mL of horsetail in 1 cup/250 mL of water) helps relieve gout pain.

▶ Try **mud** and **sulfur bath mixtures** (from a pharmacy or health food store) in body temperature water to alleviate pain. Do this twice a week.

▶ Rub painful joints with **camphor spirits** (a solution of camphor and rubbing alcohol).

oil wrap for osteoarthritis

one Soak a cotton cloth in hot water and wring it out.

two Mix rosemary, marjoram, and lavender oils in equal proportions, and put 10 drops of the mixture onto the cloth.

three Wrap the hot oil pack around your afflicted joints once a day for about 10 minutes.

four Repeat the application several times as needed.

Sports such as swimming and water gymnastics minimize strain on your joints.

45

Muscle Pain

Are you limiting your workouts to the weekend? Then you've probably learned that infrequent physical exertion often reaps its revenge the following day in the form of sore, stiff muscles.

Achy muscles are a harmless but unpleasant phenomenon that usually disappears by itself after a few days, and is best alleviated through heat applications. If you train regularly and feel fit, you're not likely to suffer unduly from this malady. But muscle cramps can also be due to overload, or other causes such as circulatory disorders or a mineral deficiency.

SORE MUSCLES

▶ Take it easy during the first **12–48 hours.** Sore muscles don't have full function, and continued strenuous demands carry a heightened risk of injury.

▶ A hot bath can help you feel better. Add some **hay flowers or moor mud,** plus **spruce needle** or **mountain pine extracts** for a soothing effect. The caveat: avoid heat for two to three hours after a tough workout, as it will promote circulation and increase inflammation.

▶ A warm wrap with **arnica tincture** can ease the pain. First moisten a cloth with hot water and wring it out, then put a few drops of arnica tincture on the cloth and apply to the sore muscle.

▶ **Massage** can help ease sore, stiff muscles.

▶ **Ample fluid intake** flushes excess acids from your body, and supplies it with important minerals. Good choices include **herbal teas** and **vegetable and fruit juices,** diluted with mineral water containing little or no sodium.

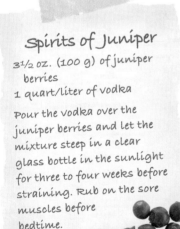

Spirits of Juniper

3½ oz. (100 g) of juniper berries

1 quart/liter of vodka

Pour the vodka over the juniper berries and let the mixture steep in a clear glass bottle in the sunlight for three to four weeks before straining. Rub on the sore muscles before bedtime.

Before intense physical activity, do a warm-up and rub your muscles with tea tree oil.

MUSCLE CRAMPS

▶ To relax a leg cramp in the calf, **carefully stretch the muscle** against the direction of the cramping, then walk back and forth a few paces. In stubborn cases, sit on the ground, pull your toes toward you, and stretch your leg out fully. After that, gently massage the muscle.

▶ Rubs containing extracts of **menthol, camphor,** or **horse chestnut** can add extra oomph to a massage to loosen up cramps; so can essential oils containing **St. John's wort, eucalyptus, spruce needles,** or **thyme.**

▶ A lack of minerals, such as **magnesium, potassium,** and **calcium,** is probably the biggest cause of nighttime leg cramps; they are abundant in fennel, broccoli, bananas, dried fruits, oatmeal, nuts, milk, cream cheese, and cheese.

▶ **Cider vinegar** provides your body with potassium: drink 2 tsp. (10 mL) of cider vinegar in 1 cup (250 mL) of water every evening for at least four weeks.

▶ If your cramps are the result of a **magnesium** deficiency, taking magnesium in the form of effervescent tablets, in consultation with a doctor, is a good idea.

Muscle Sprains

A careless moment on uneven ground can put you out of commission with a sprained ankle. But if you follow the correct first aid rules and rely on some time-tested home remedies, you'll heal much quicker.

FIRST AID

Act fast. A cold compress is the best and most effective aid for a sprained ankle, since it dulls the pain and decreases the blood flow, which lessens swelling. Ice your ankle (or whatever you've sprained) immediately. Keep the ice on for 15–20 minutes, then remove and leave off for an equal time period. Do this 4–5 times daily over the next two days. After cooling, keep the sprained body part elevated to prevent further swelling. A sprained ankle can be properly positioned by placing a pillow under the lower leg so that the leg is straight and slightly elevated.

An elastic bandage helps keep your sprained joint immobile and thus encourages healing.

HOME REMEDIES

▶ Wrap it up in an **elastic bandage**. The compression will help control the swelling. But don't make it so tight that you cut off your circulation.

▶ Chow down on **pineapple**. Its active ingredient, bromelain, can help reduce swelling and speed your healing.

▶ Apply a little **rubbing alcohol**. Rubbing alcohol cools and combats swelling, and cold wraps soaked in rubbing alcohol are a traditional treatment for sprains.

▶ Apply an **ice-cold cherry-pit bag**.

▶ When applied early, **strawflower oil** can help combat inflammation.

▶ Carefully rub a few drops of **tea tree oil** onto the skin of affected area to encourages healing.

▶ Salves and tinctures with a base of **horse chestnut**, **comfrey**, or **St. John's wort** accelerate the healing process.

▶ To make a **tincture of arnica,** let 3½ oz. (100 g) of dried arnica flowers steep in 2 cups (500 mL) of rubbing alcohol for two weeks, then strain and store in a dark bottle. For a pain-relieving wrap mix 1 tsp. (5 mL) of the tincture with 1 cup (250 mL) of cold water, moisten a cloth with it, and apply to your sprained joint for 10 minutes. Keep the tincture stored in a cool, dark place.

▶ A **liquid of oak bark** (3½ oz./100 g of bark in 2 cups/500 mL of water, boiled for 15 minutes) encourages healing.

▶ Get the **right shoes** for your sport. A tendency to sprain your ankle over and over can be a sign that you're not getting the support you need from your footwear. Shoes designed specifically with an activity in mind can provide the right amount of cushioning and traction.

Dill Salve

Dill salve alleviates pain from sprains.
2 tbsp. minced dill
1 tbsp. olive oil
a little beeswax

Mix the dill and olive oil, set aside for 24 hours, then press through a strainer. Mix with warm beeswax to form a spreadable paste. Apply the salve to the affected area.

Nausea

Nausea and vomiting are often the result of eating tainted food, consuming too much alcohol, or catching a virus. But it can also be a symptom of motion sickness, pregnancy, or simply a reaction to stress.

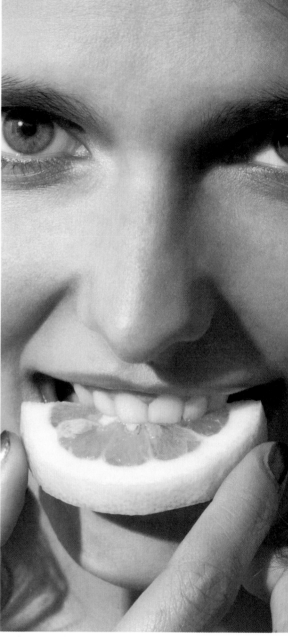

Sucking on a fresh slice of lemon can nip rising nausea in the bud.

As unpleasant as it feels to throw up, a brief bout of vomiting usually serves a purpose. It rids your body of toxic substances and, once it's over, nausea and stomach pain should disappear. Some people experience nausea when traveling by car, boat, or train. Motion sickness is especially common in children, whose balance mechanisms are more sensitive than adults'. In ancient China nausea might have been treated with monkey gallbladder (okay, they weren't always right). You can effectively combat nausea with a number of home remedies—but never suppress the urge to vomit, since that is one of your body's most powerful defense mechanisms against harmful substances.

chamomile wrap

one Fold a hand towel in two, then dip in warm chamomile tea and wring it out.

two Place the towel over your stomach area, spread a dry towel over it, and hold in place with a wool scarf.

three Let the wrap work for 10 minutes and replace as needed.

HOME REMEDIES

▶ You can effectively ward off rising nausea by deeply inhaling **the aroma of a freshly cut apple**.

▶ For sudden nausea, put a drop of **peppermint oil** onto your tongue, or dribble the oil on the back of your hand and inhale the aroma deeply.

▶ In days of yore, people kept scent bottles handy, but today people are more likely to reach for essential oils. Put 2 drops each of **lavender** or **sandalwood oil** on a handkerchief and inhale the scent deeply.

▶ To help calm your stomach crush 1 tsp. (5 mL) of **fennel seeds** in a mortar, pour 1 cup (250 mL) of water over it in a pot. Bring to a boil, and let steep for 10 minutes before drinking.

FOR MOTION SICKNESS

▶ This tea will help prevent motion sickness. You can prepare it in advance and take it along in a small thermos. Pour boiling water over 1 piece of **cinnamon bark**, and let it steep for 10 minutes before straining and drinking it.

▶ With increasing nausea it sometimes helps to slowly chew a little **ginger**.

Nervousness and Anxiety

Overstimulation, conflict, and a day packed with deadlines can jangle your nerves and leave you feeling tense. The result can be nervousness, sleep disorders, and anxiety. When it comes to reestablishing your equilibrium, these traditional teas, bath additives, and scent mixtures can help.

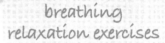

When you feel overloaded, a little self-indulgence can work wonders—perhaps a relaxing bath by candlelight or a soothing massage. But if anxiety and nervousness are taking over your life, do not hesitate to consult a professional.

HOME REMEDIES

▶ **Valerian** and **lemon balm** stabilize emotional balance when you add a few drops to your bathwater, as do **lavender, bergamot, sandalwood,** or **cedar.**

▶ For a fragrant and relaxing herbal bath, boil up about 3½ oz. (100 g) each of **chamomile, linden,** and **lavender flowers** in 2 quarts/liters of water for 30 minutes. Strain and pour into hot bathwater. Add a little music and you've got the perfect soak.

▶ **Sandalwood** reduces anxiety and nervousness. Mix 3 drops of sandalwood oil with 1 tsp. (5 mL) of **almond oil** and gently massage your shoulders, neck, arms, and legs. Better yet, get someone to do it for you.

▶ To help calm your nerves and for a restful sleep make a **sachet of hops flowers** and place it under your pillow.

▶ Three drops each of **peppermint, basil, sage,** and **lavender oils** make a calming mixture for a scent burner.

PREVENTION

▶ **Relaxation techniques** such as autogenic training, yoga, progressive muscle relaxation, and meditation exercises have a balancing and calming effect.

▶ Be sure to get plenty of **sleep** and **rest breaks**.

▶ Structure your day so there is some **time for yourself**.

▶ Taking a **leisurely walk** in the fresh air is good for the nerves.

▶ Lie in the **sun** for 10 minutes—it reduces stress and provides relaxation.

▶ **Fish oils** (omega-3 fatty acids) may elevate mood and calm anxiety. A word of warning: fatty fish can contain high levels of mercury and other contaminants, so limit yourself to two servings a week or choose a supplement instead.

breathing relaxation exercises

one Sit erect on a chair with your feet resting near each other on the floor. Let your arms hang down at the sides.

two As you breathe in through your nose, slowly spread your arms straight out to the sides and then bring your palms together over your head. Then stand up energetically.

three Rotate your hands so they're back-to-back. Lower your arms straight to the sides. As you do so, slowly sit back down and expel the air through your mouth.

four Wait a couple of seconds, then repeat the entire exercise for a total of ten repetitions.

Teas made from lemon balm, St. John's wort, hops, passion flowers, or valerian can restore your sense of inner calm.

Respiratory Ailments

Pollution, stress, smoking, smog, and office buildings with poor air quality can all leave you gasping for breath. The good news: nature offers plenty of weapons to combat asthma, bronchitis, and chronic coughs, or complement medical treatments.

The health of our lungs and respiratory system is affected by the quality of the air we breathe and the effects of poor air quality are far-reaching. The following conditions can benefit from home remedies.

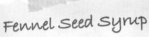

Fennel Seed Syrup

A time-tested home remedy for cough and bronchitis.
1 tbsp. (15 mL) fennel seeds
1 tbsp. (15 mL) Iceland moss
1.5 quarts/liters water
9 oz. (250 g) rock candy

Boil the herbs in the water until about half the fluid turns to steam. Strain and boil it down with the rock candy to form a syrup. Let cool, pour into a bottle, and close the lid tightly. The syrup will keep in the fridge for several weeks. Take 1 tbsp. (15 mL) every three hours, as needed.

ASTHMA

Unless you've been struck by Cupid's arrow, your sudden feeling of breathlessness is likely to be caused by asthma. This medical condition results in increased mucus production, narrowing the airways in your lungs. Infections, allergies, stress, anxiety, and stimuli such as dust, smoke, and cold can all trigger life-threatening asthma attacks. Asthma must be treated medically. But as scary as this condition can be, keep in mind that leading a healthy lifestyle can strengthen your breathing passages and boost your body's natural defenses. If you do have an attack, anything that breaks up mucus and relaxes your bronchial muscles will help. The caveat: if you have allergies or your asthma is allergy-related, be particularly cautious about using animal- and plant-based remedies. These substances can trigger immune reactions and should be used only with medical supervision.

▶ Try an airway-soothing mixture of **honey** and freshly grated **horseradish** in a 1:3 ratio. Take 1 tsp. (5 mL) three times a day.

▶ To combat airway spasms and mucus, mix 2 tsp. (10 mL) of **cider vinegar** and 1 tsp. (5 mL) of **honey** in 1 cup (250 mL) of water and drink three times a day for three months.

The calming effect of fennel on a cough has been known since ancient times, and 2–5 cups of fennel tea per day are recommended for respiratory ailments.

▶ A warm **chest compress** breaks up mucus: soak a cotton cloth in water at about 120°F (50°C), wring it out, and wrap it over your chest. Cover it with a dry cloth and rest in bed for 30 minutes.

▶ Excessively dry air irritates your breathing passages. You could spend your hard-earned money on a humidifier, but **bowls of water** placed strategically around your house will evaporate into the air, providing some relief.

BRONCHITIS

Bronchitis is an inflammation of the bronchi, the tubes leading from the throat to the lungs, usually as a result of infection or irritation. To encourage healing, drink plenty of fluids. Teas and other hot drinks can soothe irritated airways and liquefy mucus, making it easier to cough up. In addition to traditional herb, sage, or chamomile teas, home remedies that make use of common ingredients like onions and sugar can be remarkably effective, and steam inhalations may soothe a persistent cough.

▶ Grind 1 tbsp. (15 mL) of **anise seeds** in a mortar and mix with 1 tbsp. (15 mL) of dried **thyme**. Pour 1 quart/liter of water into the mixture.

Let the tea steep 5 minutes, then strain, sweeten with honey, and drink throughout the day.

▶ Peel and slice a large **onion**. Sprinkle the slices with a thick coating of **brown sugar**, layer them inside a glass jar, seal tightly, and place in a warm spot overnight. Take 1 tsp. (5 mL) of the mixture three times a day. Keep the remainder in the refrigerator.

▶ **Chamomile** soothes irritated respiratory passages. To inhale it, drop a handful of dried chamomile flowers in a bowl with boiling hot water and let steep for 10 minutes before carefully inhaling the steam. As an alternative to chamomile flowers, add 1–2 drops of **eucalyptus, thyme,** or **cypress oil** to the hot water before inhaling.

COUGH

Despite the billions of dollars spent on over-the-counter cough syrups every year, doctors say those same treatments are largely ineffective against a nagging cough. For relief of persistent symptoms, the gentle, soothing home remedies that your grandmother swore by are just the ticket. Teas made from plantain, thyme, or mallow can quiet a dry cough. And hot baths and cough remedies made from medicinal plants or ingredients may well speed you along the road to recovery.

▶ To make your own cough syrup, combine 3 tbsp. (45 mL) of **lemon juice** and 1 cup (250 mL) of **honey** in ¼ cup (50 mL) of warm water. Take 1 or 2 tbsp. (15–25 mL) every three hours. *Note: honey should not be given to children under two years of age.*

▶ For adults, **warm beer** can ease a dry cough and send you off to dreamland. Before going to bed, warm up about 16 oz. (500 mL) of beer with 4 tbsp. (60 mL) of honey—don't let it boil. Sip slowly.

▶ To make a cough tea, combine about 1 oz. (30 g) of **dried thyme**, 3/4 oz. (25 g) of **marshmallow root,** 1/3 oz. (10 g) of **crushed fennel fruit,** 1/3 oz. (10 g) of **Iceland moss**, and 1/3 oz. (10 g) of **licorice root.** Pour 1 cup (250 mL) of water over 1 tbsp. (15 mL) of the mixture, let steep for 10 minutes, then strain. Drink 1 cup (250 mL) morning and evening.

▶ A **lemon wrap** may help—but if you have sensitive skin it could cause skin irritation (if so, immediately remove the wrap and wash your skin with warm water). Nonetheless, it's worth a try: dribble the juice from two lemons on a cotton cloth and wrap it over your chest with a wool scarf tied to hold it in place. Give it an hour to work its magic before removing.

▶ Just 3 drops of **eucalyptus oil** and a little water in a fragrant oil burner can soothe your breathing passages.

A glass of warm elderberry juice, flavored with honey and lemon juice, helps with bronchitis.

A CHANGE OF AIR
There are times when you really are "under the weather." A change of climate can have a positive impact on chronic respiratory ailments. The salt content of sea air, for example, can help dissolve tough mucus in your breathing passages. What's more, sea air is largely free from pollutants and allergens. The clean, clear air and sunlight of the mountains can also benefit tortured respiratory passages.

Shingles

About 20 percent of people who had chicken pox will later develop shingles, usually when they're over age 50. The infection causes a burning, blistering rash and, often, mild to severe pain that can last for several weeks.

Shingles occur when the chicken pox virus finds its way to your nervous system. You may have no symptoms for years. But the minute your immune system is compromised by age, disease, or stress, you can break out in a burning, painful rash that leaves you itching all over. You will need medical care to deal with the condition, but lots of rest and natural remedies can help speed the healing process.

Apply tinctures or plant juices to your rash with a cotton swab, a cotton ball, or a clean cloth.

▶ Blisters heal more quickly when they are sprinkled with a little diluted **tincture of pot marigold** (1 part tincture, 4 parts water).

HOME REMEDIES

▶ **Clay** or **healing earth poultices** alleviate pain and dry up blisters. Stir the clay or healing earth with a little water to form a thick paste, spread it finger-thick on a cloth, cover with gauze, and apply, cloth-side down, on the rash. Replace the pack as soon as it warms up. Apply twice daily.

▶ Try various essential oils to alleviate pain. Mix 2 drops each of **bergamot** and **eucalyptus oils** and 2 tbsp. (25 mL) of **almond oil**. Use a cotton ball to dab the mixture onto the blisters.

▶ Apply linen cloths soaked in soothing **chamomile** or **yarrow tea** to the rash.

▶ Dribble a little **St. John's wort** or **tea tree oil** on a linen cloth and apply to the affected skin for 30 minutes to aid healing.

PREVENTION

▶ To make sure viruses don't have a chance, **strengthen your body's defenses**: regular exercise, adequate rest, and a vitamin-rich diet will help.

▶ Avoid extended **sunbathing**, since ultraviolet rays are stressful to the body.

CONSULT A DOCTOR

Shingles is the product of the *herpes zoster* virus. If you have a rash on your forehead or anywhere near your eyes, see a doctor immediately to avoid the risk of damaging your corneas. Although you can always expect some pain—unfortunately it comes with the condition—if the pain is unbearable, it could indicate the presence of nerve damage (post-zoster neuralgia). Seek medical help. Home remedies can support your doctor's treatment. Equally important is plenty of rest—physical exertion can serve to reinforce the problem.

An Herbal Wrap

Encourages the rash to heal.

What you need:
- 3/4 oz. (25 g) oak bark
- 5/8 oz. (20 g) lady's mantle
- 5/8 oz. (20 g) chamomile
- 5/8 oz. (20 g) sage
- 1/4 oz. (10 g) sweet yellow clover
- 1 quart/liter cold water

Pour the water over the ingredients and bring to a boil. Steep 5 minutes and strain. Dab the warm liquid onto the affected skin with a cotton ball or soak a cloth in it and cover the area.

Gentle herbal remedies can help blisters heal.

Skin

Essential to your health, beauty, and well-being, your skin is an important part of who you are and is crucial for your body's survival. Your skin acts as a barrier that protects you from the outside world, so be kind to it.

Despite scientific advances in treatments for skin problems, many people still prefer to rely on natural ingredients and home remedies.

CUTS AND SCRAPES

A careless moment in the kitchen can result in a cut finger; a fall from a bicycle can cause a nasty scrape. Fortunately we have the wisdom of past generations to call on when it comes to treating minor boo-boos effectively.

FIRST AID

The most crucial aspect of wound care is to clean and disinfect thoroughly. Carefully remove any foreign objects from a cut, scratch, or abrasion with disinfected tweezers. Then disinfect with an antiseptic solution (from a pharmacy). To stop bleeding, wrap a clean cloth or towel around the affected area and apply pressure.

HOME REMEDIES

Twenty-four hours after the injury, the wound—which by now should be closed—can be treated to aid healing. You'll find any number of commercial antibacterial ointments at the pharmacy, but why not try one of Mother Nature's simple, low-cost remedies?

▶ **St. John's wort** or **tea tree oil** compresses have proven their worth to many generations of healers. Add 5–8 drops of oil to a clean dishcloth and cover the wound for several hours (with St. John's wort) or 24 hours (with tea tree oil). Repeat regularly.

▶ For a **yarrow wrap**, add 3½ oz. (100 mL) of boiling water to 1 tbsp. (15 mL) of dried yarrow blooms, and strain. Moisten a cloth with the solution, gently wring it out, and apply to injured skin.

▶ You may already know that **cabbage** is a nutritional all-star, but its leaves have many healing properties as well. A cabbage wrap alleviates pain and promotes healing. To prepare, rinse a few inside leaves from a head of cabbage and remove the central rib. Soften the leaves with a rolling pin, then apply to your wound for several hours at a time, using a bandage or cling wrap to hold them in place. Use twice a day.

▶ To speed up healing, scald a **lavender teabag**, let it cool, and place it on your wound.

▶ **Vitamin C** helps wounds heal more quickly. So treat yourself to an extra serving of strawberries or a delicious juicy orange. After all, it's good for you!

PREVENTION

▶ Wear **protective gloves** when working with any sharp objects.

▶ Store **knives** in a knife block or in a container with the blades pointing downward.

▶ Make sure your **tetanus shot** is up to date.

bandage with chamomile tincture

one Pour about 7 tbsp. (100 mL) of rubbing alcohol over ½ oz. (15 g) of chamomile flowers. Let steep for ten days.

two Carefully strain the solution and thoroughly squeeze the juice out of the blooms. Pour into a clean bottle.

three Dilute the tincture with water in a 1:4 ratio and apply to a piece of muslin. Leave on your injured skin for at least 30 minutes.

Try boiling some cabbage, then cleansing your skin with the water.

A Cleaver (Goosegrass) Bath

A bath with cleaver soothes the burning and tightness of stressed skin.

3½ oz. (100 g) cleaver
2 quarts/liters water

Boil the water and cleaver for 5 minutes, then strain and squeeze out the cleaver. Add the broth to a lukewarm bath and soak for 20 minutes.

SKIN AND THE SUN

While the sun has many beneficial qualities, its damaging effects are well-documented. The ozone layer, which protects us from excessive exposure to ultraviolet (UV) radiation, isn't as thick as it used to be. The reasons why are another story, but today's reality is that more of the sun's UV radiation reaches the earth's surface. And these rays cause a variety of health problems, including skin cancer, so we should take steps to protect ourselves.

FIRST-AID MEASURES

Since sunburn is a first-degree burn, anything that cools your skin will help relieve the pain—from a wet T-shirt to a cold linen cloth soaked in saline solution and placed over the burn. To make the solution, mix 1 tsp. (5 mL) salt to 2 quarts/liters of distilled water.

HOME REMEDIES

▶ Wraps with **milk**, **yogurt**, or **buttermilk** soothe pain and cool skin. Apply at least twice a day for 30 minutes. Thin slices of **cucumber**, **potato**, or **apple** also cool hot skin.

▶ Rub your burn with the cut surface of a **lemon** or a **tomato**—the vitamin C encourages healing.

▶ Place a wrap soaked in cooled **black tea** or **witch hazel tea** (1 tbsp./15 mL of witch hazel in 1½ cups/375 mL of water) on reddened skin, several times a day.

▶ Mix together a few drops of **evening primrose** and **lemon oil** in equal proportions and apply the mixture daily.

▶ Gels or creams containing **aloe vera** or **arnica** can bring relief from pain.

Seek out the shade, even at the beach, and don't expose yourself to direct sunlight for more than a few minutes.

▶ A lukewarm bath with 8 tbsp. (125 mL) of **healing earth** as an additive cools and encourages healing.

▶ Drink plenty of fluids, preferably **cool herbal teas, mineral water,** or **diluted fruit juices.**

▶ For severe headaches, sunburn in babies and little children, severe pain, and burn blisters, **consult a doctor**; never pierce or pop the blisters.

PREVENTION

▶ **0–2 (Low) UV Index:** minimal protection required. Wear sunglasses and apply a sunscreen with a SPF factor of 15+. Cover up if outside for more than an hour.

▶ **3–5 (Moderate) UV Index:** wear a hat, sunglasses, and a sunscreen with a SPF factor of 30+. Cover up if you'll be outside for 30 minutes or more. Reduce time in the sun between 11 A.M. and 4 P.M.

▶ **6–7 (High) UV Index:** protection is a must! Wear a hat, sunglasses, and apply a sunscreen with a SPF factor of 45. Try to avoid direct sunlight between 11 A.M. and 4 P.M.

▶ **8–10 (Very High) UV Index:** extra precautions required—unprotected skin burns quickly and can suffer long-term damage. Avoid going outside between 11 A.M. and 4 P.M., but if you must, stay in the shade and cover up. Wear a hat, sunglasses, and apply a sunscreen with a SPF factor of 45+.

▶ **11+ (Extreme) UV Index:** take exceptional precautions. Stay inside, but if you must go out, stay in the shade. Cover up—wear a hat, sunglasses, and apply a sunscreen with a SPF factor of 60.

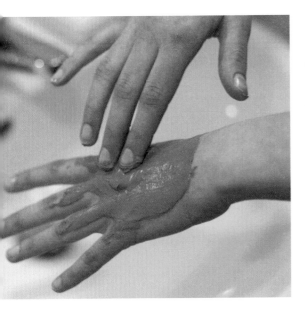

ECZEMA

This chronic skin condition, characterized by an itchy, red, scaly rash, is not immune to natural remedies. Cleansers, salves, and plant-based poultices can soothe the itching and inflammation, and help moisturize dry skin.

BASIC SKIN CARE

If you are prone to eczema, your skin needs oil and moisture to restore its natural balance. *Note: if you have allergies, animal and plant ingredients can trigger an allergic reaction, so use them with caution.*

▶ **Soap-free cleansers** are gentle and therefore far less irritating to the skin.

▶ Plant-based salves with **jojoba** or **evening primrose oil** are good moisturizers.

TREATING ECZEMA

▶ Press raw **cabbage leaves** with a rolling pin until the juice comes out. Warm the leaves in a strainer held above steam and apply twice daily.

▶ To soothe itching and reduce inflammation: pour 1 cup (250 mL) of boiling water over 2 tsp. (10 mL) of **heartsease**. Steep for 10 minutes, then strain and cool to lukewarm. Soak a cloth in the fluid, squeeze it out, and wrap the eczema for 15 minutes.

▶ Pour 1 cup (250 mL) of cold water over 2 tsp. (10 mL) of **walnut leaves**. Boil for 5 minutes, strain, and cool to lukewarm. Soak a cloth in the liquid, wring it out, and apply to the rash for 15 minutes.

A paste made from healing earth and water is easy to apply and does wonders for skin affected by eczema.

▶ Stir 3 tbsp. (45 mL) of **healing earth** and an equal amount of cold water into a thick paste. Apply to eczema for 20 minutes. Rinse with cool water, then treat your skin with an anti-inflammatory salve containing vitamin E.

▶ **Chamomile** or **pot marigold ointments** can moisturize skin and sooth the relentless itching. The healing effect is strengthened when you keep products in the refrigerator and use them cold.

▶ Oil baths (maximum bathing time of 10 minutes, at no higher than 95°F/35°C) with **chamomile** or **rosemary oil** return moisture to your skin.

▶ An **oatmeal** bath leaves your skin feeling soft and supple, and calms the itch: pour about 18 oz. (500 g) of oatmeal into an old nylon stocking, tie shut, and add to your bathwater.

THINGS TO AVOID

▶ **Alkaline soaps**, cosmetics containing alcohol, or synthetic grooming products dry your skin out even more and make it susceptible to secondary infections from bacteria, viruses, or funguses.

▶ Frequent contact with water and **hot baths** over 95°F (35°C).

▶ Intense **sunbathing**.

▶ Handling **chemicals** without protective gloves.

good to know

CAUSES OF ECZEMA
Contact eczemas are an allergic reaction to specific foodstuffs, metals, cleaning agents, or cosmetics. Atopic eczemas are usually inherited. Around 10 percent of the population is affected by it. The most common atopic eczema is neurodermatitis, which requires medical care.

Oatmeal helps to calm and soothe inflamed skin.

Sleep

Normally your body needs at least seven to eight hours of sleep to regenerate fully. But if you find yourself tossing and turning all night, you're bound to feel tired and distracted the next day. Here's some tried-and-true sleep Rx that's just as effective today as it was for grandma.

A Slumber Drink

Drink a full shot glass before bedtime as an effective tool to help you doze off and sleep through the night.

- 1/3 oz. (10 g) valerian root
- 1/3 oz. (10 g) hops cones
- 1/3 oz. (10 g) lemon balm
- 1/3 oz. (10 g) St. John's wort
- 1/6 oz. (5 g) lavender flowers
- 1 stick of cinnamon
- 1 quart/liter red wine

Grind the ingredients in a mortar and pour into a bottle along with the cinnamon and red wine. Shake the bottle every day for 10 days, then strain.

Stress, worries, or hormonal changes during menopause are often the root cause of an inability to fall asleep or a tendency to wake up repeatedly. Sleep disturbances are frequently temporary, but sometimes they drag on for weeks, months, or even years and become a nightmare for the victim. You may not be able to control all the factors that are interfering with your sleep, but mom was right on the money when she gave you warm milk before sending you off to bed. Sometimes a calming drink and a change to your bedtime routine can be enough to summon the elusive sandman.

HOME REMEDIES

▶ Slowly sip a cup of calming **valerian**, **hops**, **lemon balm**, **hawthorn**, or **St. John's wort** tea before going to bed. If you wish, you can sweeten the beverage with a little honey.

▶ Try another sleep tea made from 1⅓ oz. (40 g) of **valerian root**, ⅔ oz. (20 g) **hops cones**, ½ oz. (15 g) each of **lemon balm** and **peppermint leaves** and ⅓ oz. (10 g) of **bitter orange peel**. It will make it easy to get to sleep and then sleep through the night. Use 1 tsp. (5 mL) of the mixture per cup (250 mL) of tea.

▶ Have a tipple. Hops produce their calming effect not only in the form of teas and scent bundles, but also in **beer**. In moderation, alcohol adds to hops' soporific qualities A small glass (about 6½ oz./185 mL) in the evening can work wonders—but drinking more could have the opposite effect.

▶ An hour before bedtime, sip a glass of **warm milk** containing ⅔ oz. (20 g) of finely ground **almonds**.

▶ Take a dip. It's difficult to fall asleep if your feet are cold. **Warm socks** can help, as can **contrasting footbaths** before going to bed. Dip your feet into warm water (100°F/38°C) for five minutes, then into cold water (54–60°F/12–16°C) for 20 seconds. Repeat, ending with another dip in the warm water.

▶ Take a warm, relaxing bath containing **linden flowers** about a half-hour before going to bed.

▶ A snooze-inducing scent mixture for a scent burner consists of 4 drops of **chamomile oil** and 2 drops each of **lavender, sandalwood,** and **neroli oil**. Place the scent burner in your bedroom an hour before bedtime or add the drops to a small bowl of warm water to disperse the scent.

▶ Dribble a few drops of **lavender oil** onto a **spelt cushion** and lay your head on it. Your body heat will cause the oil to evaporate gradually, bringing on drowsiness.

You may need to make some lifestyle changes in order to sleep well.

a money-saving hint

Just before they bloom, clip a couple of branches from a lavender bush, dry them, and hang the fragrant clippings in your bedroom to encourage sleep.

▶ Here's a trick you can use to put one over on sleep: lie down on your bed in complete darkness, keep your eyes open, and **force yourself to stay awake**—usually the reverse will happen and you will quickly fall asleep.

▶ Modern methods such as **autogenic training** help to induce sleep through autosuggestion.

TIPS FOR A GOOD NIGHT'S SLEEP

▶ Keep your bedroom **quiet**, **dark**, and **not too warm** (no more than 63°F/17°C).

▶ Before going to bed, thoroughly **air out the bedroom**.

▶ There should be **no television** in your bedroom—it belongs in the living room.

▶ Going to bed and getting up at regular times provides a **healthy sleep rhythm** and synchronizes your body's biological clock.

▶ Make sure your **mattress** is of good quality, and test it out by lying down on it before making a purchase.

▶ Use sheets made from **natural materials** (like cotton or linen) to avoid night sweats.

▶ Get **lots of exercise** during the day, preferably in the fresh air to ensure that you're tired at bedtime.

▶ Take a short **walk** before going to bed.

▶ Avoid **fatty foods** in the evening, as heavy food weighs on your stomach.

▶ Don't consume **alcohol** in excess, or **coffee, black tea,** and **cola** containing caffeine. They are stimulants and interfere with sleep.

▶ Avoid **wrestling with problems** in the evening—worrying spoils sleep. Make a to-do list of all the things you need to address the following day, then relax!

▶ Establish a routine. Kids need to be run off their feet during the day to be tired at night, but the hour before bedtime should be low-key. Aim for a **calm bedtime routine** that might include a bath and a book.

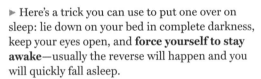

Sleep Sachets

A sleep sachet provides a pleasant, aromatic route to a refreshing slumber.
1 handful lavender flowers
1 handful hops cones
1 handful lemon balm
1 handful of St. John's wort
1 small pillowcase

Mix the dried herbs and enclose them in the cushion. Use as a pillow or place underneath your pillow.

Stomach Complaints

Hustle and bustle, improper nutrition, stress, and too little exercise can result in stomach upset. It's best not to let things go that far. If you're already uncomfortable, don't pop a pill right away—your sensitive stomach is likely to react just as well to nature's much gentler medications.

STOMACH ACHE

It's an unfortunate fact of life that many of the foods we like best, our stomach likes the least. Eating too much at once can also leave you with a tummy ache, since your stomach has trouble handling the extra volume. But if you drink plenty of mineral water and unsweetened herbal teas (preferably at least 2 quarts/liters per day), eat a healthy diet, and don't feast too often, your stomach will thank you.

▶ Sip **fennel**, **chamomile**, **lemon balm**, or **peppermint tea** with and in between meals.

▶ Eat a small piece of fresh or pickled **ginger** for nausea. Or if you prefer, grate roughly 2 tsp. (10 mL) of fresh ginger and let it steep in 1 cup (250 mL) of water for about 10 minutes before drinking.

▶ All those cultures that value the after-meal burp have been right all along. **Bubbly water** or **soda** can aid you in your endeavor.

▶ Prepare an anti-inflammatory tea from 1 tsp. (5 mL) of **licorice root** and 1 tsp. (5 mL) of **valerian**: pour 1 cup (250 mL) of boiling water over the ingredients, cover, and let steep for 10

People who subject their stomach to fatty foods risk a fire within.

minutes. Strain and sip one cup slowly at mealtimes. *Note: do not use during pregnancy.*

▶ **Chamomile tea** can help ease cramps.

▶ As granny could have told you, a steaming bowl of **oatmeal** is good for an upset stomach—it's mild-tasting, warm and soothing, and carries a load of vitamins and minerals, as well as fiber.

▶ **Vitamin A** helps rebuild damaged mucus membranes in your stomach lining. Good sources include carrots, green cabbage, mache, spinach, bell peppers, apricots, and honeydew melon.

▶ The medicinal use of **licorice** dates back several thousand years. At least 14 studies indicate that taking licorice extract can stimulate the body's defense systems against ulcers, rebuild damaged mucus membranes in the stomach, increase intestinal health, and inhibit ulcer-causing *heliobacter pylori*.

▶ Massage your stomach in gentle, circular motions with 1 tbsp. (15 mL) of **almond oil** mixed with 3–4 drops of **chamomile oil**.

---

good to know

NUTRITIONAL FALLACY
In the past, most doctors believed stress and dietary factors caused stomach ulcers (peptic ulcers), with their symptoms of bloating, pain, and nausea. The prescription: get rest, reduce anxiety, eat bland food, and eliminate coffee and alcohol. Recent research, however, has revealed that the culprit in one out of five cases of peptic ulcer is actually a bacteria called *heliobacter pylori*. A simple test is enough to confirm the diagnosis and, after treatment with a course of antibiotics, only a small proportion of patients relapse.

Replace fatty foods with fresh grains and fibers to take a major step towards calming a usually unruly stomach.

▶ A gentle stomach massage in a circular motion with **chamomile** or **lavender essential oil** (3–4 drops mixed with 1 tbsp./15 mL of almond oil) alleviates pain.

▶ **Coffee, alcohol,** and **spicy** or **fried foods** may be "repeat offenders." Watch your diet and avoid food triggers.

▶ Eat **smaller meals** more frequently, and take your last meal at least three hours before bedtime.

IRRITABLE BOWEL SYNDROME (IBS)

Doctors don't fully understand the mechanism behind irritable bowel syndrome. What they do know is that it is marked by continuing problems with constipation, bloating, diarrhea, heartburn, and nausea. It's likely that stress has a certain influence on IBS and certain foods seem to make it worse. On the plus side, it won't kill you, and with a little help from age-old wisdom, you may be able to get your unruly bowels in check.

▶ Lingering over your meal allows **enough time to digest**. When you are relaxed, you're less likely to swallow air, which can increase abdominal discomfort.

▶ Avoid excessively rich foods and divide your food intake into **several small meals** a day.

▶ **Alcohol** and **cigarettes** are poison for a nervous stomach.

▶ Avoid **coffee** and **black tea**. They stimulate digestion, and that's not good if you're prone to diarrhea.

▶ Avoid **strong spices**, as well as sweets, smoked foods, donuts, and fried foods.

▶ The aptly named **chamomile roll cure** can provide relief when used in the morning over the course of several days (see box at right).

HEARTBURN

Sometimes your stomach rebels against rich, highly spicy, or fried foods, especially when you gobble them down too quickly.

The result can be heartburn, aptly named because you feel a burning sensation just under your ribcage, often accompanied by a feeling of fullness, nausea, and stomach pain. In addition to traditional home remedies such as peppermint and fennel tea, a change in your eating habits and other gentle, natural solutions may help put out the fire.

▶ **Nux vomica** is a homeopathic remedy for relieving heartburn. You'll find it at your local health food store.

▶ Sip a cup of tea made from **elder blossoms**, **linden blossoms**, and **peppermint** (mixed in equal proportions) to relieve cramps and calm your stomach. To prepare, pour 1 cup (250 mL) of boiling water over 1 tsp. (5 mL) of the mixture.

▶ **Black tea** with a **pinch of salt** and a **soda cracker** calms the stomach.

chamomile roll cure

one In the morning make a tea from 2–3 tsp. (10–15 mL) of dried chamomile and 1 cup (250 mL) of water.

two Go back to bed and then sip the tea on an empty stomach.

three Lie on your back for 5–10 minutes, then for an equal time on your left side, stomach, and right side.

four Keep drinking chamomile tea throughout the day.

Strengthening Your Body's Defenses

A strong immune system can fight off most viruses—but when it's weakened, viruses can get the upper hand. A healthy diet and lifestyle can strengthen your body's defenses, aiding prevention or assisting if a virus does get hold.

Healthy Eating

- Vitamin C is essential to your immune system. You'll find it in many fruits and vegetables, but particularly good picks are citrus fruits, kiwis, bell peppers, and fruit juices (especially orange, guava, and cranberry juices).

- Eat a varied diet with plenty of fruits, vegetables, whole grains, plant oils, milk products, fish, and lean meats. You'll be providing your body with a full supply of substances to fortify your defenses: vitamin E, beta-carotene, zinc, and selenium.

- Avoid nicotine and alcohol: both weaken the immune system, and tobacco smoke is a Class A carcinogen.

a money-saving hint

Grow vitamin-rich herbs such as basil and parsley on the windowsill—then you always have an economical source.

Reducing Stress

Stress, conflict, and worry are poison not only for your mental well-being, but for your body's defenses. In order to ease the burden on body and soul:

- Build in regular breaks during the day for a little "me time."

- Learn a relaxation technique, such as yoga, progressive muscle relaxation, or Qigong.

- Get adequate rest, always going to sleep and rising at the same time every day.

Toughening Up

Even a good, old-fashioned barefoot stroll through the grass can perk up your immune system.

- Start each morning with a contrast shower: turn on the warm water, then, after two minutes, switch to a cold shower for 15 seconds. Repeat the process three times. End on cold water.

- Avoid car exhaust—it chokes immunity—and don't spend too much time in poorly-ventilated indoor places where chemicals are being used (such as beauty salons and gas stations), or where new materials, such as carpets, have recently been installed.

- Drink at least six 8 oz. (250 mL) glasses of water a day to boost your immune system and lessen feelings of fatigue.

Plenty of Exercise

The fastest way to feel energized is to exercise—you'll feel the effects right away. A simple 10-minute walk will decrease tension, banish fatigue, and boost mental alertness for hours afterward. Make it a daily routine, and pretty soon, you'll be toning muscles, strengthening your heart, and improving the functioning of most organs and bodily systems. Exercise immediately lightens the workload of the immune system, speeding the elimination of germs and other threats by stimulating circulation, making you breathe deeply, accelerating perspiration, and increasing muscle activity. Try bicycling, swimming, or taking a brisk daily walk.

From the Pharmacy

Compounds made from purple coneflower (*Echinacea purpurea*) activate your immune system and strengthen your body's defenses. Take echinacea daily for a period of about eight weeks. If you take it longer, the desired effect will be reversed; when your immune system is stimulated for too long it soon becomes exhausted. Note: Don't take echinacea if you're allergic to coneflowers.

Teeth

Too much sugar produces acids that attack and damage tooth enamel. The result is tooth decay. The good news: the risk of cavities decreases with advancing age. The bad news: gum and periodontal diseases start showing up more frequently.

Rhatany Root Tincture

Prevents inflammation and strengthens gums.

1²/₃ oz. (50 g) rhatany root (minced)

Vodka

Put the root into a small bottle and completely cover with vodka. Seal and let steep for two weeks; shake occasionally. Strain the fluid into a small bottle, thoroughly squeezing out the roots. Apply some of the tincture on inflamed gums several times a day using a cotton swab.

GRINDING YOUR TEETH

Teeth aren't built for the punishment of constant grinding—they're designed to touch briefly when you're chewing or swallowing. Anger, worry, and poorly-fitting false teeth are the most frequent causes of tooth grinding, which can lead to tooth wear and gum problems.

▶ Head to the dentist to find out whether **tooth misalignment** or **fillings** or **crowns** that don't fit properly are the root of the problem.

▶ Try **relaxation techniques** if psychological strain is causing your teeth grinding. They may provide relief.

▶ Use a **mouth guard,** fitted by a dentist, to reduce the impact of tooth grinding at night.

GUM INFLAMMATION AND PERIODONTAL DISEASE

Pressure sores and injuries from dentures, plus plaque and tartar, can lead to inflammation of the gums, accompanied by redness, pain, bleeding, and even receding gums, if left untreated.

▶ Gargle with **sage oil**. It disinfects and alleviates pain. Put 4 drops into ½ cup (125 mL) of warm water and gargle with it several times a day.

▶ For a simple mouthwash, dissolve 1 tsp. (5 mL) of **table salt** in a glass of water.

▶ Put 5 oz. (150 g) of **quince seeds** in 1 quart/liter of water, boil for 15 minutes, strain, and let cool. Rinse your mouth three times a day with it.

TOOTH PAIN

Home remedies can alleviate the pain of a cavity, but they can't eliminate the hole in your tooth—see a dentist for help with that.

▶ Tooth pain improves quickly when you dribble a little **clove oil** onto a cotton ball and hold it to the painful tooth.

▶ It's even simpler and just as effective to place a **clove** on your aching tooth and carefully bite down on it.

▶ Roll a **savoy cabbage leaf** with a rolling pin until soft and then press it onto the outside of the appropriate cheek.

▶ Rub the gums surrounding your painful tooth with a crushed **garlic clove**.

▶ Rinse your mouth three to five times a day with an analgesic mixture of **arnica**, **sage**, and **chamomile**. Mix together ⅓ oz. (10 g) arnica, 1 oz. (30 g) sage, and 1⅓ oz. (40 g) chamomile. Pour a cup of hot water over 1 tbsp. (15 mL) of the mixture, then strain and cool.

▶ Ice cools and soothes pain: press an **ice pack** onto your cheek or **suck an ice cube**.

▶ Chew a small piece of **violet** or **calamus root** to release pain-soothing substances.

Eat an apple a day to strengthen your gums.

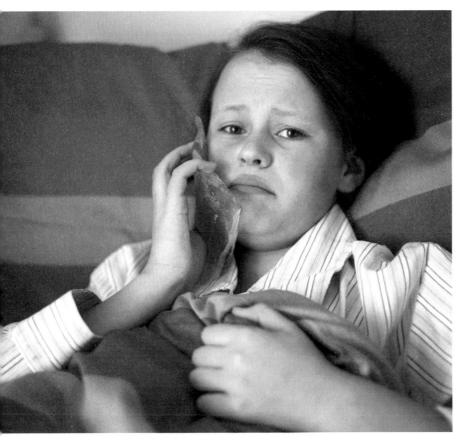

A cold pack provides quick relief from tooth pain.

▶ **Willow bark** and **meadowsweet** contain substances related to the painkiller acetylsalicylic acid (a component of many synthetic pain medications). Tea from these herbs relieves tooth pain.

PREVENTION

▶ Have your teeth **cleaned and checked** by a dentist and a dental hygienist at least once a year, even if you are experiencing no problems; go every six months if necessary.

▶ To cleanse your mouth of bacteria, rinse it thoroughly several times a day with **tea tree oil** (3–4 drops of tea tree oil in a glass of warm water) after brushing your teeth.

▶ Regularly use mouthwash containing **sage** or **chamomile** to clean and disinfect.

▶ **Massage your gums** regularly with your fingers to strengthen them. Apply gentle pressure and work in circular motions.

▶ A diet low in **sugar** deprives bacteria of their livelihood and keeps your teeth healthy.

▶ **Brush your teeth** two to three times daily, after each meal.

▶ When you brush, use **toothpaste containing fluoride** to harden your teeth.

▶ **Replace your toothbrush** regularly (at least every two months), since bacteria from your mouth will cling to it.

▶ If you are on the go during the day and have no chance to brush, chew some special **teeth-cleaning** or **sugar-free gum** to stimulate saliva production and help remove food particles.

▶ Eat tooth-friendly foods. After meals, eat **nuts** or **cheese**, which counteract acidity, or a fibrous food, such as **celery**, which removes plaque.

a money-saving *hint*

Avoid grinding your teeth at night by using this simple trick: chew some hard bread crust or a carrot before going to bed to tire out your chewing muscles.

proper teeth cleaning

one Use dental floss or a dental water jet to remove food particles between your teeth.

two Use the red-to-white technique when brushing: always clean from the gum and down toward the tip of the tooth.

three Brush the chewing surfaces of your teeth.

four Thoroughly rinse your teeth and gums with mouthwash.

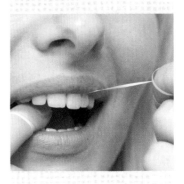

The Ideal Home Pharmacy

Next time you have an ache or pain, don't rush to make a costly trip to the pharmacy. You can equip a home medicine cabinet for a song. And often, nature's simple remedies can be just as effective as anything you'll find at the store. In addition, herbs are extremely versatile and can be a sensible complement to other treatments.

Medicine Cabinet Must-Haves

The following belong in every well-prepared parent's home pharmacy:

- Hot water bottle
- Thermometer
- Disposable gloves
- Tweezers, scissors
- Adhesive bandages in several sizes
- Sterile compresses
- Gauze bandages, elastic bandages
- Bandage clips, safety pins
- Triangular bandage
- Eye patch

Recommended Commercial Preparations

For ailments that require quick intervention, have the following medications on hand:

- Antihistamines in case of allergic reaction
- Disinfectants for minor injuries
- Pills to control pain and fever
- Medications for constipation and diarrhea
- Gel for burns and cuts

a money-saving hint

At the pharmacy, always ask for less expensive, generic drugs, when available.

Natural Remedies

When it comes to stocking your home medicine chest, you should supplement your basic equipment with natural remedies.

- The following essential oils have a place in every medicine cabinet: St. John's wort oil (nervousness/depression), tea tree oil (healing of wounds), and eucalyptus oil (respiratory passages). Use 3–5 drops of each for wraps, additives to bathwater, or inhaling. Pick up essential oils from pharmacies or health food stores.

- The most important tinctures for your medicine cabinet come from pot marigold blooms, chamomile, and St. John's wort. Use them externally or internally. Chamomile soothes such things as stomach and cold symptoms, and St. John's wort helps with nervousness and depression. A rule of thumb: for internal applications, use 10 drops, three times a day in water or juice. For external treatment of things such as skin injuries, dilute the tinctures in a 1:4 ratio and use with compresses or add to bathwater (e.g., chamomile for insomnia or stress). Tinctures can be pricey, but you can easily make your own supply. You need about ½ oz. (15 g) of herb per 3½ oz. (100 mL) of rubbing alcohol and dark, sealable glass bottles for storage. Kept cool, they will last for about a year.

- Prepare curative teas from 1 tsp. (5 mL) of dried flowers and leaves of various herbs and 1 cup (250 mL) of hot water (see box at top right).

a money-saving *hint*

Grow, harvest, and dry your own herbs.

Curative Teas

Chamomile	Stomach and digestive ailments
Linden	Feverish cold and illnesses, stomach and intestinal cramps, nervousness, headaches (particularly migraines), infections
Lemon balm	Sleep disturbances, queezy stomach and intestinal problems, nervousness
Peppermint	Nausea, vomiting, inflammation of the stomach lining, intestinal gas
Plantain	Cough, hoarseness, whooping cough

Proper Storage

Store your medicinal arsenal in a dry, dark, and cool place, or in a lockable cabinet—preferably out of the reach of small fingers. Check the contents regularly to ensure that the expiry dates of medications have not passed and there is enough on hand for an emergency.

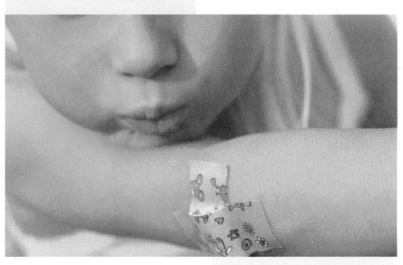

Emergency Numbers

Keep a list of the most important emergency numbers handy or on speed dial: emergency response (police, fire, and ambulance), family doctor, nearest hospital/poison center, emergency room, and pharmacy.

Throat

Your throat hurts, it's painful to swallow, and your voice is just a croak—sore throats are unpleasant and typically the companions of cold or flu. But natural remedies can often provide fast relief.

A sore throat is a common complaint that could be caused by viral or bacterial infection, allergy, dry air, or by inhaling smoke or other airborne pollutants. A sore throat is often the first sign of a cold and can be accompanied by fever and congestion.

SORE THROAT

Sore throats can run the gamut from a mild scratching to severely inflamed mucous membranes in your throat and pharynx. Fortunately, you just have to open your cupboard door to find a range of proven remedies for this common ailment.

▶ Drink lots of fluids to keep your mucous membranes moist. Hot **herbal** or **fruit teas** (especially anti-inflammatory **sage tea**) are ideal drinks. Sweeten to taste with **honey**.

▶ **Honey** has a natural antibacterial effect that makes it a particularly effective home remedy. Allow 1 tsp. (5 mL) of honey to run slowly down your throat several times a day to chase sore throats away.

▶ Heat helps support the body's natural defenses. Wear a **scarf** when you feel a sore throat coming on, and avoid drafts and cold.

▶ Dry air further irritates mucous membranes. To keep humidity levels in your house high, place **moist cloths on the radiators** and **bowls of water** on the windowsills. Add a couple drops of essential oils for a soothing effect.

▶ **Gargling** soothes pain and swelling in your throat and pharynx. Mix 1 tsp. (5 mL) of **salt** with 2 cups (500 mL) of water to make a solution for gargling. Or try an old home remedy: 2 tbsp. (25 mL) of **cider vinegar** in 1 cup (250 mL) of water. Sweeten with honey.

▶ **Garlic** has antiviral and antifungal properties, so it can be particularly effective at relieving a sore throat caused by a virus. Add to food or blend a few cloves of garlic into a veggie cocktail. The good news: it makes no difference if it's fresh or dried.

▶ A very effective home recipe for sore throat is a mixture that tastes better than the ingredients might suggest: ½ tsp. (5 mL) of freshly grated **horseradish** is stirred into a glass of warm water

Onion Milk with Thyme and Cloves

Onion milk alleviates pain and inflammation.

1 quart/liter milk
1 onion
1 sprig of thyme
2 cloves

Cut the onion into large pieces and add to a pan with the milk, sprig of thyme, and cloves. Bring mixture to a boil, then remove from the stove and let steep for 10 minutes before straining. Drink onion milk three times a day.

Pour boiling water over chamomile flowers and inhale the steam to open up your breathing passages and alleviate pain.

along with 1 tsp. (5 mL) of **honey** and a pinch of **ground cloves**. Drink slowly.

▶ Toss your **toothbrush**. Bacteria trapped on a toothbrush may cause a lingering sore throat.

HOARSENESS

There are many possible causes for that frog in your throat: strained vocal chords, excessively dry ambient air, or a viral infection, to name just a few. Resting your vocal chords may be all that is needed—so speak softly and as little as possible. In addition, an array of simple remedies can speed up the healing process. If there is no improvement, you should consult a doctor.

▶ Hot tea of any kind can soothe a sore throat—especially **sage tea**, which should ideally be made fresh every time from dried sage leaves. Slightly warmed **mulberry juice** (from a health food store) also alleviates discomfort.

▶ If your mother treated your sore throat with a soothing mug of **hot milk and honey**, she was

right on the money. Drinking this beverage several times a day will quickly ease hoarseness.

▶ Tasty, economical, and effective: cut an **apple** into slices, lightly fry it in a little butter or oil, sprinkle with plenty of sugar, and eat.

▶ A **potato wrap** speeds healing. Boil, peel, and mash 2–3 potatoes. Spread the warm spuds onto a cloth and wrap around your throat with a wool scarf to hold them in place. Wear until the potatoes cool three times a day.

▶ Make a refreshing throat compress by soaking a linen cloth in warm **thyme, sage,** or **mullein tea**. Gently wring out the cloth and wrap around your throat, covered by a wool scarf.

▶ Add a few drops of either **lavender** or **eucalyptus essential oil** to 1 cup (250 mL) of boiling water and inhale to ease hoarseness.

▶ **Ice cream** is also a favorite pain remedy, and not just for children. Or try a hot drink flavored with **lemon** and **honey**.

Varicose Veins

Since varicose veins cannot be undone without medical intervention, prevention is just as important as treatment. A little old-fashioned advice can at least help keep your varicose veins from getting any worse.

Those swollen, darkened veins in your legs can be traced to the faulty functioning of your veins' valves, which causes blood in your legs to accumulate.

Take to the stairs to help stimulate blood circulation and strengthen calf muscles.

a cold knee shower

one Direct a cold stream of water (with the shower head removed) along the outside of the right leg from the back of the foot to a hand's breadth above the knee. Hold it there for 10 seconds.

two Move the stream downward on the inside of your leg.

three Repeat the process with your left leg.

four Finally, briefly rinse the soles of your feet.

five Dry off and put on warm wool socks. Rest for 20 minutes.

HOME REMEDIES

▶ Very important: **keep your legs elevated** as frequently as possible to encourage the blood backed up in the veins to flow out.

▶ Stir together 1 cup (250 mL) of warm water, 1 tbsp. (15 mL) of **cream**, and 5 drops of **lemon essential oil**. Soak linen cloths with the mixture, wring them out slightly, and apply to your calves.

▶ Massage your legs from bottom to top using a mixture of 5 drops of **cypress**, **lavender**, and **juniper essential oil** with about ¼ cup (50 mL) of **olive oil**.

▶ Get a **chair that fits your body**. When you sit in a chair that is too deep for you, the edge of the seat presses into your legs constricting blood flow.

▶ Go low. **Low-heeled shoes** require your calves to do more work, greatly aiding circulation.

▶ Rub your legs twice a day with **pot marigold salve**.

▶ Researchers have found that supplements containing **horse chestnut extract** (from a pharmacy or health food store) can combat leg pain and swelling as efficiently as compression stockings.

▶ Raise the foot of your bed or **elevate your feet** with a pillow to encourage blood flow.

PREVENTION

▶ Avoid **standing or sitting for a long time**.

▶ Don't **cross your legs**. It can slow circulation to and from your lower legs.

▶ Wear **support stockings** prescribed by a doctor.

▶ Sit on a chair, stretch out your legs, and repeatedly **bend and stretch your feet** to activate the vein pumps.

▶ **Get moving**. Activities such as hiking, swimming, bicycling, and cross-country skiing promote circulation and prevent blood from pooling.

▶ **Climbing stairs** is active training for your calf muscles—avoid elevators and escalators!

▶ **Lose weight**. Carrying around extra pounds puts additional stress on your circulatory system.

Warts

Pediatricians used to sometimes advise their small patients to draw their wart on a postcard and send it far away—a psychological boost that might have helped. These days, medical responses to a wart consist mainly of burning, scraping, cutting, or freezing. These are painful techniques that can leave scars. In most cases, warts respond better to natural, tried-and-true remedies.

Warts occur when viruses, usually the papilloma type, invade skin cells. They may be unsightly, and they occasionally itch. A plantar wart on the heel or ball of the foot can cause pain when walking, because the weight on the foot presses it inward. Warts often disappear within six months to two years without treatment.

HOME REMEDIES

Treating warts requires patience—unfortunately, there is no cure-all. Resist scraping or picking them off. If you have a case of painful plantar warts (warts that grow inward and often appear on your feet), you may require medical treatment.

▶ **Bloodroot** is considered a classic wart cure. The milky sap that dribbles from the cut edges of leaves and stems can be applied directly to the wart. *Note: only use bloodroot externally—it is poisonous when ingested.*

▶ **Pot marigold salve** works well for warts on your face, since it contains relatively mild substances.

▶ Apply a few drops of **tea tree**, **lavender**, or **clove oil** to the wart.

▶ Brush pure **castor oil** onto the affected areas several times a day to keep the viruses from reproducing.

▶ A paste made from **baking powder** and **castor oil** can help; brush it onto the wart several times a day and cover with a dressing.

▶ Mix together **Epsom salts** and **cider vinegar** in a 1:4 ratio and dab onto the wart several times a day to promote healing.

HELP FROM THE PANTRY

▶ Rub warts with a peeled raw **potato**.

▶ Alternatively, brush the skin growths with the juice of an **unripe fig**.

▶ Apply the inside of a **banana peel** to a wart on the sole of your foot and secure it with a bandage.

▶ Cut a **lemon** into slices and put them into a glass. Add **cider vinegar** to cover. Let the lemon slices steep for two weeks, then rub the wart with them.

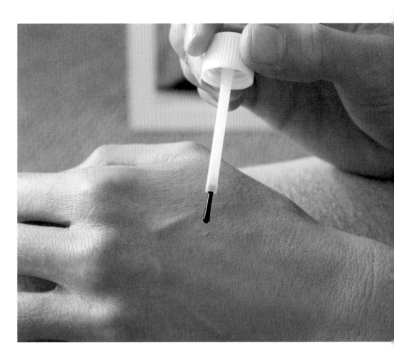

Apply oils and mixtures with a small brush to avoid spreading the warts through touch.

Women's Reproductive Health

Women have the exciting ability to create new life, but the hormones that control the reproductive cycle can trigger discomfort. Fortunately, there are a number of traditional ways to combat these kinds of pain.

From adolescence on, a woman's reproductive system has a major impact on her life. Her complex hormonal balance may be disrupted as she progresses from the onset of periods to childbearing to menopause. Here are some time-tested remedies.

MENSTRUAL DISCOMFORT

Breast pain, bloating, acne, cramps, and a feeling of intense irritability—these are just a few of the symptoms that may signal the start of your period. And often PMS (premenstrual syndrome) is just the beginning. Once your period arrives, the discomfort is ramped up even further; you may experience more intense cramping and pains in your head, back, and stomach.

▶ **Monk's pepper** (chasteberry) has been used for gynecological conditions since the time of Hippocrates. It helps regulate hormonal balance, soothes the discomforts of PMS (such as breast tenderness and itchy skin), and even inhibits severe bleeding.

▶ Warm **foot, sitz, and full baths** increase comfort and reduce cramping. Additives might include

Ginger tea can help combat nausea during pregnancy.

relaxation-inducing **lemon balm** or **lavender**; **chamomile** or **yarrow** to counter severe bleeding; or **thyme** or **hay flowers** to bring on menstruation.

▶ **Massages** can help ease pains and cramps: gently massage your lower abdomen and back with **St. John's wort, evening primrose,** or **lavender oil.**

▶ Tea made from **shepherd's purse** helps regulate severe menstrual bleeding.

▶ Tea made from **deadnettle** soothes severe bleeding and cramps.

▶ A tea made from **valerian root, chamomile,** and **peppermint**, mixed in equal amounts, soothes severe bleeding accompanied by cramps.

▶ Tea made from **tansy** and **pot marigold** helps stop cramping.

▶ Tea made from **rue** and **yarrow**, mixed in equal amounts, may help regulate menstruation and eliminate pain.

PREGNANCY

Although a natural condition, pregnancy can be difficult for some women.

▶ In the first trimester of pregnancy, many women are plagued with **morning sickness**. This simple trick can help: take a package of cookies or soda biscuits to bed and nibble a few right after waking up in the morning. Then rise, have a leisurely breakfast, and sip some peppermint tea.

▶ **Stretch marks** may appear on your breasts and your expanding belly. Gentle massages with **jojoba** or **evening primrose oil** keep your skin moist and elastic.

▶ A warm wrap with lavender oil helps soothe **breast tenderness**.

▶ **Swimming** or a gentle **back massage** can soothe pelvic pain.

▶ **Magnesium**, found in wholegrain products and dried fruits, helps eliminate cramping in your calves.

MENOPAUSE

An inevitable part of aging, menopause generally hits women some time between the age of 45 and 55. The precipitous drop in hormones that is the hallmark of menopause can also trigger a series of uncomfortable symptoms, including hot flashes, vaginal dryness, insomnia, and mood swings.

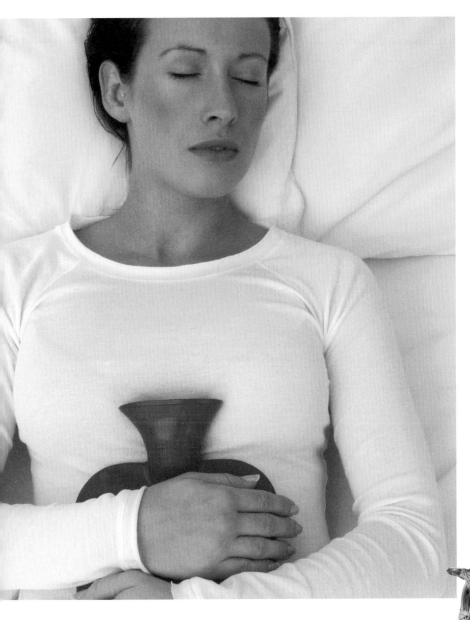

Our grandmothers regarded heat as a universal remedy; during menstruation, a hot water bottle placed on your lower abdomen eases cramps.

good to know

BLACK COHOSH

The roots of black cohosh contain triterpane glycosides, a popular treatment for premenstrual discomfort, menstrual irregularities, and painful menstruation, as well as hot flashes during menopause. Women around the world have been using the herbal supplement for generations and a wealth of modern evidence backs up their choice. In many studies, black cohosh outperformed conventional therapies such as hormone pills and antidepressants in combating menopause symptoms. Note, however, that it takes four to six weeks from first consumption for the effects to appear.

▶ Various tea preparations help people get through menopause. **St. John's wort tea** stabilizes mood, **valerian tea** has a calming, balancing effect, **sage tea** reduces sweating attacks, and **lemon balm tea** can help with sleep disturbances.

▶ **Contrast footbaths** may help fend off those pesky hot flashes. Fill two foot basins with **hay flowers** or **hops flowers** and water—one hot (100°F/38°C) and the other cold (50°F/10°C). Alternate placing your feet in the warm water for 5 minutes, and the cold for 10 seconds.

▶ Nutrition plays a role in hot flashes; eat plenty of fresh food and abstain from **coffee**, **alcohol**, and **nicotine**, which can lower your estrogen level.

▶ **Red beets** contain substances that work like female sex hormones and can reduce menopausal discomfort.

▶ **Soy** and **red clover** contain phytoestrogens—plant-based compounds that bear a chemical resemblance to estrogen. Asian women have long reaped the benefits of soy, making them far less prone to hot flashes. So by all means, incorporate soy milk, soy flour, and tofu into your diet, or pick up some clover pills.

A Natural Approach to Good Health   **71**

All Natural
Body Care

A daily body care regime is critical to a well-groomed appearance, and nature offers just about everything you need to look and smell great. Here are time-tested formulas to keep your skin, hair, and nails healthy and beautiful.

Age Spots

Age spots usually appear on the back of your hands, but can also show up on your arms and face. You can lighten and even eliminate them using natural care products—but these treatments requires plenty of patience.

Increased pigmentation is a result of years of exposure to ultraviolet rays; it generally shows up later in life.

These unsightly brown splotches, sometimes referred to as "liver spots," should really be called "sun spots"—they're actually the result of too much sun exposure.

HOME REMEDIES

It's possible to conceal age spots with makeup; there are also costly medical procedures, such as laser removal, that give more lasting results. But home remedies are still worth a try. Start by testing them out on less noticeable places, like your hands, before using them on your face.

▶ Try applying **pure lemon juice** on age spots twice a day. Or, try **buttermilk** for a similar effect.

▶ An easy-to-make and easy-to-use paste to lighten age spots can be made by mixing ⅓ oz. (10 g) each of **powdered ginger** and **rose petals** with about 3 oz. (80 g) of **powdered cleaver** (from a health food store). Stir 2 tsp. (10 mL) of the mix into a small amount of warm water to make a spreadable paste. Apply to the spots, cover with a cloth, and leave for about 30 minutes before thoroughly rinsing your skin clean.

▶ Make a natural bleaching agent by mixing together about 1 tsp. (5 mL) each of **honey** and **plain yogurt**. Spread the mix on your age spots once a day, and leave for 30 minutes before rinsing well.

▶ Other simple solutions include rubbing age spots several times a day with a piece of **papaya**, or using gels containing **aloe vera** (from a pharmacy). They can be helpful because they contain substances that stimulate the growth of healthy cells.

Lemon-Based Bleaching Agent

1 egg white
2 tsp. (10 mL) lemon juice
½ tsp. (2 mL) vitamin E oil

Beat ingredients together and spread on age spots. Let work for 20 minutes, then rinse thoroughly. This daily regimen, when repeated over the course of a few weeks, may even help remove age spots altogether.

PREVENTION

▶ **Free radicals** contribute to the occurrence of age spots. Since their development is aided and abetted by ultraviolet radiation, you should avoid intensive **sunbathing**.

▶ Adding certain vitamins to your diet, while avoiding some other substances, can be very helpful in preventing age spots. Avoid **alcohol** and **nicotine**—they encourage the formation of free radicals. A **well-balanced diet** provides your body with "radical catchers" such as vitamin C and pro-vitamin A (in fruits and vegetables), vitamin E (in plant oils and grains), and selenium (in nuts, legumes, and grains).

Blemishes

The ancient Greeks used vegetable-based treatments, while the Romans preferred mineral baths—but both helped heal blemishes. Traditional methods of fighting pimples, spots, and blackheads can prove very effective.

Natural ingredients are at the forefront of today's skincare research and can be found in many of the latest beauty products. You can achieve the same results using these simple methods.

HOME REMEDIES

There are a number of remedies to help in the battle against pimples, spots, and blackheads.

▶ To calm reddened, irritated skin, use the anti-inflammatory properties of **mallow**. To make a healing mask, beat 1 egg white till stiff and infuse with 3 tbsp. (45 mL) of mallow tea. Apply with a brush, let work for 15 minutes, then rinse off.

▶ To combat acne, create a **yeast mask** by crumbling ²⁄₃ oz. (20 g) of brewer's yeast. Combine with 2 tbsp. (25 mL) plain yogurt, then mix in 1 tsp. (5 mL) of honey. Apply the mask to your moistened face, and rinse thoroughly after 20 minutes.

▶ To treat inflamed skin, a liquid made of 2 tsp. (10 mL) of **stinging nettle** (from a health food store) and 1 cup (250 mL) of boiling water will help. Steep for 10 minutes and wash the affected area three times a day with the cooled broth.

Brewer's yeast is used to make clarifying masks.

▶ Before we began to rely on drugstore products as our allies against acne, people dabbed natural remedies onto pimples several times a day. The best-known ones include **thyme oil, raw potato slices, lemon juice**, and freshly-cut **garlic cloves**.

PREVENTING PIMPLES

Follow these tips to help prevent the outbreak of pimples.

▶ Refresh your skin daily using **mild cleansers**.

▶ Thoroughly remove makeup every night, and avoid any products that contain **oil**.

▶ Limit **sun exposure** and use appropriate sunscreen.

▶ Monitor your **diet.** Determine whether alcohol, nicotine, coffee, black tea, and fatty foods fuel your breakouts.

Be careful with facial steam baths—too much heat could scald your skin.

A Facial Steam Bath

A weekly deep cleansing of the pores can soothe blemished skin.

2 tbsp. (25 mL) chamomile
2 tbsp. (25 mL) peppermint
2 tbsp. (25 mL) thyme
2 tbsp. (25 mL) horsetail
3 quarts/liters water

In a large bowl, pour boiling water over the herbs and let steep briefly. Cover your head with a towel and carefully hold it over the bowl for 10 minutes to let the steam open up your pores.

Cellulite

Dimples on the face are usually considered attractive; dimples on your thighs and buttocks, not so much. Cellulite is very common for women and has been for years. That's why our grandmothers found ways to deal with it.

Massage with a sisal glove in the morning and evening to help in the fight against cellulite.

Cellulite shows up when a pocket of fat beneath the skin pushes on the connective tissue, creating a cottage cheese effect. Women are particularly prone to cellulite because their connective tissue is softer than that of men. Usually the troublesome bumps appear on the buttocks, hips, and thighs.

HOME REMEDIES

There are a number of methods for fighting cellulite, including some which use potatoes, sea salt, and numerous massage oils.

▶ To make an effective massage oil, pour a little more than 3/4 cup (200 mL) of **wheat germ oil** over a handful of fresh **ivy leaves** and let steep for two weeks in a sealed container in a warm location. Strain and mix in 2 drops of **rosemary oil.** Rub into your trouble spots daily, using circular motions.

▶ Other oils such as cinnamon, lavender, chamomile, clove, rosemary, and sandalwood (for more on essential oils, see page 99) can be mixed with a base oil (such as almond oil) to create a **massage oil** for cellulite patches.

▶ **Potatoes** possess remarkable healing powers, including the ability to tighten your connective tissue. To take advantage of this, peel one raw potato and spread thin slices onto the skin affected by cellulite. Cover with a cotton cloth and let work for 15 minutes.

▶ Create your own mixture to tighten the subcutaneous tissue by boiling about

3 tbsp. (45 mL) of **ivy leaves** in 2 quarts/liters of water for 2 minutes, then strain. Moisten cotton cloths with the cooled liquid and apply to the affected areas once a day for 20 minutes.

▶ Massaging **sea salt** into your moist skin can also be effective. Do it after taking a shower, then rinse off with warm water.

PREVENTION

Diet and exercise are key to preventing cellulite. First and foremost, people carrying excess pounds must slim down—being overweight is a risk factor.

▶ Exercise promotes circulation and keeps your skin and connective tissue taut. **Weight training** is particularly helpful, and specific exercises can be designed to target trouble spots.

▶ Cut back on **hydrogenated** and **saturated fat, sugar,** and **salt**—they encourage fat and water buildup, leading to dimpled skin.

▶ Drink plenty of **fluids** to flush out waste and provide your skin with moisture from the inside. Eat a **low fat, high fiber** diet containing plenty of green vegetables and fresh fruits.

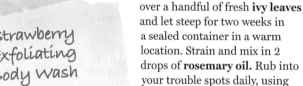

Strawberry Exfoliating Body Wash

An exfoliating body wash has a revitalizing effect on cellulite.

2 oz. (60 g) strawberries
2 oz. (60 g) cucumber, unpeeled
2 tbsp. (25 mL) buttermilk
1 tbsp. (15 mL) yogurt
1 egg yolk
1½ oz. (50 g) ground almonds

Puree all the ingredients in a blender or grind them in a mortar. Store in a sealable container and use in the shower. The mixture can be stored in the refrigerator for up to three days.

a money-saving hint

Don't toss used coffee grounds—they make an excellent exfoliating body wash.

Deodorants

Using your own blend of natural ingredients is healthier and less expensive than using store-bought deodorants, and still helps to gently refresh your skin and prevent odors.

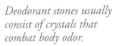

Underarm perspiration is caused by secretions from the apocrine and the eccrine sweat glands. The amount you perspire is largely based on the body's efforts to regulate temperature. The hotter the temperature, the more you sweat. This is how the body cools itself.

BASIC FORMULA

Essential oils are an important element of many deodorant formulas. The essential oils of **citrus plants,** such as lemon, bergamot, lemongrass, lime, neroli, and grapefruit, are pleasantly cooling. **Rose** or **lavender oils,** on the other hand, lend a delicate, feminine aroma to deodorant, while **sage** and **cypress oil** have an astringent and contracting effect that helps reduce sweating. They can keep you smelling great all day.

Homemade deodorants are best stored in a pump bottle and shaken before each use.

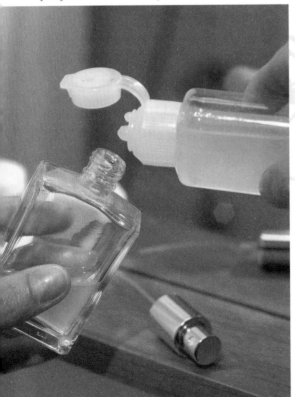

▶ To make a basic, but fragrant, deodorant, mix about 3 tbsp. (45 mL) of vodka and 3 tbsp. (45 mL) of either **witch hazel, cornflower,** or **rose water.** Add to the mix 40 drops of essential oil. For best results, steep the deodorants for about a week before using.

Deodorant stones usually consist of crystals that combat body odor.

VARIATIONS

▶ To make a very simple deodorant, mix 2–3 drops of essential oil, such as **rose** or **lavender oil**, with a little water and dab it on your underarms.

▶ Another option is to use **deodorant stones** or **crystals,** which are made from crystallized natural mineral salts that kill odor-causing bacteria. Deodorant stones are inexpensive, but may clog your pores if applied too liberally.

▶ To make a homemade deodorant bursting with a **fresh summer scent**, mix 3 tbsp. (45 mL) each of dried sage and dried lavender, the juice and grated rind from half a lemon, and 3 drops each of lemon and neroli oil in a sealable container. Pour in 1 cup (250 mL) of witch hazel and steep for a week. Strain, and add 2 tbsp. (25 mL) of cider vinegar.

▶ **Cider vinegar** by itself is also useful to counter excessive sweat. Sprinkle cider vinegar onto a cotton cloth and rub your underarms with it. Another easy method to nip sweat production in the bud is to drink **sage tea** regularly.

good to know

THE PROPER USE OF DEODORANTS
Apply deodorants to clean skin in order to prevent odor-producing bacteria from multiplying too quickly. Keep odors at bay by shaving your underarm hair, but wait a day before applying deodorant to avoid skin irritation. Using too much deodorant can leave you with clogged sweat glands and may cause inflammation.

Eye Care

The skin around your eyes is extremely sensitive and requires special care. Eye creams provide moisture to this delicate skin, which must be kept properly hydrated.

Eye creams both moisturize the delicate skin around the eyes and treat dark circles and wrinkles.

CARE PRODUCTS

▶ **Plant-based eye creams** are available in most pharmacies: they contain eyebright, pot marigold, aloe vera, and oils such as wheat germ, avocado, and macadamia. Apply them morning and night.

▶ For a homemade **fragrant skin oil** that will leave you looking dewy, mix about 3½ oz. (100 mL) of avocado oil and 3 drops of rose oil.

▶ Using easily-spreadable **plant oils,** such as almond, apricot, jojoba, and coconut oil, is an excellent way to moisturize the sensitive areas around your eyes and keep your skin smooth. Apply a few drops directly on your skin or moisten a gauze bandage or cotton pad with oil and place it onto your closed eyes and the surrounding skin.

CIRCLES UNDER THE EYES

Whether the cause is lack of sleep, allergies, or even just aging, no one looks their best with dark circles under the eyes. Dark circles appear when your blood vessels show through the delicate skin under your eyes.

▶ Eye creams or gels containing **horse chestnut** or **butcher's broom** promote circulation, helping to banish circles under your eyes.

▶ Mix 1 tbsp. (15 mL) of **egg white** mixed with 3 tbsp. (45 mL) of **plain yogurt** to make a refreshing eye mask. Dab onto the circles under your eyes and let the mask dry, then rinse with warm water.

Almond oil can help prevent wrinkles.

good to know

Before applying an eye moisturizer, cream, or oil, clean the area around your eye by dabbing it carefully with a plant-based cleanser on a cotton pad. Since the skin around your eyes is very delicate, eye care products should not be rubbed in. Instead, carefully apply them with your fingertip and pat them in gently below the eye, starting from the outside in.

Drinking mineral water can help prevent unwanted crow's-feet.

▶ To make an invigorating eye compress, pour 1 cup (250 mL) of boiling water over 1 tsp. (5 mL) each of **eyebright** and **linden flowers**. Steep for 5 minutes and strain. Moisten two cotton pads or balls with the cooled liquid and place onto your closed eyes for a few minutes.

▶ One easy way to eliminate circles under the eyes is to place fresh, cold **cucumber slices** onto your eyelids. If you're in a hurry, use **concealer** to cover circles and provide a little visual first aid.

CROW'S-FEET

As we grow older, our skin becomes dryer and wrinkles form around our eyes. It helps to moisturize regularly, but crying, laughing, blinking, and winking leave traces, wrinkling delicate skin and creating crow's-feet. And don't try to get by without wearing your glasses—continued squinting also produces wrinkles.

▶ To delay those dreaded crow's-feet as long as possible, keep your skin smooth through daily care. Pure **avocado** and **almond oil** and **aloe vera gels** moisturize and prevent wrinkles.

▶ For a homemade wrinkle cream, stir together a little **almond oil** and **lanolin**, and apply to the skin under your eyes before bedtime.

▶ Once a week, treat the skin around your eyes to a nourishing **skin-firming mask**. Mix together 1 egg yolk, 3 drops of lemon juice, and ½ tsp. (2 mL) of olive oil, and apply the mixture with a brush. Leave on for 15 minutes, then rinse with warm water and refresh with cold water.

EYELASH CARE

Thick, dark, long lashes—this beauty ideal is easy to achieve with mascara.

▶ Use **mascara** with **mink** or **almond oil** to strengthen your eyelashes.

▶ Carefully **remove eye makeup** in the evening. Dab a little water onto a soft cloth and wipe off mascara by rubbing gently toward your nose.

▶ To ensure healthy eyelashes, carefully apply a little **olive** or **castor oil** with a cotton swab for some deep moisturizing—but be careful not to get the oil in your eyes.

Facial Cleansing

Beautiful skin doesn't just happen—a good skin care regimen is vitally important. Always remove sweat and makeup from your face with a cleanser. Then refresh and clarify using a toner, before finally applying a cream, gel, or skin oil.

Wash cleanser residue off your face using plenty of warm water.

Harsh cleansers, such as soaps or toners with a high alcohol content, do not only remove the dirt and grease on your skin—they can also strip your skin's natural oils. Opt instead for mild products that match your skin type.

CLEANSING NORMAL SKIN

You likely have all the ingredients you need to make your own cleansing milks in your refrigerator or cupboard—just follow these easy steps.

▶ Stir together about half of a single-serving container of **plain yogurt**, 1 tbsp. (15 mL) of **olive oil**, and 2 tsp. (10 mL) of **lemon juice**. Apply with a cotton ball, and rinse with warm water after about 2 minutes. A supply of this cleansing milk can be kept in the refrigerator for two to three days.

▶ Slightly warm up 1½ oz. (50 g) of **buttermilk** and dissolve 1 tsp. (5 mL) of **honey** in it, then stir in 1 tsp. (5 mL) of **lemon juice**. Dab the mixture onto a cotton ball and cleanse your face with gentle, circular motions. Leave on for 2 minutes before rinsing with warm water.

CLEANSING GREASY SKIN

▶ To prepare a degreasing cleansing milk, pour 1 cup (250 mL) of boiling water over 1 tbsp. (15 mL) each of **lady's mantle, chamomile,** and **sage**. Strain after 5 minutes and allow to cool. Top off the liquid with about 7 oz. (200 mL) of **buttermilk** and bottle. Shake before using and apply with a cotton ball. Leave on briefly before rinsing with warm water. The mixture can be kept for up to three days in the refrigerator.

▶ To make a **stinging nettle milk** that will promote circulation and clear up oily skin, heat up a handful of fresh stinging nettle leaves in about 1¼ cups (300 mL) of milk. Strain the milk just before it comes to a boil and let cool. Apply the mixture with a cotton ball, then rinse.

▶ **Fennel lotion** has been around for a long time, thanks to its ability to improve skin's appearance. To make it, steep 3 tbsp. (45 mL) of fennel seeds in about ⅔ cup (150 mL) of buttermilk over very low heat for 30 minutes. After the infusion cools, strain and apply with a cotton ball.

▶ Alternatively, create a paste that will help improve skin's appearance by stirring together 1 tbsp. (15 mL) of finely crushed **flaxseeds**, 1 tbsp. (15 mL) of **oat bran**, 1 drop of **lemon oil**, and a little hot water. Apply to your face as a cleanser.

CLEANSING MATURE AND DRY SKIN

High-quality oils cleanse gently and return moisture to your skin.

▶ For dry skin, add 3½ oz. (100 mL) of **aloe vera gel**, 3 tbsp. (45 mL) of **almond oil**, and 3 drops of **lavender oil** to a bottle and shake vigorously. Apply with a cotton ball, let sit for several minutes, and rinse off the excess oil with warm water.

▶ For mature skin, melt ⅓ oz. (10 g) of **beeswax**, 1½ oz. (50 g) of **lanolin**, and ⅓ oz. (10 g) of **cocoa butter** in a hot double boiler. Add 2⅔ oz. (80 g) of **almond oil** and heat to 140°F (60°C). While stirring, add 2⅔ oz. (80 mL) of **rose water** heated to 140°F (60°C). Continue stirring the mixture until cool, then apply to skin.

CLEANSING SENSITIVE SKIN

▶ To make a cleansing lotion containing skin-friendly **pot marigold**, mix about ⅔ cup (150 mL) of warm water with ½ cup (125 mL) of **oatmeal**, 1 tbsp. (15 mL) of glycerin, and 2 drops of **pot marigold** tincture.

▶ For a fragrant cleansing lotion, heat a handful of fresh **violet blooms** in about 1¼ cups (300 mL) of milk. Just before it comes to a boil, remove from heat and strain. Let cool before applying.

TONER

A toner will remove leftover cleansing milk and help clarify your skin. Use a cotton ball or pad to dab a small amount onto your skin. Toners are generally left on skin to dry, not washed off like a regular cleanser.

▶ For normal skin, add 5 tbsp. (75 mL) of **witch hazel** and 3 tbsp. (45 mL) each of **rose water** and **orange blossom water** to a bottle and shake. Alternatively, you can rub your skin with a piece of fresh **cucumber**.

Toners containing aloe vera are particularly gentle on sensitive skin.

▶ For an **astringent** or **anti-inflammatory toner** that is perfect for oily skin, add ¼ cup (50 mL) of sage water, 1 tsp. (5 mL) of rubbing alcohol, and 1 drop each of tea tree and sage oil to a bottle and shake. Alternatively, use **dandelion tea.**

▶ For dry skin, add 3 tbsp. (45 mL) of **pot marigold tincture**, 6 tbsp. (90 mL) of **orange blossom water,** and 1 drop of **lavender oil** to a bottle and shake vigorously.

▶ To avoid irritating sensitive skin, apply a formula of 1 oz. (30 mL) of **pot marigold tincture,** 4 tbsp. plus 1 tsp. (70 mL) of distilled water, and 3 drops of **chamomile oil**.

▶ For mature skin, add ¼ cup (50 mL) of **orange blossom water,** 1 tsp. (5 mL) of **cider vinegar,** and 2 drops each of **seabuckthorn** and **incense oil** to a bottle. Be sure to shake before each use.

Calming Lotion

This flower lotion is cooling and refreshing for both normal and sensitive skin.
4 tbsp. (60 mL) witch hazel
4 tbsp. (60 mL) rose water
2 tbsp. (25 mL) lemon juice
2 drops lavender oil
2 drops rose geranium oil

Add ingredients to a bottle and shake vigorously. Apply a small amount of the lotion after cleansing.

The active agents in lady's mantle can be a boon to oily skin.

Facial Masks

Cleansing and nourishing facial masks have long been used to enhance a youthful appearance. The ingredients used thousands of years ago are similar to those we have at our fingertips today—and they're found mainly in the refrigerator, pantry, and fruit basket.

Masks and exfoliators remove the dead skin cells that build up on the surface of the skin, revealing more lustrous skin beneath.

NORMAL SKIN

▶ To make a **tea-based mask**, mix together 1 tbsp. (15 mL) of plain yogurt, 1 tsp. (5 mL) of black tea, and ½ tsp. (2 mL) of lemon juice. Apply the mask, cover with a warm, moist cloth, and let it work for 15–30 minutes, depending on skin sensitivity.

▶ Another classic in beauty care combines **yogurt** and **honey**. Mix together and apply 1 tbsp. (15 mL) of plain yogurt, 1 tbsp. (15 mL) of sunflower oil, 1 tsp. (5 mL) of plain honey, and 1 tsp. (5 mL) of lemon juice.

---

the right way to apply a mask

one Apply a facial mask only to freshly cleaned skin, leaving space around your eyes and mouth.

two Leave the mask on for 15–30 minutes. During that time, tune out and relax—try listening to some of your favorite music.

three Carefully wash off the mask with warm water before applying a moisturizing cream, gel, or skin oil to preserve your renewed skin.

▶ To take advantage of the cleansing power of fruit in mask form, dissolve 1 tbsp. (15 mL) gelatin in ½ cup (125 mL) **apple juice** in a double boiler. Cool until it reaches the consistency of a gel. Apply mask and let dry, then rinse off with warm water. Note that you can use **pear** or **peach juice** instead of apple.

▶ To make a nourishing mask, mix an **egg yolk** with 1 tsp. (5 mL) of **honey** and a few drops of **olive oil** and apply to your face. After 15 minutes, rinse with warm water.

OILY, BLEMISHED SKIN

▶ Using **healing earth** (from a health food store) is an effective way to calm inflamed skin. Stir together 2 tbsp. (25 mL) each of healing earth and water to create a spreadable paste.

▶ Also effective against inflamed skin is a mask made from **tea**, **egg**, and **carrot**. To make the mask, beat one egg white until stiff and finely grate half a carrot. Mix the two loosely, stir in 1 tsp. (5 mL) of calming chamomile and anti-inflammatory yarrow teas, and apply.

▶ **Brewer's yeast** has long been touted as an effective remedy for oily skin. To make a traditional brewer's yeast mask, stir together about ⅔ oz. (20 g) of brewer's yeast, ⅔ oz. (20 g) of yogurt, and 1 tsp. (5 mL) of honey.

Healing earth is a time-tested home remedy for oily or blemished skin.

Facial masks provide your skin with moisture, combat pimples, and contribute to a well-groomed appearance.

▶ Concoct a **soothing mask** that will ward off pimples, blackheads, and inflammation by stirring together 3 tbsp. (15 mL) of oat flour with 3 drops of antiseptic tea tree oil, 2 drops of sage oil, and an equal amount of warm water. Apply thickly.

▶ A mask using **ground almonds** works like a gentle exfoliating scrub, cleansing your skin of residue and oil. To make the mask, mix 2 tbsp. (25 mL) of honey, 3 tbsp. (45 mL) of finely ground almonds (use a food processor or coffee grinder), and the juice of half an orange. Use to scrub your face gently, avoiding your eyes. It should last for one week in the fridge.

▶ **Cetaphil cream** (from a pharmacy) is also a good tool to fight oily, blemished skin. Stir together 1 tsp. (5 mL) of the cream, 1 tsp. (5 mL) of fresh grape juice, and ½ tsp. (2 mL) of honey, and apply.

MATURE SKIN

Fruit masks are the perfect picker-uppers from the orchard to render saggy skin firm and smooth.

▶ Peel and puree a ripe **peach** and mix with a little facial cream to make a thick paste you can apply to your face, leaving it as soft as the fruit's skin.

▶ Grate an **unpeeled apple** and stir together with 1 tbsp. (15 mL) of cider vinegar and 1 tsp. (5 mL) of cornstarch for a wrinkle-defying mask.

DRY SKIN

▶ Dry, thirsty skin responds very well to a number of natural formulas. To make a mask with a great natural moisturizer, puree half an **avocado** with 1 tsp. (5 mL) each of **honey** and **table cream**.

▶ **Oatmeal** cleanses and provides moisture. To make a mask, soak 2 tbsp. (25 mL) of fine oat flakes in a ½ cup (125 mL) of buttermilk for about 30 minutes. Apply a thick layer of the mixture to clean skin.

▶ For a rich **honey mask**, mix together 2 tsp. (10 mL) of honey, 2 tbsp. (25 mL) of plain yogurt, and 1 tsp. (5 mL) of wheat flakes.

▶ To make a spreadable paste that will revitalize dry skin, stir together 2 tbsp. (25 mL) of **healing earth** with 1 tsp. (5 mL) of nurturing **almond oil** and an equal amount of water.

▶ For better skin tone, spread on a thick mask made from 2 tbsp. (25 mL) of **healing earth** mixed with 5 drops of **wild rose oil** and an equal amount of **rose water**.

▶ Raw, peeled **potato slices** have long been used as moisturizers. Simply apply the slices to your face for a few minutes after it is cleansed.

SENSITIVE SKIN

Sensitive skin is not uncommon. With so many chemical-laden products out there, natural options are a must.

▶ To make a **peppermint mask** that promotes circulation and clears up your skin, stir together 2 tbsp. (25 mL) of finely ground oatmeal with 3 drops of peppermint oil and an equal amount of hot water. Spread the mask on thickly.

▶ To make a mask with a calming effect, stir together 2 tbsp. (25 mL) of **healing earth** and an equal amount of lukewarm **chamomile tea** to produce a spreadable paste. Apply and cover with a warm, damp cloth.

For Care of Mature, Dry Skin

½ banana
1 tsp. (5 mL) honey
1 egg yolk
1 tbsp. (15 mL) yogurt
1 tbsp. (15 mL) wheat flakes

Puree the banana and mix with honey, egg yolk, yogurt, and wheat flakes. Apply to face, cover with a cloth, and let work for about 15 minutes.

Fingernails

Like your hands, your fingernails are a personal calling card—and chewed nails and torn cuticles don't make a very good impression. Help your nails shine with regular care and a diet rich in vitamins.

Many women—as well as men—feel more attractive and better groomed with manicured hands. Just follow these tried-and-true methods.

THE ESSENTIALS OF NAIL CARE

▶ For a basic **hand and nail scrub,** heat up 2 tbsp. (25 mL) of cocoa butter and mix with 2 tbsp. (25 mL) of ground almonds and 5 drops of lemon oil. While it's still warm, massage it into your hands and nails, and rinse with warm water. Always scrub before every basic manicure.

▶ Ideally, you should give yourself a **manicure** every other week. Start with a gentle exfoliating scrub to remove scaly skin and dirt, and then push your cuticles back. Shape your nails with scissors or a file (filing from the edge of the nail and toward the center). Follow up by massaging your hands and nails with a moisturizing gel, such as **aloe vera**.

▶ Basic daily cleaning is necessary and simple. Scrub your nails with a **soft brush** and coat them with a little **olive** or **almond oil.**

▶ Don't cut your **cuticles**—just carefully push them back. You will have better luck if you soften them first with a little **olive oil.**

▶ Alternatively you can **soften your cuticles** by mixing together 1 egg yolk, 1 tbsp. (15 mL) of fresh pineapple juice, 1 tsp. (5 mL) of lemon juice, and 2 drops of lemon oil. Apply with a brush or cotton swab. Rinse after 15 minutes.

▶ It's a matter of personal preference whether you file or clip your nails. Use an **emery board** or a **glass nail file** (or even a diamond file for very strong nails). Metal files can make your nails brittle and fingernail clippers are not much better—they can cause your nails to become grooved and frayed.

Use only high-quality scissors for manicures.

Treat your nails to a warm oil bath once a week.

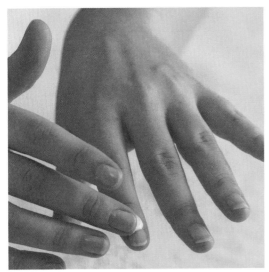

Your fingernails take on a healthy sheen when rubbed with beeswax.

► Your fingernails will appreciate a **therapeutic oil bath**, made easily by warming up ¼ cup (50 mL) of macadamia, almond, or olive oil and adding 1 drop each of geranium, seabuckthorn, and lavender oil (from the pharmacy or a health food store). Dip your fingers in the oil bath for 2 minutes, then massage your hands with the remaining oil.

► To make a **nourishing poultice** that should be applied to your nails once a week, thoroughly mix 1 egg yolk and 2 tbsp. (25 mL) of wheat germ oil, and then stir in 1 tbsp. (15 mL) each of grated carrots and lemon zest. Apply the poultice to your nails and the backs of your hands and cover with a cloth. Rinse with warm water after 30 minutes.

► Finish by shining the nails with a **chamois nail buffer** or a **polishing file**, or apply clear nail polish.

BRITTLE NAILS AND SOFT NAILS

Anyone who has them knows how frustrating they can be. There are, however, simple ways to strengthen brittle nails. Start by coating your nails with a little warm **olive oil** mixed with a couple of drops of **lemon juice** every evening. Wear soft cotton gloves and let the mixture work overnight.

► To strengthen stressed fingernails, mix together 2 tbsp. (25 mL) of **silicic acid gel** (from a health food store) and 1 tbsp. (15 mL) of **beer**. Apply to your nails and let work for 5 minutes, then rinse.

► **Vitamin B$_7$ (biotin)** also strengthens your nails. It is abundant in brewer's yeast, soy products, organ meats, and egg yolk.

► Avoid growing **long nails** and **fast-drying nail polish**. The latter makes your fingernails brittle.

► Soft nails can be toughened up by rubbing them once daily with a mixture of **cider vinegar** and **lemon juice**.

THE RIGHT WAY TO APPLY NAIL POLISH

Look for nail polish with as few chemical ingredients as possible. The Chinese may have already had the right idea 3,000 years ago, when they began painting their nails with a mixture of egg white, gum arabic, gelatin, and beeswax.

When using nail polish, keep in mind these helpful pointers:

► Before applying nail polish, it is always a good idea to prime your nails with a protective, nurturing **base coat**.

► Apply the nail polish in **two coats**: start with a stroke in the center of the nail and then do the sides in 2–3 strokes.

► Nail polish lasts longer when you apply a protective **top coat.**

► Nail polish remover should be **acetone-free** and should contain oil to keep your fingernails from drying out too much.

Nail Oil

For flexible, strong nails.
2 tbsp. (25 mL) almond oil
1 tsp. (5 mL) jojoba oil
5 drops lavender oil
5 drops lemongrass oil

Mix all ingredients and massage into nails morning and evening.

Foot Care

Our feet carry us throughout life. In fact, during an average lifetime, most people will walk the equivalent of the world's circumference three times. Your tender tootsies have earned a reward. Footbaths, scrubs, and lotions keep your feet healthy and looking good.

Corns, calluses, bunions, and ingrown toenails are not only unsightly and uncomfortable, but they can also make it difficult to buy shoes that fit. These problems are preventable, and many natural home remedies can ease them. By caring for your hard-working feet, you make sure that walking and other forms of exercise remain pain-free and pleasurable.

REGULAR CARE

▶ Treat your feet with a nurturing **foot lotion** and use daily. To make the lotion, bring 1 cup (250 mL) of milk, a handful of peppermint leaves, and 2 tbsp. (25 mL) of rosemary needles to a boil. Let steep for 15 minutes, then cool and strain. Mix 3 drops of peppermint oil into the herbal milk and pour into a sealable bottle. Rub your feet with this lotion morning and evening—it will keep in the refrigerator for about four weeks.

▶ To make a **weekly foot scrub** that will remove scaly skin and make your feet smooth and supple again, mix together 1 tbsp. (15 mL) of almond oil, 1 tsp. (5 mL) of sea salt, and 3 drops of eucalyptus oil. Massage into your feet for a few minutes, then rinse them thoroughly. It's a good idea to do a foot scrub before a pedicure.

▶ Calluses can be painful. To avoid them, remove hardened skin occasionally with a **pumice stone**, preferably after a shower or bath. (To further soften a callus, tape a cotton ball soaked in vinegar to your foot overnight.) After gently filing down the callused skin, massage **olive oil** into your feet to keep the skin supple.

TIRED, STRESSED, AND SORE FEET

▶ A **foot massage** makes your feet feel good. To make a simple massage oil, mix together 2 tbsp. (25 mL) of almond oil and 3 drops of lavender oil and massage your feet with gentle, circular motions. Begin with the sole of your foot and proceed from the toes toward the heel. You can also use a **massage brush** or **foot roller**.

Herbal Wash

A remedy for painful feet.

2/3 oz. (20 g) mugwort
2/3 oz. (20 g) chamomile
2/3 oz. (20 g) peppermint
2/3 oz. (20 g)
   linden blossoms
1 quart/liter cold water

Pour the cold water over the herbs, heat, and boil for 15 minutes. Before straining, cool to lukewarm, then wash your feet with the herbal liquid.

After a pedicure, moisturize your tired feet.

A foot roller feels great on your tired soles.

8 oz. (250 g) of sea salt. Mix the ingredients well. Dissolve 2 tbsp. (25 mL) of the bath salts in about 2 quarts/liters of warm water and soak your feet for 10 minutes. Store the remainder of the salts in a tightly closed container.

▶ A **sand and sea salt scrub** removes callused and scaly skin on the soles of your feet. To make the scrub, thoroughly mix 1 cup (250 mL) of fine sand, 2 tbsp. (25 mL) of sea salt, about ¾ cup (175 mL) of olive oil, and 2 drops each of rosemary, peppermint, and lemon oil. Rub into the soles of your feet with circular motions before rinsing with warm water and rubbing dry.

▶ Brittle skin can be painful and, if left untreated, can lead to more problems. To make a soothing **herbal oil**, heat ½ cup (125 mL) of olive oil, add ⅓ oz. (10 g) each of **pot marigold** and **lavender** blooms, and let steep for 3 minutes over low heat. Strain the cooled oil and thoroughly squeeze out the flowers. When warm to the touch, apply a thin coat to your feet.

▶ To help swollen feet, cook up some tasty **asparagus**—it's a natural diuretic. **Bananas** will make a difference, too; they are a natural source of potassium, which helps relieve fluid retention.

FOOT CONDITIONING

Your feet are like any other parts of your body—they require regular exercise. **Walking barefoot** is one way to stimulate circulation and toughen your feet.

▶ To strengthen your feet, spread some **marbles** out on the floor and roll your feet back and forth on them. Then try to grasp the marbles with your toes.

▶ Wearing **properly-fitting shoes** at all times is crucial.

▶ Another **massage oil**, especially for dry skin, consists of 3 tbsp. (45 mL) of olive oil, 1 tsp. (5 mL) of cider vinegar, ½ tsp. (2 mL) of chamomile oil, and ½ tsp. (2 mL) of alum. Stir all ingredients into a hot double boiler, cool, and rub into your feet.

▶ To **refresh tired feet**, try a fragrant herbal mixture of ⅔ oz. (20 mL) each of peppermint and pot marigold tinctures, ⅓ oz. (10 mL) of rosemary tincture, 10 drops each of lemon, cypress, and peppermint oil, plus 3½ oz. (100 mL) of witch hazel. Add all ingredients to a bottle with a spray top and shake vigorously. Spray your feet several times daily, as needed.

▶ To get your tired, swollen feet back up to speed, try an **elder blossom footbath**. Boil two handfuls of elder blossoms in 1 quart/liter of water with a handful of peppermint leaves. Cool, strain, and pour liquid into a small basin of warm water. Soak for 10 minutes.

▶ Take a therapeutic footbath by filling a bowl with warm water and adding a few drops of **chamomile** or **lavender oil**. Just as simple is a warm footbath with 1 quart/liter of **milk** or **whey** added. The bath can rehydrate cracked skin on your feet.

▶ To make **stimulating bath salts,** dissolve 2 tsp. (10 mL) each of rosemary and spruce needles in 2 tbsp. (25 mL) rubbing alcohol, then add about

perfect pedicures

one Take a 10-minute foot-bath with warm water and a few drops of the essential oil of your choice.

two Gently remove callused skin. A pumice stone, which has been used for skin care since the time of the ancient Greeks and Romans, works well for this, or use a special callus plane from a specialty store.

three If necessary, soften your cuticles with a little olive oil and push them back with a cuticle stick.

four Trim your nails. Always cut or file them straight to keep them from becoming ingrown and painful.

Fragrances

Fragrances have played an important role in human attraction for thousands of years. On special occasions, the ancient Egyptians would wear cones of scent on their heads that melted in the heat, exuding exotic aromas. Today, men and women are still seduced by fragrant mixtures of flowers, fruits, woods, and spices.

Succulent fragrances stimulate your mind. You'll feel refreshed and revitalized when you apply any of these traditional formulas. Smells sway emotions, modify perception, and are the ultimate wake-up call for your senses.

BASIC FORMULAS

▶ Mix together about ¼ cup (50 mL) of vodka, 1 tsp. (5 mL) of distilled water, and about 25 drops of the essential oil of your choice, and shake vigorously. The resulting fragrance is immediately ready to be enjoyed.

▶ **Sandalwood** and **cedar** are favorites for masculine scent mixtures. For a flowery aroma, use **patchouli, geranium,** or **lavender oil.** Opt for **orange** or **bergamot oil** to obtain a charming fresh scent, and use **violet** or **rose oil** to achieve heavy, sensual notes.

▶ Oxygen, heat, and light destroy fragrances. Keep homemade perfume in a **tightly-sealed bottle** in a cool, dark location (like in a drawer), and it'll last around three months.

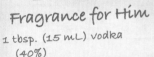

Fragrance for Him

1 tbsp. (15 mL) vodka (40%)
10 drops chamomile oil
10 drops geranium oil
10 drops clary sage oil
10 drops bergamot oil
10 drops neroli oil
5 drops coriander oil
about 3½ oz. (100 mL) witch hazel

Put the vodka and the essential oils into a glass bottle and shake well to dissolve the oils. Add the witch hazel and shake once again. Let steep for a week and shake before each use.

HOMEMADE FRAGRANCES

▶ **Eau de Cologne**, a time-tested classic, can be made at home. Mix 1¼ cup (300 mL) of water with 12 drops each of bergamot and lemon oil, 10 drops each of orange and geranium oil, 6 drops of rosemary oil, and 3 drops of neroli oil. Shake vigorously and set mixture aside for two days. Then add about

The fragrant oils used to make perfumes can be found in health food stores.

Make a soft, tantalizing perfume from violets.

Apply strong aromas such as patchouli or jasmine to the insides of your wrists or behind your ears.

of **lavender** or **rose flowers** for the violets, if you prefer those scents.

▶ For a fragrant **rose water,** pour 1 quart/liter of boiling water over 3½ oz. (100 g) of fresh rose petals and steep for an hour, then strain. Bring the rose water back to a boil and pour it over another 3½ oz. (100 g) of rose petals. Store the cooled rose water in a dark bottle.

PERFUMED HANKERCHIEFS

Perfumed handkerchiefs may sound old-fashioned, but it is a tradition that is certainly worth reviving!

▶ You can make a suitable fragrance by pouring 3½ oz. (100 mL) of rubbing alcohol over 10 cloves, 2 cinnamon sticks, ⅔ oz. (20 g) of violet root, and ⅔ oz. (20 g) sandalwood in a sealable container. Let the mixture steep for two weeks, shaking occasionally, then strain and mix with 3½ oz. (100 mL) of rose water. Sprinkle **just a few drops** onto a handkerchief as needed.

USING FRAGRANCES

Consider these guidelines when using fragrances:

▶ In contrast to heavy evening perfumes, the subtle aroma of **less intense fragrances** are suitable on your body from head to toe.

▶ Never use too much perfume, or the scent will become overpowering. A **couple of drops** from a vial or **2–3 squirts** from a pump bottle are perfectly adequate.

▶ In order to make the most of a scent, apply perfume to **clean skin**.

⅓ cup (75 mL) of distilled water, shake once again, and let steep for about a week before using.

▶ To produce a feminine fragrance with a subtle vanilla aroma**,** slit open 2 **vanilla beans** and soak in about 3½ oz. (100 mL) of vodka. Remove the vanilla pods after three days and add 1 cup (250 mL) of distilled water.

▶ To make a classic summer perfume that relies on the pure, fresh scent of **citrus fruits**, mix together 1 tbsp. (15 mL) of vodka, 10 drops each of orange, neroli, lemon, mandarin orange, and rose oils, plus 5 drops of bergamot oil, then add about 3½ oz. (100 mL) of orange flower water. The scent needs a week to develop fully.

▶ For a distinctive **violet perfume,** pour about 1⅓ oz. (40 mL) of rubbing alcohol and ¼ cup (50 mL) of distilled water over 3½ oz. (100 g) of violet flowers and let steep for a full week. Strain the liquid and mix with 3½ oz. (100 mL) of distilled water. You can also substitute two handfuls

Hair Coloring

Women have been using nature's bounty to color their hair since the Bronze Age. As concerns grow over the safety of harsh chemical hair dyes, substances like henna have enjoyed renewed popularity. Not only are they easy on your hair and scalp, they can provide a great variety of silky, shimmering shades.

Dealing with natural hair dyes will require a bit of trial and error. It is a good idea to first color a lock of your hair to check the color before applying to your entire mane. To ensure that your shade is neither too light nor too intense, stick with the specified exposure time.

BRIGHTEN AND TOUCH UP BLOND HAIR

▶ To make a **lemon-based wash** that will lighten and add shine to blond hair, mix ⅔ cup (150 mL) boiling water with the juice and grated peel of a lemon, and steep for 30 minutes. Strain and stir in 1 tsp. (5 mL) of **cider vinegar**. Slather evenly on your freshly washed hair and rinse with warm water after 10–15 minutes. Repeat once a week.

▶ Mix together a spreadable paste that will turn blond hair shiny. Pour a little boiling water over about 5 oz. (150 g) of **chamomile blooms** and steep for 30 minutes. Then strain and put the flowers into a bowl with 3½ oz. (100 g) of dried, finely-ground **rhubarb**. Add 1 tbsp. (15 mL) of **olive oil** and an equal amount of hot water, and mix. Apply with a brush and cover hair with plastic wrap for 30 minutes. Rinse out and wash your hair.

Red Coloration

Henna turns dark brown hair a rich, attractive red.

1 cup (250 mL) red henna powder
1 cup (250 mL) black tea
1 tbsp. (15 mL) olive oil

Mix the henna, warm tea, and oil and apply immediately. Cover your head with plastic wrap and a large towel and leave on for two hours. Rinse hair with warm water and wash.

Henna powder comes from the dried and ground leaves of the henna bush.

BRUNETTE HAIR DYE

▶ To make a shimmering brown dye, blend ½ cup (125 mL) of **natural henna** with 1 cup (250 mL) of finely ground **walnut shells**. Stir in enough boiling water to make a spreadable paste. Add 1 tsp. (5 mL) of **lemon juice** and 1 tbsp. (15 mL) of **olive oil**, stir, and apply with a broad brush. Cover your hair with plastic wrap and let sit for 20–30 minutes before thoroughly rinsing and washing your hair.

▶ Create a medium brown dye with a light red luster by mixing 3½ oz. (100 g) of crushed **onion peel**, 1½ oz. (50 g) of finely-ground **sandalwood,** and 1 tbsp. (15 mL) of **olive oil**. Pour in enough boiling water to create a spreadable paste and apply with a broad brush. Cover your hair with plastic wrap and leave on for 20–30 minutes before rinsing and washing your hair.

DYING YOUR HAIR
DARK BROWN OR BLACK

▶ To make a dark brown or black dye that will work on all natural hair colors, mix 3 tbsp. (45 mL) of **black tea**, ½ cup (125 mL) of **black henna powder**, 1 tbsp. (15 mL) of **olive oil**, and 1 tsp. (5 mL) of **cider vinegar**. Add enough boiling water to produce a spreadable mixture. Apply with a broad brush, cover your hair with plastic wrap, and leave on for about 30–40 minutes before rinsing and washing your hair.

When dying your hair, be sure to protect your forehead under the hairline to avoid staining your skin.

▶ Create a rinse that will result in a darker shade with a subtle luster by steeping 4 tbsp. (60 mL) of dried **sage**, 2 tbsp. (25 mL) of dried **rosemary**, and 1 tbsp. (15 mL) of **lemon juice** in about 1²/₃ cup (400 mL) of water over low heat. Strain after 30 minutes, cool, and use as a rinse after washing your hair.

COLORING AND DARKENING GRAY HAIR

▶ Gray hair can also be colored, producing **high-lighting effects**—the white hairs take on color differently from those that are not yet gray.

▶ To darken gray hair, mix 3½ oz. (100 mL) of boiling water with 4 tbsp. (60 mL) of dried **sage** and 1 tsp. (5 mL) of **black tea.** Let steep for 30 minutes, then strain. Moisten your hair with the lukewarm solution and rinse after 30 minutes.

Color rinses with herbal mixtures leave your hair with a silky sheen.

Hair Conditioners

Nurturing conditioners and fortifiers add vitality, suppleness, and silky luster to your crowning glory. Fortunately, nature provides the right ingredients for every hair type.

Rinses, poultices, hair tonics, and other conditioners can make dull hair shine. Pick treatments appropriate to your hair type.

OILY HAIR

▶ Make a **lemon rinse** by mixing 1 quart/liter of boiling water with the peels from 2 lemons and steep, covered, for 20 minutes. Strain and squeeze out the lemon peels thoroughly. Let the lemon water cool to warm before rinsing.

▶ To make a conditioner containing **essential oils,** which can help regulate the activity of your oil glands, mix 3 tbsp. (45 mL) of cider vinegar with 2 drops of sage, juniper, and lemon oil and 7 oz. (200 mL) of warm water. Rinse your hair with it, then rinse again with tap water.

▶ To rid your hair of oil and make it smell wonderful, make a **vanilla rinse** by mixing 3½ oz. (100 mL) each of white rum and beer, 2 eggs, 1 tsp. (5 mL) of lemon juice, and ½ tsp. (2 mL) of vanilla pulp. Massage into your hair. Rinse after 10 minutes and wash your hair thoroughly.

▶ A **tea tree oil poultice** will reduce oily buildup. To make one, mix ¼ cup (50 mL of almond oil with 3 tbsp. (45 mL) of lemon juice and 10 drops of tea tree oil, comb through wet hair, and leave on for 30 minutes. Rinse, then wash.

▶ Reduce oil production by applying an **oil cure** every 10 days. Mix 2 tbsp. (25 mL) of jojoba oil and 10 drops each of juniper and tea tree oil, and apply to your dry, unwashed hair and scalp. Comb through, cover your hair with plastic wrap and a towel, and leave on for 30 minutes. Wash your hair with a mild shampoo.

FINE HAIR

▶ Make a weekly **egg and beer poultice** that can add body to lank locks by stirring together 3 tbsp. (45 mL) of beer and 1 egg. Massage into hair, and cover with plastic wrap and a towel, and leave on for 30 minutes. Then wash your hair gently with a mild shampoo.

▶ To make a **hair fortifier** that will add luster and body to fine hair, dissolve 1 tsp. (5 mL) of honey in 7 oz. (200 mL) of warm stinging nettle tea and add 1 tsp. (5 mL) of fruit vinegar. Massage the liquid into washed, still-wet hair and let it dry.

LUSTERLESS, DULL HAIR

▶ For shiny hair try a **cider vinegar rinse**. Mix 1 tbsp. (15 mL) of cider vinegar, 5 drops of lavender oil, and 2 cups (500 mL) of warm water and rinse your washed hair with it. Do not wash out.

▶ You can also quickly make a **luster rinse** with **tea**. Mix 2 cups (500 mL) each of chamomile and orange blossom tea and apply while still warm.

NORMAL HAIR

▶ To make a **henna poultice** that will leave your hair with a silky luster, stir together 1 tbsp. (15 mL) of neutral henna with 1 egg yolk, 1 tsp. (5 mL) of olive oil, and enough warm water to make a spreadable paste. Massage into washed hair and leave in for 15 minutes. Rinse with warm water.

▶ For a healthy scalp and lustrous hair, mix 3 drops each of **neroli, chamomile, lavender,** and **sage oil** in the palm of your hand and spread through your freshly-washed hair. Do not rinse off.

▶ To make a **natural hair fortifier,** mix together 2 cups (500 mL) of warm water, 1 tsp. (5 mL) of honey, 1 tsp. (5 mL) of cider vinegar, and 3 drops of lemon oil. After shampooing, spread through your hair and let it dry—do not rinse it out.

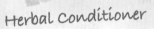

Herbal Conditioner

Use this conditioner for oily hair after every shampoo.
1 tsp. (5 mL) burdock root
1 tsp. (5 mL) chamomile flowers
1 (5 mL) tsp. sage
1 tsp. (5 mL) peppermint
1 tsp. (5 mL) lavender flowers
1 tsp. (5 mL) rosemary
2 cups (500 mL) water
1 tbsp. (15 mL) lemon juice

Mix the herbs and the boiling water, and steep for 30 minutes. Then strain and add the lemon juice. Use warm and do not rinse out.

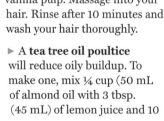

Wrap hair in plastic and a towel after applying a poultice.

DRY, STRESSED HAIR

▶ **Avocados** are outstanding sources of moisture. To make a deep conditioner, puree the flesh of 1 avocado and mix with 2 egg yolks and 1 tbsp. (15 mL) of molasses. Knead the paste evenly into your wet hair and rinse thoroughly after 30 minutes. Apply once weekly.

▶ **Bananas** also make a nurturing conditioner. Mix one crushed banana with 1 tbsp. (15 mL) of avocado and massage the paste into your hair and scalp. Cover your hair with plastic wrap and a towel, leave on for 20 minutes, then rinse hair with warm water and wash with a mild shampoo.

▶ **Thyme** protects your hair from drying out. To make a thyme rinse, pour 1 quart/liter of boiling water over 3 tbsp. (45 mL) of thyme (fresh or dried). Steep for 10 minutes, then strain and cool to lukewarm. Apply after every shampoo.

DANDRUFF

Those annoying flakes of dandruff are usually the result of an excessively dry or oily scalp and/or inappropriate hair care products.

▶ To make a **dandruff-fighting rinse**, mix 1 tsp. (5 mL) each of comfrey, rosemary, and stinging nettle (fresh or dried) with 7 oz. (200 mL) of witch hazel and steep for five days. Massage into your scalp after every shampoo and do not rinse out.

▶ To make a **stinging-nettle-based hair tonic,** mix together 1/4 cup (50 mL) stinging nettle tincture and 2/3 cup (150 mL) water and apply directly to your scalp with a cotton ball. It should be applied only after every second or third shampoo.

▶ Apply a **linden flower tea rinse** (4 tbsp./60 mL linden flowers in 2 cups/500 mL of water) after every shampoo to eliminate dandruff.

▶ Make an **essential oil remedy** by mixing 1 tbsp. (15 mL) of almond oil with 2 drops each of cedar, rosemary, and lemon oil. Massage into your scalp. Rinse after two hours.

To eliminate split ends, rub in a mixture of cocoa butter and lanolin before every shampoo.

Hair Washing

When it comes time to lather, rinse, and repeat, there are many gentle shampoos based on old formulas for every type of hair—without chemicals and side effects.

A mild, neutral shampoo from the pharmacy is a good starting point for many nurturing or fortifying formulas. After washing, let hair air dry—and if you must use a hair dryer, avoid the hot setting.

And when it comes to healthy hair, what you put on your tresses isn't the only thing that counts—your diet matters, too. Make sure you get plenty of vitamin B2, biotin, and zinc from foods such as salmon, dark leafy veggies, and legumes.

OILY HAIR

If your scalp produces too much oil, your hair will become limp, lank, and greasy shortly after shampooing. Strong shampoos dry out your scalp, encouraging more oil production, but pH-neutral shampoos have the opposite effect, controlling oil levels. Since oil can form an ideal breeding ground for bacteria, it is best to wash greasy hair at least every two days.

▶ To make a **mild herbal shampoo** for oily hair, pour 1 quart/liter of boiling water over a handful each of sage, rosemary, and peppermint (fresh or dried). Steep for 30 minutes, strain, and mix with about 2/3 cup (150 mL) of neutral shampoo before bottling the mixture.

▶ For a **fragrant shampoo,** mix 3½ oz. (100 mL) of neutral shampoo with 3 drops each of cedar, bergamot, and lavender oil.

FINE HAIR

▶ The active agents in **stinging nettle** can help fortify hair lacking volume and body. To make a shampoo, put 3½ oz. (100 mL) neutral shampoo, 1 tsp. (5 mL) honey, ¼ cup (50 mL) of stinging nettle tincture, 20 drops of lavender oil, and 2 cups (500 mL) of distilled water into a bottle and shake.

Massage shampoo into your hair and scalp with gentle, circular motions.

DULL, LIFELESS HAIR

Chemical hair treatments can render hair limp and lank, without a healthy sheen.

▶ Make a **nurturing shampoo** that will give your hair luster by mixing 2 tsp. (10 mL) of wheat germ oil and 2 tsp. (10 mL) of honey. Dissolve 1 tbsp. (15 mL) of olive oil soap flakes in 3½ oz. (100 mL) of hot water and mix in 1 tsp. (5 mL) of lemon juice. Pour the ingredients into a bottle and shake before use.

NORMAL HAIR

▶ To make a **mild, fragrant shampoo** that is ideal for normal hair, mix 3½ oz. (100 mL) of neutral shampoo with 2 drops each of neroli, lemon, and ylang-ylang oil, and let steep for a week.

▶ **Baking soda** is an outstanding cleanser because it absorbs dirt very effectively and leaves hair with a silky sheen. For a **clarifying shampoo,** stir 1 tsp. (5 mL) of baking soda into about 2 tsp. (10 mL) of shampoo, and wash hair thoroughly.

▶ To make a **fortifying shampoo** from the good old days, beat 1 egg yolk with a fork till foamy and mix with 2 tbsp. (25 mL) of beer, 1 tbsp. (15 mL) of cognac, and 5 drops of lemon oil.

DRY, OVER-PROCESSED HAIR

If the glands in your scalp secrete too little oil, your hair will become dry and brittle. Too much sun, salt water, chlorine, frequent blow-drying, and chemical hair treatments can ramp up the damage. A dry hair shampoo generally contains substances such as egg yolk or oils that boost your hair's moisture level and bring back the shine.

▶ Make an **egg shampoo** by beating together 2 egg yolks with 2 shot glasses of rum, 1 tbsp. (15 mL) of olive oil, and the juice of half a lemon. Massage the shampoo into your wet hair and your scalp, let it work briefly, then rinse thoroughly.

▶ For a dry hair **regenerating shampoo,** mix ¾ oz. (25 g) of powdered iris root, about 2¾ oz. (75 g) of talcum powder, and 10 drops each of lemon and rosemary oil. Store in a well-sealed container.

▶ **Olive oil** has been both consumed and used for hair care in the Mediterranean for thousands of years. One old trick involves preparing your scalp before washing your hair to prevent the shampoo from drying it out. Rub a little olive oil into your scalp and leave it on for 30 minutes. Rinse with warm water, then wash hair with an easy-to-make, moisturizing shampoo composed of 2 eggs and 1 tbsp. (15 mL) of avocado oil.

▶ Make dry hair soft and silky by soaking a **washcloth in whole (3.25%) milk** and rubbing it into your washed, damp hair. Rinse thoroughly after 15 minutes.

▶ Treat **dandruff** with an infusion of rosemary and thyme. Place 2 tbsp. (25 mL) of dried rosemary and 2 tbsp. (25 mL) of dried thyme in a bowl and add ⅔ cup (150 mL) of boiling water. Cover the bowl and allow to steep for 15–20 minutes. Strain into a 10 oz. (300 mL) clean plastic bottle with a tight-fitting lid. Add ⅔ cup (150 mL) cider vinegar and shake before each shampoo.

▶ Make a **dry shampoo** with 1 tbsp. (15 mL) cornstarch or finely ground oatmeal. Apply to your hair and rub it through to absorb as much oil as possible. Comb hair to remove tangles, then thoroughly brush until all excess cornstarch or oatmeal is removed.

Soapwort Shampoo

Soapwort has been used to lather up for generations.
10 soapwort stalks with leaves
2 cups (500 mL) water
2 handfuls of fresh herbs

Chop soapwort finely and bring to a boil in water. Strain after 15 minutes. For greasy hair, add peppermint or white deadnettle. For dull hair: parsley or rosemary. For dry hair: marshmallow or comfrey. For normal and fine hair: stinging nettle or horsetail. Allow to cool while covered. Strain again and bottle.

Many shampoo formulas contain egg yolk. The lecithin in the yolk gives hair vitality.

Hand Care

Hands are always on display, so it pays to keep them beautiful. But it's not easy; every day your hands are exposed to the elements or harsh cleansers. Since they contain very little subcutaneous fatty tissue, hands are particularly sensitive and need conscientious care.

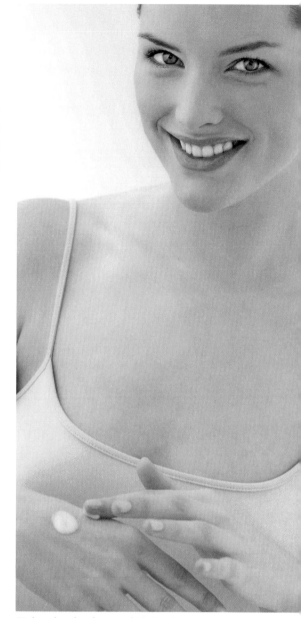

The skin on your hands is subject to similar aging processes as facial skin, but well-maintained hands can remain supple, move very gracefully, and stay attractive. So go ahead and pamper your hands with these soothing home remedies.

TLC FOR ROUGH HANDS

▶ Chapped hands become velvety-soft again when treated with a **fennel infusion**. In the morning, pour 1¼ cup (300 mL) of boiling water over about ½ cup (125 mL) of fennel seeds, steep for 10 minutes, strain, and cool. Soak your hands in the infusion for 2 minutes after every washing.

▶ To rejuvenate dry skin, use a **yogurt and egg poultice** once a week. Mix together 2 tbsp. (25 mL) of yogurt, 1 tbsp. (15 mL) of cream cheese, 1 egg yolk, 1 tbsp. (15 mL) of honey, and 2 tbsp. (25 mL) of lemon juice. Apply a layer almost ⅛ in. (3 mm) thick to hands. Wash off with warm water after at least 15 minutes.

▶ For an **exfoliating scrub** that will smooth rough skin, stir 1 tsp. (5 mL) of sugar with a little lemon or grapefruit juice, and rub your hands with it before rinsing with warm water.

▶ To make an **oil and honey massage** that leaves your skin noticeably softer, mix 1 tsp. (5 mL) of honey, 2 tsp. (10 mL) of almond oil, and 2 drops of seabuckthorn oil. Massage into your dry, chapped hands. Let it work overnight—wear cotton gloves—and rinse with warm water in the morning.

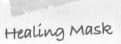

Healing Mask

For smooth, soft hands, apply this mask weekly.

½ cucumber
1 egg white
1 tbsp. (15 mL) yogurt
1 tbsp. (15 mL) avocado oil
1 tsp. (5 mL) lemon juice
2 drops peppermint oil

Peel and puree the cucumber, then beat the egg whites until stiff. Mix all the ingredients and spread on your hands. Leave for 15 minutes before rinsing hands with warm water.

To keep hands soft, use a daily hand cream.

▶ For a **moisturizing emulsion** that will cleanse, stir 1 tsp. (5 mL) of honey and the juice from half a lemon into 3½ oz. (100 mL) of warm milk.

▶ Make a **daily hand cream** by pouring the juice from 2 lemons through a cheesecloth. Mix the clear juice with an equal amount of almond oil. Melt 2 tbsp. (25 mL) of beeswax in a double boiler, add the lemon-almond oil, and stir until the liquid cools. Add 5 drops of citrus oil (e.g., lemon, grapefruit, neroli, or lemongrass). Pour into a clean jar and store in the refrigerator—it will keep for three days.

► Back in the olden days, badly cracked skin was treated with a hand cream made of **milk**, but soaking your hands weekly in warm **olive oil** will also render skin soft again.

TIPS FOR COMBATING SWEATY HANDS

Sweaty hands are not uncommon. Luckily, there are many simple, natural solutions.

► A **fenugreek hand bath** calms overactive sweat glands. Soak ¾ cup (175 mL) of fenugreek seeds in 1 quart/liter of cold water for six hours, then strain. Bring to a boil and leave to cool. Bathe your hands in the liquid for 15 minutes twice daily.

► Mix 1 tbsp. (15 mL) of **lemon juice** and 1 tsp. (5 mL) of **rubbing alcohol.** Apply regularly (at least once a day) to combat sweaty hands.

► Rub your hands with **diluted cider vinegar** (vinegar mixed with an equal amount of water) to reduce sweating. Apply three times a day.

► Apply **rubbing alcohol** three times a day.

ELIMINATING SPOTS AND ODORS

Our hands are always on display, making how they look and smell important. Follow these tips to keep them clean and odor-free.

► Remove stubborn nicotine spots by rubbing them with a little **lemon juice.**

► Use a paste of 1 tsp. (5 mL) of **olive oil** and 1–2 tsp. (5–10 mL) of **sugar** to remove age spots.

► Try a paste made from **confectioner's (icing) sugar** and **lemon juice.**

► Soak smelly hands in **milk.**

► Rub your hands with **moist salt** or **coffee grounds** to remove the odor.

► Before cutting onions or garlic, rub hands with a little **olive oil** to prevent absorbing the smell.

► To keep your hands from developing spots, rub them with **vinegar** before cutting or coring fruit.

PROTECTING YOUR HANDS

Our hands are precious, which is why we should take steps to protect them. How hands are washed and dried, when to use creams, and water temperature are critical.

► Harsh soaps interfere with the skin's natural acid protection coating; a gentler and better choice is a **mild, pH-neutral soap** or a natural-base cleansing lotion.

► Avoid washing your hands in water that is either **too hot** or **too cold** to keep skin from cracking and drying out. After every washing dry your hands thoroughly; don't forget the areas between your fingers.

► Apply a little **moisturizing cream** every time you wash your hands, and especially before going to bed. Be sure to rub cream on your cuticles.

► Alternatively use a fragrant, homemade oil of 1 tbsp. (15 mL) of **olive oil** with 2 drops of **chamomile** or **lavender oil.** Avoid harsh soaps or toners with a high alcohol content, which remove not only the dirt and grease on your skin, but also your skin's natural oils. Opt instead for mild products that match your skin type.

► When doing housework, use soft **latex gloves** to keep your hands dry and protect them from harsh detergents and household chemicals.

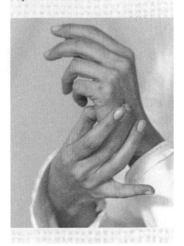

relaxing massage

one Wash your hands, dry them, and apply a mild hand cream.

two Massage your palms with your thumbs in forceful, circular motions. Then turn your hands over and gently rub between the fingers with your thumbs.

three Splay your fingers, stretch them out completely, then relax them. Repeat several times.

four Use one hand to stroke each finger on the other hand from the tip to the wrist. Then shake out your hands.

Sturdy, thorn-proof gloves are essential for gardening.

Homemade Beauty Products

The cosmetics industry can be a minefield of overly harsh ingredients. Using natural cosmetics gives you the advantage of plant-based oils for moisture and nutrients and essential oils for delightful scents. Here are the most common ingredients used to make homemade beauty products—and their benefits.

Plant-Based Oils

- Apricot kernel oil makes an excellent massage oil and has a faint scent of almonds. It is appropriate for all skin types, but particularly for dry, sensitive skin.

- Avocado oil promotes cell regeneration and mixes well with other oils.

- Jojoba oil, a liquid wax made from the seeds of the boxwood, controls moisture, and doesn't leave skin with an oily sheen. It is suitable for every skin type.

- Macadamia nut oil is rich in fatty acids, making it an ideal ingredient for creams.

- Use almond oil for massages and to care for all skin types.

- Olive oil nurtures every skin type, but in particular regenerates dry, rough skin.

- Wheat germ oil is rich in vitamin E, which combats the aging of dry, mature skin.

Active Agents

These plant oils, available at pharmacies and/or health food stores, have healing and/or nurturing qualities. They should therefore be added to cosmetics only in very small amounts.

- St. John's wort oil comes from fresh blooms. It is used frequently as a massage oil, and can soothe sensitive, blemished, dry, or rough skin.

- Evening primrose oil heals, stimulates, and improves the appearance of skin. It is also sometimes used in conditioners for brittle, overprocessed hair. It is made from the seeds of the evening primrose.

- Seabuckthorn oil comes from the berries of the seabuckthorn bush, a Russian olive plant. It does wonders for mature, dry, and cracked skin.

- Black cumin seed combats bacteria and fungi on irritated, inflamed skin.

- Wild rose oil comes from rose hips and provides rough skin with ample moisture. It also encourages cell regeneration.

Essential Oils

These common oils, found in most health food stores, provide the finishing touch to so many homemade beauty products: a delightful scent. Which one you choose is up to you!

Bergamot Oil	The finest of all citrus oils with a sweet, citrus-fresh scent
Geranium Oil	A soft, flowery, feminine touch
Lavender Oil	A pure, fresh, flowery scent used in many products
Neroli Oil	A fresh, flowery scent with a touch of bitter-sweet orange
Rose Oil	A sweet, flowery scent; a very feminine oil
Rosemary Oil	An intense scent similar to camphor; use sparingly
Sandalwood Oil	A warm, heavy, and long-lasting scent used by both men and women
Incense Oil	A heavy oil with a touch of lemon and camphor
Ylang-ylang Oil	An exotic, sensual scent, ideal for perfume, deodorants, and bath additives; use sparingly
Lemon Oil	A pure, fresh scent with a subtle and sweet touch; ideal for cleansing

Useful Ingredients

- Cetaphil cream is a soft, unscented cream that washes off with water; it is well suited as a base for making creams.

- Beeswax gives creams, salves, lotions, and lipsticks a thicker, more solid consistency.

- Vinegar reduces itching, cools, and refreshes. It regulates the pH value of your skin, acts as a natural antiseptic, and promotes blood circulation. The vitamins and minerals it contains also make organic cider or other fruit vinegar an ideal additive for cleansers and baths.

- Glycerin is a clear, syrupy alcohol used as a lubricant in creams and lotions.

- Cocoa butter melts at low temperature and makes a good base for soaps and creams.

- Lanolin—the pure oil from sheep's wool—is a moisturizing skin care all-star in large part because of its water-repellent properties.

Mineral Ingredients

- Healing earth, found in health food stores, is a fine-grained soil consisting of white and red clay, loam, and aluminum silicates. The sterilized powder is mined from Ice Age loess deposits and can be used both internally and externally to absorb toxins. In the latter case it can be used in wraps, compresses, face masks, baths, and hair care products.

- Rhassoul and kaolin, found in some health food or natural products stores, are natural clay cleansers that provide a gentle, non-sudsy alternative to shampoos and soaps.

Lip Care

The thinnest skin on your entire body is on your lips—in fact, they have just three layers of cells compared to the 16 layers on most of your face. Since your lips have neither sweat nor oil glands, they dry out easily and need lots of TLC to keep them soft.

Our lips are often exposed to sun, wind, and other irritants, but luckily for us there are a number of easy, natural ways to keep lips soft.

CARE AND PROTECTION

▶ Carefully massage your lips with a **soft toothbrush** every morning. You can even add a little **honey** to the toothbrush to make your lips softer.

▶ The active ingredients of **papaya** will also render your lips soft. Make a balm by pureeing ¼ of a papaya. Apply generously to your lips and the surrounding skin. Rinse with warm water after 10 minutes and apply regular lip balm.

▶ Make a **moisturizing lip balm** by melting 2 tbsp. (25 mL) of wheat germ oil, 1 tbsp. (15 mL) of beeswax, and 1 tbsp. (15 mL) of honey in a double boiler. Add 3 drops of peppermint oil and 2 drops of chamomile. Stir until thick, then let cool.

▶ For an **everyday balm,** melt 3½ oz. (100 mL) of olive oil and ¾ oz. (25 g) of beeswax in a double boiler; let cool to lukewarm. Mix in 1½ tsp. (7 mL) of honey, 20 drops of chamomile tincture, and 1 tsp. (5 mL) tincture of propolis. Stir until cool and store in a cool place.

▶ A simple, weekly **exfoliating lip scrub** consisting of 1 tsp. (5 mL) of sugar and a little olive oil will remove flaky skin and promote circulation.

▶ Always protect your lips from **ultraviolet rays** by using lip balm with a built-in sun protection factor.

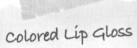

Colored Lip Gloss

2 tbsp. (25 mL) coconut oil
1 tbsp. (15 mL) almond oil
1 tbsp. (15 mL) beeswax
1 tbsp. (15 mL) cocoa butter
1 pinch pearl-luster pigment (optional)
1–2 drops red food coloring

Melt the oils, wax, and cocoa butter together in a double boiler and stir. Stir in the pearl-luster pigment and the food coloring. Put into a small container to cool.

Apply all-natural lip gloss to help protect your lips.

▶ Drink plenty of **fluids** to keep the sensitive skin of your lips tender and smooth.

▶ Avoid **licking your lips** in cold weather—the combination of wet and cold robs your lips of even more moisture, rendering them dry and rough.

ROUGH, CRACKED LIPS

▶ You can smooth chapped lips by applying some **cocoa butter** or **carrot juice** several times a day, or by placing slices of **cucumber** on them.

▶ Alternatively, mix 1 tsp. (5 mL) each of **yogurt** and **honey**, and apply to your lips. Wait 10 minutes and rinse with warm water.

▶ To make a **warm compress**, mix equal amounts of thyme, willow bark, and chamomile. Pour a cup of boiling water over 1 tsp. (5 mL) of the mixture, steep for 10 minutes, then strain. Dip a soft, sterile cloth into the warm liquid and apply to your lips for 20 minutes.

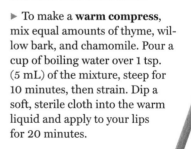

To heal chapped lips, apply a bit of honey and lick it off after 15 minutes.

Moisturizers

Ads from the cosmetics industry promise consumers a flawless complexion and perpetual youth if they use their products—but you can do just as well with quick, inexpensive, and easy-to-prepare natural formulas.

The appropriate choice of skin care creams or oils depends mainly on your skin type and age—more mature skin requires different care than youthful skin.

NORMAL SKIN

▶ For a tried-and-true skin cream, beat 1 **egg white** stiff and add 1 tsp. (5 mL) of **honey** and 3 drops of **almond oil**. Beat the mix further to produce a thick, smooth cream that will keep in the refrigerator for three to four days.

▶ Alternatively, melt 1½ oz. (50 g) of **beeswax** in a hot double boiler and add 3½ oz. (100 mL) of **wheat germ oil** and about 4 tbsp. (60 mL) of **elder flower water**. Stir the ingredients, put the cream into a small porcelain container, and store in the fridge.

OILY, BLEMISHED SKIN

▶ To make a **pimple-busting face cream**, boil 3½ oz. (100 mL) of distilled water with 1 tbsp. (15 mL) of **yarrow**. Cool the solution and filter through a fine sieve, before adding 1 oz. (30 mL) of **witch hazel** and stirring the mixture slowly into 3½ oz. (100 g) of **Cetaphil cream**. Store in a porcelain container in the refrigerator.

▶ Make an **anti-inflammatory cream** by pouring ½ cup (125 mL) of boiling distilled water over ⅔ oz. (20 g) of **pot marigold blooms.** Cover and let it cool, then strain through a fine sieve, thoroughly squeezing out the blooms. Stir in 1½ tbsp. (20 mL) of **almond oil**, and blend the mixture with 3½ oz. (100 g) of **Cetaphil cream**.

MATURE SKIN

▶ **Rose gel** will quickly plump up mature skin. Heat about ⅔ cup (150 mL) of distilled water and mix in 1 tsp. (5 mL) of powdered **gelatin**. Stir in 1 tsp. (5 mL) of **rose oil** and 4 drops of **lavender oil**, plus 1 tbsp. (15 mL) of **glycerin**. Let the gel cool and store in a porcelain jar.

Homemade cosmetics do not contain additives and should be used within four weeks when refrigerated.

Yarrow contains antiseptic substances that can help combat blemishes.

▶ A **beeswax-based cream** will preserve skin's elasticity. Melt 1/3 oz. (10 g) of beeswax in a double boiler at 140–160°F (60–70°C). Stir in 1/4 cup (50 mL) of **almond oil**, 1 tsp. of **jojoba oil**, 1/2 oz. (15 g) of **aloe vera**, and 5 drops of **rosewood oil**.

DRY SKIN

▶ To treat sensitive, dry skin, mix 1/2 cup (125 mL) of **cocoa butter**, 2 tbsp. (25 mL) of **beeswax** (grated), 2 tsp. (10 mL) of **distilled water**, 3 tbsp. (45 mL) of **sesame oil**, 2 tbsp. (25 mL) of **coconut oil**, and 1 tbsp. (15 mL) of **olive oil**. Combine beeswax with water and melt over low heat, add cocoa butter, and blend. Gradually add coconut, sesame, and olive oil. Pour into a glass jar. The mix will thicken as it cools down.

▶ Alternatively, stir together 2/3 oz. (20 g) each of **lanolin** and **petroleum jelly** and add 2 drops each of **rose** and **lavender oil**; stir until the cream is smooth. Store in a porcelain container in the refrigerator for up to two months.

FACIAL OILS FOR NIGHT USE

Facial oils, when applied sparingly to squeaky-clean skin, soak in almost completely. When stored in the refrigerator, homemade oils last for about two weeks. All oils are made by adding ingredients to a small, dark bottle and shaking vigorously. They differ depending on skin type.

▶ For **normal skin:** blend about 1/4 cup (50 mL) each of jojoba and almond oil with 5 drops each of geranium, rose, lavender, chamomile, and incense oil.

Oil from the orange blossom has long been used in traditional cosmetics.

▶ For **mature skin:** pour 1/4 cup (50 mL) of almond oil, 1 tsp. (5 mL) of wheat germ oil, and 5 drops each of incense, lavender, and chamomile oil into a dark bottle. Shake well.

▶ For **dry skin:** mix 5 tbsp. (75 mL) of olive oil, 2 tsp. (10 mL) of avocado oil, and 10 drops of lemon oil.

▶ For **oily skin:** stir 1 1/2 oz. (50 g) of powdered aloe into 1 1/3 oz. (40 mL) of distilled water and add 2 tsp. (20 mL) of orange blossom water. Set aside. Stir 1 tsp. (5 mL) of honey with 3 1/2 oz. (100 mL) apricot kernel oil in a double boiler. Mix all ingredients together.

▶ For **sensitive skin:** mix 1/3 cup (75 mL) of almond oil, 2 tsp. (20 mL) peach pit oil (from a health food store), and 10 drops of neroli oil.

When making cosmetics, cleanliness is of utmost importance.

Neckline and Throat

A woman's décolletage has long been a symbol of beauty and femininity. But the skin on your neck and throat is significantly thinner and more sensitive than on other parts of the body, so daily care is required to keep it firm.

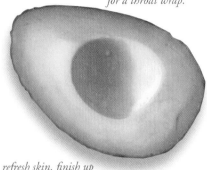

Instead of almond oil, you can use avocado oil for a throat wrap.

To refresh skin, finish up a morning shower with a blast of cold water.

and wait 30 minutes. Rinse with warm water and apply moisturizing cream to your skin.

▶ To prepare a **skin balm** for nightly skin regeneration, mix 2 tbsp. (25 mL) apricot kernel oil, 15 drops jojoba oil, 3 drops neroli oil, and 2 drops each of almond, rose, and lavender oil with 2 tsp. (10 mL) glycerin. Pour into a dark, sealable container. Gently rub a few drops into your neckline and throat before bedtime.

▶ For a flawless neckline, puree about 3½ oz. (100 g) of **raspberries** and mix with 2 tsp. (10 mL) each of **almond bran** and **honey**, as well as 1 **egg yolk**. Apply to your neckline as a mask, and rinse after 30 minutes with warm water.

▶ **Throat exercises** help keep skin firm. Reach over your head to grasp your left ear with your right hand. Carefully turn your head to the left, hold the tension for a few seconds, and then relax. Do the same with the other side.

SUN PROTECTION

The sensitive skin of your décolletage should be sheltered from the sun. To prevent slackening of the tissue and the formation of wrinkles, use sunscreen consistently on your face, neck, and throat.

There are a number of natural remedies for neck wrinkles and loose skin around the throat.

HOME REMEDIES

▶ Combat loose skin and aging with an **oil wrap.** Mix about 1 tbsp. (15 mL) of **almond oil** with 1 tbsp. (15 mL) of **honey**, spread the mixture onto a cloth, and apply to your throat for one hour. Apply weekly.

▶ Reduce neck wrinkles with **parsley milk**. Heat up 2 cups (500 mL) of **whole (3.25%) milk** and add a bunch of chopped **parsley**. Let it steep for a few minutes, then strain the milk and let it cool to lukewarm. Moisten a soft, clean cloth with the parsley milk, place it on your throat, and let it work for 15 minutes.

▶ To tighten the skin on your neckline and throat, make a **lemon cure** by beating 1 **egg white** until stiff, then stirring in the juice of 1 **lemon**. Apply

Nutrition and Beauty

A healthy, balanced diet is good for more than keeping off weight; vitamins and minerals make your skin smooth and supple, strengthen your fingernails, teeth, and gums, and keep your hair shiny and silky.

Vitamins

- A good supply of vitamin A is the basis for healthy skin and a fresh face. Vitamin A keeps skin smooth and young by stimulating cell regeneration. You can get it in the form of retinol (liver, whole eggs, milk, and some fortified food products) or from the beta-carotene contained in many fruits and vegetables (carrots, cantaloupe, sweet potatoes, and spinach). You can make it easier for your body to absorb beta-carotene by boiling or steaming foods containing the substance and adding a little butter or other fat.

- B vitamins are key for the growth of skin, hair, and nails. Vitamin B_6, in particular, helps form collagen for firm connective tissue. Biotin, which is often referred to as Vitamin B_7, is another of the B-group vitamins that protects skin and hair cells.

- Vitamin C accelerates collagen production in your cells and helps keep gums healthy. Since vitamin C is quickly destroyed by heat, foods high in vitamin C are best eaten raw.

Minerals

- Iron facilitates oxygen transport in your blood. Pale, brittle fingernails and hair loss can be signs of an iron deficiency—one of the most common nutrient deficiencies in the world.

- Potassium stimulates your kidneys and digestive system, ensuring the elimination of harmful substances, and plays an important role in keeping your skin supple.

- Calcium (contained in milk products) makes teeth strong and healthy.

- Magnesium keeps cell walls stable, preventing skin from wrinkling.

- Selenium, found in wholegrain products, can repair skin damage.

- Zinc aids vitamin A in its duties and promotes the healing of wounds as well as a strong immune system.

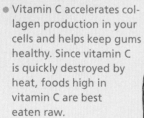

Sources of Vitamins and Minerals

Beta-carotene	orange and yellow fruits and vegetables, dark leafy vegetables
Biotin	eggs, legumes, organ meat
B vitamins	grains, soybeans, nuts, legumes
Iron	meat, wholegrain products
Potassium	dried fruits, legumes, nuts, soy products, vegetables, mushrooms, avocados, bananas
Calcium	milk and milk products
Magnesium	wholegrain products, legumes, mineral water
Selenium	brewer's yeast, wholegrain products, seafood, mushrooms, brown rice
Vitamin C	citrus fruits, kiwi, rose hips, blackberries, bell peppers, papaya, broccoli
Vitamin E	cold-pressed oils, nuts, cereal germ
Zinc	legumes, cereals, nuts, poultry, seafood

Vitamins are classified according to how they are absorbed and stored in the body. Vitamins A, D, E, and K are soluble only in fats, whereas vitamin C and the B vitamins are soluble only in water. Your best source of vitamins and minerals is food, but a multivitamin can offer insurance against gaps in your diet.

Antioxidants

Environmental pollution, cigarette smoke, ultraviolet radiation, and stress contribute to the formation of what's known as free radicals in your body. These aggressive oxygen compounds can damage tissue and cause your skin to age prematurely when present in excess amounts. Natural antioxidants such as vitamin C, vitamin E, beta-carotene, and selenium stabilize free radicals and keep them from causing damage in the body. A diet high in antioxidants also reduces your risk of developing many serious diseases. Eating a range of whole foods can help you ward off damaging toxins and free radicals. Among the top picks:

- Berries are chock full of healing antioxidants. Blueberries, raspberries, and blackberries contain proanthocyanidins that can help prevent cancer and heart disease. Strawberries, raspberries, and blackberries contain carcinogen-fighting ellagic acid. Blueberries also appear to delay the onset of senility. Eat them on their own, throw a handful in your morning cereal, make a smoothie, or enjoy them for dessert with a dab of low-fat whipped cream.

- With more vitamin C than an orange and more calcium than a glass of milk, broccoli gets a gold star for nutrition. But on top of that, it's loaded with disease-battling phytonutrients. Boil it, steam it, or make a flavorful soup.

- Garlic—aka "the stinking rose"—acts as a natural antibiotic, killing off some strains of harmful bacteria. It can also help fend off cancer, heart disease, and the effects of aging. Roast it whole and spread on a baguette, or sauté it with a little butter and toss with hot pasta. Yum yum!

Fluids

If your skin is to remain supple, clear, and fresh, it needs plenty of fluid. Adequate fluid intake also helps your internal organs filter out harmful substances. A rule of thumb: drink at least 1½ quarts/liters of fluid per day—ideally mineral water, fruit juice spritzers, or herbal and fruit teas. Freshly squeezed organic fruit and vegetable juices will boost your appearance and your health. Drink them in any combination, but don't underestimate the caloric content of fruit juices.

Oral Care

Brushing and rinsing do more than give you a healthy smile; they may also improve your long-term health. Many illnesses, some of them serious, can get their start in your mouth—reason enough to keep it clean.

People have believed for centuries that bad teeth signify bad health. It was only recently, though, that we identified the scientific connection: gum inflammation. The theory is that bacteria from dental plaque seep into the bloodstream via inflamed gums and produce enzymes that make blood platelets stickier and more likely to clot, contributing to the hardening of arteries. The good news is that this risk factor can be easily controlled.

Healthy teeth and strong gums are the product of conscientious care and good nutrition. To the chagrin of children, sugar is the number-one enemy of our teeth. Sugar damages teeth in two ways: by interfering with the absorption of calcium and causing tooth decay. Milk products, on the other

Toothbrushes with moderately sized heads are able to reach corners and angles effectively.

A toothbrush should fit comfortably in your hand to facilitate brushing.

hand, contain a healthy load of calcium, which hardens your teeth. To keep your gums healthy and strong, eat plenty of fresh fruits and vegetables; the vitamin C they contain is a fountain of youth for your teeth.

TOOTH-CARE TIPS

▶ Good tooth care does not end with tooth brushing. Cleaning between your teeth at least once a day with **dental floss** is essential. Guide the floss between teeth and wrap it in a "C" shape at the base of the tooth, slightly under the gum line. Slide the floss up to the top of the tooth several times. Finish by rinsing your mouth.

▶ Recent findings indicate there's no difference between a **regular** or **electric toothbrush** when it comes to thorough cleaning. Because of their rapid, rotating motion, electric toothbrushes clean effectively in a much shorter time—but brushing carefully for 2–3 minutes is equally effective. In either case, replace your toothbrush every two months.

▶ **Halitosis** is often caused by a coating on your tongue, but it's simple to remedy with a **tongue scraper**. Just slide the scraper over your tongue three to four times, twice a day.

HOME REMEDIES FOR TOOTH BRUSHING

▶ Fresh breath is guaranteed with a toothpaste made mainly from **healing earth** and **sea salt**. Mix together 3½ oz. (100 g) of fine healing earth and ½ tsp. (2 mL) sea salt and dribble in enough boiled water to make a creamy liquid. Add 2 drops each of peppermint and tea tree oil.

▶ For a gum-strengthening **tooth powder**, finely grate 1¾ oz. (40 g) of dried orange peel and mix with about 1 oz. (30 g) of dried peppermint leaves and ⅓ oz. (10 g) of sea salt. Store in a screw-top container. When brushing your teeth, just sprinkle a little powder onto your moistened toothbrush.

▶ For a whitening tooth powder familiar to your grandparents, mix 1 small container of **baking soda** with 2–3 drops of **caraway oil**. But don't use it too often; the acidifying ingredients in baking soda can hurt tooth enamel.

▶ You can also whiten your teeth—and strengthen your gums—by rubbing them with the inside of a **lemon peel**. Alternatively, brush your teeth occasionally with **warm sage tea**.

MOUTHWASHES

Using mouthwash after brushing can leave your mouth fresh and clean.

▶ To make a pleasant-smelling, refreshing mouthwash, mix ¼ cup (50 mL) each of water and vodka and 3 drops each of **eucalyptus, anise,** and **clove** oil in a small bottle. Add 1 tsp. (5 mL) of the mouthwash to a glass of water and gargle.

▶ For another refreshing rinse, mix 2 cups (500 mL) of vodka, 2 tsp. (10 mL) of **rhatany (krameria) tincture,** 2 tsp. (10 mL) of **peppermint oil**, about ½ tsp. (2 mL) of **cinnamon oil**, and ¼ tsp. (1 mL) of **anise oil**. Add just a dash of the mixture to a glass of water and rinse.

▶ To make a mouthwash that will strengthen your gums, mix 2 tsp. (10 mL) each of **arnica, propolis, rhatany,** and **sage tinctures**. Add 10 drops of the mixture to a glass of water and rinse.

▶ Inflammation can be soothed with a mouthwash made from 2 tsp. (10 mL) of **arnica tincture** diluted with 2 tbsp. (25 mL) of water.

Rose Blossom Mouthwash

- 5 tbsp. (75 mL) rose blossoms
- 4 tbsp. (60 mL) sage
- 2 tbsp. (25 mL) strawberry leaves
- ⅔ cup (150 mL) cider vinegar
- 3½ oz. (100 mL) rose water

Mix herbs in a sealable container and pour the heated cider vinegar over top. Steep for 10 days, strain, and squeeze out herbs thoroughly. Mix the remaining liquid with rose water and pour through a filter. Add a dash to a glass of water and rinse.

Brushing teeth is just the beginning when it comes to oral hygiene. Flossing will clean your gums and the spaces between your teeth.

Relaxing Baths

Take advantage of the power of a long soak in the tub to soothe, moisturize, and heal your skin. After you step out of the bath, follow up with a moisturizer.

First, you have to determine your skin type (turn to page 113 for more on skin types). Dry and oily skin each require different treatments, and even if your skin is normal, it still requires special care.

NORMAL SKIN

▶ Open your pores with a **yogurt-based bath additive.** Puree 1 individual serving of plain yogurt, 1 tbsp. (15 mL) of honey, 2 tbsp. (25 mL) of almond oil, and the pulp of 1 vanilla bean in a blender. Add 10 drops of orange oil and swirl into the bathwater.

▶ Invigorate your skin with a **spruce needle bath additive.** Fill a jam jar two-thirds full with fresh spruce needles, add enough sea salt to fill the jar completely, then pour in water to the top. Let steep in a warm place for two weeks and shake vigorously every day. Put 2 tbsp. (25 mL) of this mixture into a cloth bag and put it into the bathwater.

▶ Pamper yourself with a **vanilla shower gel**. Stir together 3½ oz. (100 mL) of neutral, unscented shampoo, ¼ cup (50 mL) of warm water, a pinch of salt, and 15 drops of vanilla oil.

OILY SKIN

▶ Make a **buttermilk bath** by adding to the water a puree made from 1 quart/liter of buttermilk, the juice of 4 lemons, and 4 generous handfuls of peppermint leaves.

▶ Soothe your skin with an **oatmeal bath.** Combine 9 oz. (250 g) of oatmeal, a handful of fresh sage and peppermint leaves, and 10 drops of lemon oil in a cloth bag or old pantyhose. Drop the bag in your bathwater, squeezing it out occasionally while you soak.

▶ Short on time? Simply add 1 quart/liter of fresh **whey** and 10 drops of **peppermint oil** to your bathwater.

▶ Stimulate your body with a **firming shower gel.** Stir together 1 cup (250 mL) of shower gel base (available from beauty supply stores or online) with 10 drops each of geranium and lemon oil and 5 drops each of rosemary, juniper, and sage oil.

MATURE AND DRY SKIN

▶ Get silky-soft skin with a **bath oil** made from ¼ cup (50 mL) of almond oil, 10 drops of grapefruit oil, and 5 drops each of lemon and orange oil.

▶ Soak in a **lavender bath.** Cover a handful of dried lavender flowers with water, boil for 5 minutes, and strain. Add 2 tbsp. (25 mL) of honey and 1 tbsp. (15 mL) each of cream, buttermilk, and olive oil, and add to your bathwater.

For maximum relaxation, spend about 20 minutes in a bath below 97–100ºF (36–38ºC).

Scrubs

Treat your face and body to exfoliating scrubs regularly to remove dead cells, and they will refine and clarify your skin's appearance. It's almost like being reborn!

Two thousand years ago, the Judeo-Roman historian Flavius sang the praises of sea salt, a valued ingredient in natural beauty care products.

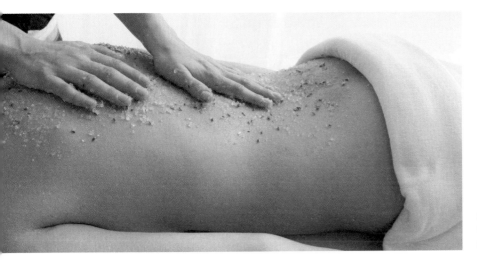

Body scrubs should be gently massaged on your skin and then rinsed off thoroughly.

Exfoliating scrubs can be made from a number of natural ingredients. Oranges, lemons, sugar, olive oil, and almond bran are ideally suited for facial scrubs. Essential oils and salt are key ingredients for body scrubs.

EXFOLIATING FACIAL SCRUBS

▶ Treat sensitive skin with **orange peel.** Grate the zest from an orange and dry carefully, then grind in a coffee grinder or a mortar. Add a little warm water and rub onto skin. Rinse thoroughly.

▶ Rejuvenate your skin with a scrub made from ingredients found in almost every home. Stir together 1 tsp. (5 mL) of **sugar** and 1 tbsp. (15 mL) of **olive oil**. Massage the scrub onto your skin, then rinse thoroughly.

▶ Make normal and oily skin clean and glowing by mixing together 1 tbsp. (15 mL) each of **almond bran** and **oatmeal** with 1 tsp. (5 mL) of **grated lemon peel**. Add a little warm water, then massage the scrub on your skin. Rinse thoroughly with warm water after 2 minutes.

▶ Smooth dry skin with a **fragrant oil scrub.** Mix 2 tbsp. (25 mL) of almond bran with an equal amount of rose water to produce a thick paste. Add 2 drops of rose oil and 1 drop of lavender oil. Gently massage into the skin and rinse with warm water after 2 minutes.

EXFOLIATING BODY SCRUBS

▶ Stimulate dry skin with a **sea salt scrub.** Mix 1 tbsp. (15 mL) of sea salt, 2 tbsp. (25 mL) of almond oil, and 10 drops of lemon oil and apply to a washcloth. Massage your skin with it while still wet from the shower and rinse thoroughly.

▶ Make a **sweetly fragrant scrub** by mixing together 2 tbsp. (25 mL) of sea salt, 1 tbsp. (15 mL) of walnut oil, 5 drops of patchouli oil, and 2 drops of jasmine oil. Apply the scrub, wrap yourself in a towel, and let it work for 30 minutes before rinsing off thoroughly.

good to know

HOW OFTEN?

Since exfoliating scrubs are abrasive, they shouldn't be used frequently. Exfoliating facial scrubs and body scrubs should be used on dry skin once a month. But you can treat normal facial skin to a scrub every two weeks, and oily facial skin weekly. After a scrub, always apply a moisturizing skin care product made specifically for your skin type.

Shaving

Daily shaving is not only time-consuming, it can also put stress on skin. Luckily, this can be remedied with the right cream, salve, or lotion. And if you cut yourself or develop an ingrown hair, any number of time-tested home cures can offer quick relief.

When using a blade razor, place it high on your cheek and move in short strokes.

Whether you shave with a manual or electric razor is a matter of personal preference. But avoid using a manual razor if you have blemished skin, since it may open pustules and could lead to infections.

SOOTHING SKIN IRRITATIONS

▶ Soothe and disinfect your skin with a pleasantly fragrant **aftershave lotion.** Pour 1½ tbsp. (20 mL) of rubbing alcohol, 5 tbsp. (75 mL) of witch hazel, 1½ tbsp. (20 mL) of rose water, and 2 drops each of clary, seabuckthorn, sandalwood, cedar, lemon, and cypress oil into a small bottle. Shake vigorously and let steep for four weeks. Apply straight or pour a little aftershave into your hand, rub in a few drops of jojoba oil, and apply.

▶ Make a **balanced aftershave lotion** by thoroughly stirring together 2½ oz. (75 g) of pH-neutral moisturizer (from a pharmacy) and 1 tsp. (5 mL) each of jojoba, apricot kernel, and almond oil, and 1 tsp. (5 mL) aloe vera gel, plus 2 drops each of chamomile, mint, and geranium oil. Store the aftershave in a jar in a cool place.

▶ Relieve and soothe irritated skin with a **witch hazel salve** (available at health food stores); the effect is increased by mixing in a few drops of St. John's wort or tea tree oil.

▶ Combat irritation and soothe your skin after shaving with creams and salves containing **pot marigold, chamomile,** or **aloe vera.** They should be available in most health food stores, as well as some pharmacies.

TREATING SMALL CUTS

If you use a blade razor, you are bound to cut yourself from time to time. When you do, stop the bleeding with the following:

▶ Dab small cuts with a cotton ball moistened with **rubbing alcohol.**

▶ Stop bleeding with a moist **styptic pencil.**

▶ **Yarrow flowers** are a tried-and-true home remedy for cuts. Grind the dried flowers to powder in a mortar. Apply to the cut and press lightly with a damp cloth.

REMOVING INGROWN HAIRS

▶ Apply a **hot compress** (e.g., a damp cloth with 2–3 drops of tea tree oil). Then pull out the hair with clean tweezers and disinfect the skin with a drop of tea tree oil. To prevent ingrown hairs, use only clean, sharp blades and always shave in the same direction your hair grows.

The trusty old shaving brush still does the job when lathering up before a shave.

Skin Care for Your Body

Legend has it that Cleopatra indulged in daily milk and honey baths. Now you can soothe and refresh your skin with time-tested, natural ingredients that provide nutrients, moisture, and subtle fragrances.

We spend a lot of time worrying about the skin on our face. However, most of our skin exists from the neck down, and it faces many of the same challenges that facial skin does. Luckily, there are many traditional treatments that soothe and restore—just choose those best suited to your skin type.

NORMAL SKIN

▶ Make a **body-nurturing cream** by mixing ½ tsp. (2 mL) of lanolin and 1 tsp. (5 mL) of cocoa butter melted in a hot double boiler. Then add ¼ cup (50 mL) of almond oil and stir frequently until mixture cools. Add fragrance by blending in 5 drops of rose oil (for women) or sandalwood oil (for men).

Body lotions made from plant ingredients are a boon to skin, contributing to its regeneration.

Squash Poultice

Provide moisture that is appropriate for every skin type.

3½ oz. (100 g)
   squash, skin removed
1 peach
1¾ oz. (50 g)
   cucumber, unpeeled
1 tbsp. (15 mL)
   cocoa butter
1 tbsp. (15 mL) honey
1 egg white

Puree ingredients in a blender. Apply to skin, wrap your body in a linen cloth or large towel, and let work for 20 minutes before showering.

▶ Make your skin soft and silky with a poultice of 3½ oz. (100 g) of **Dead Sea mud** (available at health food stores or online). Mix with 2 tsp. (10 mL) **aloe vera gel** and apply to clean, dry skin. Wrap your body in a large towel and let work for 30 minutes before showering. Use weekly.

▶ Refresh your skin with **body powder.** Mix 2½ oz. (75 g) each of arrowroot starch and cornmeal. Stir in 5 drops each of ylang-ylang and neroli oil. Store the powder in an opaque, sealable container and apply with a powder puff to clean, dry skin.

OILY SKIN

Oily skin looks shiny, with large and clearly visible pores. The overproduction of oil gets trapped inside your skin's pores and, in that oil-rich environment, bacteria proliferate, causing inflammation in the form of pimples and blackheads on your face, back and neckline.

▶ Moisturize skin with a **nurturing body oil** of 5 tbsp. (75 mL) of jojoba oil with 1 tbsp. (15 mL) of almond oil and 5 drops each of lavender and geranium oil. Apply sparingly to your skin after bathing or showering.

▶ Fight blemishes on your back and neckline with a **lavender-honey mask.** Stir together 2 tbsp. (25 mL) of whole wheat flour, 1 tbsp. (15 mL) of honey, and 2 tbsp. (25 mL) of orange blossom water in a double boiler to form a paste. Add 5 drops of lavender oil and spread on problem areas. Shower off after 20 minutes. Apply once or twice a week.

▶ Remove shine from your skin with **body powder.** Mix ½ oz. (15 g) of talcum powder, a pinch (2 g) of zinc oxide, and 2 drops of lemon oil.

MATURE AND DRY SKIN

Dry skin and mature skin are both rough and taut; they crave moisture and oil from an outside source.

▶ Moisturize your skin after bathing or showering with a **fragrant oil mix.** Combine ¼ cup (50 mL) of jojoba oil and 10 drops of essential oil. Good choices include patchouli, mandarin, neroli, lemon, myrrh, rose, or lavender oil.

▶ Treat skin with a **body oil** with a **floral fragrance**. Mix 3 tbsp. (45 mL) each of avocado, almond, and apricot kernel oil, 15 drops of rose oil, and 5 drops of lavender oil. Rub in sparingly after a bath or shower.

▶ Moisturize dry skin with a **body cream.** Melt 1 tbsp. (15 mL) each of cocoa butter and beeswax in a hot double boiler and stir in 1 tbsp. (15 mL) each of sesame, avocado, and coconut oil. Place cream in a container and keep refrigerated for up to two months.

▶ Soak up the moisture from an **exotic poultice**. Puree a banana and mix with 2 tbsp. (25 mL) of buttermilk, 1¼ cup (300 mL) of coconut milk, 2 tbsp. (25 mL) of yogurt, and 1 tbsp. (15 mL) of honey. Massage gently into skin and cover with a large towel. Rinse off after 30 minutes.

After feet, elbows tend to be the most neglected part of the body. But they, too, need care.

ELBOW CARE

We rarely see our own elbows, but that does not mean we should ignore them.

▶ Treat raw, rough elbows to a poultice on occasion. Apply a mixture of 2 tbsp. (25 mL) of warmed **honey** and 1 tbsp. (15 mL) of **lemon juice** and leave on for 30 minutes. Rinse and liberally apply moisturizing cream to your elbows.

▶ Alternatively rub your elbows with **warm almond oil**, wait 5 minutes, and wipe off with a clean cloth. Then treat your skin with a mixture of equal parts lemon juice and glycerin.

Homemade lotions, creams, and body oils make wonderful gifts when presented in decorative bottles.

Skin Types

The skin is our largest sensory organ. It excretes sweat and oil, stores fat and moisture, and protects us from heat, cold, and pathogens. There are five basic skin types, and each one needs special care.

NORMAL SKIN

Normal skin is largely free from blemishes and has adequate moisture. To care for normal skin:

▶ Clean skin with a mild, **pH-neutral soap** or **cleansing lotion.**

▶ Apply a **moistening floral water** (e.g., rose or orange blossom water).

▶ Finish with a thin application of a **not-too-rich cream** or **gel.**

SENSITIVE SKIN

Sensitive skin may be affected by the sun, detergents, and some makeup products. To care for sensitive skin, apply:

▶ **Almond** or **jojoba oil** as a moisturizer.

▶ **Orange peel** facial scrubs.

OILY SKIN

Oily skin is characterized by large pores, an oily sheen, pimples, and blackheads. But despite your overactive oil glands, your skin still needs moisture. A consistent care program includes:

▶ **pH-neutral cleansing** with a soap or lotion.

▶ A clarifying, **alcohol-free facial toner.**

▶ An oil, a light cream, or a gel with **anti-inflammatory properties.**

▶ A weekly **exfoliating scrub** and follow-up **facial mask.**

COMBINATION SKIN

If you have enlarged pores, an oily sheen, and perhaps blemishes in the T-zone (forehead, nose, and chin)—but the rest of your skin is often dry—you have combination skin. In addition to using a mild, pH-neutral cleanser, you should:

▶ Do a regular **exfoliating scrub** (once a week).

▶ Apply a **moisturizing cream** on dry skin in the cheek area and a cream for oily skin in the T-zone, preferably in combination with **astringent herbal waters** (e.g., witch hazel or sage water).

DRY SKIN

Dry skin is characterized by small pores, wrinkles, scaly areas, and a feeling of tautness. Try the following skin care regimen:

▶ Gently cleanse skin with **moisturizing lotions** or **plant oils.**

▶ Use **floral water** such as orange blossom water.

▶ Use rich **facial creams, gels,** or **oils.**

▶ Try an **exfoliating scrub** (once or twice a month).

Follow a skin care regimen that is suitable for your skin type.

Sun Protection

Sunlight may soothe the soul, but its ultraviolet rays can damage your skin. It's to blame for up to 90 percent of wrinkles, not to mention the dreaded leathery look.

UV rays are grouped into three categories—A, B, and C—according to wavelength. UVC rays have the shortest wavelength and never reach the earth. The rays we need to guard against are UVA and UVB, as these rays permeate our atmosphere and cause skin to age. UVA rays, with the longest wavelength, are dangerous because they penetrate deeply into the skin, causing damage to collagen and cells. UVB rays are shorter, but more powerful, and are most intense during the summer months. They cause sunburns, aging, and wrinkling. Research shows repeated exposure to UVB rays can affect the immune system and lead to skin cancer.

BEHAVIORAL TIPS

To protect yourself and others from sunburn:

▶ Drink lots of fluids, especially **mineral water,** to keep your skin from drying out.

▶ Introduce your skin to the sun **slowly**—it's best to begin in spring.

▶ Opt for the **shade** (or indoors) during the hottest parts of the day.

▶ Use **sunscreen** on **cloudy summer days**—clouds may fool you into believing you're not getting burned, but ultraviolet rays still pass through.

▶ Wear **lip balm** with built-in sun protection.

▶ Protect children with **sunglasses** and a **sunhat**, too.

▶ Wear clothing made from **natural fibers**—ultraviolet rays can penetrate artificial fabrics.

Always cover your eyes with UV-protected sunglasses.

▶ The closer you get to the **equator**, the higher the SPF you need. The same applies to **altitudes**: the sun's rays become stronger in the thinner air. **Reflective surfaces** (such as water and snow) also produce intense radiation.

PROPER APPLICATION OF SUNSCREEN

▶ Apply sunscreens in a timely manner, **15 to 20 minutes** before going outdoors, and let it dry thoroughly before you don your clothes. Use creams for normal skin and gels for those with sensitive skin or an allergy to the sun.

▶ Reapply cream immediately after **swimming, showering,** or **drying off**, even when using so-called waterproof sunscreens.

▶ Apply sunscreen protection **several times a day.** Be sure to apply plenty to your nose, cheeks, ears, neckline, and shoulders.

NATURAL SUN PROTECTION PRODUCTS

Let's be clear: natural sunscreens such as avocado or sesame oil and lemon juice do not provide much protection, and are generally inadequate for children or adults with sensitive skin. Use them only for moder-

ate sunbathing lasting just a few minutes, and only when your skin is already tanned. If you're headed to hotter climes, pack a high SPF sunscreen in your suitcase.

AFTER-SUN EXPOSURE

▶ Rejuvenate and return moisture to your skin after sun exposure with an **after-sun body oil**. Mix 4 tbsp. (60 mL) of base oil with 15 drops of essential oil and apply a thin coat to your face and body. Good choices for a base oil include jojoba, wheat germ, and wild rose oil; soothing essential oils include seabuckthorn and lavender oil.

▶ Provide skin with both nutrients and moisture in a **cocoa butter and lanolin lotion.** Soften 2 tbsp. (25 mL) each of cocoa butter and lanolin in a double boiler, then stir in 2 tbsp. (25 mL) each of jojoba and wheat germ oil, 4 tbsp. (60 mL) of black tea, 1 tbsp. (15 mL) of glycerin, and 5 drops of lavender oil. Let cool and store in a jar in a cool place.

▶ Regenerate your skin with a **soothing bath additive**. Puree one cucumber, 2 cups (500 mL) of shredded oats, 2 tbsp. (25 mL) of rosemary, 3½ oz. (100 mL) of black tea, and 1 tbsp. (15 mL) of olive oil in a blender. Add to bathwater at 86–93°F (30–34°C), and relax in the tub for 20 minutes.

▶ Short on time? Just add 2 quarts/liters of **buttermilk** to the bathwater.

▶ Cool your skin with a paste of 1 quart/liter of **plain yogurt** and 2 tbsp. (25 mL) of **jojoba oil**. Spread over your face and body; rinse in a warm shower after 20 minutes.

Children need the added protection of a cream with adequate SPF protection.

Care for Mature and Dry Skin

½ banana
1 tsp. (5 mL) honey
1 egg yolk
1 tbsp. (15 mL) yogurt
1 tbsp. wheat flakes

Puree the banana and mix with honey, egg yolk, yogurt, and wheat flakes. Apply to face, cover with a cloth, and let work for about 15 minutes.

A broad-brimmed hat provides some protection from the sun's rays.

A Well-Managed
Home

In today's hectic world, we are so busy with work and family that housekeeping chores tend to be done on the fly. But when it comes to cleaning, we can still look to old-fashioned methods to achieve amazing results.

Bathrooms

Cleaning your bathroom is a necessary evil. But if you use time-tested cleaners and cleaning methods, you won't need harsh chemical cleansers to keep sinks, tiles, and fixtures spotless.

The bathroom needs to be cleaned regularly, as lime and soap will leave their traces in the tub and in sinks. To keep your bathroom sparkling clean, try some of these surefire tricks:

SINKS, BATHTUB, AND SHOWER
▶ Clean your sinks daily with a mild bathroom cleaner, then rub them down with **fabric softener**—the water will run off easily, leaving no residue.

▶ Rub off stubborn dirt or lime residue with a **lemon peel** dipped in **salt.**

▶ Scrub bathtubs, sinks, and tiles with a paste of **salt** and **turpentine** to renew luster.

▶ Wipe **fiberglass tubs** with a damp cloth and a little **baking soda**.

▶ More delicate **acrylic tubs** have a reputation for being hard to clean, but as long as you shine them up regularly, all you should need is a little **dish soap** and **water**.

▶ Make shower stalls crystal-clear with a **dish soap solution** and a soft cloth. Rub off minor soap scum buildup with **vinegar,** or treat serious buildup with a paste made from **salt and vinegar,** applied with a scrub brush in a circular motion. After you've finished cleaning, rinse and dry your shower stall. Use a **squeegee** daily to prevent lime spots. Rub off minor chalk streaks with **vinegar**.

▶ Apply a little **petroleum jelly** to the shower curtain rod to allow the curtain to slide on the rail more easily. Soak new or freshly-washed curtains in **salt water** to prevent mold growth. You can treat mold stains with **vinegar, lemon juice,** or **baking soda**.

A bathroom should have an exhaust fan to reduce the chance of mold growth.

Use an old toothbrush to clean hard-to-reach places.

PLUMBING FIXTURES

▶ Achieve a scent-free shine by rubbing plumbing fixtures with a mixture of 1–2 tsp. (5–10 mL) of **lemon juice** and about 2 cups (500 mL) of **water**.

▶ Remove **lime residue** on fixtures by wrapping an old rag moistened with **vinegar** or **lemon juice** around the fixture and letting it work for a couple of hours or overnight. Remove the softened lime deposits with a **toothbrush**.

▶ Get rid of lime buildup in faucet aerators and showerheads by letting them sit in a solution of **vinegar** and **salt**. Clean the holes in the showerhead with a **nailbrush** or **toothbrush**.

Citrus Cleanser for the Bathroom

This bathroom cleanser is good for the environment; it's easy on your nose, too.

1/3 oz. (10 mL) dish detergent
5 drops lemon oil
3/4 oz. (25 g) citric acid
about 1 cup (250 mL) water

Mix the detergent and the lemon oil. Stir the water and citric acid to produce a clear fluid. Stir in the detergent-lemon oil solution and store in a bottle for up to three months.

TILES

▶ Make old tiles gleam like new by gently rubbing them with a piece of old **newspaper** or a **chamois cloth** moistened with an **ammonia solution** (1 tsp./5 mL in about 2 cups/500 mL of water). Polish with a little **cooking oil** to add shine and protect against moisture.

▶ Rub away stubborn stains with **straight ammonia solution.**

▶ Remove rust spots by rubbing them with a mixture of **water** and **vinegar.**

▶ Scour discolored grout between tiles with **ammonia solution** or **baking soda**. Dab it on with a moist cloth or old toothbrush, let it work, and rinse it off.

▶ Whiten grout by scrubbing it with a little **toothpaste** on an old, soft-bristled toothbrush.

▶ Clean silicon caulking with **powdered yeast** dissolved in water.

▶ Use very fine **sandpaper** to rub severely discolored grout—but be sure you don't damage the glaze on the tiles.

TOILET

▶ De-lime the toilet bowl by placing a layer of **toilet paper soaked in vinegar** over the deposits and brushing them off the following morning.

▶ Avoid urine scale by putting a dash of **vinegar** in the bottom of the toilet bowl once a week and letting it work overnight.

DRAIN

▶ Use a **strainer** to prevent hair from clogging your drain.

▶ Ensure pipes are clean by pouring boiling **potato water** down the drain.

▶ Sprinkle **baking soda** into the drain and rinse down with hot water to unclog pipes.

▶ Eliminate most unpleasant smells by sprinkling a little **baking soda** directly into the drain and letting it work on the odors overnight.

Beds and Bedding

If you want a good night's sleep, keep your bedding clean and spring for a good-quality mattress. After all, we do spend about a third of our lives in bed.

Clean, well-aired-out bedding makes good sanitary sense and will help ensure a good night's sleep. A good mattress should support your body, especially your spinal column. Replace it every 10 years, or you risk developing back problems due to your saggy mattress.

BLANKETS, PILLOWS, AND SHEETS

▶ **Air out** and **shake** your bedding. This distributes the filling evenly and combats **dust mites** and other small creatures that like warm, dark places.

▶ Hang **down comforters** and **pillows** on a clothesline when the air outside is fresh and dry, but not in intense sunlight, which can make the feathers brittle and porous. Keep your bedding indoors during damp weather.

▶ Wash bedding in a **washing machine** only if the washing drum is big enough to handle it—otherwise have it cleaned commercially.

▶ Wash down either in **down detergent** or **hair shampoo,** then throw it in the dryer at a low temperature with a clean tennis ball or sneaker. Do not **vacuum** down or feather blankets; you risk thinning out the filling.

▶ Wash your bedding more frequently and use pillows and blankets made from **synthetic materials** or **rayon** instead of feathers if you have allergies. These are easier to wash and dry to get rid of mites.

MATTRESSES

▶ Prevent **lumps** from forming in your mattress by turning it every three months, and flipping it twice a year.

▶ **Air out** and **clean** your mattress. Take it out of the bedroom and let it breathe. To clean it, place a **damp sheet** on the mattress, then beat it. The cloth will pick up the dust from the mattress.

▶ Dust your mattress using the **upholstery nozzle** on your vacuum cleaner—it's best to vacuum whenever you change your sheets.

▶ Buy a special **mattress cover**. It is worth the price if you have severe dust mite allergies; it will protect your mattress from mites and can be washed at high temperature.

▶ Consider mattress covers made of **molton fabric** or **terry cloth.** They are easy to remove and launder and protect your mattress against stains.

▶ Rub off fresh **bloodstains** with water, then treat with a mixture of 7 oz. (200 mL) of **cold water,** 3 tbsp. (45 mL) of **vinegar**, and 2 tbsp. (25 mL) of **powdered laundry detergent**. Dab with water and dry with a blow-dryer.

▶ Remove stains that are still **wet** by standing the mattress up and catching the drips with a **towel.**

good to know

MATTRESS FILLERS

Good mattresses come in many varieties. They may have a core of synthetic material such as foam, latex, or interior springs, or the core may be made from natural materials like coconut, horsehair, straw, or seaweed. The covering usually consists of linen, cotton, or raw silk. Mattresses with a natural core should be refurbished after about five years, since they wear out more quickly than latex or spring mattresses. If you're plagued by allergies, opt for a dust-free and anti-bacterial mattress made of foam or latex.

Brass and Pewter

Bring luster back to the pewter and brass items that adorn your home. With a couple of tricks up your sleeve, you can revive your *objets d'art,* doors, and window latches.

Brass is an alloy of copper and zinc characterized by its gold-like color and shine. Pewter is a soft, heavy metal, with a shiny silver-gray surface that is vulnerable to scratches. Both metals can be kept gleaming with a variety of traditional methods.

BRASS

▶ Wipe brass items with a **damp chamois cloth.** To clean it thoroughly, use a **vinegar paste.** Stir together equal parts vinegar, salt, and flour, and spread it on the brass. Let it work for a while, wash it off, and buff.

▶ Rub away corrosion with a mixture of 2 cups (500 mL) of **buttermilk** and 1 tbsp. (15 mL) of **salt**. Rub it repeatedly and forcefully over the corroded spots until they disappear; rinse and polish with a soft cloth.

▶ Create a beautiful shine by rubbing your brass with the cut surface of a **potato,** then buff.

▶ Eliminate **verdigris** with a solution of 1 tbsp. (15 mL) of **salt** in about 2 tbsp. (25 mL) of **ammonia.** Using gloves, dip a rag into the solution and rub onto the brass object, then wash it off.

▶ Retard tarnish and brighten brass by rubbing it with a cloth moistened with a dab of **olive oil** after each polishing.

Brass candlesticks add an elegant touch to any dinner party, as long as you keep them shiny.

PEWTER

▶ Clean pewter with **horsetail.** Just drop a handful of the herb into a bowl with 1 quart/liter of water and 1 tsp. (5 mL) of **vinegar,** then submerge the item. Leave it overnight to do its work. Let it dry and polish.

▶ Rub your pewter with the **outer leaves** of a head of **cabbage** and rinse it with clear water. Finally, treat the surface with a cut piece of **leek** and rinse again. You may want to wear some nose plugs for this cleaning job.

▶ Remove heavy dirt by immersing your pewter object in a glass or bowl of **warm beer** and scrubbing it with a soft **nailbrush.**

▶ **De-wax** pewter candlesticks by freezing them and flaking off the wax. If any wax remains, melt it with a blow-dryer set to hot, and carefully wipe away any excess wax.

Pewter regains its beauty when rubbed with cool ashes.

Carpeting

Rugs and carpets take a beating from shoes, kids, and pets. Keep them maintained on a regular basis to ensure that they feel great beneath your feet, contribute warmth to a room, and provide maximum comfort.

Rugs and carpets need to be cleaned and dusted regularly. They can also fall victim to food and bloodstains, as well as burns, oil and grease stains, imprints, and odors. Follow these tips to keep your rugs and carpets spotless:

DUSTING

▶ **Vacuum** to maintain a carpet. It's best to vacuum regularly and thoroughly, rather than waiting until the dirt becomes visible.

▶ Gently stroke new rugs with a **brush** to loosen and pick up material for the first six months.

▶ Don't vacuum authentic **Oriental rugs** too frequently, and keep the suction level low to avoid damaging the fine fibers.

RUG CLEANING

▶ **Wet-clean** every rug or carpet from time to time. Throw small, washable rugs into the washing machine. Clean the others by hand with a mild detergent, using a **soft-bristled brush** or **sponge** to release the dirt and grime. Rinse afterward with water and, whenever possible, hang your rugs outdoors to dry.

▶ Use homemade **cleaning powder** to clean rugs. Mix 3 tbsp. (45 mL) of **soap flakes** with 18 oz. (550 g) of **potato flour** or **cornstarch**, sprinkle the mixture on the rug, work it in well with an old hairbrush or scrub brush, then vacuum.

▶ Clean and freshen a rug by sprinkling it with moist **salt.** Let it work for a few minutes; vacuum.

▶ Grate **fresh potatoes** and scald them with boiling water. Strain the spuds after three hours and brush the rug with the potato water for a natural cleaning. Leave to dry, then vacuum.

▶ Give your rug a **snow bath**. Place it with the pile side in contact with the snow (which should be light and fluffy, not slushy), and beat the rug out. It should look like new.

▶ Freshen the rug's colors by rubbing it with **vinegar** and **water**.

TREATING STAINS

▶ Soak up **rug spills** immediately with a clean, dry cloth. Work the stains out from the edge toward the center.

▶ Treat **blood-** and **coffee stains** immediately by dabbing the soiled spot with a solution made from

2 tbsp. (25 mL) of **vinegar** and 4 tbsp. (60 mL) of **water**. Speed is essential when dealing with these kinds of stains.

▶ Also try **mineral water** for coffee or bloodstains. Flush the stains with some water, then dry and dab with **diluted ammonia**.

▶ Soften dried stains with **glycerin** to help loosen the stain before further treatment.

▶ Reverse the damage of a **minor burn spot** that haven't actually destroyed the pile of the rug with an **onion-based mix**. Boil up 1 cup (250 mL) of vinegar, 1½ oz. (50 g) of talcum powder, and 2 coarsely-chopped onions. Let cool, apply to the spot and let dry; then brush off the residue.

▶ Rub the rug or carpet's **fibers** gently with **steel wool** until the burned bits disappear.

▶ Repair burn holes by using a **razor blade** to cut some fibers from a hidden place in the pile of the rug, put some **all-purpose glue** into the burn hole, and arrange the fibers in it. Weigh down the area until the glue dries.

▶ Eliminate **grass stains** with a solution made of 1 tbsp. (15 mL) of **ammonia** and 1 cup (250 mL) of **water**, then dab with tap water.

▶ Soak up **grease** or **oil stains** by sprinkling them with **rye** or **cornmeal.** Let it sit for an hour, brush off, and remove the residue with tap water.

▶ Sprinkle **salt** on fresh **red wine** stains. As soon as the liquid has been absorbed, vacuum it up and dab the spot with **mineral water.**

▶ Blot up large **white wine** stains with **paper towels,** then treat them with a solution made from ¼ tsp. (1 mL) **mild detergent** and 1 quart/liter water. Blot up any excess liquid.

▶ Remove hardened **chocolate** with a knife, then dab away the residue with cold water, followed by warm water.

▶ Horrified to find a big wad of **chewing gum** stuck to the rug? Never fear. Place a plastic bag filled with **ice cubes** on it to make the chewing gum brittle enough to chip away with a spatula or spoon.

WHAT ELSE YOU NEED TO KNOW

▶ Avoid **imprints** in your carpet. Buy little, round **plastic coasters** just slightly larger in diameter than the furniture feet.

▶ You can remove imprints by placing a **damp cloth** on them and carefully **ironing** it, then brushing the fibers in the opposite direction.

▶ Don't let rugs slide. Sew **rubber canning seals** under the corners of the rugs; with larger rugs, you might add a few more along the sides and in the center.

▶ Avoid **electric shocks** by spraying synthetic-fiber carpets with a mixture of 1 cup (250 mL) of **liquid fabric softener** and about 2½ quarts/liters of water.

▶ Straighten **rug fringes** by spraying them with **starch** and smoothing with a comb.

▶ Keep **straw rugs** flexible. Spray them occasionally with salt water.

▶ Remove odors from rugs with **baking soda.** Simply sprinkle it on the surface, let it work for a half-hour, then vacuum it up. For stubborn odors, first rub the carpet with **vinegar** and **water**, then apply the baking soda.

removing furniture impressions

one Pick up the piece of furniture and move it enough that you can reach the impression.

two Place an ice cube on the compressed fibers to make them swell up, then vacuum to make the pile stand up again.

Use an old-fashioned straw rug beater to rid your rugs of dirt and dust.

Dishes

Bypass the dishwasher. Instead, handwash dishes, valuable silverware, and delicate porcelain. It's not time-consuming, and you'll save electricity. Tackle stubborn stains and baked-on residue with some old-fashioned elbow grease—and maybe a little old-fashioned ingenuity as well.

Only dishes designated dishwasher-safe by the manufacturer should be machine-washed. Wooden cutting boards and plates have no place in your dishwasher; they can't stand the heat and will lose their luster or even crack and split. You're also better off washing dirty pots and pans by hand. They take up too much space in the dishwasher and require a special, less energy-efficient wash cycle to get them clean.

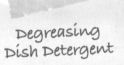

Degreasing Dish Detergent

⅓ cup (75 mL) liquid dish soap
⅓ cup (75 mL) distilled water
juice from ½ lemon

Thoroughly stir together the ingredients and put into a jar with a screw top. Put 1 tsp. (5 mL) of the soap mixture into a sink filled with water. Grease dissolves particularly well at a temperature of 120°F (50°C).

BEFORE DOING THE DISHES

▶ **Soak** dried-on food remains to soften them before rinsing. You'll find that **grease** rinses off better with **hot water,** but **proteins** and **carbohydrates** do better with **cold.**

▶ Protect delicate **porcelain** by lining your sink with a **terry cloth towel.**

▶ Rubbing **lipstick marks** with **salt** makes them much easier to wash off.

WASHING BY HAND

▶ Keep a **tea towel** and a **dishwashing sponge** (which you change frequently) nearby when washing dishes by hand. Use water that's at least 140°F (60°C) to prevent **germs** from entrenching themselves.

▶ As a general rule of thumb, wash **non-greasy items** before greasy ones. The proper sequence: first glasses, then plates, bowls, and other dishes, followed by cutlery and, finally, pots, pans and baking sheets. Fill a second sink or basin with hot, clear water for **rinsing.**

▶ Wash glazed and unglazed **earthenware pottery** by hand, without detergent if possible. And keep in mind that the glaze on earthenware pottery is heat-sensitive.

▶ Scrape **food remnants** from valuable porcelain immediately, then wash each piece separately in warm water.

▶ Never wash **gold-rimmed porcelain** with **baking soda** or other harsh products that can take the finish off.

▶ Clean **wood, bone,** and **ivory silverware handles** with special care. Rinse the metal parts with a damp sponge, but don't dip the handles into water. Place the cutlery into the drainer basket with the handles up.

▶ Eliminate **hairline cracks** in your fine china by soaking it overnight in a large bowl of **warm milk** (no warmer than you would feed a baby). Then gently handwash as usual. Those tiny lines will disappear.

REMOVING STAINS FROM PORCELAIN

Remove stains from porcelain with these simple, but effective tricks:

▶ Remove **tea stains** or leftover residue from porcelain cups by mixing hot water with 1 tsp. (5 mL) of **baking soda** in the cup, letting it sit, and then washing it out thoroughly. Or, mix together 2 tbsp. (25 mL) of **chlorine bleach** and 1 quart/liter of water. Soak the cup in the solution for no more than 2 minutes, then rinse immediately.

Work with clean dishwater for best results.

► Wipe off minor **lime residue** easily with a damp sponge and **citric acid**.

► Wash off stubborn lime residue by pouring a dash of **citric acid** and **hot water** into the container to be cleaned and letting it sit for one hour. Repeat as needed until residue is dissolved, then wash and rinse thoroughly.

► Wipe brown stains off your teapot with a paste of **vinegar** and **salt.**

► Scrub away stains with a mixture of **salt** and **vinegar** or **lemon juice.**

► Banish **nicotine stains** by attacking them with a **cork** dipped in **salt.**

CLEANING TEAPOTS AND COFFEEPOTS

► Never wash teapots with **dish soap** or in the **dishwasher**; simply use hot water. A layer of tannin residue actually enhances the aroma of the tea.

► Can't stand the look of the tannin? Remove it gently by adding **vinegar** to the teapot, letting it steep, and rinsing it out thoroughly. Another option: dip a damp cloth in **baking soda** and use it to wipe out the pot before rinsing, or scrub it with **fine steel wool** and water.

► Clean your **glass coffeepot** by adding a handful of **uncooked rice** and filling it with **dishwater**. Put the lid on and shake until stains are gone.

► Dissolve **denture cleansing tablets** in warm water to deal with stubborn lime deposits.

► Use a flexible **bottle brush** to clean the neck of your teapot.

► Eliminate **thermos bottle odors** by mixing **hot water** and **baking soda.** Let sit in the thermos.

AFTER WASHING

► **Air-dry** your dishes for best results. Place them vertically in a **dish drainer** to let the water run off. Make sure the handles of stainless silverware all point down.

► Dry dishes while they are still **warm** to prevent watermarks and bring out the shine. Use **dish towels** made from an absorbent material like **cotton** or **linen**. Generally, you'll have to wash new towels several times before they become sufficiently absorbent.

► Protect old or valuable porcelain with **paper towels** placed between each of the plates before storing them in the cabinet.

► Allow **thermos bottles** to dry thoroughly inside and store them with the top open to prevent them from developing a musty smell.

► Hang **cups** if possible to save space.

► Turn the top of **tureens, sugar bowls,** and **teapots** upside down, so that the **handle** or any other protruding part is protected inside the bottom piece.

Add a shot of vinegar to your rinse water to give dishes a beautiful shine.

gluing porcelain

one Lay out porcelain, thick quick-drying glue, and clothespins or modeling clay for attaching the porcelain pieces on a work-safe surface (newspapers, an old blanket or towel, etc.).

two Clean the broken pieces of porcelain and the areas to be glued with a lint-free rag; let dry.

three Apply a very thin layer of glue to the pieces.

four Very carefully fit the porcelain pieces together and let them dry; if necessary, hold them in place with clothespins or modeling clay. If any excess glue squeezes out of the fitted porcelain, wipe it off immediately.

Doors

They provide security, contain noise and odors, and offer privacy. In addition, there is scarcely anything in your home that is used by so many people every day as your doors. So it's no wonder that defects and signs of wear begin to appear after time.

Spray a little sewing machine oil or other liquid lubricant into the squeaky hinge on a heavy door.

Ideally every door in your home should be weather-efficient and silent. Rid your place of squeaky hinges, stubborn keys, and other door problems in a jiffy.

AROUND THE DOOR

▶ Look for a build-up of **debris** in the track of a **sliding door** if it sticks. If the debris is causing the problem, clean the track with a **wire brush** and lubricate it with a little **petroleum jelly** to ensure easy sliding.

▶ Too much **paint** making the door stick? **Sand** the edges on the door and frame lightly, and apply a thin coat of paint.

▶ Eliminate **squeaky doors.** Take out the **hinges** one by one and lay them on newspaper on the floor. **Lubricate**, then replace.

▶ If there's too much room between the door and the frame, the door will **rattle** when it is closed. In that case, adjust the metal hardware to reduce the distance between the frame and the door.

▶ Fix loose doors by affixing **weatherstripping** inside the frame. Make sure that the surface is clean and free from grease before applying.

▶ Add weatherstripping around the top and sides and a **door sweep** at the bottom if there is a **draft** around your exterior door.

LOCKS AND FITTINGS

▶ Use **powdered graphite** around a **tight latch**, but never use oil as dust adheres to it and can clog the mechanism.

▶ Muffle the sound of a particularly noisy **door latch** by gluing **felt strips** into the door frame at the level of the lock mechanism.

▶ Install a **mechanical door closer** so that the door doesn't slam when it shuts.

▶ Sticky lock mechanism? Either spray some **liquid lubricant** right into the cylinder, or use a **pencil** to apply some powdered graphite to the key and use it to lock and unlock the door repeatedly.

▶ Rub some **candle wax** onto a stubborn key, and it will slide into the lock more easily.

▶ Take off the door and apply a little lubricant, such as **petroleum jelly, soap,** or **wax,** between the two parts of a squeaky hinge. Re-hang the door and wipe off any excess lubricant.

Fabric Dyeing

Refresh well-worn clothing and rejuvenate faded fabrics with a little dye. You can buy synthetic products, but remember that effective natural dyes have been used for centuries. Often you need look no further than your own home or backyard.

Before dyeing, there are a number of factors to consider. Figure out what kind of washing machine you would be using, or whether a plastic basin is a better choice. The type of fabric to be dyed is also of great importance.

GROUND RULES FOR DYEING

Only natural fibers of plant origin—that is, cotton, rayon, linen, half-linen, and natural-fiber blends—can be dyed. Synthetic fibers such as polyester don't absorb color. When dyeing blends of natural and synthetic fibers, only natural fibers will react to the dye, so they should make up at least 60 percent of the fabric to ensure a dark enough color. Keep the following rules in mind:

▶ Always dye light-colored fabrics **darker** rather than the other way around, and don't dye **high-performance fibers** such as Gore-Tex, microfibers, or down-filled articles of clothing.

▶ Dye fabric with **synthetic colors** in the washer.

PREPARATION FOR DYEING

▶ Use a washing machine to dye. A **medium shade** will result when 2½ lb (1.15 kg) of fabric is placed in a large machine; if less fabric is in the machine, it will be darker.

▶ It's easiest to dye with a **top-loading machine.** Put the fabric to be dyed into the washing machine and spread 5 oz. (150 g) of dye powder over it. Dissolve the powder in 1 quart/liter of water and start the wash cycle at 105°F (40°C). When the washer fills with water, pour in the dissolved dye as well as 1 quart/liter of water. Once you've dyed the fabric, run it through a wash cycle.

▶ **Front-loading machines** measure the amount of water to put in the machine based on the amount of fabric being washed. Therefore, you will have to add the fabric before adding the pre-dissolved dye to the washer's dispenser.

▶ If dyeing in a **plastic basin,** weigh the fabric first; you need 2 quarts/liters of dye bath for every 3½ oz. (100 g) of fabric. Heat the water to 105°F (40°C), pour it into an appropriately-sized basin, dissolve the required amount of dye (see instructions on the package), and add 1 tbsp. (15 mL) of dye powder per quart/liter of water. Move the fabric back and forth in the dye bath for one hour. Then wash thoroughly.

DYES FROM NATURE

These natural additives can all be used with the basic dye formula (see sidebar). The more berries or flowers you use and the longer the boiling time, the darker the color.

▶ Oak leaves—dark beige to olive.

▶ Blueberries—purple.

▶ Chamomile flowers—yellow to golden-yellow.

▶ Red beets—carmine red.

▶ Sorrel—corn-yellow.

▶ Walnut leaves—medium brown.

Light-colored fabrics are easier to dye than dark-colored ones.

plant dyes

one Boil 7 oz. (200 g) of plant leaves or flowers for one hour in 2 quarts/liters of water.

two Dissolve ⅓ oz. (10 g) of alum in 2 quarts/liters of water for every 1½ oz. (50 g) of material to be dyed. Put the fabric into the solution, heat it up to 160°F (70°C), then let it cool.

three Wash fabric well, then place it in the plant brew, and let simmer on the stove for about one hour. Place the fabric in vinegar and water to set the color.

Floors

Floors come in a wide variety of materials, patterns, and colours. How you care for your floors is going to depend entirely on the material they are made from. Some, like shiny, sealed floors, take less effort to keep clean than unsealed ones. More delicate materials like wood or laminate need some special care.

We walk across them every day, so keeping floors clean is important. Tile, wood, and stone floors need to be cared for differently in order to bring out their characteristic highlights and avoid damaging them.

TILE FLOORS

▶ **Mop** the floor after **sweeping** or **vacuuming.** Start at one end and proceed toward the door. Mop in a wavy line, without lifting the mop from the floor. For very dirty floors, you may have to change the cleaning water.

▶ Choose a **sponge mop** for cleaning tile floors; they do a much better job of cleaning seams and small irregularities. For extra stubborn dirt, use a **scrub brush** and wash the tiles by hand—sometimes there's no substitute for elbow grease!

▶ Clean **stone floors** by adding a small amount of **ammonia** to the wash water. This combination also makes dull tile floors shine like new.

▶ Coat porous **terra-cotta** and **unglazed natural stone tiles** with **linseed oil** immediately after installation, and avoid mopping for two weeks. You can use this type of waterproofing for areas that are subject to heavy use, such as entryways and the kitchen.

▶ Make **stains from liquids** (e.g., tea, coffee, cola, red wine, fruit juices, and ink) disappear from porous tiles by dabbing them with a little regular **stain remover** available at any drugstore or home supply center.

fixing scratches in wood

one Rub out scratches with some fine steel wool. Take care not to rub too deeply, or you could damage the surrounding wood.

two Mix a little medium-brown shoe polish with some basic floor polish.

three Rub the mixture into the wood until the color matches the floor.

Before mopping a parquet floor, make sure it's free from dust and debris.

WOOD FLOORS

▶ Avoid **swelling** and **warping** wood floors by ensuring that very little moisture is left behind by a wet mop. Beware extremely hot water, as well, as it may cause the wood to crack and split.

▶ Tackle serious **stains** and **streaks** on sealed wood floors by adding a shot of **ammonia** to the mopping water.

▶ Sweep up **sand** and **small stones** immediately to avoid damage.

▶ Remove **scratches** in a wood floor with a little **shoe polish** and very fine **steel wool** (see sidebar on page 130).

▶ Mop sealed wood floors with **black tea** to add a matte sheen and an attractive color.

▶ Avoid **waxing** floors too often. The trick is to occasionally add 4 tbsp. (60 mL) of **furniture polish** and 1 cup (250 mL) of **white vinegar** to your mop water.

▶ Scrub oiled wood floors with a **warm soda solution** (3 tbsp./45 mL baking soda per quart/liter warm water), and then mop them with tap water. Repeat until the solution is mopped up and floors are clear. You should occasionally recoat with a thin layer of **linseed oil**.

▶ Carefully scrape off ground-in dirt with a **knife** in the direction of the wood grain. Then lightly rub the area with a dab of **turpentine,** wash, and polish with a soft cloth.

OTHER MATERIALS

▶ **Sweep** and **damp-mop laminated** floors; too much moisture will make the material swell.

▶ **Damp-mop** and **rub dry sealed cork flooring.** Apply **wax** sparingly twice a year and occasionally polish until shiny. You don't have to dry cork flooring that is **vinyl-coated.**

▶ Clean **slate** and **stone** flooring with **water** and **household cleanser.** But be careful—too much cleanser can attack color! After mopping and drying, apply some **lemon oil** to ensure the floor shines like new. Remove any excess oil with a dry rag. You can best protect a stone floor by applying a **cement sealer** and **wax.**

▶ Wash **polished limestone flooring** with a **low-pH all-purpose cleanser,** otherwise the floor will become dull. In addition, look for a cleanser with as few detergents as possible (10–20%) and no more than 4% phosphate, since both are highly nondegradable.

▶ Do not use **vinegar** for cleaning or washing natural stone floors such as **marble, travertine**, and others. They can dissolve when exposed to acidic cleaners.

▶ Clean linoleum floors with the water from **boiled potatoes.**

▶ Remove scuff marks and dirt from **baseboards** covered with polyurethane or oil-based (gloss or semigloss) paint with a **sponge** and a grease-cutting, all-purpose **dish soap**, then clean with a cloth dampened with tap water. You can also use a household spray cleaner, but remember to spray the cleaner on a clean cloth—not the baseboard—to prevent streaking and avoid getting it on the floor.

▶ If you encounter really tough stains, test an inconspicuous corner with **scouring powder** and an all-purpose, **plastic scrubbing pad**. If the test does not show any damage, apply the method to the entire baseboard.

A microfiber mop is great for hard-to-reach corners.

Footwear

Allow your feet to breathe and keep athlete's foot at bay by wearing shoes made from genuine leather or other breathable materials. Your feet need air. After all, they contain about 250,000 sweat glands and can produce up to 1 cup (250 mL) of perspiration per day.

New shoes can sometimes be a little painful. But armed with a few new shoe tricks and tips for cleaning and maintaining shoes, your recent footwear purchase should last years. If you need a new pair, proceed as follows:

Homemade Shoe Polish

You can make colorless shoe polish for smooth leather in a flash with the following ingredients:

5 oz. (150 g) petroleum jelly
1/3 oz. (10 g) beeswax
2 tsp. (10 mL) boiling water
1/6 oz. (5 g) soap flakes

Melt the petroleum jelly and wax in a double boiler, then add the boiling water and soap flakes. Then stir with a cooking spoon or a whisk until blended. Stored in a glass or a can, the mixture will keep for about six months.

NEW SHOES

▶ Buy shoes in the **afternoon**. Your feet swell through the day and you don't want to purchase a pair in the morning, only to find that by midday they're uncomfortably tight.

▶ Spray or rub them with a thin coating of colorless **water-repellent** to prevent staining before wearing new shoes for the first time.

▶ Rub **vinegar** on the inside of new leather shoes, especially dark-colored ones, to prevent any **staining**.

▶ New shoe **pinches**? Moisten a cotton ball with **rubbing alcohol or vinegar** and dampen the tight spot, then put the shoe back on for a while.

▶ Avoid wearing shoes **two days in a row** to give them time to air out.

▶ Make **cork heels** more durable by coating them with **clear nail polish.**

PROTECTIVE STORAGE

▶ Don't jumble shoes together; if you do, they'll lose their **shape** and develop mold more easily due to poor ventilation. Your best option is a closet with compartments specifically for shoes.

▶ Never put your shoes into a **plastic bag** where they won't be able to breathe; instead opt for a **cloth bag** or store your shoes inside **discarded socks.**

▶ Use **shoe trees** to keep your shoes in shape. A cheaper, but equally effective, alternative is to stuff them with pantyhose full of **balled-up newspaper**.

▶ Prevent **sagging** in the leg of a boot by stuffing it with a couple of layers of **rolled-up newspaper**.

CLEANING AND MAINTAINING SHOES

To make your own shoe shine kit, you'll need a fairly stiff brush for cleaning shoes, some soft rags for applying polishes (one for each color), and a soft brush or cloth for polishing. Here are some other cleaning and maintenence tips:

▶ Repel water from **leather soles** by occasionally coating them with **castor oil.**

▶ Smear stains on smooth leather shoes with an **onion** cut in half, then buff them.

▶ Rub stiff **calfskin** with a mixture of **water** and **milk** to make it soft again, then polish.

▶ Remove scuff marks from **patent leather shoes** by rubbing them with a cotton ball dabbed in **acetone-free nail polish remover**.

▶ Produce a bright shine on patent leather shoes by rubbing with either **petroleum jelly** or **mineral oil.** Old patent leather also recovers its shine when rubbed with half an **onion**. Remember to always buff well afterwards.

Always polish your leather shoes in the evening so that the polish can work overnight, then brush and shine the shoes in the morning.

▸ **Warm up** patent leather before wearing in the winter to keep the finish from cracking.

▸ Keep patent leather flexible with **glycerin**.

▸ Clean **deerskin, nubuck,** and **suede** with a **rubber eraser** or **crepe brush**.

▸ Carefully remove stains on **full-grain leather** shoes with a **rubber eraser**.

▸ **Waterproof deerskin** with a mix of 1 tbsp. (15 mL) of **glycerin**, 1 tbsp. (15 mL) of **fruit vinegar**, and 5 tbsp. (75 mL) of **water**. Put in a spray bottle and carefully spray your shoes with it.

COMMON PROBLEMS

▸ Dry **wet shoes** with **balled-up newspaper** stuffed inside, which will help them maintain their shape. Avoid placing them near a heat source; the leather will stiffen and crack. Once dry, remove remaining dirt with a **brush**—including on the sole—and then rub in some **shoe polish** and buff.

▸ Rub unattractive **snow** or **water stains** on smooth leather shoes with half an **onion** or a little **lemon juice**. Let it work briefly and then buff it off. Rub down stains on deerskin shoes with **salt**—but remember to clean it off thoroughly afterwards.

▸ **Handwash white fabric** or **canvas** shoes, or toss in the washing machine—but don't put them in the dryer.

▸ Dip the ends of **frayed shoelaces** in **clear nail polish** or wrap them with **clear tape** to make them easy to thread through the eyelets again.

▸ Sprinkle **talcum powder** in **sweaty shoes**, let it work overnight, and shake it out. You can also clean insoles with talcum powder—just remove them from the shoes, apply the powder the same way, let it sit, and brush it off.

Change footwear daily and store in a well-ventilated shoe rack to allow shoes and boots to air out after being worn.

Soften up dried-out shoe polish on the heater.

Furniture

Your home is furnished with items made from a number of materials, and each one requires different care. Bypass the chemical-based cleaners and polishes, and consider using instead gentle, everyday ingredients to keep all your furniture bright and clean.

Start by removing the old chemical-based cleaners from under the kitchen sink and replacing them with some of the many natural, safe cleaning products available at your local drugstore.

Furniture Polish

1½ oz. (50 g) beeswax
⅔ cup (150 mL) turpentine

Add the ingredients to a jar and screw on the lid, but not too tight. Place the jar into a bowl of hot water and move it around gently until the ingredients blend, forming a paste.

ANTIQUE FURNISHINGS

▶ Never expose antique wood to **direct sun** or treat with **conventional polishes**; because of its age, it's particularly delicate. Rather than using oils that can degrade the finish over time, polish antique furnishings with **beeswax**—available from a hardware store—specifically made to treat antique wood for long-lasting protection.

WOODEN FURNITURE

Maintain your wood furniture based on the type of wood it's made of and how it was manufactured. How you should treat veneered furniture is based on the type of veneer. If unsure, check with the manufacturer.

▶ Give shine to **teak** or **rosewood** furniture with a mix of 1¼ cups (300 mL) of **beer**, 1 tbsp. (15 mL) of **melted beeswax**, and 2 tsp. (10 mL) of **sugar**. Apply thinly with a brush, let dry, and buff with a wool cloth.

▶ Bring out the grain and coloration of **walnut** by rubbing it occasionally with **milk**. Rubbing scratches in this versatile wood with a **walnut** cut in half really works wonders.

▶ Make dull **ebony** shine like new by rubbing it with **petroleum jelly**. Let it sit for a few minutes, remove the excess, and buff with a wool cloth.

▶ Maintain **oak** by applying **warm beer**, then going over it with a wool rag. Remove stubborn soil stains carefully with **fine sandpaper**. Rub the remaining stains with **turpentine** and apply another coat of **protective varnish**.

▶ **Untreated** or **dulled wood** is porous; grease from your hands can be easily transferred to the wood. When a grease or oil stain appears, press a **cheesecloth** on it, and then apply a **warm iron** to help loosen and absorb the stain.

▶ Make a polishing mixture for maintaining **untreated** or **varnished wood**. Melt 1¼ cups (300 mL) of **beeswax** in a double boiler, let it cool a little, stir in 1¼ cups (300 mL) of **turpentine**, and let it harden. Apply sparingly to the surface with a rag and buff with a clean cloth.

▶ Rub water stains with **toothpaste**—you can even mix in some **baking soda**. For **light-colored** wood,

A shaving brush is the perfect tool for dusting wood surfaces with scrollwork, like on this classic cabinet.

Wicker furniture harbors house dust. Vacuum regularly with a brush attachment.

try rubbing a **Brazil nut** over the spot. For **dark wood**, it's better to dab a mixture of **ashes** and **vegetable oil** onto the stains with a **cork**.

▶ Remove **rings left by glasses** by mixing a little **butter** with **mayonnaise** and a little **ash** and rubbing it on the affected area.

▶ Treat **scratches** by matching the color to the wood. If **light-colored,** remove scratches with **petroleum jelly** or a mixture of 1 tsp. (5 mL) of **oil** and 1 tsp. (5 mL) of **vinegar**. For **dark wood,** substitute **red wine** for the vinegar.

RATTAN AND WICKER FURNITURE

▶ Clean **untreated cane, rattan,** or **bamboo** by first vacuuming the furnishings, then cleaning them with rags and a **mild soap solution**. (For extra cleaning power, add a dash of **ammonia** to the soap and water.) When **treating varnished wicker furniture, cane,** or chairs with **raffia** or **straw** sitting surfaces, soap and water will do the trick.

▶ Increase the **durability** of your furnishings by brushing them down once a year with **salt water.**

▶ Lighten the color of **wickerwork** by rubbing it with half a **lemon** or a mixture of **salt** and **vinegar**; rinse the furniture thoroughly after treatment.

▶ Get **sagging wicker seats** back into shape by dampening them with **hot water** and then leaving them to dry outdoors for at least 24 hours. As the fibers of the seats dry, they will tighten and shrink back to their original shape. Keep them in the shade as direct sunlight could bleach them out.

▶ Treat the **underside** of your furniture with **lemon oil** to keep it from drying out.

SMOOTH SURFACES

▶ Wipe **marble tops** with a slightly moist cloth. Treat stains with a little **lemon juice** or **lemon rind** and **salt**, but let the juice work for just a moment to keep the acids from attacking the stone. Apply a mixture of 3 tbsp. (45 mL) of **baking soda** and 1 quart/liter of warm water to dull marble; let it work for 15–30 minutes, rinse with water, and rub dry.

▶ Use a **soap and water solution** with a dash of **vinegar** to clean furniture with **plastic tops.**

▶ Dust **glass panes** on furnishings such as display cases and bookcases regularly. If they are very dirty, moisten a cotton ball with **rubbing alcohol** and rub the glass in circles to avoid streaking.

removing wax from wood

one Use a blow-dryer on the lowest fan speed and highest heat to melt the wax residue.

two Then rub the wax off with a paper towel and wipe it with a solution of equal parts white vinegar and water.

Glass and Mirrors

They attract dust, dirt, and scratches, and every touch leaves a fingerprint. But when your mirrors and glass surfaces gleam, it can make your whole house sparkle. Take charge and keep your glass surfaces and mirrors streak-, fog-, and scratch-free.

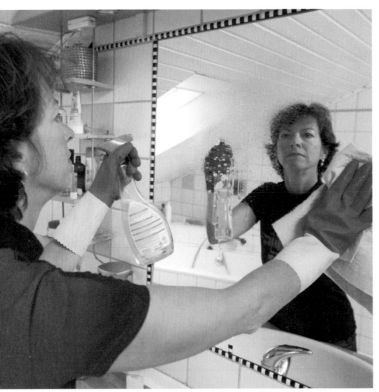

Eliminate streaks on mirrors with a solution of 1 cup (250 mL) of vinegar in 1 quart/liter of warm water.

Most homes have a considerable number of glass surfaces and mirrors. But a few household items and a little elbow grease are all that is needed to keep them all clean.

GLASS SURFACES

▶ Keep **tabletops** shining like new by wiping them with **lemon juice**, drying with **paper towels**, and polishing with **newspaper**.

▶ Polish away **small scratches** in glass surfaces with a little **toothpaste**.

▶ Remove **dried-on flyspecks** by wiping them with **ammonia** and water.

▶ Allow **wax** to harden before carefully lifting it off with a razor blade. Use **rubbing alcohol** to remove the remainder.

▶ Fill a **sharp chip** in a glass surface by covering the edge with a thick layer of **clear nail polish.**

▶ Dust **glass television** and **computer screens,** then clean by moistening a damp cloth with a little **rubbing alcohol**, and wiping and polishing the screen. But remember to read the owner's manual first to avoid causing any damage.

▶ Clean **flat screen monitors** and **television screens** with a dry, soft **microfiber cloth** (the kind you use to clean your glasses) and gently wipe the screen. If that doesn't completely remove the dirt or oil, don't respond by scrubbing; pushing directly on the screen can burn out the pixels. Instead, dampen your cloth with **distilled water** and **white vinegar** (in a ratio of 1:1) and try again.

MIRRORS

▶ Keep mirrors gleaming with **warm water** and **vinegar.** Combine 1 cup (250 mL) of white vinegar with 1 quart/liter of warm water and rub on the mirror with a soft cloth. Use **crumpled newspaper** to wipe the mixture away in slow circles. Presto! No streaks.

▶ Clean a mirror by rubbing it with a **potato** cut in half, then rinsing with water and polishing. The bonus: it will keep bathroom fog at bay, too.

▶ Keep mirrors clean without leaving streaks by wiping them with cool, strong **black tea** and drying with a **chamois cloth.**

▶ Wipe your mirror with a little **rubbing alcohol** to give it a nice luster after polishing. Rubbing alcohol also removes sticky film from **hairspray.**

▶ **De-fog** mirrors with a blow-dryer after a shower. A quick blast should clear up the problem.

▶ Prevent mirrors from fogging up by coating them with **shaving cream** or **toothpaste** and wiping them dry with a clean towel before showering.

▶ Avoid dulling mirrors by positioning them away from **direct sunlight.**

▶ Remove **hairspray** on mirrors by wiping them with a solution of **clarifying shampoo and water**, then rinsing and drying them.

Glassware

People have treasured luminous stemware and beautiful crystal collectibles for centuries, and they are proudly handed down from one generation to another. Being very fragile, they need a little special attention, and should be handled with care.

A slice of lemon will quickly clear a cloudy glass.

By observing a few basic rules, you can banish smudges and water rings on decanters, vases, and glasses—without breaking them.

▶ **Handwash** high-quality glasses rather than cleaning them in a dishwasher.

▶ If you must use a dishwasher, slide stemmed glasses in **sideways** to ensure that they don't break.

▶ Place a **dish towel** in the sink while you're washing delicate glassware to prevent chipping.

▶ Remove **lipstick marks** with **table salt** before washing glasses.

▶ Clear a **cloudy glass** by dipping it in an **ammonia solution** and thoroughly washing it out.

▶ Add a dash of **vinegar** or **lemon peel** to the wash water to make glasses gleam.

▶ Keep cold glasses from **cracking**—wash them in warm water only. **Scalding hot water** will leach the shine from crystal glasses and dull the gold or silver rims on glassware.

▶ Wash **glasses with painted decorations** quickly; keep them in the water too long, and the adornments may dissolve.

▶ Rinse out **beer, wine,** and **champagne glasses** with warm, clear water only. Detergent residue can change the taste of a drink, as well as taking the fizz out of champagne and the head off your beer.

▶ Dry glasses without leaving lint using a **linen dish towel.**

▶ **Polish** your glasses by rubbing on a thin paste of **baking soda** and **water**, rinsing thoroughly, and buffing with a soft cloth.

▶ Store wine glasses **upright** with the bowls open to the air; otherwise they may over time develop a musty smell, and there is a risk of damaging the rims if the glasses stick to the cabinet shelf.

SPARKLING CLEAN VASES AND CARAFES

▶ Help **crystal** maintain its shine by washing it only in warm water, then rinsing and drying. Or wash crystal in hot, soapy water; rinse with hot water and dry.

▶ Clean narrow-necked glass containers with a **bottle brush** moistened with **vinegar** and **water**.

▶ Remove hard-to-reach dirt in a decanter or container with **crumbled eggshells** and **lemon juice.** Let stand for two days, slosh back and forth a few times, and rinse.

▶ Combat **green algae** in a vase. Add a handful of **black tea leaves** and douse them with **vinegar**, then tip the vase back and forth until the green coating completely disappears.

▶ Buff **leaded crystal vases** with a **chamois cloth** after they have been washed.

Cloudy Glass Vase Remedy

You can combat serious dirt or clouding on glassware with a salt and vinegar paste made from:
1/3 cup (75 mL) salt
2 tbsp. (25 mL) vinegar

Mix the salt and vinegar to form a paste. Spread the paste on the inside of the vase, using your finger or a soft brush. Let it sit for 15–20 minutes, then empty and rinse with clear water.

Housecleaning

It really is a snap to keep your household under control. The key word is organization. Plan for daily, weekly, and occasional tasks, as well as spring cleaning. Follow a regular schedule, and no task will seem too daunting. You will save yourself time and energy in the long run.

Daily

Keep your household orderly so that it's easier to keep clean. These daily household tasks can be accomplished in the blink of an eye.

- Pick up scattered clothing, shoes, toys, and newspapers daily; you're well on your way to a tidy home.

- Shake bedding out thoroughly and air out your bedroom.

- After brushing your teeth in the morning, rinse out the bathroom sink with water to keep lime from building up.

- Wash all dishes, cutlery, pots, and pans used to prepare and eat meals during the day.

- Wipe down the countertops in your kitchen to keep any dirt and germs from getting a foothold.

Weekly

Pencil in these weekly housecleaning chores, and your major spring cleaning will definitely proceed much more smoothly than if you had let the work build up.

- Dust, vacuum, and wet-mop the floors in all rooms.

- Clean the bathroom thoroughly. Scrub the sinks, shower and/or tub, and toilet; wipe off tiles in wet areas and wash the floor.

- Clean the mirrors.

- Wipe out your refrigerator and thoroughly clean the stove and sink.

- Take out the trash every time there is garbage pickup.

- Return cans and bottles for refund, and put out recyclables on collection day.

- Change and wash household linens.

- Sweep the porch and/or deck and patio.

From Time to Time

Come up with a cleaning schedule in order to keep an overview of tasks that require occasional attention. Follow the schedule to ensure that nothing gets overlooked. Be sure to include the following tasks:

- Wash windows.
- Wash curtains and drapes.
- Clean doors and door frames.
- Clean upholstered furniture thoroughly.
- Maintain wood furniture.
- Wipe down kitchen cabinets.
- Perform maintenance on kitchen appliances.
- Clean lamps.
- Clean rugs and carpets.
- Dust walls.
- Take care of all cleaning equipment.

Spring Cleaning

Take on just one manageable area every day, e.g., on the first day the bedroom; the next day the bathroom, and so forth.

- Move the furniture and clean neglected corners.
- Clear out your clothes closet and weed out pieces you haven't worn in a long time. A good rule of thumb: if you haven't worn it for a year, toss it!
- Check the freezer for stale foods and discard them; then defrost (if necessary) and clean.
- Check stored food supplies in the pantry for freshness and toss out any that have gone bad.
- Clear out the basement and storage sheds and earmark usable items for a yard sale.

A System for Cleaning

Before you start cleaning, make sure that all required cleaning materials are on hand. You won't need heavy-duty chemicals, even for your annual spring-cleaning. A mild all-purpose cleaner, vinegar, lemon, and some type of furniture maintenance product will do the trick.

Set aside adequate time for housecleaning and wear comfortable, old clothing that you don't mind getting sweaty and dirty. You might also want to wear nonslip shoes and gloves, along with eye protection, depending on the type of work.

Want a time-honored system for cleaning? Observe these three rules:

- from top to bottom
- from back to front
- clean the same items at the same time (e.g., clean all the glass, wash all the surfaces, etc.)

Start by clearing the cobwebs from the ceiling, polish the wood and glass, dust, clean all upholstered surfaces, and so forth, ending with the floors. Always work from the back corner of a room toward the door. Right-handed people usually work more effectively from right to left, and lefties from left to right.

Housekeeping Accessories

The daily battle against dust and dirt can be won only if your cleaning equipment is in proper working order. Keep it clean to ensure your house will be spic-and-span and looks its best.

Follow a few simple rules to ensure that not only will your house be clean, but so will the brooms, brushes, dusters, and sponges that make it possible. After all, regular cleaning keeps washrags, sponges, and cloths from turning into a breeding ground for germs and bacteria.

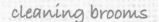

cleaning brooms

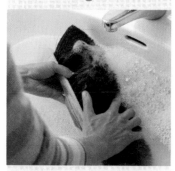

one Wash the bristles of brooms and brushes in warm, soapy water.

two Comb the washed, rinsed bristles with a fine comb. Let dry thoroughly.

BROOMS AND BRUSHES

▶ Use brushes and brooms with **natural bristles,** even though they need more care than nylon or plastic bristles.

▶ Clean broom bristles in **detergent** and **warm water.** Rinse thoroughly in cold water, and lean the broom head-up, handle-down against an outdoor wall. If it happens to be a sunny day, the rays will help kill any lingering bacteria.

▶ **Soak** new natural bristles on brooms and scrub brushes briefly in **salt water** before the first use to make them last longer.

▶ Wash older brooms and hand brushes with natural bristles occasionally in **warm, soapy water.**

▶ Soak natural bristles on your broom in **vinegar** and **water** if they have become **too soft**.

▶ **Soften stiff natural bristles** by dipping them briefly in a solution of 1 oz. (30 g) of **powdered alum** and 1 quart/liter of **water**. Can't find powdered alum? Mix **water** and **milk** in a 1:1 ratio.

▶ **Hang brooms** on the wall with the handle pointing down to preserve the **elasticity of the bristles**; this applies to both natural and synthetic bristles and dishwashing brushes.

▶ Apply **steam** to **bent bristles** to quickly straighten them out again.

RAGS, SPONGES, AND CLOTHS

▶ **Machine-wash** all rags used for cleaning and dusting at 140°F (60°C) and allow to dry thoroughly. You'll give them increased life and be able to use them repeatedly.

▶ Put **microfiber cloths** into the dryer after every third wash. Fibers that are matted from frequent washing will become fluffy again.

▶ **Soak** washrags overnight in **lemon** or **vinegar water** to keep them smelling fresh. Everyone knows that they can get stinky very quickly.

▶ Leave wet washrags to dry in the **sun** when weather permits. The ultraviolet light disinfects and kills bacteria.

▶ Boil **natural sponges** in **vinegar water** to combat unwanted germs.

▶ Kill mold and other bacteria in **sponges:** place a wet sponge in the **microwave** for a full minute. Be careful when removing the sponge as it will be piping hot. Don't try to put a dry sponge in the microwave, as the sponge may catch fire.

▶ Pick up dust and lint from dust rags by dipping them in **glycerin** after they've been washed. Let them dry and store them in a plastic bag.

DUSTERS

▶ Wash **feather dusters** in a sink filled with warm water and a squirt of **baby shampoo**. Rinse, then carefully squeeze out the water, and dry the dusters with a blow-dryer.

▶ Shake out **microfiber dusters** before washing them in soapy water. Rinse and let dry.

▶ Toss **rag dusters** in the washing machine with a **mild detergent**, and let air-dry.

Ironing

With today's modern steam irons, ironing boards, and other aids, ironing is often done in a jiffy. That doesn't mean you can't learn from some of grandma's old tricks, which make even delicate textiles and tricky seams or pleats easy to handle.

Whether you iron all your washing while watching football on Sunday afternoon, or find yourself rushing to iron one dress shirt early in the morning before heading to the office, the same basic ironing rules apply.

EQUIPMENT

▶ Help save your **back** from injury by investing in an **adjustable-height ironing board.**

▶ Place **aluminum foil** under the ironing board cover to reflect heat. It will save you a lot of time.

▶ Let your **steam iron** steam off two or three times to percolate out any lime deposits. Repeat this each time you iron.

BEFORE IRONING

▶ Put **cotton fabrics**, including your shirts and blouses, into the dryer for 15 minutes at moderate temperature and hang them up to dry. This makes ironing easier than if they're completely dried in the dryer.

▶ Spray **excessively dry fabrics** with **warm water** before ironing them—warm water spreads through the fabric more quickly than cold.

▶ Sprinkle clean laundry with **water,** then roll it up and put into a plastic bag to keep laundry damp until you're ready to iron it.

Use even strokes when ironing and don't press down too hard.

▶ Add a little **vinegar** to the water used for sprinkling to make your iron glide over laundry more smoothly.

IRONING BASICS

▶ Iron just to the **edges** of **seams** and **stitches** to ensure they don't push through.

▶ Iron **button facings** on a soft underlay from the back side; don't iron the buttons.

▶ Iron fabrics manufactured on a **diagonal** against the direction of the fabric.

▶ Protect **delicate fibers** by placing a **cloth** or **tissue paper** between the iron and the fabric.

▶ Iron **heavy fabrics** such as **wool** and **flannel** with a **damp cloth** between the iron and the fabric.

▶ Iron the **collars** of shirts or blouses first—then the inside, from the tip of the collar to the middle to avoid wrinkles on the seam. Iron the **cuffs** in the same way, followed by the arms, and then the front and back.

▶ Iron fabrics from the back side and the **creases** last longer.

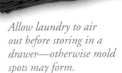

Allow laundry to air out before storing in a drawer—otherwise mold spots may form.

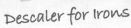

Jewelry

Jewelry has long been fashioned from gemstones, beads, and precious metals, and its appeal endures both for its beauty and, sometimes, its sentimental value. With a few simple tricks, your treasures will retain or recover their sparkle and shine like new.

Use a soft toothbrush to remove tarnish from filigreed silver jewelry, and clean gems with toothpaste.

Keep jewelry in a box lined with velvet and divided into multiple compartments to prevent damage.

Before cleaning gold, you need to know what is real gold and what is merely gold-plated. If you are considering cleaning silver, remember that it oxidizes, especially when you haven't worn a piece of jewelry for quite a while. The best care for pearls is to wear them frequently; contact with your skin helps them retain their color and luster.

GOLD

▶ Clean **gold-plated jewelry** with water only.

▶ Clean **pure gold** with a little **baking soda** on a moist cotton ball before rinsing it.

▶ Rub **matte** gold jewelry with **onion juice** to bring out its shine. Don't forget to buff it!

▶ Clean dirty gold jewelry with a solution of 2 tbsp. (25 mL) of **ammonia** and 1 quart/liter of **water**, then rinse and dry. For serious dirt, wash with a solution of 1 tbsp. (15 mL) of **rubbing alcohol** and 1 quart/liter of **soapy water**, then rinse with water and dry.

▶ Add 3 drops of **liquid dish soap** to a medium-sized bowl of warm tap water. Place gold jewelry in the bowl and let it sit for 10–15 minutes before rinsing and drying. If more power is required, use **club soda** instead of tap water.

▶ **Protect** gold jewelry from getting **scratched** by storing individual pieces in **soft paper envelopes**.

SILVER

▶ Remove **oxidation** from silver with ease. Line a deep dish with **aluminum foil**, place the jewelry in it, sprinkle with **salt**, and pour boiling water over it. Wait an hour before removing the jewelry, and buff until it shines brightly.

▶ Protect silver jewelry from **tarnishing** by wrapping it tightly in aluminum foil.

▶ To remove a small tarnish, dab some **toothpaste** on your finger and rub the tarnished part; rinse and dry with a clean cloth. For larger jobs, make a **spreadable paste** of **baking soda** and **water**, and rub on the paste with a damp sponge.

▶ To clean silver jewelry, place it in a small pot with water and ½ tsp. (2 mL) of **detergent**. Slowly heat the contents and let the jewelry "boil" for 2–3 minutes to dissolve the dirt.

▶ Leave silver in **beer** overnight, then rinse and polish to recover its sparkle. For an alluring shine you can also pour **potato water** over silver jewelry, then rinse it with warm water and rub dry with a soft cloth.

COSTUME JEWELRY

▶ If costume jewelry is very dirty, sprinkle **baking soda** onto it and scrub with a **toothbrush**, then wash and dry.

▶ Buff jewelry with a **baby toothbrush** and pick out residue from encrusted stains with a wooden, nonscratching **toothpick**.

▶ Avoid **dark discoloration** on your skin and clothing by applying **clear nail polish** to the back of costume jewelry.

GEMSTONES

▶ Clean **hard gemstones** (diamonds, sapphires, rubies) with a solution of 1 quart/liter of water and 2 tbsp. (25 mL) of **ammonia**; or dip them briefly in **rubbing alcohol,** then rinse.

▶ Never immerse **emeralds** in water. The fairly soft stone sometimes has cracks that will absorb the liquid.

▶ Delicate **opals** don't respond well to major temperature fluctuations, so don't wear an opal ring, for example, when you're doing dishes. It's best to polish them with a **chamois cloth.**

▶ Many gemstones, such as **emeralds, opals, turquoise, lapis lazuli,** and **pearls**, do not tolerate sun. Remove them before sunbathing.

PEARLS

▶ Immediately wipe off any **hairspray, skin cream,** and **perfume** that settles on your pearls.

▶ Pearls dissolve on contact with **acids**.

▶ Clean pearls with a **soft brush** and a **mild detergent solution**. Wash off and repeat if necessary.

▶ Rub pearls with **olive oil** every two to three years to help maintain the luster.

▶ A **small velvet envelope** or **soft cloth** provides protection against scratches.

AMBER

▶ Remove dirt with **warm water**, then dry the stone immediately.

▶ Cover **grease stains** with **white chalk**, then wipe off with a soft cloth after a couple of hours.

▶ Try some **olive oil.** Add 2 drops of oil onto a **clean flannel cloth**. Rub the amber until it shines brightly. If any olive oil remains, polish with a clean cloth.

▶ Avoid **steam cleaning.** Too much exposure to water turns amber cloudy.

CORAL

▶ To clean coral, dab it with **soapy water** using a **linen rag**. Rinse with water and buff with a **chamois cloth.**

▶ Coral shines beautifully when you dip it into a mild **salt solution** and subsequently buff it dry.

a rejuvenating bath for gold chains

one Dissolve a little dish soap in warm water.

two Add 1–2 tsp. (5–10 mL) of powdered chalk and stir.

three Put solution into a small bottle or any covered container.

four Place the gold chain in the solution, close it, and shake well for 1 minute.

five Remove the chain and rinse with water.

Blazing heat can bleach out aquamarine.

Kitchen Appliances

A coffeemaker, toaster, blender, and microwave—no kitchen should be without them. But even though these gadgets make life easier, they still need regular maintenance. With a few traditional tricks up your sleeve, your kitchen will be in fine working order.

Most kitchen appliances run on electricity, therefore special care should be used when cleaning them. The first step in cleaning all types of kitchen appliances is always to pull the plug, then detach all removable parts and wash them or put them into the dishwasher.

CLEANING, DECALCIFYING, AND MAINTENANCE

▶ **Decalcify** your **espresso machine** or **coffeemaker** regularly using a mixture of equal parts **vinegar** and **water.** Add the solution to the reservoir and run it through just as if you were making a pot of coffee. Repeat the process twice with water.

▶ Fill your **kettle** with the same solution (equal parts vinegar and water). For significant calcium deposits, bring the mixture to a boil. Let it sit for 30 mintues, empty it out, and rinse thoroughly. If necessary, scour with **steel wool**.

▶ Before cleaning your **microwave**, add a slice of **lemon** to a **bowl of water** and heat until steam forms, then simply wipe out the appliance with a cloth. **Vinegar** and **water** work just as well.

▶ Rub a little **cooking oil** into the **rubber gaskets** of kitchen appliances to ensure they close tightly. This task should be performed occasionally.

▶ Make your **hand mixer's beaters** easier to insert and remove by putting a tiny drop of olive oil into the installation sockets.

▶ Empty the crumb tray of your **toaster** and shake out the crumbs over the kitchen sink.

▶ Spread a layer of **baking soda** on the oven bottom to clean a **non-self-cleaning oven**. Spray with enough water to make the soda damp. Let sit for a couple of hours, then wipe clean.

▶ **Garbage disposals** are self-cleaning, but they can get smelly. To keep them running smoothly, operate with a full stream of running **cold water** and flush the ground up debris away after. At the first sign of an unpleasant odor, tear up the peels of **oranges** or **lemons** and run them through the garbage disposal.

It's time to decalcify when it takes an excessively long time for water to run through your coffee machine, or the taste of your coffee changes.

Kitchen Utensils

Using the right kitchen tools makes food preparation and cooking easier, faster, and even more enjoyable. When you purchase anything for your kitchen, take into account its quality, the material it's made of, and how easy it will be to clean.

Modern kitchen utensils can be made of plastic, metal, or wood. You can simply drop plastic implements in the dishwasher, but wood and metal implements may require special care. Items that can't go into the dishwasher should be washed with dish soap and water right after use.

KNIVES

▶ **Sharpen** kitchen knives regularly. If you don't own a knife sharpener, the unglazed bottom of a **porcelain teacup** works, too.

▶ Knives cut better if you **warm** the blade in advance.

▶ Use only **top-quality knives** for cutting foods.

▶ Don't use a **ceramic knife** to cut frozen foods, bones, or hard bread crusts.

▶ Use either a **plastic** or **wooden cutting board.** Glass, metal, and stone aren't suitable.

▶ To protect your knife blades and avoid injuries, keep knives in a **knife block,** on a **magnetic knife strip**, or in a **roll.**

▶ Protect yourself from exceptionally sharp points by capping tips with **corks.**

▶ Remove stuck-on residue with a dishwashing brush or a **cork** dipped in **salt.**

METAL UTENSILS

▶ Use a **toothbrush** to clean hard-to-reach areas in **graters** and **garlic presses.**

▶ Clean **metal flour sieves** immediately after use in **cold water**—warm water will make the flour stick like glue.

▶ If metal gets **rusty**, sprinkle it with **salt** and rub with **bacon rind.**

▶ Stick **metal shish kebab skewers** into a cork; they'll stay together, making them less dangerous.

WOOD IMPLEMENTS

▶ Don't put wooden spoons in the **dishwasher,** as heat and cleansers can damage wood. All you need is **water** and **dish soap**. Soak heavily-encrusted spoons in a solution of one part **baking soda** to 10 parts water.

▶ It is extremely important to thoroughly disinfect **wooden cutting boards** after cutting **poultry, meat,** and **fish** to avoid cross-contamination of bacteria. Rub boards with a **bleach and water solution,** then wash as usual and dry thoroughly.

▶ Wash **wooden handles** promptly and allow them to dry. Occasionally massage in some **olive** or **canola oil,** and wipe off any excess with a clean cloth or paper towel.

▶ Prevent **grease** from adhering to cooking spoons by holding them under **cold water** just before using them.

▶ Remove **dough** stuck to a **rolling pin** by sprinkling a little **salt** on it, rubbing it off, then washing and drying thoroughly.

Ladles, whisks, and salad spoons are easily reached when you stand them handles-down in a container.

Kitchens

The kitchen is the family nerve center, the heart of the home, and the most popular room in the house. It's where meals are prepared and enjoyed, a family reconnects, and where guests tend to congregate. This means it deserves special and regular attention.

A clean kitchen is an ongoing work of art! The good news: you generally don't need special equipment or chemical cleaners if you stick to a routine and deal with cooking mishaps when they occur.

SURFACE CARE

Countertops and other well-used surfaces in your kitchen require daily attention to keep them clean and bacteria-free.

cleaning the oven

one If burned-on residue is still moist, sprinkle it with salt and wipe it off with a paper towel.

two Thoroughly moisten hard, burned-on areas with a soap solution and then wipe them off.

three If burned-on residue remains, be persistent: mix 5 tbsp. (75 mL) of baking soda with two drops of liquid dish soap and 4 tbsp. (60 mL) of white vinegar until they form a thick paste.

four Apply the paste to the inside of your oven and scrub with a brush, then wipe out and thoroughly rinse.

▶ **Plastic** or **granite surfaces** are easy to care for; they can be washed off with a sponge and a **soap solution**, or even with one part **vinegar** and one part **water**. Wipe them dry immediately to avoid streaks.

▶ Wipe down **large surfaces** with a rag in each hand—one for cleaning and the other for drying.

▶ To eliminate unwanted germs from the countertop, scrub **unsealed wood surfaces** regularly with **salt** or a mixture of 4 tbsp. (60 mL) of **baking soda** and 2 tbsp. (25 mL) of **lemon juice**.

▶ Rub **wood surfaces** with a little olive oil or linseed oil after cleaning to make them **dirt resistant.**

▶ When cleaning **cabinets** inside and out, add a little **vinegar** to your soapy water to cut grease.

▶ Remove **watermarks** on wooden furniture or flooring by rubbing on a little **toothpaste** (but not the gel kind), wiping it off with a clean, damp cloth, drying it, and polishing.

SINKS

▶ Get **stainless steel** sinks spotless with **bar soap.** Other worthwhile proven methods include rubbing them with **potato peels, baking soda,** or **lemon juice.**

▶ Use a couple of dashes of **lemon juice** on a dishwashing sponge to rub down a **discolored** sink.

▶ Rub out **heat marks** in your sink with **club soda.**

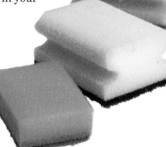

Scrubbing sponges and abrasive cleaners help combat stubborn dirt.

Keep your kitchen sparkling with the right cleaning techniques for all cabinets, counters, and appliances.

minutes, wipe, and, if necessary, remove any residue with a **glass scraper**. To preserve an attractive shine, polish your stove top with a little **vinegar**. And to keep scratches from forming, lift pots and pans from one burner to the next, rather than sliding them.

▶ Lightly rub dried-on deposits on a **gas stove's non-removable parts** with a moistened **dishwasher detergent tab**, then wipe dry. Use gloves to protect your hands.

OVEN

▶ Put a **heatproof container of water** into your still-hot oven; the moisture will make it easier to wipe clean.

▶ If you're worried that the contents of a **baking** or **roasting pan** will well over, place **aluminum foil** underneath to save yourself some elbow grease.

▶ Clean burned-on foods in a still-warm oven with **salt** and wipe the surface dry with a piece of **newspaper** or a **paper towel**.

▶ Use a **damp cloth** to soften burned-on food remnants so they can be easily scrubbed away.

▶ Rinse **cake pans** with **dish soap** and **water**. Clean tough stains using **salt** and **vegetable oil**.

▶ Scrub **burned-on sugar** with **newspaper** and **salt**, then wash with soap and water.

REFRIGERATOR AND FREEZER

▶ Maintain **rubber seals** by rubbing them with **talc** so they don't become brittle.

▶ Regularly clean the inside of your refrigerator with **vinegar** and **water,** or wipe it down with a solution of **baking soda** and **water.**

▶ If you're not lucky enough to have a frost-free freezer, mini-icebergs may form. If so, it's time to **defrost**. Empty the contents of your freezer into a cooler, then place a pot of **boiling water** inside and close the door until the ice melts. Wipe with **soap, vinegar,** and **water.**

▶ To prevent rapid ice buildup, after you defrost, wipe down the inner freezer walls with **cooking oil** or **glycerin.** When you defrost next time, the ice will easily separate from the walls.

▶ **Lime spots** disappear when you treat them with a mixture of **vinegar** and **salt**: place a paper towel over the spot, sprinkle with the solution, and let it set in. Remove the paper towel and rinse.

STOVE TOP

▶ Wipe up splashes and spills on your stove top **immediately**; you'll save yourself a lot of extra work.

▶ If food gets burned onto an **electric heating element**, place a cloth damp with soapy water onto the cold element for two hours and then wipe it clean. Deal with spills in the **grooves** of the heating element by slightly heating the element and sprinkling on a little **baking soda**, then rubbing it in with a sponge. Wipe it off with a damp sponge or cloth.

▶ **Ceramic glass stove tops** are especially easy to clean. For everyday cleaning, simply wipe them with a damp sponge. If food is burned on, dribble a little **lemon juice** on it, let it set in for a few

Laundry

Nowadays you can get clean clothes with the twist of a knob. That would have seemed like magic just a few decades ago, when laundry day required a full eight-hour shift and plenty of elbow grease. But even then, people had some helpful tricks that we can adopt today, both to save energy and protect the environment.

We all like to keep our whites clean and bright, but cleaning products like bleach contain harsh ingredients that can be tough on lungs. Keep your laundry room bleach-free by using other products on your clothing. Colors, wool, lace, velvet, and silk all require a little special care.

WHITEN CLOTHES
WITHOUT USING BLEACH

▶ Let your clothes soak in a basin of **hot water** and **lemon slices** for one to two hours, then wash as usual. If clothes are particularly dingy, boil the water, turn off the heat, add your clothing and lemon slices, and soak overnight.

▶ **White vinegar** works well, too. Pour ½ cup (125 mL) to 1 cup (250 mL) into the wash with detergent. It will whiten, help wash away detergent or soap residue, and soften the fabric.

▶ One more idea: the old-fashioned power of **sunlight** helps brighten whites and gives them that wonderful outdoor scent.

PROTECTING THE ENVIRON-
MENT AND SAVING ENERGY

Get your laundry spanking clean in an environmentally-friendly way with an energy-efficient washing machine and the following ground rules:

▶ Do not add too much **detergent** and never use more than the manufacturer's recommendation. Too much will result in a soap overflow.

Wash that little black dress according to the manufacturer's instructions, and it will stay black for years to come.

▶ Take **water hardness** into account—the softer the water, the less detergent you need.

▶ Ensure that the **water level** is set to match the laundry load. This protects the machine, especially during the spin cycle.

▶ Avoid the **prewash cycle.** It is unnecessary with most laundry.

GETTING THE LAUNDRY READY

▶ Soak **yellowed** or **graying** laundry in a natural bleach (as detailed at left).

▶ Put **delicate articles** into a **cloth bag** or an old **pillowcase** before washing.

▶ Before washing, close **zippers** and rub them with **graphite** or a little **grease** so they don't jam later on. Also, undo buttons and turn pockets inside-out.

▶ If possible, **remove stains** before doing the laundry.

▶ Soak **very dirty laundry** overnight in soapy water before washing. A dash of **turpentine** in the soapy water dissolves dirt even more.

▶ **Collars** and **cuffs** of shirts and blouses don't always come out of the wash clean. Before washing, rub them with a mixture of 1 tbsp. (15 mL) of **rubbing alcohol** and a little **coarse salt.**

FABRIC CONDITIONER

▶ Liquid fabric conditioners can be pricey, so consider a natural softener: add 1 tbsp. (15 mL) of **salt** to the last rinse.

▶ Another natural fabric softener: pour 1 cup (250 mL) of **vinegar** into the last rinse cycle.

Wash work clothes separately to avoid transferring dirt to other articles of clothing.

WHITES

▶ Laundry comes out whiter when you add a tightly closed laundry bag containing some **eggshells** or **lemon slices** to the load. Wash in hot water.

▶ Add ½ cup (125 mL) of **baking soda** to the main wash cycle. You'll get whiter whites and a nice, fresh smell.

▶ Soak discolored white laundry in **fresh milk** until it turns sour. Then rinse and wash as usual.

▶ One of the other time-proven methods is to use **dishwasher detergent** in your laundry loads instead of laundry soap. Beware that this can be hard on clothes and should be used only on heavy-duty clothing, sheets, and towels.

COLORS

Follow these tips to ensure proper care of colors:

▶ Prevent new colored fabrics from **running** by adding a dash of **vinegar** to the wash water**.**

▶ Add **sugar** to the rinse water to ensure colored laundry comes out bright.

▶ Never hang colored laundry to dry in **bright sunlight**—otherwise, the colors will fade.

▶ Protect **jeans** from wear before washing them: soak them first in a **salt solution** (1 tbsp./15 mL of salt in 1 quart/liter of water).

▶ Do not **starch** colored laundry when it is still hot, or the colors may run.

LACE, VELVET, AND SILK

These are delicate materials that require some basic ground rules.

▶ Handwash blouses and pillowcases made from **natural silk** with a special **wool** or **silk detergent.** Then rinse thoroughly and hang up dripping wet to dry.

▶ Allow **black silk to** retains its shine by washing it with **black tea** and a little **mild detergent.**

▶ Make **velvet** shine after it has been washed by brushing it down with a little **salt**.

▶ Wash **raw silk** by swishing it around in **warm, soapy water**. Roll the garment in a towel to extract as much of the water as possible, and then lay it flat to dry. Iron while still damp on the back side of the fabric.

WOOL

▶ **Sweat odor** disappears when you moisten two cloths with a **water and ammonia solution**, place the article of clothing between them, and steam it with the iron.

▶ Soak **yellowed, undyed wool** overnight in a solution of **hydrogen peroxide** and **cold water** (1:8). Then rinse out and wash.

▶ **Shampoo** is an excellent cleanser for **wool,** whether in the machine or the sink. It's gentle on the woven fabric, so the wool doesn't become matted as it would with other, harsher detergents.

▶ To **soften** a scratchy sweater, dissolve 1 tbsp. (15 mL) of **hair conditioner** in a sink filled with water and swish around the item for 2 minutes. Rinse and dry.

▶ Wool items lose their **shape** when spun dry. Instead, roll them gently into a dry towel, squeeze the excess water out with your hands, then hang on a clothes rack to dry.

cleaning velvet

one Grate pieces of chalk and sprinkle onto an absorbent paper towel. Fold the chalk into the paper.

two Place the paper towel onto the velvet and go over it with the iron to draw out the grease.

Leather

Strong and durable, leather will last a long time if treated with care. Instead of using expensive, chemical-laden leather care products, lean toward home remedies that have stood the test of time to protect your garments, gloves, belts, and bags.

Eliminate the pinch in new shoes by rubbing their insides with rubbing alcohol or vinegar.

We wear or carry leather products that come in a variety of colors and types just about every day. Follow these ground rules to ensure that they look and feel great:

washing leather gloves

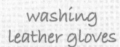

one Fill the sink with warm water and dish soap, and add a dollop of glycerin. This makes the leather softer and more stretchable.

two Put on your leather gloves and wash them in the soapy water.

three Rinse with tap water and hang on a clothes rack to dry. When they are half dry, knead them to make them soft again and lay them flat to complete the drying process.

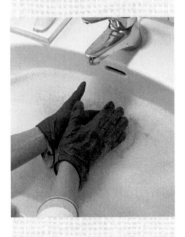

PROPER STORAGE

▶ Leather needs to breathe. Never store in a **plastic bag**.

▶ Hang **belts** in your closet or roll them in a **cloth bag**.

▶ Store leather garments that you no longer wear in **fabric clothing bags.**

▶ Fill **soft handbags** with **newspaper** to help keep their shape.

LEATHER GARMENTS

▶ Never leave leather items too long in the **sun** because intense sunlight can leave leather mottled.

▶ Allow wet leather garments to dry at **room temperature**—not in the sun or near a heat source. Otherwise, the leather may become brittle or, in some cases, even release toxic compounds.

▶ Brush **suede** well after drying. Occasionally treat suede and **nubuck** with a special **brush** that lifts the nap.

▶ Use a **rubber eraser** or **suede eraser** to rub down dirty collars and cuffs.

▶ Clean **white leather** with a little **milk**.

▶ Wash leather garments in water **no hotter than 86°F (30°C)**, and only when absolutely necessary.

GLOVES

▶ Rub **black leather gloves** with the inside of a **banana peel** to make them shine like new.

▶ Wash **suede gloves** in soap and water with a few drops of **ammonia**. Squeeze the water through the gloves carefully by hand, and then squeeze it out again before laying them flat to dry.

▶ Rub a little **castor oil** into **old, stiff leather gloves** to bring back their flexibility.

▶ Place **tight gloves** between **damp cloths** for a few hours, then put them on while still damp to stretch them out. No need to keep them on until they're dry—just wear them for a few minutes.

BELTS AND BAGS

▶ Clean **colored leather belts and bags** occasionally with a **damp cloth**, then allow to dry at room temperature, far from the sun—otherwise, they may lose their color.

▶ Clean dusty, dirty **leather suitcases** long stored in the basement with a solution of equal parts **milk** and **turpentine**.

▶ Clean your hardworking leather **briefcase** with 1 tsp. (5 mL) of **rubbing alcohol** and 1 cup (250 mL) of **water**.

▶ To maintain leather **suitcases,** apply **castor oil** generously. Let it soak in for a few hours, then buff with a soft cloth.

Lighting

Lamps don't just provide light; they add to the ambience and decor of a room, so ensure they're not shrouded under a layer of dust. Keeping lightbulbs and lampshades clean and tidy also increases brightness and saves energy.

Remove surface spots on paper shades with a rubber eraser.

Dust-covered lightbulbs lose up to half their brightness. Clean them regularly for optimal lighting.

Safety is always important when electricity is involved. Before cleaning, always pull the plug on lamps or turn off the breaker. If you use a ladder to access lightbulbs and shades, make sure it is sturdy and not standing on a rug. If possible, have someone steady the ladder.

SHADES, BULBS, AND CABLES

▶ Dust **fiber** and **rattan** shades regularly. Alternatively, gently vacuum the shades with a soft upholstery nozzle.

▶ **Paper** shades shouldn't be cleaned with a wet cloth. But discolored **vellum** shades respond well to soapy water and rubbing alcohol.

▶ Lampshades made from **parchment** don't get dirty as quickly, and are easier to clean, when they're sealed with **clear varnish**; simply wipe them down with a damp cloth.

▶ Use a roller brush with sticky tape to clean **velvet** lampshades, or vacuum them carefully on low power.

▶ Vacuum **fabric** shades or run a lint brush over them. Otherwise, have them cleaned professionally so they don't shrink.

▶ Wipe **silk** lampshades with equal parts **vinegar** and **warm water**. Make sure you wring your rag out well, so that it's just slightly damp.

▶ Don't use cleansers on **Tiffany lamps**. Instead, wipe them down with a soft, damp cloth and clean the joints with a soft toothbrush.

▶ Dust **glass, plastic,** and **metal** lampshades before washing them thoroughly inside and out with dish soap and water. Polish them with a dry, lint-free cloth. **Glass lamps** and **chandeliers** shine beautifully when you add a shot of **vinegar** to the water you're using to clean them.

▶ Use a **feather duster** or **soft brush** on **hanging lamps** or **cable systems**; for high spaces, invest in a duster with a **telescoping handle**.

▶ Clean **chandeliers** with **rubbing alcohol** applied directly to a lint-free cleaning cloth. First clean the framework, then the pendants and bulbs.

▶ Remove ceiling and wall lights with **half shades** several times a year to shake out the insects and dust and to clean the shades thoroughly.

Odors

No home is impervious to some of the less desirable aromas that emanate from kitchens, bathrooms, bedrooms, and hallway closets. Impress your guests—and yourself—with a home that is odor-free, or at least odor-controlled, with just a few easy tricks.

Keep milk from boiling over by smearing the top edge of the pot with butter.

The kitchen and bathroom are the main offenders in the war against odors. But don't forget that you can easily carry odors, including tobacco and a variety of pollutions, into your home from outside.

Proper ventilation is your primary weapon against kitchen odors. But you can deal with stubborn smells with a few simple tricks that would have been familiar to your grandmother. In fact, most of them can be curbed during the cooking process.

COOKING

▶ Mask odors by boiling **water** and a little **cinnamon** in a small pot while cooking.

▶ Stretch a dishcloth moistened with **vinegar** over the pot in which you're cooking **fish** and other strong-smelling foods.

▶ Cooking **cabbage**? Drop a **bread crust** into the cooking pot to absorb odors. For **cauliflower**, try half a **lemon**.

▶ Sprinkle boiled-over **milk** with **salt** to keep it from boiling over again.

▶ After cooking, combat food odors by briefly moistening the heating elements with

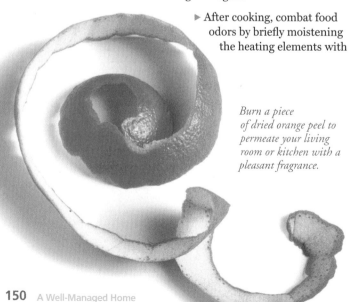

Burn a piece of dried orange peel to permeate your living room or kitchen with a pleasant fragrance.

a little **vinegar,** or boiling some vinegar in water. You might also try wrapping a few **cloves** and a **cinnamon stick** in aluminum foil and placing the package directly on the hot heating elements.

KITCHEN ODORS

It's not just the food itself that creates strong odors; where we store and cook food also contributes to the problem.

▶ Combat musty smells in kitchen cabinets by washing them with **vinegar** and **water**, or bag up **coffee grounds** from the coffeemaker; the coffee will neutralize any remaining odor.

▶ Eliminate odors in your oven: put a **bowl of white vinegar** on the rack, or place a few **orange peels** in a warm oven. Want to blast out nasty smells in a hurry? Rub down your oven with **half a lemon**.

▶ Avoid hair-raising odors in the refrigerator by always wrapping foods separately and making sure that containers are tightly covered. If the occasional bad smell seeps through anyway, try placing a bowl of **vinegar,** half an **apple,** or a little **baking soda** in an open bag or on a plate or bowl in your fridge.

▶ Sprinkle a little **baking soda** in the bottom of your dishwasher to eliminate unpleasant odors the next time you run the machine. Just as effective: add a few drops of **concentrated orange oil** during the next wash cycle.

▶ The smell of **onions** or **garlic** can cling to a wooden cutting board. To freshen it up, rub it with half a **lemon,** and rinse. Lemon will work wonders for your hands as well.

► Destroy musty smells that can develop in **clay** and **ceramic pots** by rinsing them out thoroughly with **hot vinegar.**

► Refresh stale-smelling **thermos bottles** by rinsing them with tap water, and then filling them with hot water and a little **baking soda.** Let the solution sit in the thermos for 5 minutes before thoroughly rinsing with tap water.

► Banish grungy smells from the **trash can** by adding **citrus peels** or **baking soda.**

BATHROOM SMELLS

► Burn **matches** or light a **candle** to help curb musty smells in the bathroom. A **potpourri** of fragrant herbs and spices, such as cinnamon, rosemary, thyme, cloves, or lavender also does an excellent job covering up nasty odors.

► Add a dash of **toilet cleanser** or **vinegar and water** to the bottom of the brush holder to keep the toilet brush from getting smelly. Hang **towels** and **washcloths** to dry and change them frequently so they don't smell musty.

TOBACCO ODORS

► **Vinegar** helps to counter the lingering smell of cigarette smoke. Boil it in a pot on the stove and after it cools, pour it into small decorative bottles or bowls to be spread around the house.

► Rinse out **ashtrays** with a vinegar solution as well, and sprinkle **coffee grounds** in the bottom of your ashtray to help absorb the smell of ashes.

CLOTHING

► Start with clothing storage. A piece of **soap** or a small sachet of **lavender, cedar chips,** or even **coffee grounds** will imbue your clothes closet with a pleasant smell. Also, try to hang your **coats** and **jackets** outside to air before hanging them back up in the closet.

► Most of us are intimately acquainted with the problem of **stinky athletic shoes.** One simple remedy is to sprinkle a little **baking soda** in your shoes, let them stand overnight, then vacuum it out. If you have particularly sweaty feet, change your shoes regularly. When you're not using your sneakers, stuff them with a pair of socks filled with **kitty litter** to absorb the odor and wick away moisture. A final option is to place shoes in a **zipper lock bag** in the freezer overnight to kill odor-causing bacteria.

OTHER ODORS

Household odors are not limited to the kitchen and bathroom, or to just tobacco and shoes. These helpful hints will help chase away other bad smells in your home:

► Keep musty odors at bay by burning a **bay leaf,** placing a piece of **citrus fruit peel** on a hot heating element, or hanging a **vanilla bean** in your room.

► If the exhaust from your **vacuum cleaner** smells stinky, change the bag and simply vacuum up some **lavender flowers** or **peppermint leaves.** Alternatively, dab a **cotton ball** in a little perfume or aromatic oil and vacuum it up.

► Absorb the smell of **animal litter** by adding a little **baking soda** to the litter box.

► Add a piece of **charcoal** to **vase water.** This will keep it from smelling foul.

► Moldy smells vanish from **plastic containers** when you wash and dry them, fill them with **crumpled newspaper** or **coffee grounds,** and freeze them overnight.

► Rinse musty-smelling **leather suitcases** with **vinegar** and leave them open to the fresh air for a few days.

► Eliminate the smell of **oil-based paint** by setting several bowls of peeled, sliced **onions** around the room.

a money-saving *hint*

You can impart a fresh, clean smell to your dishwasher by including a little lemon juice or lemon peel in each load. Lemon is a natural deodorizer and degreaser—you may never have to buy expensive deodorant for your dishwasher again.

Fragrant lavender will keep moths out of your cupboards.

Pests

They may be invisible, they may bite, and they may be lingering in your home. But humans have been dealing with creepy-crawlies for generations, so there are a number of simple ways to rid your house of these uninvited guests. Read on for some tried-and-true home remedies to drive them away.

Place an orange stuck with cloves on the windowsill to keep flies from coming into the house.

They may be after your food, your blood, the wood that holds your home together, or even your clothing. Here are some natural ways to keep those pesky creatures far from your home.

ANTS

▶ Ants follow a scent trail, marching in a straight line one-by-one. Disrupt the trail by sprinkling **mint tea leaves, crushed cloves,** or **chili powder** at the point where they enter your house. Once they lose the scent trail, they can no longer find their way in.

▶ Draw a line with a piece of **chalk** or **baby powder** through the ants' route; the tiny party-crashers won't be able to cross it.

▶ Ants will gobble down strewn **baking soda** and feed it to their young, causing their stomachs to rupture and cutting down on their population.

▶ Ants can't resist a solution of **sugar, yeast,** and **water**; it, too, makes them burst.

▶ Effective baits against ants also include **honey, water,** and **syrup.** Set them out in a shallow dish; ants get trapped in the sticky solution and die.

FLIES

▶ The best solution is to install **screen windows and doors** and try to keep food covered.

▶ Set out bowls of **vinegar** (replace them daily).

▶ Use **blue** tablecloths; believe it or not, flies avoid this color.

▶ The smells of **basil, peppermint, lavender,** and **tomato plants** also ward off flies.

▶ Coat meat with **lemon balm** or **basil** before grilling it and all the flies will take off.

FLEAS

▶ If fleas have taken up lodging in your **sofa** or **armchair**, place a **bucket of water** in front of the furniture and run a **lint roller** over the upholstery in the direction of the bucket. The fleas will jump into the water and drown.

▶ Put a dish of **lemon slices** into a closet to keep fleas away.

▶ If your rug is infested, sprinkle it with **salt,** let it work for a while, then vacuum.

WOODLICE

▶ Put a bottle of **sweet liqueur** or **leftover wine** in the basement; the creatures will climb in and become intoxicated. You can discard them along with the bottle and repeat the process as needed.

▶ Leave **hollowed-out potatoes** or **turnips** as a lure. You can crush them along with the woodlice that have crawled inside.

MICE

▶ Before reaching for a mousetrap, try driving mice away with **chamomile flowers** or **peppermint.** Growing peppermint plants near your entrance works well as a deterrent.

▶ **Peppermint oil, turpentine,** and **camphor** are all scents that are supremely unappetizing to mice. Dab a little on some cotton balls and place them strategically in areas where mice might enter.

---

good to know

HOW TO KEEP DOGS AND CATS FREE FROM PESTS
After every walk, check your pooch for fleas and ticks. If you suspect the presence of insects, put some walnut leaves in the dog's bed. If your dog or cat becomes infested, mix up 2 tbsp. (25 mL) of vermouth and 1 quart/liter of water, let the solution steep for two to three hours, and rub it on the animal's fur.

Moths stay away from fabrics when you make a sachet of lavender flowers or place a sprig of lavender in your closet.

MITES

▶ Mites dislike both **fresh air** and **light**. Regularly shake out bedding and blankets thoroughly.

▶ **Vacuum** rugs or beat them and wash them on a regular basis.

▶ Replace carpets with **wooden floorboards** or **tiles**.

MOTHS

▶ Drive away moths with **dried citrus peels** or **cedar chips** in small bags.

▶ Moths won't take up residence in fabrics that are used frequently, so **shake out** linens and clothing regularly.

▶ Remove supplies infested with **pantry moths** immediately and wash out your kitchen cabinets with **vinegar and water**.

MOSQUITOES

▶ Keep mosquitoes from getting into your house or cottage with a **screen**. If they do get past the front door, a **mosquito net** will help prevent them from biting you while you sleep.

▶ Keep the pesky stingers away from terraces and balconies by hanging up a cloth sprayed with a few drops of **clove** or **laurel oil**. Alternatively, pour the oil into small bowls or an oil lamp.

CARPET BEETLES

▶ **V**acuum regularly to keep hair and lint from collecting and providing food for carpet beetle larvae.

▶ Seal **cracks** in parquet flooring and spray **neem oil** (available at most garden centers) along floor moldings. This makes the larvae stop eating and prevents them from growing and reproducing. Be warned, it will take time.

COCKROACHES

▶ For a minor infestation, use a **cloth moistened with wine or beer** as bait. When the insects have gathered on the cloth, pour boiling water over it.

▶ Combat cockroaches with a lethal "roach dinner." Mix one part powdered **boric acid**, one part **white flour,** and one part **white sugar** and place in bowls under the fridge, in the backs of drawers, and behind the stove.

SILVERFISH

▶ Sprinkle a little **plaster** on damp cloths and place them in the bathroom or the kitchen at night; in the morning, shake them and their load of insects off outside.

▶ Grate a **potato** on a piece of **newspaper** to attract silverfish, then just fold the paper up and toss the whole lot in the outside garbage.

WASPS

▶ Wasps make themselves scarce when they detect the odor of **heated vinegar.**

▶ The insects also keep their distance from **lemon slices studded with cloves**.

▶ Make a **wasp trap.** Fill a narrow-necked bottle with a sugar solution or diluted fruit juice and a little detergent and vinegar. Wasps will happily go in, but can't get out.

BEDBUGS

▶ Before calling in the pros, you might try spraying **rubbing alcohol** where bedbugs thrive. It may contain the problem by killing some bugs on contact.

▶ Placing clothing, shoes and boots, toys, stuffed animals, backpacks, and other non-washables in the **dryer** for 20 minutes or more on high temperature may kill bedbugs.

▶ Wash and dry clothing and linens at **high temperatures** (over 113°F/45°C).

Pots and Pans

Stores today are filled with a huge selection of pots and pans manufactured from a variety of materials. When deciding what to buy, take into account the advantages and disadvantages of each; a good set of pots and pans can last a lifetime.

With such a varied choice of pots and pans, you should remember that special care is needed to clean and maintain different types of cookware. Some are more popular than others. Aluminum is lightweight, conducts heat well, and is fairly inexpensive. The most popular form of cookware is likely stainless steel. It is inexpensive, long-lasting, and resists wear and tear. Some traditional care methods will go a long way to protect any set of pots and pans.

GENERAL CARE

▶ Don't use **metal implements** while cooking, since they can cause surface damage, particularly to nonstick pans.

▶ Wash dirty cookware with **dish soap** and **water**, using a **dishwashing sponge** or **brush**. For enamel and stainless steel, use **steel wool** for heavy-duty cleaning.

▶ Soften dried-on and especially burned-on food remnants overnight with **water** and a little **salt**. Boil the mixture in the pan, let it cool, wipe it out, and rinse.

▶ Take special care when cleaning cookware with **wooden handles** that may swell and split when soaked.

ALUMINUM POTS

▶ Never wash aluminum pots in the **dishwasher** or with **abrasive cleaners**; you risk discoloring or scratching the finish. Instead, scrub very lightly with a little **soapy water** and **steel wool.**

Get better cooking results and save money in the long run by buying high-quality cookware.

▶ Bring back the shine by boiling **spinach** in an aluminum pan for a few minutes. Don't eat the vegetables though—aluminum forms toxic compounds with fruit acids, so avoid using aluminum pots for cooking fruits or vegetables.

▶ Don't **soak** your aluminum pots too long and avoid **storing food** in them, as they can be prone to discoloration.

ENAMEL POTS

▶ Before the first use, enamel pots should be boiled for an hour with a **vinegar-salt solution** (1½ oz./50 g of salt; 2 tbsp./25 mL of vinegar; 1 quart/liter of water) to increase their durability. Faulty enamel coatings allow harmful heavy metals to leach into your food.

Removing Rust from Cast Iron

If, despite your careful treatment, rust spots form on cast-iron cookware, use a lemon solution sure to remove them. Mix together:

1 tbsp. (15 mL) lemon juice
2 cups (500 mL) water

Dip a brush in the solution and coat the rust spots. Then maintain the cookware as usual.

▶ Pouring **cold water** into hot enamel cookware will cause the enamel to crack.

▶ Coat any stains on enamel pots with a paste of **baking soda** and **water** and let sit for an hour, then boil for 20 minutes (leaving the paste in the pot) and wash with hot, soapy water. Boiling **orange** and/or **lemon peels** for 20 minutes in a pot three-quarters-full of water also removes stains (but don't eat them). Finish by rinsing thoroughly.

STAINLESS STEEL COOKWARE

▶ Rinse out immediately after cooking, as **salt** can attack the surface.

▶ Stainless steel shines like new after rubbing with a moist cloth sprinkled with **baking soda**.

▶ Rub stains and small scratches off cookware with a paste made from 1 tbsp. (15 mL) of **dish soap** and 1 tbsp. (15 mL) of **baking soda**. Rinse it off with **cold water.**

CAST-IRON POTS AND PANS

▶ **Season** cast-iron cookware before the first use: clean **pots**, rub in some **vegetable oil**, and heat them in the oven on the top rack. For **pans**, add 1–2 tbsp. (15–25 mL) of oil and heat it on the element until the oil smokes. Wipe out with paper towels after it cools.

▶ After use, wash pots and pans in **warm dish-water,** dry immediately, and rub with **cooking oil**.

▶ Keep your cookware from rusting. Store it in a **dry** place.

COPPER COOKWARE

▶ Immerse new pots and pans in **boiling water** and allow to cool.

▶ Rub any tarnished spots shiny with **half a lemon and a little salt.**

▶ You can also try a paste of **vinegar and salt** to make copper shiny. Let it work for 30 minutes, wash off with cold water, and then dry with a chamois cloth.

COATED POTS AND PANS

▶ Wash with **warm water** and rub sparingly with **vegetable oil.**

▶ Remove dried-on remains. Boil 3 tbsp. (45 mL) of **baking soda** in about 2/3 cup (150 mL) of **water** in the pan, pour out the liquid, and wipe out the baking soda residue along with the leftover food.

▶ Avoid scratches by placing **paper towels** between pans when you store them.

KETTLES

▶ Lime deposits don't stand a chance when you fill your kettle halfway with **water** and **vinegar** and boil the contents. Turn off the heat, let the liquid work for a couple of hours, and wash thoroughly.

▶ Avoid calcification by placing **a pebble** or **a piece of marble** in the kettle.

Don't use steel wool on your cookware unless you're sure it can take it—some materials are more delicate than others.

good to know

AVOID BURNING FOODS
Prevent burning the food you're cooking by lightly coating your pots and pans with oil and salt after each washing and wiping them with a paper towel. Foods won't cook on so hard, and subsequent washing will be quicker and easier.

Sewing

Do you have a shirt button missing, pants that need a patch, or socks that need to be darned? Long considered a craft art, sewing is a skill that everyone should know. It's easy to learn, and knowing how will help you extend the life of your clothing.

THE SEWING BASKET

You don't really need a large basket to mend your clothing; basic sewing basket items will fit into an old shoe box or cookie tin. Here are some tips about what you need and how to store it:

▶ Keep **sewing** and **darning needles** of various sizes in a **pincushion** or piece of **soap**. Yes, soap! It coats needles, helping them pass easily through thick, firm fabrics.

▶ Try using a **magnet** as a pincushion; you can also use it to gather up lost needles.

▶ Store **pins** and **safety pins** in a small **matchbox**.

▶ Store a selection of **silk and cotton sewing thread**, plus **darning thread** in common colors, as well as some **yarn** for thick fabrics.

▶ Add a **thimble, darning egg, seam cutter, scissors,** and perhaps a **needle threader** to complete your sewing kit.

▶ Stay organized by stringing **buttons** together by color. If not, as time goes by, buttons will accumulate in the sewing basket, making it difficult to find the one you want. Store extra ones for specific articles of clothing in transparent, labeled bags.

SEWING ON PATCHES

At some point in time, articles of clothing, otherwise in excellent condition, will need patches. Usually elbows, knees, and the crotch area are first to fall. When sewing on patches, consider the following:

▶ Hand stitch **iron-on patches** along the edges when patching **stretchy fabrics.**

▶ Sew together **holes** in **knitted items** before applying a patch, to ensure they don't get larger.

▶ Sew on an **inside backer** made from previously discarded denim when patching a favorite pair of well-worn jeans.

▶ Use a **sewing machine** to attach patches to tough fabrics such as **denim**.

BUTTONS AND BUTTONHOLES

▶ Before you lose a loose button and have to dig up a replacement, sew the original on properly.

A well-stocked sewing basket is an absolute necessity in every house.

▶ Avoid damaging a favorite blouse when cutting off buttons by inserting a **comb** between the fabric and the button before snipping the threads.

▶ Stiffen thread by rubbing it with **candle wax;** that way, it's easier to thread onto a needle.

▶ Sew on a button with four holes in a **crisscross shape** so if one thread breaks, the second keeps the button in place.

▶ Use a **matchstick** as a spacer between button and fabric. Once you've fastened the button, remove the matchstick. Then secure the button with multiple strands to reinforce it and finish with a couple of extra stitches on the back of your fabric with the ends of the thread.

▶ Avoid tearing out fabric on the button facing, especially on coats, by sewing an **additional flat button** onto the **inside** when sewing on a button.

▶ Sew a **frayed** or **oversized buttonhole** with a couple of horizontal stitches at the upper and lower edges of the hole so that the head of the button just fits. Sew up the ends of the thread on the back side.

REPAIRING A SEAM

If you need to repair a seam, proceed as follows:

▶ Press the folded seam with an **iron** and secure it with **pins.**

▶ Sew the folded inner edge of the seam in a **cross stitch pattern,** from the back side to the top of the face fabric.

▶ Keep your stitches **small and neat** to ensure that they're not visible on the outside of the fabric.

▶ Avoid pulling the stitches too **tight**. This will keep the seam flexible and protect it from tearing out again.

▶ Use an **iron** a **damp cloth** to steam the seam.

PROTECT HEMS FROM WEAR AND TEAR

Iron-on selvage is usually quite stiff and may prevent your pants or skirt from hanging properly. In order to protect the hems of good pants from wear and tear, sew on a selvage band as follows:

▶ Try on the pants or skirt with the appropriate shoes. Mark the desired hem with **chalk** or **straight pins**, then lightly iron it in place.

▶ Use a **sewing machine** to sew on the selvage band along the ironed edge so that about $1/32$ in. (1 mm) protrudes beyond the hem.

▶ **Hand sew** the hem like any other seam.

QUICK HELP

Here are some extra sewing tips that will come in handy when you least expect it:

▶ Thread easily by spraying the end of your thread with **hairspray.**

▶ Stop **runs** in fabric before they get any worse by adding a little **clear nail polish** or a little **glue**. But keep in mind that you won't be able to sew them later, so use this technique only when you have no other options.

▶ Rub **sticky zippers** with **beeswax** to get them gliding smoothly again.

▶ Spray **used zippers** with **starch** and iron them smooth so they can be sewn in easily.

▶ Lightly hit the head of a **snap** with a hammer to make it hold better.

▶ Replace **elastic bands** by fastening the new band to the old one with a safety pin. As you pull the old one out, the new one is pulled in.

▶ Make threads more durable by rubbing them with **paraffin** or **wax**.

▶ You don't have the right-colored thread? Always choose a shade **darker** than the original—never use a lighter color.

▶ Use some new **shoelaces** to make hanging loops for heavy jackets. Just cut them to the appropriate length and then attach them with strong thread inside the collar.

how to darn

one Stitch over, then under the hole in the first undamaged row to form parallel threads running lengthwise.

two Weave parallel threads running crosswise through the lengthwise threads until the hole is completely filled.

Shades, Curtains, and Drapes

Window coverings shield your family from prying eyes, keep the cold out on winter nights, and protect you from the summer's heat. By maintaining them carefully, you can extend their life and keep them looking great.

There is a tendency to sometimes ignore shades, curtains, and drapes, but they, like every other item in your house, collect dust, hair, and pollution. Regular maintenance will ensure clean window coverings.

DUSTING

▶ Dust curtains and drapes regularly with the **upholstery nozzle** on the vacuum cleaner to ensure they don't have to be washed or cleaned quite so often.

▶ Curtains made from **synthetic fabrics** attract dust. Use **cold salt water** to dissolve it.

Detergent for Curtains

1½ oz. (50 g) soap
10 quarts/liters water
4 tbsp. (60 mL) ammonia
4 tbsp. (60 mL) turpentine

Dissolve the soap in hot water and stir in the ammonia or turpentine. Pour the solution over curtains laid flat in the bathtub, and leave for about an hour before rinsing. This detergent is particularly well suited to delicate curtains.

WASHING

▶ Soak colored curtains in **salt water** to prevent fading and help dissolve dirt.

▶ Wash delicate curtains **by hand** in the bathtub with plenty of **hand soap.**

▶ Protect curtains in the washing machine by putting them in a **pillowcase**.

▶ Always wash curtains using your machine's **delicate cycle,** with plenty of water; that way, they won't wrinkle as much.

▶ Allow hand-washed curtains to **drip dry** and never wring them out. To ensure that they hang properly, weight the bottom edges with **clothespins** before hanging them.

▶ Prevent **shrinking**: stretch out **cotton** curtains while they are still wet.

▶ **Stiffen** curtains with a 1:3 **sugar-water solution** added to the last rinse, or put them in water used for boiling **rice**.

▶ Give your curtains a wonderful fragrance by adding a few drops of **perfume** or **essential oil** to the wash cycle.

COMBATING YELLOWING

▶ Yellowed curtains recover their gleaming white color even without chemical bleaches when you soak them in a **baking soda solution** (about 1 cup/250 mL baking soda in 10 quarts/liters of water) before washing them. You can get the same effect by adding a glass of **cola** or 2–3 **denture cleansing tablets** to the curtains' wash cycle.

▶ **Salt**, the cure-all, also helps with this; simply soak smoke-yellowed curtains overnight in a salt solution (about 18 oz./550 g of salt in 10 quarts/liters of water) and then wash as usual.

▶ If older curtains lose their whiteness, give them an attractive **cream** color instead; just add an infusion of **linden flower tea** to the rinse cycle. The intensity of the color depends on how long you let the tea steep.

Hang just-washed curtains while still damp so they don't have to be ironed.

Silver

Silverware, silver place settings, and decorative items made from this precious metal have been treasured over generations—but with age comes tarnish. Thankfully, removing it requires only a bit of tender loving care. For that, we have the wisdom of the past to call on.

Storing and cleaning silver place settings, silverware, and decorative silver are key to refurbishing and maintaining treasured belongings.

STORAGE

▶ Always **dry** silver thoroughly before storing it away. For silver place settings and other silverware, a **drawer lined with velvet** is a good choice—preferably one that closes tightly.

▶ Buy **rolls with felt pockets** for storing silverware. **Felt** also keeps silver from tarnishing quickly.

▶ Keep silverware in **tightly-sealed plastic bags** or wipe on a very thin layer of **glycerin** to prevent tarnishing. Store it in a place that isn't subject to major temperature fluctuations.

▶ Tuck a sachet of **activated charcoal** into the plastic bags to act as an air filter—look for it at your local pet store. Replace the sachet once a year.

▶ Silverware made from soft silver is easily scratched by harder steel, so **store it separately.**

FIRST AID FOR TARNISHED SILVER

▶ When silver shows the first traces of tarnish, immerse it in either **sour milk** (milk with a couple dashes of **vinegar**) or **buttermilk** for 30 minutes; then wash it off and polish with a soft cloth.

▶ Treat minor spots of tarnish with a paste of **cornstarch** or **baking soda** and **water.** Let the paste work for a few minutes, then rinse it off and wipe dry with a soft cloth.

SILVER PLACE SETTINGS AND SILVERWARE

▶ Silver tarnishes upon contact with **egg, broccoli, and fish**; wash it immediately after use.

▶ **Egg spots** on silver vanish quickly when you rub them with **damp salt**. Then rinse the silverware thoroughly with tap water.

▶ Remove spots on silver **coffeepots** with very fine **steel wool** and a little **vinegar.**

▶ To clean your silver **teapot,** fill it with **boiling water** and add a little **baking soda.** Let it work overnight and rinse thoroughly.

DECORATIVE ITEMS

▶ Clean **embossed** or **punch-marked** silver pieces with **lukewarm, soapy water** and a **soft brush**.

▶ For **verdigris** on copper, brass or bronze, gently rub on a mixture of **salt** and **lemon juice**, then buff off.

▶ Wipe silver pieces with **intentionally-darkened decorations** with a **cloth** for polishing silver—that way the darkened indentations remain dark.

make your own silver dip

one Half-fill a sink with warm water.

two Insert a piece of aluminum foil in the sink, along with 2 tbsp. (25 mL) of salt and 3 tbsp. (45 mL) of baking soda.

three Dip your silver in the solution. Most tarnish will simply slide off, but you may have to soak some stains for 5 minutes at a time.

four If stains remain, remove silver from dip, clean with soap and a rag, and insert again.

five Remove the silver and wipe with a soft cloth until shiny.

Fine decorations and edges on silverware are best cleaned with toothpaste and a soft cloth.

Stain Removal

We've all been irritated by a stain on a new tablecloth or a new shirt. Don't despair—milk, fruit, coffee, and other typical stains may seem disastrous, but they can be remedied quickly and easily.

Universal Stain Removal

1 cup (250 mL) rubbing alcohol
3½ oz. (100 mL) ammonia
2 tsp. (10 mL) naphtha

Mix the ingredients together in a sealable bottle. Keep out of the reach of children.

BASIC RULES

Not all stains should be treated the same way. A rule of thumb: the fresher and damper the spot, the easier and more completely you can remove it.

▶ **Water-soluble stains** are the most common. All you'll need to remove them is tap water, at least when they're fresh. Treat **albuminous stains** (protein-based stains such as blood, mayonnaise and egg) only with cold or warm water.

▶ Treat **older stains** with a mixture of 2 tbsp. (25 mL) of **water** and 3 tbsp. (45 mL) of **vinegar**. Leave mixture to dry and then rinse. When removing a stain, start from the outside and work toward the middle. Avoid using hot water, or you risk setting the stain (especially if you don't know what kind of stain it is). To avoid leaving an outline of the stain, blow-dry the wet area.

▶ If possible, scrape a **dried stain** with a **spoon** or soften it with **glycerin** before treating it.

THE ABCS OF STAINS

Stains come in a variety of shapes, sizes, and types. Just about any liquid or solid from the refrigerator or pantry can stain. The garden and garage are also full of potential stain materials.

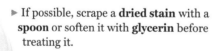

Fresh red wine stain? Sprinkle salt on the stain immediately, followed by a little mineral water, white wine, or champagne, then wash the item.

▶ Remove **beer stains** with a thin soap solution containing a little **ammonia**, then rinse with water.

▶ Wash **bloodstains** on clothing immediately in **cold water**—hot water will cause the protein in the blood to congeal and attach firmly to the fibers. For particularly stubborn stains, moisten the clothing in cold salt water. Dry bloodstains should be soaked in cold water, then treated with **salt water** or **soda water**. When cleaning delicate fabrics, use a paste of **water** and **potato flour** or **cornstarch**: spread it on the stain, let it work for a few minutes, rub it off, and rinse thoroughly with tap water.

▶ Rinse off **burn marks** on washable fabrics with cold water, sprinkle with **salt**, and dry them in the sun. Treat burns marks on delicate fabrics carefully with diluted **vinegar**.

▶ **Grease stains** can include makeup, butter, margarine, mayonnaise, cooking oil, and engine oil. Promptly sprinkle grease stains with **cornstarch** or **healing earth** to absorb the grease, then brush away the saturated starch. You can also try rubbing the stains off using hot water mixed with a little **dish soap** to dissolve the grease. For delicate fabrics, place a paper towel on both sides of the stain and **iron** it. Stains are best removed from **wool** fabrics by rubbing them off with a little **mineral water** and a **terry cloth towel**.

▶ Remove tough **lipstick stains** by dabbing them with **eucalyptus oil** and leaving it to soak in before laundering. **Boil** white table napkins, handkerchiefs, or washcloths marred by lipstick stains.

▶ Rub **tar stains** with **lard** before washing the item. For an extra boost, add 2 tbsp. (25 mL) of **baking soda** to the laundry detergent. Oil, tar, and grass stains can also be treated with a few drops of **eucalyptus oil**.

▶ Treat fresh **grass stains** with **ammonia**, but first test the sensitivity of the fabric on an inconspicuous place, such as an inside seam. Another option: apply a halved **potato** to the grass stain to allow the starch to dissolve the stain, then launder as usual. Soak older grass stains on white fabrics with a mixture of one part **egg white** and one part **glycerin** before washing.

▶ Soak **coffee stains** on table linens or clothing in **cold salt water** while they're still fresh. Dab older stains with **glycerin** and wash them out, or, in the case of upholstery and rugs, pat them dry.

▶ Soak dried **cocoa stains** in **warm milk**, then

Treat a shirt with dry, caked-on mud by first shaking and pulling off as much excess dirt as possible outdoors. Then wash with soap and warm water.

holding the soiled item over a bowl and dribbling very hot water onto it. Alternatively, soak it in **buttermilk** and launder as usual. You can also use buttermilk to remove stubborn fruit stains from your **hands**. For **dried fruit stains**, dribble with **lemon juice** and rinse after 30 minutes. If the stain still doesn't come out, try treating it with an **ammonia solution** (2 tbsp./25 mL of ammonia in 1 quart/liter of water) or **glycerin solution** (equal parts of glycerin and water).

▶ Apply **lemon juice, vinegar,** or **soda water** before laundering fabric with **red wine stains.**

▶ **Red dye stains** from cherry popsicles or maraschino cherries can turn a favorite treat into a laundry conundrum. Mix equal parts **hydrogen peroxide** and **cool water** in a spray bottle; spray on the stain and leave for 30 minutes, then rinse with equal parts **vinegar** and **water**. Peroxide is a bleach, so always test a spot first. If the technique doesn't work the first time, try again.

▶ Treat **sweat stains** with a **vinegar-water mix** (2 tbsp./25 mL of vinegar to 3 tbsp./45 mL) of water) or **ammonia solution**.

▶ Scratch off **wax spots,** then place a paper towel under and over the spot and **iron** until all excess wax is absorbed by the paper. If necessary, replace the paper towel. Remove any remaining stain from **colored wax** by dabbing it with **rubbing alcohol,** always rubbing from the outside in.

wash with detergent containing **enzymes**.

▶ Remove **chewing gum** by placing the affected clothing in the freezer in a plastic bag. Once the gum is frozen, it's easy to scrape off.

▶ Clean up **glue** immediately. For clear glue spills, try **cologne** or **oil-free nail polish remover**; in other cases, **turpentine, rubbing alcohol,** or **lighter fluid** may do the trick.

▶ Rinse **milk spots** with **cold water** before throwing the stained clothing into the washing machine. Dab non-washable fabrics first with cold water, then with **ammonia**, and finally with warm water.

▶ Treat **fruit stains** when they are still fresh by

Traditional Cleaners

Synthetic cleaning products abound in supermarkets today—some with hefty price tags. Many were actually created based on the properties of existing natural cleaning products, all of which can help keep your home clean and sanitized.

Most of the cleaning materials mentioned in this book can be bought at the local drugstore or supermarket, and you can easily mix up the solutions yourself. The caveat: wear gloves and a face mask when working with ammonia, talc, or turpentine products. Avoid swallowing, breathing, or absorbing these products through your skin, and store your homemade cleaning materials out of reach of the kids (just as you would the store-bought products). It is always a good idea to check their shelf life regularly.

Vinegar

The word vinegar comes from the Old French *vin aigre*, or "sour wine." The substance—made by fermenting ethanol—has been used for seasoning food since earliest times. In fact, traces of it have been found in 3,000-year-old Egyptian urns. But vinegar doesn't just liven up your salad; it's a great natural cleaning product, as well as a disinfectant and deodorizer. To make an all-purpose cleaner for tables, countertops, tubs, and tiles simply mix equal parts vinegar and water in a spray bottle, or pour the substance directly into the toilet bowl to remove discoloration. Just be sure to test it on an inconspicuous area before use. Vinegar should never be used on marble and, when improperly diluted, it may eat away at tile grout. But for the most part, vinegar is effective, easily accessible, and cheap!

Glycerin

This colorless, odorless, rather thick non-toxic alcohol is also known as glycerol. Glycerin is commonly used in pharmaceutical and personal care products like cosmetics, soaps, and toothpaste, as well as in certain food products. Glycerin, in its pure form, can be used to treat a number of minor medical conditions, including calluses, bedsores, rashes, and cuts. But the substance is usually used at home to soften up tough, dried-on fabric stains from things like coffee, berries, and lipstick. It is also used as an antifreeze on windowpanes; rub windows with glycerin before the temperature drops and they won't freeze over.

Ammonia

Ammonia, or ammonium chloride, is the ammonium salt of hydrochloric acid and a crystalline solid. It has been used in everything from fertilizer to rocket fuel. That may make it sound like a dangerous chemical, but in fact, ammonia has been used as a household cleaner for a very long time. Commercially, it's most commonly found as the watery solution ammonia (ammonium hydroxide). Use liquid ammonia at home for stain removal or when cleaning stainless steel, glass, and porcelain—it leaves a streak-free shine. It is also used to combat mold and pests.

Talc

Also known as magnesium silicate hydrate, talc is the softest mineral. It feels soapy, which accounts for its alternate name: soapstone. As a finely ground filler, talc is used in the paper and cellulose industry, the paint and varnish industry, and in the production of rubber, plastics, and ceramics. It is also used in the pharmaceuticals industry and in food production. In its ground-up form (talcum powder) it is used as a body powder or makeup base. In the home, it makes for a gentle scrubbing agent and can be used to treat rubber seals or to silence squeaky wooden floorboards and stairs. Don't breathe in talcum powder or you risk causing serious inflammation in your breathing passages.

Turpentine

Turpentine, also known as spirit of turpentine or wood turpentine, is a mixture of resin and essential oil from various species of pine. Turpentine oil, produced by distilling turpentine, is particularly effective for dissolving grease. The colorless-to-yellowish fluid has numerous applications in your home, e.g., as a floor polish, shoe polish, or an effective solvent for stain removal. Don't dispose of turpentine products by pouring them down the drain—it's not good for the environment or your pipes. Check with your local authorities for proper disposal methods before you throw it away.

a money-saving *hint*

Toothpaste makes an easy and economical silver polish.

Upholstery

The upholstered seat in your living room is likely to get slept, jumped, and spilled on. Given the amount of abuse it takes, the maintenance of its upholstery and fabric is especially important.

It is not surprising that upholstered furniture requires regular care, considering how many hours we spend on the couch gazing at the tube, reading a book, and socializing with friends.

MAINTAINING UPHOLSTERY

▶ Clean upholstered furniture regularly with the **vacuum cleaner**; but reduce the suction to avoid damaging the underpadding.

▶ **Beat the dust** out of upholstery outdoors to prevent dust from spreading through the room and settling on the furniture.

▶ Before beating large upholstered furniture, cover it with a **damp cloth** to catch the dust being released. If you moisten the cloth with **vinegar** and **water**, the colors will take on new freshness.

▶ Moisten furniture's **pressure points** with a little **hot water,** cover with **white paper,** and iron dry. Be careful not to burn the points.

▶ Clean dirty couch **cushions** every year with a **vinegar solution** made from one part vinegar and one part water. Apply it with a cloth and then wipe off with tap water.

▶ Machine-wash or dry-clean **removable covers** when necesary. Observe the care directions. Brocade, chintz, velvet, silk, and wool tweed must be dry-cleaned.

▶ After washing cushion covers, **iron** them from the inside and put them back on the cushions while still damp; they will stretch better and dry without wrinkling.

▶ Rub soiled spots on **wool** or **linen covers** with a **soft rubber eraser.**

▶ Clean **dark velvet upholstery** covers with a brush moistened in **cold coffee**; then moisten a cloth with tap water and pat the velvet to pick up any excess.

▶ Clean **synthetic covers** by dipping a cloth dampened with **water** and a little **baking soda** and gently rubbing the cushion with it. Go over it again with a **water and soap solution**.

▶ Remove **lint** and **pet hair** with a **damp sponge**, or a piece of **tape** wrapped around your hand with the sticky side out.

REMOVING STAINS FROM UPHOLSTERY

▶ Immediately remove **residue** and vacuum up **spills**. Remove **stains** by working toward the middle to avoid leaving an outline.

▶ Sprinkle **fresh grease and oil stains** with **cornstarch**. Let it set until the grease is absorbed and then brush it off.

▶ Dab **older grease stains** with **ammonia solution, rubbing alcohol,** or **cologne**, then carefully rub with water.

▶ Treat **milk spots** immediately with **cold water** or a lather of **moisturizing soap** and **warm water**. To finish, pat dry.

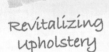

Revitalizing upholstery

¾ oz. (25 g) soap flakes
2 cups (500 mL) water
3½ oz. (100 mL) glycerin
3½ oz. (100 mL) rubbing alcohol

Heat the water and dissolve the soap flakes. Let cool, then stir in the glycerin and rubbing alcohol. Store the mixture in a container. As needed, dissolve 1 tbsp. (15 mL) of the mixture in water, stir with a whisk, and apply the foam with a sponge.

When vacuuming the couch, use a crevice nozzle to clean between the seat and arm.

MAINTAINING LEATHER UPHOLSTERY

▶ Clean **washable leather** with a **soap solution** (1 tsp./5 mL of liquid soap in 1 quart/liter of water). Wring out the cloth thoroughly. Allow the furniture to dry, then buff.

▶ Maintain **dark leather** by rubbing **castor oil** into it thoroughly once or twice a year.

▶ Treat **light-colored leather** with **petroleum jelly**. Let it work for about an hour before removing the excess with a soft rag.

▶ Make **scuffed leather upholstery** shine again. Treat with a mixture of equal parts **beaten egg white** and **linseed oil**.

▶ Produce a **natural leather polish**. Boil some **linseed oil**, let it cool, and mix with an equal amount of **vinegar**. Apply with a soft cloth and buff.

▶ Special **nourishing creams** for **older leather** can be purchased at furniture stores or online. Allow them to work their magic for about 24 hours after application, then buff. But make sure you wipe them well so nothing rubs off on your clothing.

REMOVING STAINS
FROM SMOOTH LEATHER

▶ Remove **water-soluble stains** with a damp rag and **moisturizing soap foam**, then thoroughly wipe with warm water.

▶ For stubborn dirt or stains, work up a foam with **saddle soap** and rub it in with a sponge in circular motions. Go over the spot again with tap water and apply leather conditioner after it is dry.

▶ Treat **older grease stains** on colorfast leather with **baking soda**. Dip a cloth into hot water, wring it out, sprinkle on a small amount of baking soda, and then carefully rub the grease from the edge toward the middle. Go over it with a warm, moist cloth.

▶ Pour a little **milk** on a clean cloth and dab it on leather to remove marks from a **ballpoint pen**. It should work in most cases.

▶ Try rubbing an **ink spot** with a clean cloth dampened with a little **warm water**. If that doesn't do the trick, carefully treat the stain with a small amount of **turpentine**.

REMOVING STAINS
FROM FULL-GRAIN LEATHER

▶ Sprinkle **fresh grease stains** with **talcum powder**. The powder will absorb the grease, allowing you to simply brush it off. Repeat as needed.

▶ Treat **grease stains** on full-grain leather or deerskin with **fine-grained sandpaper** or a **rubber eraser**. But take care not to rub too long or bear down too hard with sandpaper as you risk damaging the leather.

▶ Remove **water stains** on full-grain leather by allowing them to dry, then roughening them with a **brush**.

Check to see if leather is washable: if water soaks in when you dribble it on an inconspicuous spot, avoid using water to clean it.

Walls

Regular maintenance keeps walls and ceilings clean, and make rooms appear light and airy. Whether walls are painted, paneled, brick, stucco, or wallpapered, keep them in top form to avoid renovations and make all the walls in your home bright and welcoming.

Keeping walls and ceilings dust- and cobweb-free should be part of regular housekeeping chores. Beyond regular maintenance, walls and ceilings with different surfaces require more detailed care.

MAINTENANCE ROUTINE

▶ **Dust** walls and ceilings regularly.

▶ No feather duster? Tie a dust rag to a **broom**.

▶ Spray your feather duster with **water** to help better adhere spiderwebs.

▶ Suck up spiderwebs with the **crevice nozzle** on your vacuum cleaner.

▶ Test all **cleaning products** on an inconspicuous spot before removing stains. This is important because if the product stains the wall and it cannot be removed, at least it will be hidden from view.

▶ If you plan to put up **wallpaper**, go for the **scuff-resistant** variety. This will make cleaning much easier, and will cut down on time spent on maintenance.

▶ If you have to **wet-wash** the walls, be extra safe and shut off the **electricity**.

BRICK

▶ Brush brick walls occasionally with a **scrub brush** and sweep up loosened grout.

▶ Do not **wet-wash** brick walls—the moisture will soak into the porous masonry, possibly leading to mildew and potentially other damage.

STUCCO

▶ Dust plaster moldings and decorations regularly, preferably with a **feather duster.** Use a **soft paintbrush** to clean corners and curves.

▶ **Wet-wash** stucco only when necessary. First check that the finish is solid enough, then spray it with a little soap and water so you're able to reach even the cracks. Finally, spray with a small amount of water and dab up all liquid with a dry cloth.

PAINTED SURFACES

▶ Remove dirt or stains on walls painted with **oil paint** with soapy water. Use **turpentine** to carefully dab off ink and grease marks.

▶ Wash **walls painted with latex** with soapy water containing a couple of dashes of **ammonia**, then wipe with water and pat dry. You'll find a soft **scrub sponge** helpful around light switches.

▶ Wipe down walls painted with **lacquer** from top to bottom with a small amount of warm water.

A clean paintbrush works well for dusting hard-to-reach corners on decorative molding.

▶ Never wet-wash **whitewashed walls**; it will take the color off.

▶ Rub fresh stains off **painted walls** or **rugs** with a **rubber eraser** or a fresh piece of **white bread.**

WALLPAPER

▶ In heavy traffic areas such as the kitchen and the stairwell, it's a good idea to coat fabric or paper wall coverings with a **clear glaze** to make them easy to wash. The same applies to a child's room and areas around a light switch. Remember: check the wallpaper for **colorfastness** beforehand. This will save time in the long run.

▶ If a specific **section** of wallpaper is very dirty, it might be easier to simply remove it and replace it with a new piece. Make sure the remaining wallpaper and the patches abut each other, rather than overlapping at the edges.

▶ **Dust textured vinyl wallpaper** before cleaning. Then wipe it with a damp cloth, sponge, or soft brush and warm detergent solution, rinse with water, and dry thoroughly. The key: don't let it get too moist.

▶ Dust **grease stains** on textured wallpaper with **talcum powder,** allow it to work, and brush off the powder. Wipe off any excess powder with a damp cloth or remove with a quick vacuum.

▶ Never **soak fabric** or **cork wallpaper**—they will swell. Instead, carefully wipe them off with a damp cloth. If too much water is applied, pat dry with a clean cloth.

▶ Treat **cork wallpaper** like washable wallpapers if they are sealed with a **matte varnish**. This is one way to avoid the potential problem of soaking cork wallpaper.

▶ Carefully **vacuum** wallpaper made from **grass** or **burlap** on low power and avoid wet-washing them.

PANELING

▶ Don't ever let **waxed surfaces** become too wet. Otherwise treat them as you would waxed floors or furniture.

▶ Wipe **sealed, painted,** or **varnished paneling** with soapy water. Avoid any **abrasive powder,** which can leave scratches.

▶ Treat **wood coated with clear lacquer** once a year with **furniture polish.**

Wash walls using gentle circular strokes with a damp, soft sponge and an all-purpose wall cleaner.

▶ If minor **mold spots** have formed on wood panels, dry them with a blow-dryer and scrub with a soft brush. Finally, polish them with a soft cloth and **furniture polish.** Note that mold can be very dangerous if it grows out of control. Make sure that the room is well-ventilated and be sure to wear a protective face mask. If you are ever in doubt about the severity of the mold, do not hesitate to call in a professional to deal with what can be a serious problem.

▶ Remove layers of old polish with **fine steel wool** and **turpentine**. Rub with the grain of the wood.

removing grease stains from wallpaper

one Place a super-absorbent paper towel on the grease stain or small wax pencil scribble.

two Go over it with a not-too-hot iron for as long as it takes for the spot to disappear. Move the paper around occasionally and replace it if necessary.

three Dab the remaining stain carefully with turpentine, or rub it off with a cloth and some baking soda.

Windows

Proper technique and the right accessories help make this housekeeping chore simple and rewarding. No special cleaning products are required to make and keep your windows clean and streak-free, and keep sills and frames looking like they've just been installed.

When windowpanes are especially dirty, lather them generously with a water and detergent solution and squeegee them free of streaks.

Before the window-cleaning begins, a little prep work is needed to help make the whole job easier. First remove the curtains from the windows and any knickknacks from the windowsills. Also cover sensitive surfaces to protect them from drips. Do yourself a favor, get a real chamois cloth; it absorbs water more quickly and is easily squeezed out. With proper care it will last for years.

LONG-LASTING CHAMOIS

▶ Keep your chamois cloth soft and smooth by using it only with **water**, or solutions made with water and **vinegar** or **alcohol.** Detergents remove the leather's oils and leave it stiff.

▶ Rinse out your chamois with **warm salt water** after every use to keep it soft.

▶ Never **wring out** a chamois cloth. Instead, squeeze it gently, open it up, shake it out, and let it slowly air-dry.

WINDOWSILLS

▶ Apply a **soft soap solution** on windowsills to battle everyday dirt.

▶ Remove **water stains** with a soft cloth moistened with a solution of equal parts **rubbing alcohol** and **tap water.**

WINDOW FRAMES

▶ **Vacuum** the window frame joint with the appropriate nozzle on the vacuum cleaner before starting to clean with liquid.

▶ Wipe wood window frames treated with **clear glaze** or **varnish** with a **damp cloth.** Replace the water frequently, and to get them extra clean, rub them with a solution of equal parts **rubbing alcohol** and **tap water.**

▶ Clean **painted** window frames with a solution of 2 tbsp. (25 mL) of **ammonia** in about 2 cups (500 mL) of **water.**

▶ Clean **wooden** window frames, then **dry** with a soft cloth.

▶ Rub off **flyspecks** on wood frames using a **rough rag** moistened with water. Another option: clean them with a mixture of **reduced-fat milk** and **cold water** in equal proportions.

▶ Stick with **hot, soapy water** for washing **aluminum** or **plastic frames;** scouring powder will scratch the frames.

WINDOWPANES

▶ Clean dirty panes regularly with a **vinegar solution** of 1 quart/liter of warm water and 1 cup (250 mL) of white vinegar. The vinegar dissolves the dirt and keeps flies away.

▶ Clean extremely dirty windowpanes first with **warm dishwater,** then wipe them down with **tap water,** making sure you don't leave streaks.

▶ Add a squirt of **glycerin** to the wash water to help windows resist dust and ensure they won't fog up in winter.

▶ Mix a few drops of **ammonia** with the wash water. This keeps windows from **frosting.**

New stained glass is strong enough to be washed using traditional cleaning methods.

▶ Expel streaks and leftover drips with a lint-free **rag**, **newspaper**, or **chamois cloth**.

▶ When **squeegeeing** windows, moisten the edge of the squeegee to keep it from squeaking and improve contact with the glass.

▶ Polish washed windowpanes with an old pair of **pantyhose** to really bring out the shine.

▶ Clean **small windowpanes** (skylights, louver windows, transom windows) only with a **chamois cloth**: thoroughly wet the chamois in the wash water, squeeze it out, and work from the edge toward the center of the glass. Immediately wipe dry to prevent streaking.

▶ Wash **skylights** when it's raining hard for maximum effect: carefully tilt the wet window and lather it with wash water, then shut it again and let the rain rinse it off.

▶ Rub **dulled** windows or mirrors with **olive** or **linseed oil** to get their shine back. Leave on for an hour, wipe dry with tissue paper, then clean as you would normally.

▶ Eliminate **grease stains** on windowpanes with half an **onion**. The sulfides in the onion are powerful cleaners.

▶ Oust **flyspecks** from glass panes with a clean cloth moistened in **warm black tea**. A couple of squirts of **rubbing alcohol** will also dissolve them, making it quick and easy to wipe them off.

▶ Is there **glazing compound** left on your windowpane from when the glass was installed? The solution: rub it off with a little **ammonia** or **turpentine** on a cotton ball.

▶ Scrape off **stickers** on new panes by first soaking them with warm water and then removing them using a **glass scraper**. If any old, brittle stickers remain, remove them by rubbing with **olive oil** until the pane is clear.

▶ Remove **fresh paint splashes** with **turpentine** or **nail polish remover**. For dried paint, turn to a **glass scraper**, such as those used to clean ceramic stove tops.

SPECIAL CASES

▶ **Modern stained glass** is so strong that it can be cleaned as you would normal glass panes. Take greater care with **old stained glass**: simply wipe it carefully with a damp cloth. If the old glass is actually painted, don't wash it at all or you risk removing the color. Instead, dust the panes with a **soft brush**.

▶ Clean **frosted glass** with **hot vinegar water** to give it a dull sheen; then carefully wipe dry.

▶ Dust **etched glass** with a **soft brush**, and clean the textured side of the glass with a **chamois**. You can simply squeegee the smooth side.

Add half a raw onion to your wash water for gleaming windowpanes.

The Traditional *Kitchen*

Many of us have forgotten about time-honored ways of preparing food—from drying to pickling—that are both nutritious and easy on the pocketbook. Read on for tips from yesteryear that are still useful in today's kitchens.

Bread

Bread is one of the oldest prepared foods. In the past few decades, homemade bread has become a delicacy —especially when it's warm, fragrant, and fresh from the oven. It doesn't take many ingredients, or too much effort, to bake delicous breads in your own home.

A good-quality mixer with appropriate attachments speeds up the bread-making process.

To make bread dough, in addition to flour or whole grains, you need water, salt, and a leavening agent such as yeast, sourdough, or baking powder. As a rule of thumb, the more thoroughly you knead the dough, the looser and finer the crumb. Make sure you give your dough enough time to rise undisturbed at an even temperature of about 72°F (22°C). But keep in mind that it's not the elapsed time that determines when the bread is ready to bake, but rather the volume of the dough; it should be roughly double in size.

Set sourdough bread aside for a day or two; it will taste better and be easier to slice.

BASIC RECIPE FOR WHEAT BREAD

To make wheat bread, you'll need 18 oz. (500 g) wheat flour or wholegrain wheat, ⅔ oz. (20 g) yeast, 1 pinch of sugar, about ¾ cup (175 mL) warm water, and 1 tsp. (5 mL) salt.

▶ Stir 5 tbsp. (75 mL) flour with the crumbled yeast, sugar, and water in a bowl and **let rise** in a warm location for 15–30 minutes.

▶ Sift the remaining flour and salt over it and **knead** until the dough no longer sticks to the side of the bowl.

▶ Knead it a little longer on a flat work surface until the dough feels **elastic** and **dry.**

▶ Shape your dough into a ball and place in a large bowl. Cover with a cloth, and let rise again until it **doubles in volume** (about 30–60 minutes).

▶ After kneading again, form into a **loaf** on a baking sheet and let rise for 30–60 minutes.

▶ Finally, lightly brush the loaf with water and **bake** for about one hour at 400°F (200°C).

SUCCESS WITH DOUGH

▶ Avoid mixing **salt** and **yeast** right away; salt can stunt the activity of yeast.

▶ Add any number of flavorings to your dough according to taste: **coriander, caraway,** or **pepper.** Or try tossing in 2 tbsp. (25 mL) of **sunflower seeds** or **flaxseeds** for a tasty change.

▶ Press firmly with your fingertip on the dough and if the impression remains visible after you remove your finger, you will know your bread is risen and **ready to bake.**

▶ Prevent air bubbles from forming while the dough rises by **punching it down** vigorously before shaping it, then again kneading it carefully and thoroughly with the heels of your hands for a few minutes more.

▶ Use **baking soda** or **baking powder** for leavening quick breads, which don't require long periods of time for rising. But they must be baked in a loaf pan; otherwise, the dough will spread all over the baking sheet.

▶ Make your own **sourdough starter**—dough from an old batch—that is mixed with the bread's traditional ingredients to provide leavening. When making sourdough breads the starter is needed (*see recipe on next page*).

▶ Keep **yeast breads** for one to three days, as they taste best fresh.

BASIC RECIPE FOR HEARTY RYE BREAD

When baking with dark flour, yeast alone won't do the trick; you will need to either buy a pre-made sourdough starter or make one yourself to use as a leavening agent. To make a sourdough starter for rye bread:

▶ Dissolve ⅔ oz. (20 g) yeast in 2 cups (500 mL) warm water and mix in about 10 oz. (300 g) of wholegrain rye. The starter foams as it ferments and must remain covered and undisturbed for three days at room temperature.

▶ Mix together the other ingredients: 10 oz. (300 g) **wholegrain rye** and 14–16 oz. (400–450 g) **wheat flour**, 1 tbsp. (15 mL) **salt**, and 1 tsp. (5 mL) **ground coriander** or **caraway.**

▶ Stir together 3½ oz. (100 g) sourdough starter, 1½ oz. (40 g) yeast, and about 24 oz. (700 mL) water; knead with the flour mixture, and then **let the dough rise** for about two hours at room temperature.

▶ Add some tasty **ground nuts.** This will make the **wholegrain** bread not only tastier, but also a little lighter.

▶ Knead your dough thoroughly once again after it has spent a night in the **refrigerator**. Shape it into loaves, and **let it rise** for one to two hours.

▶ **Bake** for 20 minutes at 425°F (220°C), then reduce the temperature to 375°F (190°C) and bake for another 60 minutes.

▶ Thump the **underside** of the bread to see if it's done; it should sound muffled and hollow.

▶ Let sourdough bread **cool down** in the turned-off oven for best results.

▶ Sourdough breads **taste better** when they are a day or two old. Rye-mix breads keep for 8–10 days, pure rye breads even longer.

Rising dough should be placed it in a bowl large enough to protect it from a draft.

BAKING TIPS

▶ Bake dough within **three hours** to avoid having the dough collapse**.**

▶ Form **rolls** by shaping the dough into a fairly thick rope, cutting it into pieces, and rolling each one into a smooth ball with your cupped hand.

▶ Place a **bowl of water** in the oven during baking to make bread and rolls crisp (but not hard).

▶ Brush your loaves with a little **water** or **egg yolk** for an attractive shine**.**

a money-saving *hint*

Sliced bread stays fresher longer when you wrap it in a cloth. It also helps to put a peeled potato or half an apple in the bread box to keep bread moist. Before warming up day-old rolls, brush them with water or milk to make them wonderfully crisp again.

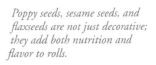

Poppy seeds, sesame seeds, and flaxseeds are not just decorative; they add both nutrition and flavor to rolls.

Cold Storage

A cellar or cool pantry was once the only place to store produce to eat later during the cold winter months. Nowadays it's still worthwhile buying fresh, seasonal fruit and veg when plentiful and inexpensive. And some of yesterday's cold storage methods still work best.

Aside from saving much-valued space in the refrigerator, putting fresh food in cold storage helps guarantee a healthy diet and acts as a backup in case anything prevents you from buying fresh food at the supermarket.

THE BEST CONDITIONS

For storing supplies, all you need is a cool, well-ventilated basement storage room or a frost-free garage. The optimal ambient temperature is 39–41°F (4–5°C) with humidity of 80–90%.

▶ Place one or more **buckets filled with water** in your cellar, if it isn't damp enough.

▶ Leave a box of **damp sand** in cement spaces that are dry and warm.

▶ Before storing supplies, wash your shelves with **baking soda and water** or **vinegar** to keep mold from spreading.

▶ Store only **undamaged fruits and vegetables**. When you're stocking up on Chinese cabbage, endive, white and red cabbage, as well as savoy, be sure to remove all rotting leaves and any that appear unhealthy in order to avoid illness.

▶ **Check fruits and vegetables regularly** during storage. Immediately remove spoiled items, and clean the storage space if needed.

STORING FRUIT IN THE CELLAR

With the exception of apples, pears, and grapes, fruits are not suited to long winter storage in the cellar because they suffer cold damage starting at 50°F (10°C). Storing fruit in the same area as fermenting liquor or pickles in a barrel will also damage the fruit.

▶ Place **apples** individually with stems up on wooden shelves, or wrap them individually with tissue paper and store in wooden boxes. Make sure the fruit doesn't touch and that there are no rotten ones; one bad apple really will spoil the whole bunch. Apples should last for about six months or so after the harvest depending on the variety.

▶ Treat **pears** in the same way. Store them while they are still firm. As soon as they yield to slight thumb pressure on the stem end or begin to change color, move them to a warmer place; they will reach their full ripeness in a couple of days.

▶ You can keep **grapes** for a fairly long time as long as they can hang freely. First pluck out the rotten grapes and close the cut surface on the stem airtight with candle or sealing wax.

SQUIRREL AWAY VEGGIES

▶ Store **potatoes** in a wooden box that is well-ventilated on the top and bottom, or in a wire basket. Keep them in the dark, as light will produce green spots on the potatoes that are harmful to your health. Throw out any affected spuds. Potatoes can withstand temperatures down to 35°F (2°C); if it gets colder, cover them with straw or hay. Unfortunately, when potatoes are stored improperly they lose their vitamin C content.

▶ Cover **carrots** with damp sand in a box to give them prolonged life.

▶ Hang **squash** in a pair of old (clean) pantyhose to decrease the strain of their own weight.

Nuts can be kept for many months in a breathable bag in a dark, cool place.

Store carrots and other root vegetables in boxes filled with sand. Make sure you remove all leaves first.

▶ Tie **cabbages** together by the stem and hang them on wires or beams with the heads hanging downward if possible. They can also be stored on wooden shelves with good ventilation, but be sure to check them frequently and remove damaged leaves.

▶ Store **endives** and **root vegetables** in a bed of sand on the floor.

▶ **Tomatoes** stay fresh for a long time when you place them on boards on the floor without touching one another. In the fall you can even pull up green tomatoes along with the stalks, tie the roots together, and hang them in a cool, well-ventilated area. In time, you'll have vine-ripened tomatoes.

STORAGE IN THE YARD

If your cellar is too small and you don't have a garage, store produce in the yard. A shady place near your house is the best choice.

▶ Carefully place small amounts of vegetables or fruit in wooden boxes and **bury them in a pit** right under the surface of the yard.

▶ Line the box with **fine-mesh wire** to keep mice and other creatures out.

▶ The **moisture** in the ground keeps the produce fresh. Apples, carrots, and celery can be stored for many months.

MANY PREFER DRY CONDITIONS

Produce such as garlic, onions, and citrus can't tolerate moisture, making them unsuitable for storage in the cellar.

▶ After the harvest, dry **onions** on a wire rack in a patch of sun for a few days, then hang them individually, head-down, in old pantyhose with knots in between to keep them separate. Store in a cool place and, when you need one, just snip it off.

▶ Dry and store **garlic** in the same way. Never store garlic in the fridge or a sealed plastic container. In both cases, the garlic will quickly soften, and possibly develop mold.

▶ When wrapped in tissue paper and stored in cardboard boxes, **oranges** and **clementines** can last a long time in a cool and dark environment. Check them periodically and remove any that begin to rot.

▶ Choose oranges that are heavy for their size; these are full of juice and will not dry out as much during storage.

good to know

THEY DON'T ALL GO TOGETHER
Be careful with certain combinations in the storage area: apples, pears, and tomatoes should be stored far away from other fruits and vegetables. They give off ethylene, which hastens the ripening of other fruits and vegetables. Cabbage and lettuce, for example, can quickly develop leaf yellowing and rot, and carrots take on a bitter taste.

Cooking Tips

Do you steer clear of cheaper cuts of meat because you're worried they'll be tough and dry? In less-affluent times, people were frequently more creative about using the entire animal. They developed a multitude of ways to turn cheaper cuts into menu magic.

Whether your meal is fried or roasted, broiled or braised, these helpful hints can make your kitchen experience easier, less time-consuming, and less taxing on your wallet.

BRAISING, STEWING, OR FRYING

Braising is a good way to turn less expensive cuts of meat into delicious meals. You first brown the meat on all sides and then add a little simmering liquid such as broth, wine, or stock.

▶ Use about 1 tbsp. (15 mL) liquid at a time and scrape up the flavorful bits on the bottom of the pan. Keeping the **amount of fluid to a minimum** helps it retain the meat's flavor.

▶ Whether braising or stewing, **sear meat before cooking** to lock in moisture and flavor.

▶ If you want a thicker stew, dredge your meat in **flour** before browning.

Steaming is a quick and easy way to prepare seafood and vegetables.

▶ Before frying **flank steak**, marinate the meat for at least several hours and **cut across the grain** when serving.

▶ Bring out the tenderness in **ribs** by **parboiling** the meat before grilling.

THRIFTY FISH CHOWDER

Some fish are expensive, but a creamy fish chowder with plenty of hearty potato chunks is a good way to make it go further.

▶ Cut two strips of **bacon** into ¼ in. (5 mm) cubes and sauté in a soup pot until the fat is liquefied (3–4 minutes).

▶ Add ½ large **onion,** chopped and cook over medium heat until it's translucent. Then add 2½ tbsp. (35 mL) flour and stir vigorously until the fat is evenly browned, but not burned.

▶ Slowly whisk in the **stock**, making sure there are no lumps, and keep stirring until the mixture comes to a boil. Then add ¼ cup (50 mL) wine.

▶ Add ½ lb. (250 g) **potatoes** (scrubbed, peeled, and diced) and simmer 15 minutes or so, or until you can easily pierce them with a knife.

Lamb chops and steaks turn out especially tender when they're basted or marinated with oil before frying.

▶ Stir in ¾ cup (175 mL) already-warm **light cream** and bring the chowder back to a simmer before stirring in ½ lb. (250 g) haddock filets or other white fish. Heat gently for 5 minutes until the fish is cooked (don't let it boil). Season with salt and pepper and serve with fresh, crusty bread.

FRYING MEAT, POULTRY, AND FISH

▶ Prevent **fish** from **warping** by cutting the skin on an angle in several places before frying.

▶ Take **meat** from the refrigerator about **30 minutes** before cooking, whether roasting or frying.

▶ **Sautéing** is basically quick-cooking in a small amount of fat. Choose oil with a high smoking point, such as canola or peanut oil.

▶ When **deep-frying,** keep an eye on the temperature; excessively hot grease gives rise to dangerous toxins and excessively cold grease gets soaked up by the food. After cooking, allow deep-fried food to drain briefly on a paper towel.

ROASTING AND BROILING IN THE OVEN

Tender cuts of meat are better suited for roasting or broiling, which allow them to maintain the maximum amount of flavor.

▶ Meat for a nice roast should be **marbled** and have a **rim of fat**. Remove any connective tissue (the silverskin) because it becomes tough at high temperatures.

▶ When turning a roast, avoid **poking** it and losing the juice.

▶ Use the **meat stock** from browning your roast as the basis for gravy.

▶ Insert a **meat thermometer** to determine if the meat is done.

▶ You can also use a **toothpick** or **skewer**: if it feels warm when you pull it out, the meat is still rare; if it's hot, the meat is cooked through.

▶ Roast on a **rack** when possible to allow even heat circulation and browning.

▶ Roast beef or lamb with the **fat side up** to allow natural basting.

▶ Large roasts continue cooking for up to 10 minutes after you take them out of the oven. Let the roast **sit** before carving—the meat stays juicier.

▶ Before **broiling**, marinate lean meat, fish, and vegetables or brush them with oil. Add seasonings before broiling, but salt afterward.

▶ Always baste a **broiler chicken** with its own juices. A mixture of olive oil, lemon, pepper, and garlic gives it a Mediterranean twist.

▶ The drier your **chicken's skin**, the crispier it becomes when cooked—so **pat skin dry** and leave the chicken to sit in your fridge for several hours before cooking, if possible.

▶ You can also insert **seasoned butter** between the skin and the breast meat of the chicken. The technique makes basting unnecessary, and the skin still turns out crispy and the meat tender and juicy.

To seal juices in, brown your roast, then pour in broth and cook in the oven.

Dough Basics

If you're wary of attempting your grandma's favorite recipes because of fear of failure, just follow these tried-and-true tips. Before you begin, read through the entire recipe and preheat the oven. Measure ingredients exactly and follow directions carefully. With a little effort, you can turn out delicious baked goods every time.

The ingredients of a cake batter should be room temperature. Only with a shortcake dough should the butter be cold.

Once you master the art of making dough, there is no limit to what can be prepared in the kitchen. Here is what you need to get started.

TIPS ON BATTER AND DOUGH

▶ Partially **replace butter with oil** or add 1 tbsp. (15 mL) of **vinegar** to cake batter to make cake turn out especially light. To get the same result, substitute **mineral water** for half of the **milk**.

▶ Baking pans **slightly warmed** in the oven are easier to grease.

▶ Before baking, poke **yeast**, **shortening**, and **puff pastry doughs** several times with a fork to keep them from forming bubbles.

▶ After rising, **yeast dough** should no longer stick to your fingers when you knead it. **Shortcake dough** should be smooth after kneading; if it crumbles, it is too dry.

▶ **Don't open the oven** in the first 20 minutes, or your cake may fall.

▶ A cake rises beautifully when you place a heat-resistant container of **water** into the oven with it.

▶ To test whether your cake is done, pierce the dough with a **toothpick**. If no dough clings to it when you pull it out, the cake is ready to come out of the oven.

▶ Cakes should never be **cooled too quickly** or they may collapse. Leave them in the oven with the door open until they cool.

CLASSIC BAKING POWDER BISCUITS

These simple biscuits take just minutes to make and don't require extra time for leavening. Eat them warm from the oven with butter and jam.

▶ Sift 2 cups (500 mL) **sifted flour.** Add 2 tsp. (10 mL) baking powder and ½ tsp. (2 mL) salt and sift again.

▶ Cut in 4 tbsp. (60 mL) **butter** or **shortening** with a pastry cutter (or two knives) until you have pea-sized crumbs.

▶ Gradually add ¾ cup (175 mL) **milk**, stirring until a loose dough forms.

▶ Turn out onto a lightly floured board and **knead lightly** for about 30 seconds.

▶ Roll out your dough to about ½ in. (2.5 cm) thick and **cut out shapes** with 2 in. (5 cm) cookie cutter.

▶ **Bake** on an ungreased baking sheet in preheated 400°F (200°C) oven for 12–15 minutes.

BASIC BREAD

Bread dough isn't complicated, but it needs plenty of time to rise. Here is a fool-proof recipe for delicious home-baked bread.

▶ Combine 2¼ tsp. (11 mL) active dry yeast, 1 tsp. (5 mL) sugar, and ½ cup (125 mL) lukewarm water, and **let stand** 5 minutes, then stir thoroughly.

▶ Heat 1 cup (250 mL) **milk** to lukewarm. Stir in 2 tbsp. (25 mL) **butter**, 2 tbsp. (25 mL) **sugar**, 1½ tsp. (7 mL) **salt**, and ½ cup (125 mL) **warm water.**

Use a pastry cutter to cut butter into your cookie batter; it helps other ingredients combine.

Use your fingers to gently press your pie dough in the pie plate and eliminate any air pockets.

▶ Add **milk mixture** and 2 cups (500 mL) **bread flour** to dissolved yeast mixture. Beat with wooden spoon or electric mixer until smooth and elastic. Then gradually stir in another 2½ cups (625 mL) flour to make a soft dough that doesn't cling to the sides of the bowl.

▶ Turn dough out on floured board and roll into a ball. **Knead** dough until smooth, elastic, and no longer sticky (for about 10 minutes), adding more flour if needed.

▶ Place dough in a greased bowl. Cover with a dish towel and **let rise** in a warm place (75°–85°F/ 24°–29°C) until doubled (45–60 minutes).

▶ **Punch down** dough and turn it out onto lightly floured board, divided into two portions. Then cover again and let stand for 10 minutes before shaping two loaves.

▶ Place loaves **seam-side-down** in two greased loaf pans. Cover with a dish towel and let rise again in a warm place until dough is 1½ in. (3 cm) above the top of pan in the center (45–60 minutes).

▶ **Bake** at 400°F (200°C) on lower oven rack for 25–30 minutes. Remove from the pans immediately and cool on wire racks.

▶ *Note: Keep in mind that yeast dough is sensitive and cannot withstand drafts or cold, so keep your doors and windows closed while it rises.*

▶ *Note: Yeast dough can store in the refrigerator for one day. In the freezer it will keep up to five months.*

SHORTBREAD DOUGH

Work shortbread dough with cold hands to keep it from sticking to your fingers.

▶ **Knead** about 1¼ cups (300 mL) sifted flour, ²/₃ cup (150 mL) sugar, 1 egg, and ¾ cup (175 mL)

butter by hand to form a smooth dough. Shape into a ball, wrap up in foil, and **refrigerate**.

▶ Don't knead the dough for too long. If it gets too crumbly, add 1 tbsp. (15 mL) **cream cheese**.

▶ Sprinkle the dough with flour, knead thoroughly again, and **roll it out thin.** Put it onto a greased baking sheet sprinkled with flour and **bake** in an oven heated to 400–425°C (200–220°C) for 10–15 minutes.

▶ Shortbread dough will keep in the refrigerator for **about a week**. Frozen dough should thaw in the refrigerator.

SPONGE CAKE

When making sponge cake dough, make sure the sugar is thoroughly dissolved. Your grandmother needed serious elbow grease for that task, but nowadays an electric mixer makes quick work of it.

▶ Separate four **eggs**. Beat together 1 cup (250 mL) **sugar** with the egg yolks until very light and add 4 tbsp. (60 mL) **water** and 1 tsp. (5 mL) **grated lemon rind**.

▶ Sift together 1 cup (250 mL) **cake and pastry flour** and 1 tbsp. (15 mL) **baking powder**. Add to the batter.

▶ Beat the egg whites until **stiff peaks** form; fold gently into the batter.

▶ Put the prepared dough into a greased baking pan sprinkled with bread crumbs and fill it **no more than two-thirds full**. Bake in a 325°F (160°C) preheated oven for 30 minutes.

▶ *Note: Raisins, currants, and chocolate chips won't sink so much if you sprinkle them with flour before adding them to the cake dough.*

yeast dough

oひと Add 4 cups (1 liter) sieved flour to a bowl; form a crater in the middle.

two Mix 1½ oz. (40 g) yeast and 1 cup (250 mL) milk. Stir in 4 tbsp. (60 mL) flour and a pinch of sugar. Pour mixture into the crater.

three Cover the bowl with a dish towel and let rise in a warm place for 30 minutes.

Drying Food

Drying food is a time-honored method of preserving a variety of fruits, vegetables, and herbs so they can be enjoyed in winter well past harvest. This natural form of preservation concentrates and enhances flavors.

Zucchini Fries

2 medium zucchini, cut into ¼ in. (5 mm) slices

½ cup (125 mL) seasoned dry bread crumbs

⅛ tsp. (0.5 mL) ground black pepper

2 tbsp. (25 mL) grated Parmesan cheese

1 tsp. (5 mL) curry powder

2 egg whites

Preheat the oven to 475°F (245°C).

In one small bowl, stir together the bread crumbs, pepper, Parmesan cheese, and curry powder. Place the egg whites in a separate bowl; lightly stir the egg whites using a fork or whisk. Dip zucchini slices into the egg whites, then coat them in the bread crumb mixture. Place zucchini on a greased baking sheet.

Bake for 5 minutes, then turn the fries and bake for another 5-10 minutes, until browned and crispy.

When drying foods, warm air is used to remove the water and harmful bacteria that eventually cause spoilage. Removing the water also concentrates the flavor and aroma in the skin of fruits and vegetables. Dried fruits and vegetables have to be checked regularly for mold, as the skin still contains a fair amount of water—unless they were dried at high temperature, which unfortunately sacrifices taste. After drying, small plums are usually little more than skin and pit, and it is generally difficult to separate the pit from the skin. You're better off choosing larger, late plum varieties and halving the fruit so it dries faster.

WHAT CAN BE DRIED?

▶ Dry only high-quality, fresh, ripe produce, preferably **organic**.

▶ Harvest produce for drying only on **dry, sunny days.** Wet produce decays quickly and takes extra time and effort to dry.

▶ Pick **herbs** in the late morning or early afternoon, when their water content is lowest.

▶ **Windfall fruit** isn't suitable for drying.

▶ **Stone fruits** and **seed fruits** are easy to dry, although you may wish to peel seed fruits.

▶ Avoid the tedious job of picking one **berry** at a time by drying the entire cluster; the berries will practically fall off by themselves.

▶ Look for a **full, ripe aroma** with all berry varieties—otherwise the dried fruits won't have any taste.

▶ The aroma of **herbs** changes when they dry; many, like dill, chervil, tarragon, basil, and cress lose their scent altogether.

PREPARING GOODS FOR DRYING

▶ Compare the items in a batch of goods. They should be of comparable **size** and **thickness** so they dry at an even rate.

▶ Place fruit into **lemon water** made from 1 tsp. (5 mL) lemon juice and about 2 cups (500 mL) water immediately after cutting it so that the fruit does not lose its color.

▶ Dissolve 1 cup (250 mL) sugar in the same amount of water to make, alternatively, a **sugar bath.** Bring the mixture to a boil and let cool before briefly immersing the fruit.

▶ Always lay out produce for drying in a single layer, with the **cut side** facing up.

▶ Pit, blanche, and skin **apricots** and **peaches**

▶ **Beans** need to be blanched in advance in order to retain their color and aroma. You can also blanch other vegetables before drying.

▶ Thread **apple slices, mushrooms,** and **chili peppers** onto a cotton thread and hang to dry.

▶ Dry the plucked leaves of **herbs**, or hang the stems in bunches and pick the leaves off after drying.

AIR DRYING

▶ Dry in the fresh air or in an attic during **hot, dry months.** Arrange the produce to be dried on trays or, even better, on gauze stretched over a wood frame and covered with muslin.

▶ **Allow air to circulate freely** around the produce during the drying process.

▶ Drying takes **two to three days** outdoors; in the attic, **up to two weeks.**

▶ If **no juice** seeps from the fruit when you break it into pieces, it's dry and you can then store it away in containers.

ACCELERATED DRYING IN THE OVEN

▶ Place your produce **directly onto the oven rack** when oven-drying (baking sheets don't work well because they interfere with air circulation). Prop the oven door just slightly ajar with a cooking spoon to allow the moisture to escape.

▶ Place a layer of **parchment paper** between the rack and the produce to be dried. Don't use tinfoil since fruit acids can attack metal.

▶ Dry fruits and vegetables at a maximum of 140°F (60°C); because of their essential oils, herbs should be dried at no higher than 95°F (35°C). The **lower the temperature**, the fewer vitamins are lost in drying.

▶ **Turn** the produce once during the drying process, and take the opportunity to put the rack back into the oven in a different direction to allow for even heat distribution.

▶ **Mushrooms** are dry when they look wrinkled and feel leathery.

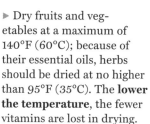

Tie herbs such as bay leaf and rosemary in bundles and hang them to dry in a well-ventilated location.

Produce on the top grate of a food dryer dries more slowly than on the shelves below, making occasional redistribution necessary.

Mushrooms with a relatively low water content, such as yellow boletuses, are good for drying. When ground up, they can be used as seasoning.

Entertaining

Stressing out about your next get-together? Preparation is key. Don't be intimidated; whether you're planning a cocktail party, a formal dinner, or a cozy reunion with old friends, the better prepared you are as a host, the greater your party will be.

Preparations should begin long before the day of the party. How will you invite people? What will you need? And when will you do the shopping?

BEFORE THE PARTY

▶ For a small circle of friends, an **invitation by phone** is fine. For larger or more formal events, a **written invitation** makes the occasion a little more special.

▶ Think about your **needs** well before the occasion: for a fairly large guest list, will you need bistro tables where people can stand, plus additional glasses or silverware? Also, you can rent or buy **folding chairs and tables** at a reasonable price and enhance them with tablecloths and chair coverings.

▶ Once you have your shopping list ready, pick up your **drinks** and **non-perishable foods** a week or two before the party to reduce last-minute stress. **Perishables** should be bought two to three days before the party and stored in the refrigerator.

▶ You can make **place cards** and **table decorations** before the party, as long as you're not using fresh flowers.

MEAL PLANNING

▶ Take into account the season and the number and types of courses you're serving when preparing a menu. The **more courses** you plan, the **smaller the portions** and the lighter the individual menu items should be.

▶ Make small, easy-to-grab appetizers for a **cocktail party**, since people usually have only one hand free.

▶ For parties of six people or more, **avoid pan-frying** so that you're not chained to the kitchen—opt instead for a roast, stewed meat, baked fish, or poultry.

▶ Avoid making dishes for the **first time** when entertaining. This is especially true for people with less cooking experience.

▶ Lighten your workload on the day of the party by planning to serve food that can be prepared one to two days in advance. **Soups**, many **desserts**, and **salad dressings** can be kept in the refrigerator until guests arrive.

THE DAY OF THE PARTY

▶ Pace yourself on the day of the party. A special **checklist** will help.

▶ **Set and decorate the table** early rather than later. You never know what hurdles you may encounter. You can even do it the night before.

▶ Have **bowls and plates** at the ready in the kitchen, and keep **serving utensils** near the table.

▶ Make sure the **drinks, glasses,** and **cold snacks** are on the tables before guests arrive when throwing a cocktail party.

▶ Open **red wines** at least two hours before the meal so that their flavors can develop.

▶ Take **cheese** for a cheese platter out of the refrigerator one to two hours before serving it to enhance the flavors and textures.

▶ **Light your candles** shortly before guests arrive and check one last time that everything is ready.

A successful family party includes a menu with something for all ages.

GARNISHING FOODS

Delight your guests and stimulate their appetites with creative garnishes made from a variety of fruits and vegetables, eggs, and cheese.

▶ Make **tomato baskets.** Cut two long slices across the top of a tomato so that a small "handle" remains across the center. of your basket, remove the core and cut the base flat to make a solid stand. Stuff tomato with meat, vegetable, rice, and/or cheese mixtures.

▶ Peel fine strips from raw, peeled **carrots** and put them in a bowl of ice water. Put the bowl in the refrigerator and let sit for a couple of hours. Remove the bowl from the refrigerator just before presentation, drain the carrots, and pat dry with a paper towel or clean cloth.

▶ Cut funny shapes out of **hard-boiled eggs** or pieces of **cheese** with a small, pointed knife.

▶ Make four evenly-spaced vertical cuts into the top of a cleaned and trimmed **radish,** then put it into cold water; it will open up like a rose.

WHEN THE GUESTS ARRIVE

▶ Greet the first guests with a **pre-dinner drink** and a few **hors d'oeuvres.** Then, take the time to chat until everyone has arrived. This should break the ice for guests who may not know one another. If you have enough time, introduce guests to each other. This will help them start their own conversations and give you the opportunity to prepare more hors d'oeuvres, as well as the much-needed time to put the finishing touches on meal preparation.

Pour wine into a carafe at least two hours before serving.

▶ Before serving dinner, **warm your plates in the oven** for 5 minutes to keep the food from cooling off too quickly during the meal. Be careful that the plates are not too hot when serving.

▶ Cover warmed-up **bread** with a clean dish towel to keep the heat in.

▶ Leave the glass on the table and hold the bottle **above the rim of the glass** without touching it when pouring drinks.

▶ Fill wine glasses only **one-third full** so that the aroma of a good wine will open up properly.

A cheese and fruit platter is an eye-catching centerpiece that allows guests to serve themselves.

Food Safety

Kitchen hygiene is just as important for home cooks as it is for restaurant chefs. Harmful bacteria can multiply on food prep surfaces and equipment, causing your food to spoil and endangering your health.

Cleanliness in the kitchen begins with you. Wash your hands with soap and water before working or cooking, and between individual prep stages.

IMPORTANT RULES

▶ Always wash **kitchen utensils** in hot soapy water between prep stages.

▶ **Plastic cutting boards** are more hygienic than wooden ones—germs can settle into the cracks in wooden boards.

▶ Use **two different cutting boards** for raw and cooked foods.

▶ Wash or replace **dishcloths, dish towels,** and **sponges** frequently because bacteria reproduce explosively in warm, moist environments.

▶ Maintain the cold chain: Pick **frozen and refrigerated foods** up last at the supermarket. Once you get home, put them in the fridge or freezer before putting your other groceries away.

▶ Don't leave **raw foods or leftovers** at room temperature for any length of time, or germs will spread and possibly make you sick.

▶ Take out the **garbage** regularly.

Wash chicken thoroughly before preparation to help prevent salmonella.

WHERE SPECIAL CARE IS REQUIRED

▶ Be careful when preparing **meat, fish, poultry,** and **eggs** to ensure harmful bacteria won't have a chance to breed.

▶ When thawing meat, fish, or poultry, place it on a plate in the fridge, **unwrapped but covered**. Discard the liquid from thawing, as it may contain harmful bacteria. Thoroughly wash the meat under running water and prepare immediately.

▶ Cook **meat, hamburger,** and **fresh sausages** all the way through; the core temperature in the meat must be 160°F (70°C) for at least 10 minutes to kill off salmonella.

▶ Use only very fresh **eggs** for dishes requiring raw eggs, and store the prepared egg dish for no more than 24 hours in the refrigerator.

▶ **Shellfish** should be cooked on the day of purchase. Wash thoroughly before cooking and follow the proper cooking times.

Raw meat requires special care. Hamburger and some seafood should be prepared the same day it's bought.

Freezing

The invention of the freezer revolutionized food storage and made it possible to keep nearly any food item for an extended period, making it easy to whip up a favorite meal or snack, no matter the season.

Peas are one of the best vegetables for freezing. They taste nearly as good as when fresh.

Foods meant for the freezer should be fresh, or in the case of cooked foods, should be packaged up and put into the freezer right after they cool down. Never re-freeze foods that have already been frozen and thawed.

THE RIGHT WAY TO FREEZE

▶ Use only **sturdy bags, plastic containers, aluminum foil pans,** and **special freezer containers** for freezing.

▶ Never fill a plastic container to the top with sauce, soup, or other liquids. They will **expand** and lift the lid or split the container—and cause a spill in the freezer.

▶ Fill **freezer bags** only partway so that the contents freeze faster and the bags are easier to stack.

▶ Prevent **freezer burn** by getting as much air as possible out of the bags before sealing the bags and storing in the freezer.

▶ It's best to freeze **multiple small amounts** and thaw packages as needed. This will decrease wastage, as once frozen food has been thawed, it has to be consumed or thrown out, not frozen again.

WHICH FOODS TO FREEZE AND HOW TO DO IT

▶ **Meat portions** should be no more than 4 in. (10 cm) thick and weigh no more than about 5½ lb (2.5 kg). Depending on the fat content, meat can be frozen for 6–12 months. **Lean meat** lasts the longest, because fat gradually becomes rancid at low temperatures.

▶ Place a piece of **foil** between sliced meats to keep them from sticking together. They will keep for two months in the freezer.

▶ Freeze only **freshly-caught, raw fish** that has been scaled, cleaned, and washed in advance. Use for up to six months.

▶ Blanche **vegetables** (see the box below) to reduce the danger of **freezer burn.** Blanched vegetables will keep in the freezer for up to 10 months.

▶ **Mushrooms, red cabbage,** and **legumes** become even easier to digest after being frozen. They lose the substances that often lead to flatulence.

▶ Freeze **berries** on a baking sheet, then drop them into bags. Fruit can be kept for up to 12 months in the freezer.

▶ **Shortcake pastry** can be frozen either raw or baked. As for yeast dough, allow it to rise once before freezing.

▶ **Bread** and **rolls** are easy to freeze and will keep for three months. If you freeze **sliced bread,** it can be defrosted as needed.

WHAT THINGS SHOULD NOT BE PUT INTO THE FREEZER?

▶ **Raw or cooked eggs** can't be frozen. Egg yolk and beaten egg white can, however, be frozen in appropriate plastic containers.

▶ **Milk products** don't belong in the freezer, the one exception being **cheese.**

▶ Keep **exotic fruit** away from the freezer. When exposed to extreme cold, **bananas** turn brown and **citrus fruits** get spots.

▶ Avoid freezing water-heavy fruits and vegetables such as **tomatoes, potatoes,** and **onions,** which also take on an unappetizing color or become soft.

▶ **Radishes** lose their taste and their typical crispy quality. **Leaf lettuce** collapses when frozen.

blanching vegetables

one Bring 5–10 quarts/liters of water to a boil, then dunk prewashed vegetables in the boiling water.

two Remove the veggies from the boiling water after 2–3 minutes and place them in a cold-water bath.

three Let drip-dry thoroughly before packing.

Grains

All around the globe, people draw nourishment from seven main grain varieties: wheat, rye, barley, rice, corn, millet, and oats. But in recent years, we've also happily rediscovered traditional whole grains like bulgur, spelt, rye, and quinoa.

Spelt is hardier than wheat and can withstand harsher climate conditions. It contains little gluten, so it is more digestible for some people.

Grains can be eaten either in their whole form (whole grain), crushed, or ground. With whole grains, only the hull is removed; with refined grains, the germ layer is removed as well. Whole grains are a better choice because they have a very high fiber content.

STORING GRAINS

▶ Protect grains against moisture and insects by storing them in **cool, dark places** in **clean, airtight containers**.

▶ Store whole grains in the **refrigerator** for up to four months; refined grains last in the **pantry** for up to a year.

PREPARING AND COOKING GRAINS

▶ Rinse grains thoroughly before cooking to remove **dirt** and **dust particles.** Continue to rinse until the water is no longer cloudy, and throw away any off-color grains.

▶ With the exception of rice and millet, most grain varieties need to **soak** to make them easier to digest. Add grains and water to a pot in a 1:2 ratio, and gently simmer. Soak the grains until they are softer and swollen to about double their original size.

▶ Strain any **excess liquid** that is not absorbed, and save it for cooking later; it contains many valuable nutrients.

▶ **Roast grains in the oven** before cooking them to make them easier to digest and faster to cook later on. Cover the grains with water in a bowl and soak for about 12 hours. Then spread them on a baking sheet, let them dry thoroughly, and put them into an oven heated to 160°F (70°C). Leave the oven door cracked a bit and stir the grains occasionally to ensure that they are evenly cooked, and to prevent them from burning.

▶ Constantly **stir grains** during preparation, as many types tend to stick to the bottom of pots.

▶ After cooking, **allow grains to sit** briefly in the covered pot, then **fluff** them with a fork as you would a pot of rice.

▶ Cook grains ahead of time. Warm up previously-cooked grains in the **microwave** in just a minute or two; add a sprinkle of water, cover with microwave-safe plastic wrap, and fluff them again when the cooking time is up.

A small hand mill allows you to grind as much grain as you wish.

VARIOUS GRAIN TYPES

▶ In northern climates, **wheat** and its subspecies, such as **rye** and **oats**, are most common.

▶ **Spelt** is a protein-rich grain that makes a particularly robust pasta, gives bread a nutty taste, and is also good as a side dish and in stews.

▶ **Whole wheat kernels** (wheatberries) should be presoaked and then cooked, but they make a tasty rice substitute and can add crunch to a salad and a nutty flavor to chili or stews.

▶ **Rye** is high in fiber and low in gluten. It can be made into flour for bread or served in flakes as a breakfast grain (like oats).

▶ Because of its low gluten content, **barley flour** is unsuitable for baking. But you can make tasty soups, stews, and pilafs with whole barley.

▶ **Millet** is one of the oldest grain varieties. Use the kernels like rice or incorporate them into a salad. Bread made with millet flour is particularly crispy.

▶ From a nutritional standpoint, **oats** are one of the most valuable grains in northern climates, mainly because they contain a protein and fat that are good for you and easy to digest. Oatmeal, oat bran, and oat flour are made from oats.

▶ **Bulgur** (a form of wheat) can replace rice in most recipes, thicken soups and stews, and be used in salads and breads, even desserts.

▶ Once called "the gold of the Incas," protein-rich **quinoa** has a fluffy, somewhat crunchy texture that makes it a wonderful rice substitute or wheat-free alternative to bulgur in tabbouleh and other salads.

BREAKFAST GRANOLA

Swiss-style muesli is a very healthy breakfast food. It's easy to make and you can modify the ingredients according to taste.

▶ Soften 6 tbsp. (90 mL) of **flaked grains** (rolled oats, rye and/or other) in ¾ cup (175 mL) water overnight, then thoroughly stir in 6 tbsp. (90 mL) **milk** or **soy milk** and the juice from 2 **lemons**.

▶ Grate 2 **apples** finely and mix them with the grain flakes. Add **sugar** to taste and 2–3 tbsp. (25–45 mL) of **grated nuts.**

▶ You can vary the ingredients depending on the **season**, replacing the apples with other fruits and substituting **yogurt** or **rice beverage** for the liquid.

▶ If you want to replace flakes with whole grains, stir the grains in with the liquid and **let the muesli steep** for at least four hours.

	good to know	
SOAKING AND COOKING TIMES		
VARIETY	COOKING TIME SOAKING TIME	
Millet	5–15 minutes 10–20 minutes	
Bulgur	2 minutes none	
Spelt	30–45 minutes 30–45 minutes	
Barley	30–45 minutes 30–60 minutes	
Rye	30–45 minutes 30–60 minutes	
Quinoa	15 minutes none	

A healthy diet should include fiber-rich whole grains, fruits, and vegetables.

Herbs

Herbs add a dash of color and flavor to food, and reduce the amount of salt needed for seasoning. They also contribute nutritional value in the form of minerals and vitamins. Go lighter on herbs with strong flavors, and add tender green herbs to a dish just before serving.

Herbs quickly lose their flavor when not handled properly. Process them quickly after they've been picked or purchased, and always chop the tender leaves with care.

HANDLING HERBS

▶ Chop herbs on a **moistened wood** or **plastic cutting board.** The flavors get lost in the wood of a dry cutting board.

▶ Harvest herbs at **midday,** when their essential oils are most intense.

▶ Wrap herbs in a **damp dish towel**; they will keep in your refrigerator's vegetable crisper for one to three days.

▶ **Dry**, **freeze** or add herbs to **oil** for longer storage.

THE MOST COMMON KITCHEN HERBS

▶ No herb is more ubiquitous than **parsley.** It is used to season soups, stews, casseroles, salads, pasta, and potato dishes. Just toss in a sprig near the end of the cooking time, or tear up the leaves with your fingers.

▶ Flavorful **basil** has a pungent taste that works well in sweet and spicy foods like stir-fries and spaghetti sauces. Simply tear it apart or cut it into strips to add to salads and marinades, or blend it in a food processor to make pesto.

▶ **Cilantro** qualifies as one of the most widely used herbs in the world. Its strong flavor adds a boost to southwestern, Asian, Latin American, and Middle Eastern cuisine. Sprinkle the fresh leaves on a finished dish.

▶ **Rosemary** has an astringent, clean scent and tastes great in Mediterranean cooking. Add the needle-like leaves to lamb, wild game, and pork, or use the stripped branches as a kind of skewer to grill meat, poultry, or fish.

▶ **Dill** is great with fish, shellfish, vinaigrette, cucumber salad, and of course, with pickles. It tastes strongest in summer. Sprinkle on before serving.

A herb chopper quickly minces delicate herbs and preserves their flavors.

If you don't have a garden, grow herbs in decorative clay pots on the windowsill or the balcony.

▶ **Marjoram** promotes digestion and goes very well with meat dishes and robust summer veggies like eggplant, tomatoes, and red and green bell peppers. It can't be frozen but, when dried, it can be added at any stage of cooking.

▶ **Tarragon** is native to Siberia and North America. It adds a distinctive flavor to vinegar, mustard, and béarnaise sauce, and goes well with poultry and shellfish. The herb's bittersweet and spicy aroma is lost when dried.

▶ Fresh and spicy **chervil** goes in salads, soups, and herb butter, as well as egg and cheese dishes.

▶ **Bay leaves** tend to be used in soups, stews, and spaghetti sauce, but their aromatic flavor is also great with fish and in many East Indian dishes like biryani. Bay leaves stimulate your appetite and also act as a preservative. You usually add the leaves whole.

Divide chopped herbs in an ice cube tray, then fill with water and freeze. Dissolve as needed in soups or sauces.

▶ There are many different varieties of mint, but **spearmint** and **peppermint** are the most frequently used. Mint highlights the fine taste of spring vegetables, peas, green beans, and salads, and adds a fresh, elegant touch to desserts and fruit bowls.

▶ **Oregano** belongs to the same family as **marjoram** and is regularly served up on pizza and in tomato dishes. Use this light, tart herb sparingly—it's easy to go overboard.

▶ Add peppery-tasting **sage** near the end of the cooking time for roast pork and poultry. It also goes well with tomatoes and beans.

▶ **Chives** taste like a combination of onions and leeks. Use the herb to dress up salads, meat broths, vegetable soups, sour cream, potato salads, and mashed potatoes, as well as scrambled eggs. The younger the straws, the more tender the consistency and the more intense the taste.

▶ Use **thyme** in soups and stews, with vegetables, and in casseroles and fish dishes. Fresh **lemon thyme** goes well with fish and poultry.

Jams and Jellies

For many people, a breakfast without a nice jam or jelly would be unthinkable, and nothing beats homemade. Making jam is a fairly simple affair that involves chopping or mashing fruit and boiling it with sugar. Jellies, on the other hand, make use of pure fruit juices.

Sterilized jars with screw tops make fine containers.

Although all fruits contain natural pectin, the trick to getting a jam or jelly to gel lies in striking the proper balance between acids and pectin.

Cleanliness is crucial when processing fruit. Even the tiniest contamination of fruit or utensils could cause the product to go bad.

IMPORTANT TOOLS

▶ In addition to a **cutting board** and **knife,** you need a **scale**, a **large pot**, a **stirring spoon**, and a **skimmer**.

▶ Copper pots are excellent heat conductors, but they react with acids, so a **stainless steel pot** is a better choice.

▶ A **funnel** and **ladle** make it easier to jar your jams and jellies.

FRUITS GEL DIFFERENTLY

In principle, nearly all fruits are good for making jams and jellies. The higher the **pectin** content of the fruit, the shorter the cooking time. Some fruits require you to add pectin in the form of lemon juice, other fruits, or pectin concentrate.

▶ Apples, blackberries, red currants, gooseberries, and citrus fruits are **high in pectin**, so they gel very quickly.

▶ Apricots, raspberries, black currants, yellow plums, nectarines, peaches, and plums have a moderate amount of pectin; a little **lemon juice** helps them gel.

▶ Pineapple, pears, strawberries, elderberries, cherries, pumpkin, and grapes have a **low pectin** content. Add the juice from a **lemon** to these fruits, or combine them with other quick-to-gel fruits that are high in pectin.

MAKING JAMS

▶ Making jam is easy: simply add one part **jam sugar** (also called jelly sugar), a mix of sugar, pectin, and citric acid, to two or three parts fruit.

▶ **Weigh** your washed, cleaned, and minced fruits and put into a very **large pot** so the contents don't boil over.

▶ Cook **harder fruits** such as pineapple, pears, and apples halfway through with little water.

▶ Stir in a little **lemon juice** to preserve the bright colors of the fruits.

If you don't want tiny seeds in strawberry, raspberry, or blackberry jam, strain it after drawing out the juice.

► Add **jam sugar** to the fruit, stir everything thoroughly, and wait a few minutes while the fruits draw out some juice.

► While **stirring continually,** bring the contents to a boil. Nothing should stick to the bottom of the pot and burn.

► Add ½ tsp. (2 mL) of **butter** to the fruit mixture and it won't boil over.

► Simmer the contents for 5–10 minutes, stirring constantly, and use a **skimmer** to scoop out the unwanted foam.

► After the **gel test** (see box at right), depending on the results, either remove the pot from the burner or cook the jam for a few more minutes if it's too runny.

► Immediately pour your prepared jam into **hot, clean jars,** wipe any spilled jam from the rim of the jars, and seal them securely.

► If you stand the jars on their lid for a few moments a **vacuum** forms that will protect the jam from mold.

► You can also make delicious jams and chutneys from **pumpkin, carrots,** and **tomatoes.**

► Rich spices such as **ginger, vanilla,** and **cardamom** can add a unique flavor to jams, and fresh herbs such as **mint** or **lemon balm** also lend a special touch.

MAKING JELLIES

► To get the **fruit juice** necessary for a jelly, add your cleaned, minced fruit to a pot with a little jam sugar to draw out the juice.

► Bring the mixture to a boil and simmer until all the fruit **floats to the top.**

► Pour the fruit mixture and its fluid into **a strainer lined with cheesecloth** and collect the juice in a bowl. Don't squeeze out the juice or your jelly will be cloudy.

► Boil the juice with an equal amount of **jam sugar** for 5–10 minutes.

► After the gel test (see box above), **pour into jars** and seal.

► You can **increase the amount of juice** you get by returning the fruit mixture to the pot after it has been strained, covering it with water, and simmering it again.

the gel test

one Put a small dollop of the boiling fruit mixture onto a plate rinsed in very cold water.

two Let the sample cool down by placing it briefly in the fridge.

three If the dollop congeals and no water forms around it, then the mixture is ready for canning.

Ginger, cardamom, and vanilla can accent the flavor of jams and jellies.

Juice

Homemade juices are chockablock with valuable nutrients that can be enjoyed by even the pickiest eater. Add a little sugar, and fruit juice becomes a long-lasting fruit syrup—a tasty addition to smoothies and desserts.

Making juices is child's play with modern juicers. But choose a good quality model that is easy to clean.

The vitamins, proteins, carbohydrates, essential fatty acids, minerals, and other nutrients contained in many juices provide energy, strengthen your bones and your immune system, and cleanse your skin. But don't overdo it; keep in mind that fruit drinks contain a whole lot of calories due to the fruit sugars.

FRESH IS BEST

▶ Avoid **prepackaged juices** which are pasteurized to make them last longer. Many vitamins and minerals are lost in the process.

▶ Opt for fresh juices which contain absolutely **no additives**, but include all the nutrients of the squeezed fruit—as well as enzymes and fiber, which aid in digestion.

▶ Consume freshly-squeezed juices quickly—otherwise, the vitamins will soon evaporate.

▶ Keep fresh juices in **dark, sealed containers** in the refrigerator for up to three days.

▶ Add a little ascorbic acid—**vitamin C**—from the pharmacy or health food store to help the juice retain its color—and provide extra antioxidants.

MAKING JUICE

▶ **Cold pressing juice** in an electric juicer is the best way to make fresh juice. Just load the cleaned fruit or vegetables into the chute on the juicer. A grater at the bottom shreds the fruit, while centrifugal force spins the juice through strainers. The residue is collected in a basket.

▶ Preserve the complete vitamin and nutritional value of the fruit by avoiding appliances that use **steam**—heat destroys vitamins.

▶ You don't need a machine to make juice. The traditional method involves **stewing fruit in a pot** with some water until it bursts or becomes soft. At that point, strain the mixture through cheesecloth or a sieve, capturing the juice in a bowl. Boil the juice with sugar to sweeten if necessary, pour it into bottles while still hot, then seal them.

TIPS FOR FRUITS AND VEGETABLES

▶ Use **organic fruits and vegetables** for juicing to ensure the skins and peels aren't contaminated with harmful substances. If you're not using organic, peel the fruit before juicing.

▶ After cleaning and washing the fruits and vegetables, **dry them thoroughly** to prevent watering down the juice.

▶ Only fruit with a very tough skin should be peeled; otherwise, just remove the core and cut it up. A **fruit press** is useful for firm fruits.

▶ If you find that **grapefruit juice** tastes too bitter, mix it with **pear juice** to take the bite out of the bitter compounds.

▶ Make vegetable juice appealing to kids by mixing **carrot** or **tomato juice** with fruit juice.

▶ Relieve heartburn, aid hair and nail growth, ensure beautiful skin, and improve vision by drinking **carrot juice**. What's not to like?

Fresh apple juice changes color quickly, so drink it fast.

Citrus fruit is easy to squeeze by hand, but fruit presses and juicers are available for making larger quantities.

▶ Juice the fruit in the usual way, and then mix it with an equal amount of **sugar**. Boil again and pour into clean bottles or jars.

▶ You can use the **canning process** to give syrup a longer shelf life.

▶ Fruit syrups make lovely **gifts** when presented in a pretty bottle.

HERB SYRUP

▶ It's equally simple to make syrup from herbs such as **lemon balm, mint, rosemary,** and **lavender.**

▶ Depending on the recipe, the washed herbs are usually simmered in water and **steeped overnight.** Mix with the recipe-recommended amount of sugar and lemon juice and pour into containers after boiling.

▶ Drink the syrup diluted with water, or use it to add pizzazz to a variety of **desserts.**

Blueberry Syrup

3 cups (750 mL) blueberries (or any other berries of your choice)
1½ cups (375 mL) water
1½ cups (375 mL) sugar
½ cup (60 mL) corn syrup
1 tbsp. (15 mL) lemon juice

Sort and wash fruit, then run it through the blender or mash it and mix with the lemon juice. Add to a large pot along with the water. Bring the contents to a boil, then lower the temperature and simmer for 15–20 minutes. Strain through a fine mesh sieve. Return berry juice to the saucepan and add remaining ingredients, stirring to dissolve the sugar. Bring to a full rolling boil for a full 2 minutes, then pour directly into sterilized jars or bottles.

▶ Stimulate your immune system with **bell pepper juice**. They have three times as much vitamin C as lemons and oranges.

▶ **Beet juice** has antibacterial properties. The betaine (a protein building block) it contains can also strengthen your liver and help your body flush out toxins.

▶ Mix together **apple** and **pear juice** to provide a gentle remedy for **constipation.**

FRUIT SYRUP

Fruit syrups are easy to make and taste delicious added to sparkling mineral water, poured over pancakes or crèpes, and drizzled on ice cream or angel food cake.

▶ Use **fully-ripened fruit** for producing syrup; it will yield more juice and is far more flavorful.

Fresh blueberries can easily be made into a delicious syrup.

Kitchen Mishaps

Even a kitchen witch can't prevent all kitchen mishaps. So if the roast is burnt, the potatoes are too salty, or the soup is too watery, try some of these home remedies. With a little improvisation you can solve most problems—even if your guests are already at the door.

You can't prevent all misfortunes in the kitchen. Luckily, when they do pop up, those many little mishaps can be remedied quickly and easily. Some, however, are easy to avoid altogether.

PREVENTING COOKING MISHAPS

▶ **Milk** won't burn if the pot is rinsed out with **cold water** before heating it up.

▶ Add a little **canola oil** to the pan to prevent **butter** from browning.

▶ **Beef broth** will stay clear if you boil a clean **egg shell** with it.

▶ **Boiled sausages** won't split if a little **milk** is added to the boiling water.

▶ Keep a **roast** from getting tough by basting it only with **hot liquids.**

▶ Rub your frying pan with **salt** before cooking **hash browns** and **eggs**. This will ensure that they don't stick to the pan.

▶ Keep **fried fish** from sticking to the pan by dusting it with **flour** or putting a little **salt** into the frying oil.

▶ **Fish** holds together better during cooking if you dribble it first with **lemon juice** and set it aside for a moment. The acid in the lemon juice cooks the fish slightly, creating a thin seal.

QUICK HELP

▶ Add a dash of **vinegar** to the pot of water if an **egg** bursts while boiling; the whites will immediately thicken.

▶ Wrap **cracked eggs** securely in **aluminum foil** before boiling.

▶ **Tough stewing meat** becomes tender when you add a dash of **vinegar** to the water.

▶ Quickly beat an **egg yolk** and a little **salt** stiff, and stir into homemade **mayonnaise** drop by drop to prevent it from congealing.

▶ **Egg whites** won't stiffen? Add a few drops of **lemon juice** and a little salt.

▶ Put excessively firm **semolina dumplings** into cold water for 10 minutes. They'll swell up more and become tender when boiled.

▶ Hold **noodles** that stick together over steam to separate them.

▶ If **gelatin** clumps together, warm it up carefully while stirring constantly or mash it through a strainer.

▶ Place a **cake** (pan-side down) on a warm, damp cloth for 10 seconds, then invert it onto a plate to ensure that it comes out of the pan more easily.

If your soup or gravy contains too much fat, let it cool down and then skim it off the top.

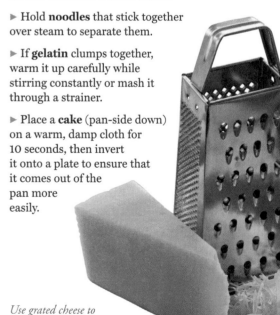

Use grated cheese to rescue burned casseroles.

After your cake cools down, scrape off burned spots with a grater and then cover it with a glaze.

▶ Remove the **grease** quickly from an excessively fatty gravy, sauce, or soup by skimming the top of the liquid with a couple of **lettuce leaves** or pieces of **paper towel.** The fat will stick to them.

BURNED FOODS

▶ If your **boiled** or **salted potatoes** are burned, carefully remove all but the last layer of unburned potatoes, put them in a pot of fresh water to finish cooking, then add a dash of **salt.**

▶ Don't stir **scorched sauces.** Quickly pour the unburned sauce into another pot and add a piece of **dry bread** or a **raw, peeled potato.**

▶ If you burn the top of your **roast,** cut out the burned parts and roast the meat in a clean pot with more **fresh fat.**

▶ Have you burned the casserole? Remove the topmost layer, sprinkle it with **cheese, bread crumbs,** or **ground nuts** and dabs of **butter** and finish baking it.

▶ Put a pinch of **salt** into a pot of slightly-burned **milk** to absorb the taste.

TOO THICK OR TOO THIN

▶ Thicken excessively thin gravies or soups with 1 tsp. (5 mL) **cornstarch** or **instant potato flakes.** Stir them first with water to make a smooth paste and then add to the gravy. Don't pour it all in at

once; add small amounts and stir until you have the right consistency. Bring to a boil and season as needed.

▶ Gravies that are too thick can easily be thinned with **water, broth, milk,** or **cream.** Add seasoning if necessary.

▶ Put **lumpy gravy** through a fine **strainer** to render it smooth again.

TOO SALTY OR SPICY

▶ In most cases you can neutralize saltiness with a mixture of **cider or wine vinegar** and **sugar** in equal proportions.

▶ Thin oversalted soups or gravies with **water, wine, milk,** or **cream.**

▶ Grate a **potato** into soups or stews to reduce excessive saltiness.

▶ Add 1–2 **raw egg whites** to salty broths; they congeal and soak up the salt. Then put the broth through a strainer or simply skim off the egg white.

▶ Add a **grated carrot** or **potato** to overly-spiced meat broth and bring to a boil.

▶ Add a sprig of **parsley** to a dish that is too garlicky for 10 minutes or so, or until it evens out the taste.

good to know

EMERGENCY EQUIPMENT
Sometimes you not only have to rescue a dish, you also need to stretch it so there's enough for everyone. For soups and stews, add lentils or beans, vegetables, or pasta. Make salads go further with fruit, tuna, olives, lentils, and nuts. A little sour cream or plain yogurt can often rescue bland soups.

Kitchen Safety

More accidents happen in the kitchen than anywhere else in the home. Cutting yourself with a knife, slipping on the floor, or burning yourself with a hot pan are among the many potential dangers. Minimize the risk by employing a few precautionary measures.

Supervision is key to kitchen safety. Learn how to carefully handle sharp kitchen utensils and make sure you know what to do in case of emergency When it comes to stove safety, never leave a pot on the stove unsupervised—especially if it's a gas stove. Turn off unneeded burners immediately.

PREVENTING BURNS

▶ Do not leave the **handles of pots and pans** hanging over the edge of the stove. It is a recipe for disaster—they could be easily knocked off as someone walks by.

Always use potholders or oven mitts to avoid oven burns.

▶ Keep an eye on any pans with **hot oil** in them: they catch fire easily and are a common cause of kitchen fires.

▶ Step back and **let the hot air escape** when you open the oven.

▶ Do not let **hot liquid** slosh out when removing pots and pans from the oven.

▶ Never place hot foods on the **edge of the stove, table,** or **work surface** where they can easily be tipped over.

▶ Keep **dish towels** away from stove burners, as they can easily catch fire.

▶ Regularly wash or replace **exhaust fan filters.** They quickly become flammable when saturated with grease.

▶ Keep your hands, face, and body out of harm's way when using the **steam release valve** on a pressure cooker.

▶ For safety's sake—and for some peace of mind—it's best to use a **kettle** that shuts itself off automatically when the water boils.

▶ Never overheat oil in a **deep fryer.** Also, replace contaminated grease, as it is more susceptible to flaming up.

▶ Make sure the **deep fryer's heating coils** are totally immersed in oil or there is a strong risk that the oil will catch fire.

▶ Run **cold water** in the sink while draining potatoes or vegetables so that the rising steam won't scald your hands.

TAKE CARE WITH KNIVES AND SCISSORS

▶ Store knives and other sharp objects in a **knife block** out of the reach of children.

▶ Don't drop knives in **dishwashing water**; if they're obscured by suds, you may accidentally grab them by the blade.

▶ Wash knives with a **brush** right after use. For dried-on food, let knives soak first in a container of **warm water.**

▶ Read the **instruction manuals** to find out how to remove the blades safely from food processors, shredders, slicers, meat grinders, and other kitchen devices with blades.

▶ Guide the knife **away from your body,** with your fingertips held at an angle, while cutting.

Use a hand guard to protect your fingers when using a mandoline.

▶ Sweep up and discard **broken glass** immediately. Gather very small pieces with a water-moistened cotton ball.

▶ If a glass breaks in the dishwashing water, **drain the water** and rinse away any excess soap suds before removing the pieces.

OTHER DANGERS

▶ Keep **household chemicals** out of the reach of children. Since these often highly toxic substances are dangerous to adults as well, make sure that they are clearly labeled and don't store them near foods or in containers normally used for foods.

▶ Wipe up **splattered grease** and **spills** on the floor immediately to ensure that no one slips.

WHAT TO DO IN AN EMERGENCY

▶ If something happens, above all, keep a cool head and **remain calm.**

▶ Smother the flames of a **grease fire** with a dish towel or a pot lid, then remove the pan from the heat source. Don't use water or a foam fire extinguisher, as this has the potential to splatter the grease outside the contained pan, and spread the flames.

▶ Turn off the oven immediately in the event of an **oven fire.** Keep the oven door closed—the lack of oxygen with suffocate the fire.

▶ Treat bruises from a fall by applying a **cold pack** or a bag of ice wrapped in a towel. Never apply ice cubes directly to your skin. Reusable **gel wraps** are good, too, but for severe falls, go to the emergency room, or call for help if you cannot get to the emergency room unaided.

▶ Apply **warm water** or the cut surface of a **cold, raw potato** to soothe pain from a burn and prevent burn blisters from forming.

▶ For minor burns, apply a little **honey**. Research shows that this will help the wounds heal faster.

▶ Cover open burn injuries with a **sterile, non-stick bandage** and cool with an **icepack**. For severe burns, go to the ER right away.

▶ Stop bleeding and simultaneously clean a cut by holding the part of your body that is burned under **cold, running water.** Then cover it with an adhesive bandage to prevent infection. Note that fairly large cuts may require stitches.

The stove should be off-limits to kids.

Leftovers

If you're one of the many that hates leftovers, here's good news: every refrigerator and pantry contains a range of simple ingredients useful for turning leftovers into tasty meals.

Casseroles and salads are the most common ways to use up leftover potatoes, pasta, and rice. But you can also transform them into delicious soups and desserts.

USING UP LEFTOVER POTATOES, PASTA, AND RICE

▶ Convert a whisked egg and a little cheese, leftover meat, and potatoes into a delicious **omelet**.

▶ Try making **potato patties**: mash leftover potatoes, mix with an egg, salt, pepper, garlic, parsley, and a diced onion, shape into round disks, bread, and then deep fry in canola oil.

▶ Puree leftover potatoes with broth and season to taste with cream or milk, herbs, and/or grated cheese to make a delicious **potato soup**.

▶ **Parmesan cheese** gives baked casseroles a great taste. But because of its dry texture, it burns quickly. Either mix it with bits of butter on the casserole, or add it later on in the cooking process.

▶ Add 2 tbsp. (25 mL) capers or sliced olives, a can of tuna, and some diced tomatoes to leftover pasta, then season with vinegar, olive oil, salt, and pepper to put together a light summer **pasta salad.**

▶ **Salads** and **pasta** taste particularly good when you let the flavors meld before eating. The same applies to **potato** and **rice salads.**

▶ Make a hearty **rice dish** from leftover rice, eggs, pork or chicken, onions, and frozen veggies. For an Asian touch, use sesame oil for stir-frying and season with soy sauce and/or toss in a little curry paste.

▶ Add a can of black beans and some salsa to leftover chicken or hamburger to make a delicious topping for **tacos** or a filling for **burritos**.

▶ Transform day-old rice into **rice pudding**: mix 2 cups (500 mL) of milk per cup (250 mL) of rice and simmer gently on the stovetop so the milk doesn't burn, but the mixture is heated through. In a separate bowl, mix together 2 eggs, 1/4 cup (50 mL) of sugar and 1/2 tsp. (2 mL) of vanilla. Whisk into the rice mixture and heat through before transferring to a casserole dish. Bake in a preheated oven at 350°F (180°C) for 20 minutes.

▶ Whip together **delicate rice pancakes** by mixing leftover rice with flour, milk, and eggs and cook like normal pancakes. Serve with cinnamon and sugar or marmalade.

Casseroles are a classic way to use up leftovers. There are practically no limits on the ingredients you can use.

Croutons made from leftover bread complement fresh salads or pureed soups.

VEGETABLE VARIETY

▶ For a simple **casserole**, layer leftover vegetables with potatoes, pasta, or rice in an ovenproof dish and pour cheese or béchamel sauce over it. Sprinkle with bread crumbs and bake.

▶ Make a **pureed soup** from leftover vegetables: heat the cubed veggies in a little broth, puree, and stir in milk for a creamy consistency. Season to taste and serve with crunchy **croutons** made from day-old bread.

VARIATIONS FOR OLD BREAD

▶ Brush your day-old bread with a little **water** or **egg yolk** before reheating in the oven for an attractive shine.

▶ Soften stale rolls in **vegetable** or **beef broth** before using them in meatballs or meatloaf to make the dish especially tasty.

▶ If rolls or bread are not too stale, turn them into **croutons** for salads or soups. Just cut them into bite-sized cubes and toast in a pan with a little bit of olive oil or butter. Heat them until they're crunchy and have browned slightly. The addition of onions, crushed nuts, or parmesan cheese provides an extra flavor boost.

Grated cheese enhances casseroles, salads, and soups made with leftovers.

▶ In summer, when tomatoes are ripe and juicy, nothing beats a **bread salad**. Chop stale slices of white bread into bite-sized chunks and mix with diced tomatoes, onions, olive oil, and wine vinegar. Season with salt, pepper, and herbs, and let it sit for at least 15 minutes.

OTHER LEFTOVERS

▶ Serve day-old **roast chicken** or **turkey breast** on a green salad, with some combination of veggies, chickpeas, walnuts, pine nuts, raisins, cranberries, and cheese. Keep it simple—serve with a classic balsamic vinaigrette.

▶ **Chicken pot pie** is a great way to use up leftover chicken and veggies. Make a thick sauce with milk, flour, and butter, along with a dash of salt and pepper. Mix in diced chicken and leftover or sautéed veggies and pour into a lightly-greased baking dish. Top with a premade pie crust: just seal the crust to the sides, cut a few vents in the dough, and bake until bubbly and golden brown.

▶ **Cooked grains** are a nutritious and filling addition to any soup.

Turn stale rolls and white bread into bread crumbs for use in casseroles, meat loaves, and meatballs.

good to know

ARE FOODS MADE WITH MAYONNAISE PRONE TO SPOILING?
Turns out this is an old wives' tale. When you turn your leftover chicken into chicken salad, the mayonnaise actually helps prevent spoilage. Why? Because commercial mayonnaise is somewhat acidic. The upshot: when you're heading out for a picnic or setting out a buffet, you don't have to avoid mayonnaise—just be conscious of keeping the food cold. And if you know that there will be leftovers, cover the dish and get it in the refrigerator as quickly as possible.

Liqueurs

Making herbal and fruit liqueurs is an adventure, and your homemade versions will be just as delicious as commercial brands. Other alcoholic specialties, such as brandied fruit and rum pot, make delicious treats when enjoying dessert or a roast.

When making liqueurs, you'll need fresh, high-quality ingredients and to keep your utensils and your prep area clean. Store liqueurs and brandied fruits in bottles or jars, while rum pot (fruit preserved in rum) ages nicely in a ceramic pot.

WHAT'S REQUIRED?

▶ The closures on containers deserve particular attention: they must be **clean** and **close tightly.**

▶ For steeping fruit liqueurs, you also need **large canning jars** with a wide neck and a capacity of at least 2 quarts/liters.

▶ **Filter** liqueurs through tea or coffee filters, a thin linen cloth, a fine metal strainer, or through a normal strainer lined with 1–2 paper towel sheets.

▶ Add **sugar** in the form of syrup, white or brown rock candy, crystalline sugar, granulated white sugar, or honey. All these sugars will dissolve with time.

▶ **Vodka** is a good liquor for steeping a liqueur or for canning fruits. It has a fairly neutral taste, so it does a great job of releasing the aromas and flavors of the ingredients. Depending on its strength, you may choose to dilute it with water.

▶ Other liquors, such as **fruit brandies, tequila, rum,** or **brandy,** can also be used.

▶ Fruits like **sour cherries, currants,** and **strawberries** are particularly good for steeping in fruit liqueurs. But let your imagination run free: other **berries, small yellow plums, papayas,** and **lemon peels** also make wonderful liqueurs.

▶ **Always wash fruit**, since you must often steep them with their peels intact.

▶ If a desired fruit is not in season, **frozen fruit** works equally well.

BASIC RECIPE FOR FRUIT LIQUEUR

▶ Add the fruits to a large container along with about 1¼ cups (300 mL) of **sugar** per 18 oz. (500 g) of fruit.

▶ Once the mixture draws out the juice, pour in the **alcohol**. Carefully stir the mixture; cover tightly.

▶ Let the contents steep in a **sealed jar,** then filter and bottle it.

Never use fruit with rotten spots or bruises.
Be particularly careful with raspberries.

VARIATIONS FOR LIQUEURS

▶ Give your liqueur a delicious, nuanced taste with ingredients like **vanilla** and **cinnamon sticks, citrus peels,** a piece of **ginger, cloves, cardamom,** or a few drops of **bitter almond oil.**

▶ Use **herbs or spices** such as fennel, cloves, bloodroot, coriander, gentian root, peppermint, anise, ginger, cinnamon sticks, vermouth herb, caraway, or dandelion, if you like things spicier. Pour about 2 cups (500 mL) vodka over 1½ to 3½ oz. (50–100 g) herbs or spices, add sugar to taste, and filter after two to three weeks.

▶ If the liqueur needs to ferment, you can also add a little **high-proof schnapps.**

▶ If you want to **adjust** an excessively strong liqueur after it has steeped, add some fruit or a little sugar and let it steep again. It's best to add the sugar in the form of **simple syrup** (one part water to one part sugar, shaken in a bottle until sugar dissolves), rather than less soluble sugar granules.

STEEPING A RUM POT

Set a rum pot to steep in **late spring** so that you can enjoy spring and summer fruits preserved in rum during the Christmas holiday season. A rum pot is just the thing for ice cream, pudding, or pancakes.

▶ To start your rum pot steeping, add to a sterilized wide-mouthed jar about 1¼ cups (300 mL) of sugar per 18 oz. (500 g) of fruit, and pour **high-proof rum** over the mixture. Seal the jar and store it in a dark, cool place.

▶ Add other **seasonal fruits** in the summer and fall (two parts fruit to one part sugar). Fill with enough rum to cover all of the fruit.

▶ Add a few **cinnamon sticks** and **star anise** in October, then set your rum pot aside.

BRANDIED FRUIT

Fruit steeped in alcohol tastes great by itself, as a delicious garnish for meat and game dishes, and as a delectable complement to fine desserts. Just remember that the fruit is saturated with alcohol, so avoid feeding it to the kids!

Liqueurs can be filtered through a thin linen cloth, a very fine metal strainer, or a strainer lined with paper towels or a coffee filter.

▶ Add about 1¼ cups (300 mL) of sugar per 18 oz. (500 g) of fruit. If you want the fruit flavor to be more prominent, **reduce the amount of sugar**.

▶ Use **brown** or **white rock sugar** to create a unique flavor.

▶ **Layer** the prepared fruit and sugar in jars and cover with alcohol.

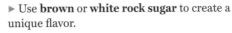

▶ If you use a **fruit brandy** for steeping, make sure the fruit and brandy are a good flavor match.

▶ When making brandied fruits, **avoid cheap brandies** as they can spoil the taste.

▶ If you don't serve the fruit-infused alcohol with the fruits, you can use them for **punch** later.

Rum pots, which can be made with a wide variety of fruits, should be made in spring to be ready for Christmas.

Meat, Fish, and Poultry

Successfully cooking meat, fish, and poultry involves proper preparation. Take the time to marinate meat overnight to ensure it will be tender and moist. And always wash fish and poultry thoroughly to guarantee that your meal will be healthy as well as tasty.

Once you have decided what to cook, calculate how much meat or fish you need, taking into account that it will shrink during the cooking process.

WHAT'S IN A SERVING?

▶ With **red meat**, generally figure on about 7 oz. (200 g) per person, or 10 oz. (300 g) for a roast with the bone in.

▶ Depending on the size, one roaster chicken or duck will feed three to four people. One goose is usually enough for six hearty eaters; a rule of thumb is about 12 oz. (350 g) per person. With turkey, count on about 1 lb (500 g) per person, which allows for leftovers the next day.

▶ With fish filets, figure on about 8 oz. (250 g) each, or 12 oz. (350 g) for a whole fish.

PREPARING FISH

Don't overcook fish if you'd like it to remain tender and juicy.

▶ Test fish for doneness by inserting a **meat thermometer** at an angle into the thickest part of the fish. The internal temperature should be at least 140°F (60°C), but at 150°F (65°C), the fish loses its flavor and moistness.

▶ Don't have a meat thermometer? Stick a wooden **toothpick** into the fleshiest part of the fish. If it meets little resistance and comes out clean, your dish is likely done.

▶ Make it easier to cut fish into chunks for chowder or bouillabaisse by **freezing** it for 45 minutes first.

▶ Thaw frozen fish in the **refrigerator** or cook it frozen; thawing at room temperature increases the likelihood of contamination.

▶ When roasting a **whole fish**, wash it thoroughly inside and out, salt, season with herbs, and rub it with olive oil. Bake in a preheated oven at 425°F (220°C). You'll know it's done when the eyes turn opaque and the flesh near the backbone flakes when prodded with a toothpick.

FRYING FISH

▶ Dredge your fish in seasoned **flour**, beaten **egg**, and finally **bread crumbs** before frying.

▶ If you're out of eggs, use **lemon juice** instead. The coating will stick just as well, and the fish will have a lovely lemony zest.

▶ Try chopped **hazelnuts**, slivered **almonds**, or crushed **cornflakes** instead of bread crumbs.

▶ Always bread fish **shortly** before cooking—otherwise, the bread crumbs will flake off.

▶ Absorb excess grease by briefly placing the cooked fish on a **paper towel.**

Garlic and herbs enhance the flavor and aroma of meat.

Use toothpicks to dress smaller birds. The bird will keep its shape and the stuffing will stay in place.

A GOOD MEAT MARINADE

Marinades serve a dual purpose: to tenderize the meat and add a mouthwatering flavor. Most marinades contain some form of acid, like lemon juice, vinegar, or wine, which break down muscle fibers in the meat. Another excellent tenderizer comes from the enzymes in ingredients like onions, ginger, and papaya. Marinades have yet another function: you can use them later as gravy.

▶ For a simple marinade, stir together 5 tbsp. (75 mL) each of **oil** and **vinegar**, and a pinch each of **pepper** and **sugar**. Place your meat in a deep container or sturdy freezer bag, then drench it with marinade. Let sit in the refrigerator overnight, turning occasionally.

▶ Use **salt** sparingly in a marinade to avoid drawing the moisture out of the meat.

▶ **Boost flavor** by adding extra ingredients like honey, mustard, wine, lemon, onion, spices, herbs, and fruits such as apples and oranges.

▶ Marinate **veal** and **organ meats** for a maximum of two hours, and other types of meat for three to four hours—even overnight. **Game** can steep in a marinade for one to three days.

▶ Don't use **metal containers** or **bowls** for marinating as they react chemically with the acids in the marinade and may impart an unpleasant (and perhaps unhealthy) flavor to the meat.

PREPARING FISH

▶ Cut the **lateral** and **dorsal fins** off when serving a fish whole.

▶ **Scale** a fish by holding it by the tail while you scrape from the rear toward the head, using a scaler or a knife with a serrated edge.

▶ **Boning** is more complicated. Open up the abdominal cavity and cut the perpendicular bones away from the meat on both sides. Then separate the central bone from the head and tail and carefully remove it along with the other bones.

CUTTING, MARINATING, AND STUFFING BIRDS

Have a sharp knife and good poultry shears on hand for cutting up fowl.

▶ Lay the bird on its back, cut through the skin between the drumsticks or wings and breast with the knife, then use poultry shears to **snip off the bones** at the joint.

▶ Use your knife to carefully **separate the breast meat** on both sides of the breastbone.

▶ Marinate white meat in **white wine** and **herbs**; and dark meat in **red wine**.

▶ Give chicken a **Mediterranean** flavor by rubbing olive oil, lemon, garlic, and herbs on and under the skin.

▶ Good stuffings for fowl use **savory** ingredients such as sausage meat and chestnuts, as well as apples, pears, and even dried fruits.

▶ **Salt** and **pepper** the abdominal cavity before you start stuffing.

▶ With large fowl like **turkeys,** also stuff the head end to make sure that dressing is well-distributed, then pull the skin across the opening to seal it in.

filleting fish

one Cut off the head just behind the gills.

two With your knife blade pointing away from you and across the body of the fish, slice toward the head, using the backbone to guide your knife.

three Release the upper fillet completely from the bones with a second cut, and put it aside.

four With a final cut, guide the knife flat beneath the central bone and free it up from the second fillet.

Non-Alcoholic Beverages

Water is the basic ingredient for all refreshing drinks, and it is essential to our good health. But drinking only water can prove tiresome, so when you want to quench your thirst, try a variety of delicious beverages.

Refreshing drinks should quench your thirst but not spike your blood sugar. Commercially-produced drinks often contain too much sugar. Take a page from your grandmother's recipe book and make your own.

a money-saving *hint*

Get your water from the tap. Unless the supply in your area has a peculiar smell or taste, it is probably just as good for you as bottled water, and it costs far less. To get rid of tap water's bleachlike flavor, fill a jug or bottle and let the water sit uncovered for several hours.

WATER, THE ELIXIR OF LIFE

Advertising by bottled water companies gives consumers the impression their product is safer and healthier than tap water. As a result, world consumption of bottled water has grown by leaps and bounds in the last 10 years. In fact, you may be better off drinking the elixir of life straight from the tap.

▶ Bottled water creates too many **discarded plastic bottles** that go straight into the dump.

▶ Since bottled water isn't fluoridated, it may lead to increased incidents of **dental decay**.

▶ Some bottled water companies actually use filtered **municipal tap water.**

Lemon and mint add a tangy flavor to tap water.

HOMEMADE LEMONADE

▶ Whip up **homemade lemonade** by grating the peels of 6 organic lemons and boiling them with 1¼ cups (300 mL) sugar and about 2 cups (500 mL) water. Simmer for a few minutes, cool, add the juice from the lemons.

▶ **Strain** the lemonade concentrate and pour it into a glass pitcher. Fill it up with **ice cubes** and lots of **cold water.**

▶ **Limes** and **oranges** are also great for making a refreshing drink.

▶ **Honey, ginger,** or **rose water** will give lemonade a unique flavor.

HEALTHY FRUITY DRINKS

Get more vitamins and minerals into your diet by drinking freshly-made fruit juices or whipping up thick and frothy smoothies from frozen fruit.

▶ Make a delicious **fruit drink** by cutting up your choice of fruits and whirring them in a blender with the juice from half a lemon, along with ¼–½ cup (50–125 mL) of sugar. Adjust the amount of sugar to the type of fruit and the sugar content of the juice.

▶ For a **fruit punch** that will serve a crowd, pour a bottle of apple or grape juice into your punch bowl and cool for several hours, stirring several times. Shortly before serving, add another bottle of juice and a bottle of mineral water, followed by ice cubes.

▶ Keep your punch cold by freezing **slices of citrus fruits** and using them in place of ice cubes.

▶ Blend **frozen fruit** such as bananas, strawberries, raspberries, or mango with a little plain yogurt, juice, milk and a touch of honey to make a frothy **smoothie.**

TEA

After water, tea is the most widely-consumed drink in the world. The term "herbal tea" usually refers to an infusion of leaves, flowers, fruit, herbs, or other plant material that doesn't include traditional tea leaves.

▶ Connoisseurs tend to buy their tea in **specialty shops** for the quality and selection.

▶ Infuse **black tea** with boiling water and let steep for 3–5 minutes.

▶ Steep **green tea** in hot water at 176°F (80°C) for only 2 minutes.

Keep punch cold without watering it down by adding ice cubes made from fruit juice.

COFFEE BEANS

▶ The amount of **coffee** you need will depend on personal taste, water quality, and the type of coffee maker you're using. Generally, when using a drip coffee maker, count on about 1 tbsp. (15 mL) of coffee per 1 cup (250 mL) water. With hard water that contains lime, use more coffee.

▶ Store coffee beans in a **dry, cool, dark location,** and keep them in a **tightly-closed container**— otherwise they'll go stale.

▶ Store **vacuum-packed coffee** for several months if unopened; frozen coffee will last up to a year.

▶ **Ground coffee** loses its flavor quickly and should be used within six months.

▶ Use a **coffee grinder** or **spice mill** to make freshly-ground coffee, and brew a fragrant and satisfying cup of joe.

▶ Use **strong tea blends** or run the water through a **filter** when water has a high lime content.

▶ Store tea in a **dry, tightly-closing container**. Special metal or porcelain containers and opaque bags are ideal for this.

▶ Don't keep tea for **daily consumption** in the **refrigerator**; the sensitive leaves can be damaged by fluctuations in humidity.

▶ For **long-term storage,** place unopened tea in the **vegetable crisper** in the refrigerator.

▶ Always store the **same type of tea** in certain containers—otherwise tea, will quickly pick up other flavors, which can ruin its subtle nuances.

▶ Make lovely herbal teas with **rose hips** and **mint.** Depending on the season you can boost their flavor: in summer use **lemon** or **lime peels** (mint), in winter use **cinnamon** or **cloves** (rose hip).

FOR HOT DAYS

▶ For **iced tea,** brew 3–4 tsp. (15–20 mL) tea leaves in 1 quart/liter of water and let steep for 3 minutes.

▶ Stir in the juice from 1½ **lemons,** sweeten to taste, then shock it by pouring it over about 25 **ice cubes.** The tea cools quickly and doesn't become bitter.

▶ Flavor it according to taste with **apple juice, fruit nectar, citrus fruits,** or **mint leaves.**

Loose tea is more flavorful than bagged tea. It also contains more minerals and vitamins.

Oil and Vinegar

Flavored vinegars and oils add pizzazz to everyday foods. Olive oil with a citrus flavor subtly enhances fried fish, and herbal vinegars provide a nice finishing touch to salad dressings.

The best oils for flavoring are those that have no taste of their own, such as mild, refined olive, sunflower, or canola oil. Good, clear wine vinegars or cider vinegars with at least 5% acid are the best base for flavored vinegars.

WHAT YOU NEED

▶ **Bottles, tops, pots,** and other utensils must be clean, and the **herbs** or other ingredients must be fresh.

▶ Use tops made of **cork, plastic,** or **glass** to seal bottles used for oil and vinegar. Metal deteriorates because of the acid in vinegar.

FLAVORED OILS

▶ Put **lightly-crushed herbs** loosely into a canning jar and pour oil over them. You need about 5 oz./150 g herbs per quart/liter of oil. You can get nearly the same results with **dried herbs** as from fresh.

▶ Let the oil **steep for two weeks** in the closed jar, stirring it once a day.

▶ **Garlic, chili peppers,** or **citrus peels** can also be used for flavoring oils.

▶ Make a **basil oil** by heating the oil to 104°F (40°C) before pouring it over basil.

▶ Use **peanut** or **refined sesame oil** as a base for flavored oils with Asian flavors.

▶ Strain the oil through a **cheesecloth** and pour it into bottles.

▶ Oils can be kept for **a year** if unopened and stored in a cool, dark place. A smell and taste test will clearly show if they're still fresh.

FLAVORING VINEGAR

▶ Heat the vinegar until it **bubbles** (you need about 5 oz./150 g herbs per quart/liter of vinegar). Once it cools to 104°F (40°C), pour it over the crushed herbs in a canning jar. Make sure the jar is tightly-closed.

▶ Let **steep for two to three weeks** and shake from time to time. Then strain and pour into bottles.

▶ In addition to herbs, you can flavor vinegar with numerous spices. **Thyme** and **tarragon** go well with **garlic, chili flakes,** and **peppercorns.**

▶ Put the spices into a small **cloth bag**, add it to the boiling vinegar, and let simmer for about 10 minutes.

▶ For a hint of sweetness, dissolve 2–4 tbsp. (25–60 mL) of **sugar** or **honey** in 1 quart/liter of hot vinegar.

▶ **Spiced vinegars** can be kept for several years unopened, but with time they will mature and become milder.

Chili Vinegar

1 quart/liter vinegar
2 large mild chili peppers
3 dried hot chili peppers
1 tsp. (5 mL) peppercorns
1 scallion, cut into strips

Bring the vinegar to a boil, then pour it over all ingredients and let steep in a closed jar for two weeks. Shake daily. Strain and pour into glass bottles.

Add a couple of sprigs of herbs to bottles of oil for decoration and to enhance the taste.

Pasta and Rice

Noodles and rice have been menu staples in numerous cuisines for centuries. Both come in many different forms and can be combined with all sorts of meats, vegetables, sauces, cheeses, and spices to make a nourishing meal.

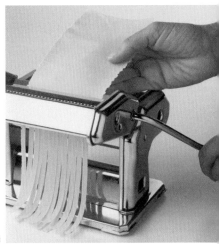

A pasta machine makes it much easier to roll out pasta dough and cut it into fine ribbon noodles.

Nothing beats the taste of fresh, homemade pasta. While it requires some effort, it's not rocket science. Plus, working with your hands to make food from scratch can actually be very therapeutic. Read on for two basic pasta dough recipes.

BASIC RECIPES FOR PASTA DOUGH

▶ For **pasta without egg:** mix about 6 oz. (175 g) durum wheat semolina with about 4½ oz. (140 g) flour and a pinch of salt. Add ¾ cup (175 mL) water and knead into a smooth, elastic dough.

▶ Add a little more **water** if the dough is too dry. It should be solid but not sticky.

▶ Let it sit for about one hour, then **roll it out** as thick as you want, cut it into the desired **shape**, and let it dry.

▶ Pasta made from **durum wheat** is particularly good with **thick sauces.**

▶ For **egg noodles:** knead about 8½ oz. (260 g) wheat flour, 3 lightly-beaten eggs, 1 tsp. (5 mL) of salt, and 1 tbsp. (15 mL) of olive oil into a smooth dough. It is done when the top is shiny and it loosens from the work surface. After letting the dough sit, roll it out, cut it up, and let it dry.

TIPS FOR THE PASTA KITCHEN

▶ Brew **coffee** when you make pasta—having moist air in the kitchen at the same time makes production easier.

▶ **Turn dough over** several times to make the process of **rolling it out** easier.

▶ Work on pasta dough **in sections** and put the rest of the dough in **aluminum foil** to keep it from drying out too much.

▶ Egg noodles can be **colored** and **flavored.** Beet juice, for example, turns noodles dark red; tomato puree, light red; carrot or pumpkin puree, orange; saffron, yellow; spinach, green; mushrooms, brown; and squid ink, black. Mix these ingredients with eggs, oil, and salt and knead them in with the flour. The dough may need additional **flour** to compensate for moisture from the added ingredients.

▶ Use a **large, deep pot** so the noodles can float freely while they boil.

▶ Pasta **swells** to about 2½ times the original volume during cooking. Make sure you add it to water at a full rolling boil.

▶ **Stir** pasta around as soon as it's in the water so it keeps its shape and doesn't stick together.

▶ **Don't add oil to the water.** Although adding it prevents boiling over, it won't stop your pasta from sticking together. Instead, oil blocks the pores so that the noodles don't hold the sauce well.

▶ Pasta dishes have a zestier flavor if you add a little **soup stock** to the cooking water.

To make tortellini, roll out the dough and cut small squares before adding a dab of filling in the middle. Carefully fold the dough over the filling. Moisten the edges in advance so that they stay together.

TYPES OF RICE AND COOKING METHODS

Rice has shaped the culture, diet, and economy of Asia. As one of humankind's oldest cultivated plants, it is the subject of numerous festivals, rituals, and ceremonies, and is undoubtedly the most important food staple.

▶ **Long-grain** or **basmati rice** has long, slender grains and a dry, glassy core. For best results, wash it thoroughly and soak for at least a half-hour before cooking. Then bring one part rice and two parts salted liquid to a boil, lower the heat, and cook, covered, for 15 minutes.

▶ Before **parboiled rice** is husked and polished, hot steam is used to force about 80 percent of the vitamins and minerals contained in the silver outer membrane into the rice grain so that it is very high in nutrients. To cook it, bring one part rice and two parts salted liquid to a boil, then lower the heat. Cook, covered, for 20 minutes.

▶ **Short-grain rice** is chalk white and soft and sticky in the core. It produces plenty of starch when cooked and can be used for risotto and sweet dishes. Soak it for 20 minutes prior to cooking. Use one part rice to one part water. Bring water to a boil, then reduce heat and cook, covered, for 10 minutes or until done.

▶ **Brown rice** comes in short, medium, and long-grained versions.

It is nutrient-dense and high in fiber. Generally, you'll need to soak it overnight or for four hours. Bring one part rice and two parts salted liquid to a boil, then lower the heat. Cook, covered, for 15–20 minutes.

TIPS FOR THE RICE KITCHEN

▶ **Don't stir rice** in the pot while you're cooking it—the result will be a starchy mess.

▶ When making rice, remember that most rice varieties **triple in size**. A side dish of cooked rice is about 1/2 cup (125 mL).

▶ Rice is tastier when prepared in **broth, tomato juice,** or a mixture of **water** and **wine.**

▶ You can repurpose cooked rice as **fried** or **baked rice** with the help of oil and spices, as well as additions such as eggs, leftover meat, and veggies. It's also good in soups.

▶ Add a pat of **butter** to the water to keep rice from boiling over.

▶ If rice is too moist after cooking, let it dry for 10 minutes on a **baking pan** in the oven.

▶ **Store** rice in a dry, well-ventilated place away from strong-smelling foods, as it easily absorbs other flavors.

The water-to-rice ratio and cooking time are different for each type and brand of rice; always follow the package directions.

Rice comes in husked and unhusked varieties. Wild rice consists of the seeds from a type of grass that grows wild.

Potatoes

Potatoes, which originated in South America, have long been considered food for the poor. But because of its versatility, the ubiquitous spud has turned into the queen of side dishes. The world's fourth largest crop is filling, economical, and nutritious—packed with potassium, vitamin C, and fiber.

Good potatoes smell earthy, not musty. In addition to carbohydrates and protein, they contain a long list of healthy minerals.

HINTS ABOUT SPUDS

▶ Choose the **right kind of potato** for the purpose you have in mind. Russets, golds, and long whites are good for baking, frying, or mashing, while the slightly waxy new potatoes taste great boiled, steamed, or roasted.

▶ Store potatoes in a **dry, dark** place. Do not keep them in the refrigerator.

▶ Potatoes that turn **green** after a week or so indicate that they're getting too much light. Move them to a heavy brown paper bag.

▶ Since **peels** are rich in nutrients, **organic** potatoes should be peeled sparingly or not at all.

▶ Add a couple of drops of **vinegar** to a bowl of water containing peeled, raw potatoes. Cover and keep in the refrigerator for two to three days.

▶ Add a little **oil** or **butter** to potatoes' cooking water to prevent boiling over.

▶ After boiling potatoes, **drain** and **cover with a cloth** to absorb the steam and keep potatoes warm.

▶ Try mashed potatoes with **buttermilk** or **chicken broth** instead of milk or cream. They impart an interesting flavor and contain less fat and fewer calories.

▶ **Parsley** and **marjoram** are particularly tasty herbs to use with potatoes.

▶ Avoid wrapping baking potatoes in **tinfoil**. It will hold in the moisture, in effect steaming your potato.

▶ To bake potatoes in the **microwave**, wash, but don't dry them, pierce them with a fork wrap them in paper towels, and cook them on a microwave rack.

▶ Leftover **creamy soups, stews, chili,** or **veggies au gratin** make wonderful toppers, turning a baked potato into a full-on meal.

▶ Potatoes are low-fat and low-calorie. To keep them that way, opt for low-fat toppers such as **plain yogurt, low-fat sour cream and chives,** and **salsa.**

▶ Leftover mashed potatoes make a terrific **thickener** for soups, stews, or sauces. Combined with leftover meat and gravy, they can be recycled as a shepherd's pie or pot pie.

▶ Leftover potatoes can be stored in a **freezer bag** or an **airtight container** and frozen for up to 10 months.

There are some 5,500 varieties of potatoes worldwide. Thin-skinned new potatoes should not be peeled.

Crispy golden hash brown potatoes are a staple breakfast food across North America.

Preserves

Fruits and vegetables can be "put up" with a preserver, pressure canner, or oven. Keep your kitchen stocked with compotes and canned veggies throughout the year.

In addition to jars, you need the following tools for preserving fruits and vegetables: a kitchen scale, measuring cup, skimmer, and funnel for transferring the preserves into jars. A jar lifter makes it easier to remove jars from the hot water, and don't forget labels for the filled jars.

PREPARATION

▶ Chose **special canning jars** with a rubber seal, glass lid, and spring closure.

▶ Check all canning jars for **scratches and chips.**

▶ Check the **rubber gaskets** used to form an airtight seal on the jars for brittle spots.

▶ Before adding preserves, **boil** the jars and gaskets in **vinegar and water** and let them drip dry, bottom-up, in a dish drainer.

▶ You can also sterilize jars in the **oven**: just place them on a baking sheet lined with paper towel for 10 minutes in an oven preheated to 325°F (160°C).

▶ If you choose to boil them in a pot, make sure your **canning jars** are all the **same height** and they don't touch the top edge of the pot.

▶ Put jars in **warm water,** then crank the heat; they can **crack** if placed directly into boiling water.

▶ When **preserving in the oven,** place the jars on a shelf or baking sheet. Don't preheat.

Compote has a unique advantage: People who are sensitive to acids tolerate it better than fresh fruit.

Special metal baskets for putting jars into a pot or the oven are very useful.

FRUIT COMPOTES

In theory, all types of domestic fruit can be safely preserved because they're naturally acidic and the added sugar will help to preserve them. Fruit compotes are a delicious winter treat over ice cream, angel food cake, or pancakes.

▶ Boil down about 4 lb. (2 kg) fruit with 1 quart/liter of water and 2¼ cups (550 mL) sugar into a **syrup.**

▶ Adjust the amount of **sugar** to the natural sugar content of the fruit so that the compote has a balanced taste.

▶ Place your washed and chopped fruits in **lemon water** to keep them from oxidizing.

▶ **Layer the fruit** no higher than 1 in. (2.5 cm) under the **rim** of the jar.

▶ Add **sugar syrup** to the jars, seal them, and put them into the pot or the oven at 200°F (90°C) for about 30 minutes.

CANNING VEGETABLES

You can get particularly good results from preserving cucumbers, carrots, peppers, and tomatoes. Beans, peas, cabbage, mushrooms, and celery are also good choices. The caveat: you must can non-acidic vegetables in a pressure canner, or you may end up with a bad case of food poisoning.

▶ Layer your vegetables tightly in the jars, and cover with a **boiling salt solution** consisting of 1 tbsp. (15 mL) salt and 1 quart/liter of water.

▶ Leave a **headspace** of about ½ in. (1.5 cm) when filling. Too much headspace may result in discoloration of the top layer; too little headspace may make the veggies swell and break the seal.

▶ Most vegetables can be preserved at a temperature of 200°F (90°C) for 90 minutes. **Cabbage, celery, peas,** and **beans** need two hours, but **tomatoes** and **cucumbers** need only 30 minutes at 185°F (85°C)—otherwise they become too soft.

▶ Shorten **preserving time** by blanching or half-cooking your veggies in advance.

TROUBLESHOOTING

▶ If the canned vegetables aren't **crisp**, the **salt solution** isn't strong enough.

▶ If the veggies **turn dark**, remember to use distilled water next time. Even iodized salt can produce a dark coloration.

AFTER PRESERVING

▶ **Remove the rings on canning jars** only after complete **cooling** (usually overnight).

▶ Check to ensure the **jars are sealed** by pressing down gently on the center with your finger. If it pops up and down (it may even make a popping sound), it isn't sealed. If the lid has been sucked down, you're good to go.

▶ If there is **no vacuum**, put the jar into the refrigerator and be sure to eat the contents within a short period of time.

▶ If your canning jar **resists opening**, place it right-side up into a pot of hot water to reduce the inner pressure. The jar will open more easily.

▶ You can keep preserved fruit or vegetables in a dark, cool location for **up to a year**.

Before preserving, remove stems and pits from cherries to keep them from losing too much juice.

When preserving red cabbage, first cut the leaves into small strips and cook them until al dente.

a money-saving hint

Instead of canning jars, you can use jam jars or vegetable jars with screw tops. The important thing is that they form an airtight seal and are free from damage. Just be aware that acids can attack the metal and release substances that leach into the preserves. As with canning jars, clean and boil your jars and lids thoroughly.

Preserving in Vinegar and Oil

You can easily preserve fruits, vegetables, and herbs in vinegar or oil as people have done for centuries. This method of preserving produces delicious foods and gives bacteria little chance of thriving.

Cleanliness plays an important role in any method of preserving foods. Select vinegars and oils carefully, as they clearly influence the taste.

PRESERVING BASICS

▶ Choose mild, refined oils such as **olive, sunflower, grapeseed,** and **sesame**; they won't overpower the flavor of the ingredients.

▶ Add some **herbs** or **spices** for a stronger taste when pickling or preserving foods.

▶ Pick light, distilled varieties of **vinegar** with good flavor, such as **cider, white wine,** or **malt.**

▶ Practically anything with a reasonably firm peel can be pickled. Fruit such as **pears** and plums, or mixtures of **vegetables** and **fruit**, taste wonderful in a sweet-sour broth.

▶ Never use dishes made of **aluminum, copper,** or **brass** when pickling. The acid in the vinegar will attack the surface, and your pickles will be contaminated by heavy metals.

▶ Before consuming the fruits of your labor, let the pickles or preserves **steep** for a **month.** After opening, eat up the contents promptly.

BASIC RECIPE FOR SOUR PICKLING

▶ To keep veggies crisp and prevent them from watering down the vinegar with their high water content, place them first in a **salt brine** for around 24 hours. Mix together 1 quart/liter of water and about ¼ cup (50 mL) of salt, and put the vegetables into a bowl and cover them with the brine. Then rinse them thoroughly and process as usual.

▶ For the **vinegar solution,** boil up a little over 2 cups (500 mL) vinegar and 1 cup (250 mL) water, 1 tsp. (5 mL) salt, plus any spices and herbs.

▶ Briefly **blanch** about 2 lb. (1 kg) washed and sliced vegetables in the solution.

▶ Remove them with a skimmer and **layer them in a jar** to within 1 in. (2.5 cm) of the rim.

Preserved delicacies in beautiful jars make great gifts for close friends.

Sweet-sour pickled fruits must be boiled if they're to be kept for more than six months.

▶ Commonly used spices include **peppercorns, mustard seeds, garlic, bay leaf,** and **chili flakes**. You can layer fresh spices between the vegetables.

▶ You may not want to add some spices directly to the jars; instead, suspend them in the pickling liquid in a small **spice packet** or a **ceramic tea ball** and remove before filling the jars.

▶ Boil the vinegar solution again and pour it into the jars. The liquid should **cover the vegetables completely.** Seal the jars and stand them on their lids for a few minutes, then turn.

RECIPES AND TIPS FOR SWEET-SOUR PICKLING

▶ Add 2–3 tsp. (10–15 mL) of **sugar** to the sour vinegar solution, according to taste, and then follow the same method as with sour pickling.

▶ Stone fruit such as **plums** can be layered in the jars raw. Fill up the jar with the hot vinegar solution and then seal.

▶ Good spices for sweet-sour pickling also include **cloves, ginger,** and **allspice.**

▶ **Honey** or **fruit juice concentrate** can replace some of the sugar.

▶ Sweet-sour fruits pickled in vinegar go well with all **meat dishes**.

SEALING IN OIL

▶ **Oil** provides an airtight seal for the ingredients, thus improving their shelf life. Depending on the recipe (and especially with seafood), additional preserving through salting, cooking, or marinating in oil may be necessary.

▶ If you want to preserve 2 lb. (1 kg) **vegetables**, you need 2 cups (500 mL) oil, 1 tbsp. (15 mL) salt, and spices and herbs according to taste.

▶ After washing and rinsing produce, cut it into bite-sized pieces and briefly **steam**.

▶ Dry **tomatoes** in advance in the oven. Lightly brown **eggplants** or **bell peppers** under the broiler and peel them. They don't need to be steamed.

▶ **Layer the veggies in the jars** with spices and herbs and pour in enough **oil**—heated to about 170°F (75°C)—to completely cover them.

▶ **Press down firmly** with a spoon so that all air bubbles rise and the jars can be sealed airtight.

▶ You can vary the spices: peppercorns, thyme, and lemon peel go well with **mushrooms**. **Tomatoes** taste great when seasoned with basil, mint, rosemary, and chili; **eggplants** go well with garlic and lemon.

▶ To pickle **seafood** in oil, cook it first in seasoned vinegar to kill any bacteria.

▶ Since seasonings and herbs release their **flavoring agents** into the oil, it can be used for seasoning other dishes.

good to know

PRICKING PICKLED FOODS
Cucumbers and plums turn out spicier and crispier if you prick them all around with a toothpick.

Mushrooms take on an intense flavor when pickled in oil with bay leaves and juniper berries.

Sauces, Gravies, and Vinaigrettes

A good sauce or dressing can bring new color, flavor, and sometimes texture to an otherwise ordinary meal. Sauces are essential companions for salads, pasta, rice, and roasts, and they are easy to vary with different combinations of spices.

When you deglaze meat juice with wine or broth, it takes on a more concentrated taste.

Wine, flour, cornstarch, or pureed vegetables all contribute to good gravies, and a tasty vinaigrette always starts with oil and vinegar.

DEGLAZING

Deglazing is the simplest way to get the base for a meat gravy.

▶ After browning, remove your meat from the pan and add **water** or some other liquid.

▶ Bring to a boil while stirring constantly to dissolve the **meat drippings.**

THE TRICK TO THICKENING GRAVY

Thickening gives gravy the right consistency and improves the flavor. Here are a few surefire tricks to getting the perfect gravy:

▶ **Puree vegetables** cooked in the meat stock to thicken your gravy and add taste.

▶ Adding 2 tsp. (10 mL) of **cranberries** gives gravy a fruity kick.

▶ When braising meat, add a few small pieces of **bread** to the pot; they'll disintegrate and make the meat stock creamy.

▶ **Flour** and **cornstarch** are good thickeners. Just stir them into a little water and add to the gravy before bringing it to a boil. If you use half flour and half cornstarch, gravy turns out thinner and lighter.

▶ A **roux** is the name for a method of mixing equal amounts of fat and flour, then cooking and combining them with liquid to make a base for sauces. For a **béchamel sauce,** add a little milk to the basic roux; for **brown roux,** add some stock.

▶ A mixture of **flour** and **butter** is good for thickening sauces shortly before serving. Knead them together in equal proportions and whisk small flakes into boiling sauce or gravy. Mixed flour and butter keeps for two weeks when refrigerated.

▶ Thicken boiled-down stocks with **cold butter**, stirring it little by little into hot gravy with a whisk until you get a creamy consistency. Serve the thickened sauce immediately.

▶ Shortly before serving, **sour cream, crème fraîche,** or **heavy cream** can also be beaten into a cooked-down meat stock for thickening.

▶ Mix a few spoonfuls of gravy with an **egg yolk** and add to the rest of the hot, but not boiling, gravy while stirring constantly. Do not let the liquid boil, or the egg yolk will form chunks.

▶ **Vinaigrette** is traditionally considered a salad dressing, but it tastes good with fish and meat dishes, too.

SUCCESS WITH GRAVIES

▶ Season **roux-based gravies** only after thickening.

▶ Boil a gravy thickened with roux for **at least 5 minutes** to eliminate the flour taste.

▶ Prevent a **skin** from forming on light gravies by drawing a piece of **butter** over them with a fork.

Vinaigrette is easy to get right, as long as you use the correct proportions of oil and vinegar.

▶ To enrich a gravy with **butter**, remove the pot from the burner and add the butter one piece at a time, letting it melt while swirling the pot a little.

▶ Beat gravies vigorously with a **whisk** to ensure they're creamy and free of lumps.

▶ To test the **consistency** of your gravy, stick a **wooden spoon** into it. The gravy should stick to it easily.

▶ You can **make gravy go further** by adding stock, vegetable broth, sour cream, cream, crème fraîche, wine, sherry, or even the water from cooking vegetables or pasta.

THE PERFECT VINAIGRETTE

Vinaigrette is still the classic salad dressing, but it relies on high-quality ingredients in the right proportions to work its magic.

▶ If you remember this one simple rule, you'll never have to consult a vinaigrette recipe again: use **vinegar** and **oil** in a 1:3 proportion. If you're adding **mustard**, use about 1 tsp. (5 mL) per 4 tbsp. (60 mL) salad dressing.

▶ Stir some **salt** and **pepper** into the **vinegar**, and whisk in the **mustard**. Then gradually pour in the **oil** while stirring constantly, until the vinegar and oil combine to form an emulsion.

▶ Always **beat in the oil last** to ensure your dressing retains its creamy consistency.

▶ If the ingredients start to **separate** from one another, beat the vinaigrette vigorously again.

▶ If the vinaigrette is **too oily**, add more vinegar and spices. If the vinaigrette tastes **sour**, add oil and salt. And remember that a little **sugar** won't hurt either.

▶ You can make a vinaigrette **in advance**. It will keep in a bottle in the refrigerator for around three weeks. Just remember to shake it thoroughly before use.

▶ You can **vary the basic vinaigrette recipe** by adding onions, garlic, nuts, dried fruit, ground flaxseeds, or herbs, depending on the salad, meat, or fish dish you will be pouring it over.

roux

one Melt or sauté about ⅔ oz. (20 g) butter in a pot and add about ⅔ oz. (20 g) flour, while stirring vigorously with a spoon.

two Keep stirring until the flour blends with the butter. For a dark roux, lightly brown the mixture.

three Add your liquid (stock, water, milk, etc.) and bring to a boil, continuing to stir the whole time until the sauce thickens.

Shopping

People who shop and store their food logically save a lot, in terms of both cash and valuable time. Making a detailed shopping list reduces the risk of buying too much or making impulse buys.

Fresh, high-quality, and usually well-priced goods are available straight from the farm or your local farmers' markets. And if you stick to seasonal and regional products, you'll get fresher goods and protect your pocketbook, as well as the environment.

PLANNING PURCHASES

▶ Post the **shopping list** in a visible spot in the kitchen. That way, anyone who needs something can immediately jot it down. And don't forget to take the list with you when you shop.

▶ Making a **meal plan** for the coming week can help you plan purchases wisely, buying only the necessary ingredients, but be flexible; try to incorporate the specials that are available in the store or supermarket ads.

▶ Never shop while **hungry**; the danger of impulse buys rises exponentially and you're likely to spend more money than you had planned.

▶ Opt for **generic brands** whenever possible. These tasty copycats are made by reputable companies and are much less expensive.

CAREFREE SHOPPING

To protect your groceries from harm, put the durable items (like cans and bottles) into your cart first and pile the fresh foods on top. You can even buy special insulating bags for frozen products.

▶ It's usually cheaper to buy **large packages**. You might even share them with neighbors or friends.

▶ To reduce garbage, choose **multi-use packaging** or buy products in **bulk**.

You can protect noodles, nuts, rice, and sugar from pests by storing them in tightly sealed plastic containers.

If your shopping list is organized according to product categories, you can dash through the supermarket much more quickly.

In terms of pure nutritional value, it's hard to beat the benefits of fish, whether it's omega-3-rich salmon, tuna, or whitefish.

▸ You'll generally find the most economical items on the **lower shelves** in supermarkets.

▸ **Commercial classifications** (like Grade A) apply only to the appearance and size of goods, not to the nutritional value of fruits and vegetables.

▸ Look for supermarket **freezer cabinets** that are neatly organized and not coated with thick ice. If the goods show any sign at all of freezer burn, walk away.

▸ **Dented cans** are best left on the shelves.

▸ Don't buy any **dairy products** with **bulging tops**—the contents could be spoiled.

▸ You can tell when **fish** is fresh by its clear, bright eyes, bright red gills, and shiny, moist skin.

▸ **Beef** should be vibrant red; **pork** should be pink.

STORAGE

Store foods properly. Temperature, light, and moisture can affect their appearance, taste, and vitamin content. Foods that are stored improperly can easily go bad.

▸ **Prepackaged goods** with a long shelf life, such as dried foods, are best kept in a dark pantry or a dry basement storage room.

▸ Even **canned goods** need to be protected from moisture and great temperature variations.

▸ Products kept in **jars, bottles,** or **clear plastic bags** should be stored in the dark.

▸ Stow **new supplies** behind those you already have on hand.

WELL-COOLED

To increase shelf life, keep foods in their proper place in the refrigerator.

▸ Foods that spoil quickly, such as **fish, meat, sausage,** and **prepared foods,** belong in the coldest place in the fridge: the meat drawer.

▸ Store all **dairy products** and **cheese** directly above the meat drawer.

▸ Foods that need only minor cooling, such as **butter, eggs, drinks,** and **ketchup,** are best stored on the top shelf or in the door compartments provided for them.

▸ **Fruits** and **vegetables** should go in the lower crisper, without packaging.

▸ Unpackage **thawing meat** and store it in a bowl or on a plate in the refrigerator, covered with aluminum foil.

▸ Fresh **fish** will keep for up to a day in the fridge; if cooked, it will last for two to three days.

▸ Store **eggs** in the fridge with the blunt end up; that way, the air remains on top and the inner membrane doesn't dissolve.

▸ To avert mold, store **blue cheeses** separately from other types of cheese.

▸ During the cooler months of the year, less delicate **fruits and veggies** can also be stored on a balcony—but they must be protected from frost and direct sunlight.

a money-saving *hint*

You'll often find some good deals at weekly markets. Keep in mind that shortly before closing time the prices on fresh goods often drop significantly.

Bread remains fresh for a long time inside a cloth bag. The bag also takes up little room.

Soup

Broths are usually a byproduct of boiling vegetables, meat, fish, or poultry in water. When you're making a stock, on the other hand, you generally boil down bones, aromatic vegetables, and spices for hours. Both are starting points for many soups.

A clear soup is a broth that can be eaten with additions such as chopped veggies, egg, noodles, chunks of meat, or dumplings. Thickened soups often use broths or stocks as a base, but they are thickened with a roux (made of flour and butter), cream, crème fraîche, pureed potatoes, or sour cream. You can make pureed soups by blending the cooked ingredients at the end so the soup is smooth.

BROTHS

Use as large a pot as possible; the ingredients must be able to float.

▶ For a **simple meat broth,** you need about 14 oz. (400 g) beef or poultry, 2 carrots, 2 leek stalks, 1 onion, and 1 stalk of celery, plus salt, pepper, and 1 bay leaf. Simmer all ingredients in 1½ quarts/liters of water for 30–40 minutes.

▶ Cook **noodles, barley,** or **rice** separately and add to the soup later—otherwise, your soup will turn unappetizingly cloudy.

▶ **Spices** such as bay leaves, cloves, and star anise are best placed in tea bell or a spice bag and hung in the pot while cooking; that way, you won't have to fish them out after.

▶ For an especially **substantial broth,** add the ingredients to the water while it's still cold.

▶ If you want to eat the meat cooked in your broth, such as **boiled beef** or **chicken,** make sure the water is boiling before adding it.

▶ A little **cognac** or a dash of **vinegar** in the cooking water makes for particularly tender boiled meat.

STOCKS

To make a stock, you also need meat bones or fish bones and carcasses.

▶ To make a **light stock,** for every quart/liter of water in the pot, add about 24 oz. (750 g) chopped bones, 1 onion, 1 bouquet garni (a bundle of herbs especially for soup), mirepoix (a chunk of celeriac, 1 carrot, and 1 leek), a few peppercorns, and 1 clove of garlic. Slowly bring to a boil, then simmer on low for four to five hours before straining.

▶ For a **dark stock,** roast the bones and vegetables first in the oven.

▶ Stocks should **simmer but never boil;** that way the stock is richer-tasting and clearer. In addition, boiling for a long time causes stock's vitamins and minerals to go up in smoke—or rather, vapor.

▶ A stock is done when it has a concentrated aroma; **chicken bones** should be coming apart.

▶ For a **fish stock,** mix 1½ quarts/liters of water with about 2 cups (500 mL) dry white wine and add vegetables, salt, pepper, parsley, and about 2 lbs. (1 kg) lean whitefish carcasses. Bring to a boil and let simmer over low heat for 20 minutes. If you cook the stock any longer, it will become bitter.

Add a finishing touch to broth in the form of fresh herbs and green onions.

A creamy zucchini soup is best served cold in the summer.

TIPS FOR BROTHS AND STOCKS

While cooking broth or stock you'll notice foam from congealed protein forming on the surface. Skim it off regularly, along with excess fat.

▶ **Remove fat** from broths and stocks by skimming it off or absorbing it with a paper towel. You can also let your broth cool, then remove any solidified fat from the top with a spoon.

▶ Clarify a finished broth by boiling a **beaten egg white** in it. The egg white absorbs suspended solids as it congeals—just remove it before serving.

▶ Another method of clarifying broths or stocks is to strain them through a **fine sieve** or a piece of **cheesecloth**.

▶ **Salt** broths and stocks **lightly**, at least at first, since they become more concentrated as liquid evaporates. You're better off carefully adding spices and seasoning at the end.

▶ Use only **whole peppercorns** in most soups; ground pepper starts to taste bitter after cooking for a long time.

▶ Use **parsley stems** for stocks; the flavor is stronger than in the leaves, which tend to turn bitter when cooked at length.

▶ Stocks or broths usually keep in the **refrigerator** for two to three days and can last up to three months in the **freezer**.

PUREED AND CREAM SOUPS

For pureed soups, root vegetables, legumes, potatoes, and pumpkin are the best choices. The starchy ingredients combine with one another, making the soup nice and creamy.

▶ For a **pureed soup,** lightly braise about 18 oz. (550 g) vegetables in a greased pan, then cook them along with root vegetables, salt, and pepper in 1 quart/liter of water. Press the soup through a strainer or puree in a blender, then season to taste.

▶ After braising the vegetables, **cream soups** can be thickened with 1–2 tbsp. (15–25 mL) flour and finished off with about 1 cup (250 mL) cream, sour cream, or crème fraîche.

▶ Thin out soups that are too thick with **milk** or a little **water**. On the other hand, you can also thicken soups that are too thin with a little sprinkling of **cornstarch**.

▶ Pureed soups can be garnished with **cream, butter, fresh herbs, croutons,** or **crumbled bacon.**

▶ When preparing a cream soup, start by making the **roux** (butter and flour), then whisk in the broth just a little bit at a time so that no lumps can form.

▶ A cream soup gets thicker the more **flour** you use. If you carefully shake the flour into the soup through a funnel, whisking constantly, the soup will be smooth. But cook it thoroughly so it doesn't taste like flour.

▶ To avoid **coagulation,** cook acidic ingredients like **tomatoes** by thoroughly boiling them. And make sure you pour the soup into the cooking pot containing the **cream**, rather than the other way around.

meat broth

one Cover the washed vegetables, spices, and meat with cold water.

two Bring the broth to a boil, then simmer for a while. Insert a spoon between the pot and the lid to let the steam out.

three When the cooking is done, remove the meat and carefully pour the contents of the pot through a strainer into a second pot.

Spices

Once-pricey spices like pepper, ginger, saffron, and nutmeg are practically essential to today's cuisine. But take note: if they're stored the wrong way or for too long, their wonderful flavors can fade.

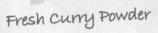

Fresh Curry Powder

2 tbsp. (25 mL) coriander seeds

2 tsp. (10 mL) cumin seeds

½ tsp. (2 mL) mustard seeds

1 tsp. (5 mL) black peppercorn

1 tsp. (5 mL) fenugreek seeds

10 fresh curry leaves

½ tsp. (5 mL) ground ginger

1 tbsp. (15 mL) ground turmeric

1 tsp. (5 mL) chili powder or cayenne pepper.

Dry roast the coriander seeds, cumin seeds, mustard seeds, black peppercorn, and fenugreek seeds over medium heat until the seeds darken and become fragrant. Stir constantly to prevent burning. Leave to cool, then grind to a powder.

Dry roast the fresh curry leaves, grind and add to the mixture along with the ground ginger, ground turmeric, and chili powder or cayenne pepper.

Using spices correctly will make a meal extra special. Here is how you can keep them fresh and put them to good use.

STORING SPICES

▶ Store spices in **airtight, opaque containers** in a **cool, dark location**—they last longer when not exposed to sunlight.

▶ Since spices tend to give off and absorb flavors, always keep the **same spice** in a given container.

▶ Stored properly, spices keep for up to **two years**, and many last even longer.

WORKING WITH SPICES

▶ Choose **whole spices when possible** (e.g., peppercorns); they retain their full flavor better.

▶ Grind spices with a **mortar** and **pestle** just before using for maximum flavor. The mortar should have a high rim to keep the spices from tumbling out. It's usually easier to grind spices if you add a little **salt** for traction.

▶ **Spice mills** are useful for nutmeg, pepper, and other hard spices. Make sure they're easy to clean.

▶ **Soft spices,** such as red peppercorns and juniper berries, can be crushed, cut, or smashed with a kitchen knife.

▶ Reserve special graters only for **ginger** or **nutmeg,** as their flavors can be easily transferred.

PROPER USE OF SPICES

Used properly, spices can help you lower the salt-content of food without reducing the flavor.

▶ Spice meats and vegetables **before cooking**; that's when they are most absorbent. **Salt** removes moisture from raw meat, though, rendering it tougher; it's wise to salt meat only after browning.

▶ **Marinades** work especially well for seasoning and tenderizing meats.

▶ Spices should heighten the taste of the food, not overpower it. So use spices in **moderation**, and make sure the flavors go well together.

▶ Many spices, such as **paprika, chili, garlic,** and **curry**, lose their flavor or become bitter when you add them to bubbling hot oil or butter. They release their aroma and taste better when lightly sautéed.

For centuries, Asian cuisine has relied on a fragrant cornucopia of spices.

COMMON KITCHEN SPICES

▶ **Cayenne pepper** consists of dried, ground chili peppers. It adds pungency to sauces and stews, such as the classic chili con carne. Just remember that you should only add cayenne shortly before serving, otherwise it becomes bitter.

▶ It's a good idea to wear rubber gloves when chopping **fresh chili peppers**. The oils in the inner membranes and the seeds can burn your hands, eyes, and lips. For milder dishes, discard the potent membranes and seeds. Dried chili peppers can be ground as needed in a mortar or spice mill.

▶ **Curry**, a mixture of various spices, is used to add a savory punch to curry or rice dishes, sauces, poultry, and meat.

▶ One of the best-loved herbs in the world, **cilantro** is used in Spanish, Middle Eastern, Indian, Asian, and South American cuisine. The leaves should be used fresh and can be sprinkled like parsley on salads, soups, and other cooked dishes.

▶ **Coriander** seeds are best bought whole and ground as needed. Coriander is the base of most curries and can be used for meat, poultry, and fish.

▶ **Cumin** gives a bite to plain rice and is used in many stews, curries, grills, and chicken dishes. It is much loved by Indian, Middle Eastern, Spanish, and Portuguese cooks.

▶ **Ginger** gives baked goods, stir-fries, rice dishes, and fruit a fresh, slightly pungent taste.

▶ **Garlic** adds its characteristic taste and aroma to countless dishes, If the tips of your garlic cloves sport green sprouts, cut the clove in half and remove the sprout before preparing the garlic.

▶ Use **caraway** to season bread, cabbage dishes, casseroles, and curry.

▶ Raw **horseradish** is particularly pungent. It gives oomph to roasts and winter soups.

▶ **Nutmeg** adds a distinctive flavor to cookies, pies, and apple sauce.

▶ The aroma of **cloves** often evokes images of Christmas, pumpkin pie, and mulled wine, but their spicy-sweet flavor also works well in marinades, red cabbage, apple sauce, and pear compote.

▶ **Paprika** runs the gamut from sweet to spicy. It releases its color and flavor when heated, but burns easily. So add paprika only when liquid ingredients are present and don't cook it too long.

▶ No cook can get by without that kitchen classic: **pepper**. Unripe green peppercorns have a citrusy aroma. Black pepper is harvested shortly before ripening and then fermented; red peppercorns, in contrast to white ones, are unshelled and more flavorful.

▶ **Saffron** adds taste to rice dishes, seafood, and lamb.

▶ Stick or ground **cinnamon** is used in Asian dishes, sauces, and many desserts.

Use a ceramic mortar. Wood absorbs the flavor of spices.

good to know
TAKE CARE WITH NUTMEG!
Nutmeg, along with its close relative, mace, is an important element in many of the world's cuisines. It imparts a nice taste and color to many dishes, from Japanese curries to a glass of holiday eggnog.

But beware: Nutmeg is poisonous when eaten in large quantities. It must always be stored well out of the reach of children. Two nutmeg seeds can be fatal to a small child.

Sweets

We know, we know: sugar should be consumed in moderation. But it's still OK to have the occasional treat. Many homemade goodies are child's play to make as long as you start with quality ingredients.

There is nothing quite like ice cream or sorbet on a hot day, or candied fruit to top off a meal.

making ganache

one In a small pot, quickly heat 2/3 cup (150 mL) cream. Bring to a boil, then take the pot off the burner to cool completely.

two In the meantime, chop up about 10 oz. (300 g) good chocolate and melt it in a double boiler.

three Stir the cream and the chocolate together to produce a smooth liquid. If necessary, stir in a little more cold cream.

GOOD THINGS FROM CHOCOLATE

Ganache, a mixture of chopped chocolate and cream or butter, is the basis for many types of truffles, and it's a cinch to make. Use more chocolate in comparison to cream for a firmer ganache.

▶ While your ganache is **still warm in the pot**, you can add liqueur, rum, sparkling wine or champagne, honey, coffee, peanut brittle, nougat, dried fruit, syrup, and many other delicious ingredients.

▶ By blending ganache made from different types of chocolate, you can make **marbled chocolates**. For example, the contrast between a layer of white chocolate with vanilla and a layer of darker ganache with orange liqueur is both beautiful and tasty.

▶ You can **decorate truffles** with just about anything as long as it tastes good and looks pretty: try icing, whole or chopped nuts, candied fruit, or colored decorations made from marzipan. You can roll the balls in cocoa powder, confectioner's (icing) sugar, or coconut, or use finely chopped nuts and chocolate crumbs.

ICE CREAM: A TREAT FOR HOT DAYS

Water is the basis for sorbet, while ice cream gets its creamy texture from milk and cream—even heavy cream. You can flavor both with sugar, fruit, and any number of other tasty ingredients.

▶ For **sorbet,** heat up about 1 cup (250 mL) water and 7 oz. (200 g) sugar and boil for 2 minutes, until the sugar dissolves. Stir in about 18 oz. (550 g) pureed fruit or 2 cups (500 mL) fruit juice and a little lemon juice. Let cool. Flavor with sugar or lemon and freeze.

▶ **Ice cream** is equally easy to make: beat 3 egg yolks with 3 oz. (85 g) sugar until foamy and thoroughly stir in about 7 1/2 oz. (225 mL) cream and 3/4 cup (175 mL) milk.

▶ Additions to these basic liquids include **pureed fruit, nuts, chocolate,** or **yogurt.**

▶ If you don't have an **ice cream maker**, put the ice mixture in a shallow metal bowl in the **freezer**. When it freezes, stir it thoroughly and freeze again. Repeat this process several times.

TIPS FOR MAKING ICE CREAM

▶ If your ice cream turns out too **grainy**, you may have used too much water or too little sugar. Alternatively, the ice cream may have frozen too quickly or wasn't stirred enough.

▶ **Ice cream loses flavor** when frozen, so the initial liquid should taste quite sweet and strong.

If you like cinnamon, roll balls of ganache in a mixture of powdered cinnamon and dark cocoa.

CANDIED FRUIT

Fruits are candied by dipping them in a strong sugar concentrate to preserve them and give them a sweeter flavor. Alternatively you can coat pineapple, apples, bananas, pears, or strawberries with chocolate.

▶ Except for **strawberries**, berries aren't good candidates to be candied because they're too soft.

▶ For fruits such as **grapes,** which can be candied whole, it's best to poke a hole in them to allow the sugar solution to penetrate them completely. Candy **orange** and **lemon** slices with the peel intact, using only organic fruit.

▶ For the **syrup**, boil 1 quart/liter of water and 2 lb. (1 kg) sugar until strings form.

▶ Suspend 18 oz. (550 g) fruit or pieces of fruit in a strainer in a steel bowl and **pour the sugar solu-tion** over the fruit until it is completely covered.

▶ Let **steep** for a day, before removing and drying the fruit. Then boil up the sugar solution and **pour it over the fruits again.**

▶ Repeat this process **five times**. The last time, boil the sugar solution down further and let the prepared fruits dry thoroughly on a cooling rack.

▶ In order to coat fruit with **chocolate**, cut it into bite-sized pieces and spear them with a wooden spit or toothpicks, before dipping them in liquid chocolate.

While melting chocolate, stir it continually to make sure it doesn't burn.

INVENTIVE SNACKS FOR KIDS

Children can be persuaded to nosh on fruit and other nutritious foods if you add a little fun first.

▶ Fashion an **edible caterpillar** by skewering melon balls, grapes, and cheese cubes on an uncooked spaghetti strand.

▶ Pour **melted chocolate** over **trail mix** to create a yummy fruit-and-nut cluster.

▶ Let the sun shine: cut **pineapple** pieces into triangles and arrange on a plate in a circle to create the rays of the sun. Spoon a little **vanilla yogurt** into the center for dipping.

▶ For the classic **"ants on a log"** treat, fill the indentation of a piece of celery with peanut butter and sprinkle raisins (or "ants") along the log.

▶ Create a flower kids will want to devour by using segments of a **clementine** or **tangerine** for the petals, a **strawberry** for the center, and **kiwis** sliced into the shapes of leaves.

Candied petals from edible plants are perfect to elegantly decorate cakes and cupcakes.

Children like ice cream on a stick. It's easy to make using basic popsicle forms.

Table and Place Settings

A carefully set and lovingly decorated table makes a dinner party a feast for the eyes as well as the stomach. Just remember that your decorations should add pizzazz without getting in the way of the meal.

Long-stemmed glasses and individual presents boost the feeling of celebration.

When setting a festive table, you should arrange things beautifully—but remember to keep it simple for both you and the guests.

TABLE LINENS

Choose your table linens according to the occasion, making sure they don't clash with the flatware, silverware, and glasses.

▶ A **tablecloth** should hang over the edge of the table about 10–12 in. (25–30 cm) on all sides. Lay a **table protector** under it to save your table from hot dishes and spills, and to keep the tablecloth from slipping.

▶ **White tablecloths** allow the greatest latitude in choosing the other decorations. To add a bit of color, place a **runner** or band of pretty fabric lengthwise or widthwise across the table.

▶ For rustic place settings, use simple **place mats**.

▶ If you need **several tablecloths** for a fairly long table, make sure that the edges overlap and that the tablecloths are all straight.

▶ For **napkins**, either tuck them into wine glasses, or fold them and lay them on the plates or to the left of them. Use napkin rings or fold the napkins into decorative shapes.

▶ With a little creativity, you can make **one-of-a-kind napkin rings.** Tie some grasses, flowers, or leaves around the napkins with a string, or transform silk ribbons into colorful napkin rings. At Christmas time, fasten small wooden toys around your napkins with red or green ribbons.

TABLE SETTINGS

▶ Place **plates** about ½ in. (1 cm) from the edge of the table. The distance between the centers of two place settings should be 24–32 in. (60–80 cm), so that you

For a simple table decoration, place flowers, leaves, and floating candles in a shallow glass bowl filled with water.

Here the orange and purple hues of the decorations are part of the Halloween theme.

can fit a good number of guests at the table without anyone feeling cramped.

▶ There should be no more than four **pieces of silverware** on the right; three on the left.

▶ Always place the **dessert silverware** horizontally above the plate. Point the handle of a fork to the left, and the handle of a spoon to the right. If you're serving fresh fruit for dessert, place a dessert fork (instead of a spoon) at the top edge of the plate.

▶ Place **bread plates,** along with a small **butter knife**, to the left of the setting if necessary.

▶ Set **glasses** above the silverware on the right-hand side in the order in which they will be used.

▶ **White wine glasses** should be positioned slightly further right and filled to two-thirds full.

▶ **Red wine** is generally served in large, wide goblets that taper slightly toward the top. Fill the glasses only a quarter-full so that the wine has room to breathe.

THE FINAL TOUCH

Don't overdo the table decorations. If your guests have to peer through the flowers to talk to you, you may have gone too far. Table decor should encourage a pleasant, festive atmosphere without hindering conversation.

▶ **Place cards** belong at the top of the place setting and can be decorated with drawings, photos, or small flowers.

▶ For children's birthdays, spell the names of guests using **alphabet cookies, candies,** or **cupcakes.**

▶ **Menus** are used mainly for official occasions, but at private parties they can round out the decorations and serve as souvenirs. Experiment with different shapes—round, oval, or triangular—or decorate them to coordinate with the invitation.

▶ For large parties, you can also write the menu in chalk on a **blackboard**.

FLOWERS AND CANDLES

▶ Use **floral decorations** that are appropriate for the season and nature of the gathering. Remember to cut them short so they don't hinder eye contact across the table.

▶ Instead of using a large bouquet, which usually has to be removed during the meal, **scatter flower petals** or arrange **small, individual bouquets** or **pots** on the table. Individual flowers and long-lasting greens such as long sprigs of ivy also dress up a festive table.

▶ Make sure **candles** are in secure candlesticks so they don't tip over.

▶ For a fairly large table, use small lanterns or **tea lights** in decorative glasses. Match the color to the floral decoration.

▶ To make a beautiful table even more festive, scatter polished pieces of **colored glass**, shiny **confetti**, or beautifully-colored **leaves** over the table cloth.

▶ On special holidays, put a small **chocolate** on every plate: an Easter egg, Santa Claus, or small heart, depending on the holiday.

Thrifty Kitchen

With a little planning, skill, and creativity, you can save plenty of cash in your kitchen—without giving up on good food. Look for savings by altering your household appliance usage, changing your shopping habits, and making savvy use of leftovers.

Cut Down on Food Costs

- Try not to let foods spoil. You can make purees, jam, smoothies, or compotes from fruit. Freeze leftover gravy and sauces (e.g., in an ice cube tray). Brown hamburger, then freeze it for later.

- Shop thoughtfully: flank steak, stewing beef, and other less expensive cuts of meat are 10 to 30 percent cheaper, but need longer marinating and/or cooking times to render them tender. Plan your meals in advance and take advantage of slow cookers to get maximum bang for your buck.

- Make use of an old cooking trick: when boiling down jam, add the juice of 1–2 lemons to save on sugar and prevent the fruit from discoloring.

- Even leftover drinks can be repurposed. Use wine that has gone sour as vinegar, and flat mineral water for making tea.

- Precook: cooking twice the amount of potatoes or noodles saves time. A day or two later you can warm them up and serve, or use in a soup or casserole.

Save Energy

- Household appliances typically use up about 30 percent of your home's energy. It's worthwhile in the long run to replace energy-wasting appliances such as old refrigerators, freezers, and electric stoves.

- A gas stove is more economical than an electric one.

- Look for good-quality, thermo-conductive pots and pans.

- Always put pots on the heating element that is closest in size, and don't forget to use a tight-fitting lid while cooking.

- Use residual heat by turning off an electrical element about 5 minutes before whatever you're cooking is done.

- A pressure cooker can save up to 30 percent of the energy used for stovetop cooking with cooking times over 20 minutes.

Try These Alternatives

- Instead of using roux (a paste of butter and flour), you can thicken gravies or soups with potato water.

- If you don't want to buy a whole carton of buttermilk for a recipe, add 1 tbsp. (15 mL) vinegar or lemon to a little less than 1 cup (250 mL) milk and let stand for 10 minutes.

- No cream in the house for making sauces? Substitute condensed milk or coffee cream. Note that these replacements won't work for whipped cream.

- You can make fruit yogurt by stirring a spoonful of jam or marmalade into plain yogurt.

- Preserved fruit makes a yummy topping on a cake.

- Almost any kind of nuts will do for pesto, including walnuts and almonds.

- You can quickly turn granulated sugar into confectioner's (icing) sugar in a coffee grinder or spice mill.

- Bread crumbs on casseroles or cauliflower can easily be replaced with ground nuts.

- You can easily make a funnel from a plastic bag by cutting off one corner.

Household Budget

Expense	Am
Mortgage payment	
Auto loan	$550
Auto insurance	$280.
Auto expenses (gas, etc.)	$ 120.(
Groceries ($100.00/week)	$100.0
Utilities	$ 433.3
Telephone	$ 110.00
Medical	$ 35.00

Budget

- Plan your menu around the supermarket specials.

- Seasonal items are not only cheaper, but also tastier and fresher because of the shorter transportation from producer to consumer.

- By tracking household spending for about a month, you can get an overview of whether your financial planning really coincides with your income and expenditures, and modify your behavior accordingly. An easy way to do it: keep an envelope in your purse or car where you can drop each and every receipt, then tally them at month's end.

- Stocking up protects your wallet. When goods become expensive, you can pull out the berries you froze in the middle of the summer.

- Buy unsliced cheese or bread. They will stay fresh longer.

- Packaged foods always cost more. Consider that prewashed salad greens will set you back an extra 50 percent or more. Is it really worth it?

Enhance Flavor

- Brush dried-out pound cake with milk and bake it briefly in the oven—it will taste fresh again—or use it up in a trifle.

- Puree uncooked mushrooms with a little broth, freeze, and use later to add flavor to sauces or soups.

- Turn a hollandaise sauce into béarnaise with a pinch of tarragon. Warmed up with 1 tbsp. (15 mL) orange peel and 2 tbsp. (25 mL) orange juice, it makes an exotic Maltese sauce.

- Steep rinsed, canned shrimp for 15 minutes in 2 tbsp. (25 mL) vinegar and a little bit of good sherry so that they lose the canned flavor.

Comfortable *Living*

There really is no place like home—it's a warm haven and retreat from an often hostile world. Here are some tips to turn your home into a comfortable refuge, whether it's by creating a bathroom spa or a bedroom sanctuary.

Bathrooms

Make the hardest-working room in your house the perfect place to escape to. Your day begins and ends in the bathroom—that's reason enough to spend a little time giving it a serene, spa-like feel. Often a few small changes are all it takes to spruce up an older bathroom.

New mirrors and lighting can freshen up a tired-looking bathroom. Change fabrics and tiles to set a new tone for the room, and always stay on the lookout for mildew, which can be dangerous.

THE RIGHT SETUP

▶ Use a **softer bulb**. Soft lights can help create the right ambience for a relaxing bath. Also, artfully-placed candles can add to the spa feel and provide flattering lighting for just about any skin type.

▶ Use light hues like **white, pale blue,** and **beige,** or **light-colored wood** to make smaller bathrooms appear larger. If you can't replace tiles or repaint the room, at least choose new accessories in lighter shades.

▶ Install a new **shower partition.** This can be done without much trouble, and it works wonders, especially in older bathrooms.

▶ Clear out the **clutter**: the only things that belong in open storage are those you use every day.

▶ Store **towels** in the **bathroom closet** if space is limited. Or for a chic, yet practical solution, roll them up, secure each with a ribbon, and place them standing up in a **basket** by the bathtub.

▶ The bathroom is the perfect spot for exotic, humidity-loving greenery like **bonsai trees** and **tropical plants.**

▶ Add **upholstered furniture** to create a trendy, inviting place to relax. **Stools** with **terry cloth seats** are moisture-resistant and provide a comfortable chair while you paint your toenails or moisturize your skin.

▶ Bring in some soothing scents like **lavender, orange,** and **vanilla** in the form of aromatherapy candles, lotions, or a scent diffuser for even more relaxation.

▶ Keep a **clock** in the bathroom—especially one that can be attached to the tiles with suction cups or hung from the showerhead—so you can always keep an eye on the time as you get ready in the morning.

▶ Get a **water-resistant radio** if you like to start your day with music.

The inviting hues of the fabrics and the modern washstand harmonize perfectly with the older tiles on the walls and floor, creating a contemporary ambience.

This functional and elegant shower shelf suits any decor and allows you to store shampoo and conditioner within easy reach.

BATH FABRICS

Well-chosen bathroom fabrics can turn the bathroom into a comfortable, attractive space and are kind to skin, depending on the fabric.

▶ Choose a **shower curtain** that complements the rest of the bathroom furnishings. **Fabric curtains** are chic and attractive compared to plastic curtains, but they need regular cleaning; if you get one, make sure it's machine-washable.

▶ Opt for attractive **matching towels** to give the bathroom a finished look. Also, thick, high-quality towels will make drying off after a bath an absolute joy.

TILES—A PROBLEM AREA

If old, cracked tiles, graying grout, or 1970's decor are setting your teeth on edge, don't immediately start the demolition. Take a cue from earlier generations and fix rather than discarding them.

▶ Try thoroughly **cleaning** the existing tiles. This will usually will do the trick. For stubborn stains, use **water** mixed with **ammonia** or **alcohol**; remove mineral deposits with **vinegar**. Rub old tiles with a little **linseed oil** to give them new shine.

▶ Repair small cracks in the tiles with **matching paint** from an art supply store. Mix a small amount of the paint with grout and apply to the tiles to fill hairline cracks.

▶ Refresh older tiles by **repainting the grout** (special grout-coloring kits are available). Keep in mind that grout paint can't be used for non-enamel tiles or on top of water-resistant joint sealer.

▶ Visually enlarge the bathroom with **adhesive mirror tiles**. They're a good choice when replacements for old tiles are no longer available. Or paint over unwanted tiles with **tile primer** and **lacquer** to cover them completely.

▶ One simple but effective solution is to cement a whole **new layer of tiles** over unsalvageable existing tiles. This will save time and money over removing the old layer and resurfacing the wall.

MILDEW? NO THANKS

The best remedy for mildew is plenty of air circulation. This gets rid of moisture so that mildew can't take hold—so turn on your bathroom fan. But that's not all you can do. Here are some surefire ways of minimizing mildew in your bathroom:

▶ Wipe condensation from the shower wall and tiles with a **squeegee** after your shower.

▶ Use **vinegar** to clean the corners between the shower or bathtub and the tiled wall from time to time as a preventative measure.

▶ Paint non-tiled wall surfaces and the ceiling with **mildew-resistant paint**.

▶ Remove the **grout** where mildew has already taken hold; clean thoroughly and seal the cleaned edges with new grout.

replacing damaged tiles

If left alone, damaged tiles can cause larger problems in a damp environment. So if you discover a cracked or chipped tile in your bathroom, follow these simple steps to stop further damage from happening.

one Completely remove the grout around the damaged tile and use a dry-cut saw to slice diagonally through the tile itself, or make several holes with a drill.

two Chip off fragments of the tile with a hammer and flat chisel until the whole thing comes loose. Remove as much of the old bonding material as possible.

three Cover the back of the replacement tile with bonding material and press it onto the wall, using tile spacers to position and fit the tile correctly.

four Let the tile cure overnight (or as directed by the manufacturer). Then apply grout and clean.

Bedrooms

To lull yourself to sleep you need to make your bedroom a sensuous haven, adding all the accoutrements of comfort and serenity in a beautiful setting. Buy a new bed, mattress, and bedding, and make sure that the individual components you choose work well together.

Getting a proper night's sleep is key to good overall health. Unfortunately, it's something that few of us get. Choose the bedsheets, pillows, headboard, and mattress that will help you nod off.

CHOOSING A HEADBOARD

True, not every bed has a headboard, but they can be the finishing touch to some bedrooms' decor.

▶ Traditional solid **wood** is sturdy and attractive.

▶ **Particle board** may be relatively inexpensive, but it's often not very stable. Also, many particle boards use toxic glues and binders that may affect the air quality in your bedroom.

▶ Check that there's no particle board beneath **upholstered headboards.**

▶ **Metal beds** can be a good investment; they're durable and stay pristine-looking longer than wooden beds.

ALL ABOUT SLATTED FRAMES

Slatted frames offer some real advantages in terms of bed height and weight.

▶ A **roll-up slatted frame** made of wooden slats joined together with **synthetic straps** is the most affordable solution.

▶ Rigid slatted frames vary considerably, depending on whether or not the frame has been **reinforced** in vulnerable spots. Some models allow you to adjust the supports to suit your sleeping position.

▶ Adjustable slatted frames let you **adjust the height of the bed** for your legs or head—an advantage if you want to watch TV or read in bed. Be aware that a well-made adjustable slat bed can easily cost a small fortune.

▶ **Futons** sometimes come with simple adjustable wood frames.

▶ Check the **number** of wooden slats to determine the quality of the frame.

▶ **Electric bed frames** let you adjust the frame effortlessly with a remote control.

CHOOSING A MATTRESS

Selecting the right mattress means not only finding one that's the right size, but also looking at the materials used and whether it fits your budget and needs. Here are the most popular mattress styles available right now.

▶ **Foam mattresses** can offer a good night's sleep. Unfortunately, they also tend to be very soft, meaning they sometimes wear out faster and can cause back pain.

Raising the upper portion of an adjustable frame makes breakfast in bed a comfy experience.

During the hot summer months, mosquito netting guards against insect bites.

▶ **Gel mattresses** are the newest developments in mattresses. They're similar to **waterbeds** for sleeping comfort, but much easier to care for. They are, however, on the pricey side.

▶ **Latex** or **high-density foam mattresses** offer a high degree of sleeping comfort. They conform perfectly to your body and sleep position while minimizing pressure on your head, shoulders, and hips. What's more, they're noise-free and if, you're sharing your bed, adjust to each individual.

▶ **Coil spring mattresses** are extremely popular because of their durability. The hollow spaces between the springs allow for constant air circulation. The higher the quality, the better you sleep. **Pocket spring mattresses** are the most comfortable, because their elasticity is confined to individual springs; each spring is sewn into its own pocket, so it moves independently of the surrounding springs.

BEDSHEETS

Just as with mattress shopping, buying the right set of sheets is a question of balancing budget with needs. You will likely want sheets or blankets of different fabrics depending on the season, as well.

▶ **Feather** and **down comforters** are warm, soft, and porous, while **sheep** and **alpaca wool,** as well as **camel hair**, provide dry warmth and are ideal if you have arthritis. **Cotton** absorbs moisture but doesn't provide as much warmth. Like **linen** and **silk**, it's better-suited for summer temperatures. Of course, **synthetic fibers** are a boon for allergy sufferers. They transmit moisture and excessive body heat to the surrounding air rather than absorbing it.

▶ **Sheets** are made from all kinds of materials, such as terry cloth, flannel, satin, silk, cotton, polycotton, and linen. **Flannel** warms you in the winter, but a **linen** or **cotton** sheet is the best choice in summer.

▶ **Fitted sheets** are very easy to put on. Their elastic bands make it easy to stretch them taut and wrinkle-free.

THE RIGHT PILLOW FOR EVERYONE

Always choose a pillow that conforms to your sleep position. If you sleep on your side, your pillow has to prop up your head, so it should be thicker than the pillow for a back-sleeper. There are even customized side-sleeper pillows available. Things to consider:

▶ If you have problems with your neck, opt for a **smaller pillow**, about 32 in. (80 cm) wide but only 16 in. (40 cm) long. Although you can position a larger pillow properly before you go to sleep, it can shift during the night, resulting in neck and back pain in the morning.

▶ If you've carefully selected a pillow but your neck pain remains, consult a **doctor**. Neck problems can be caused by a weak muscular system, which can be strengthened through exercise, but they can also be due to serious issues that require treatment.

THE CANOPY BED
Many people dream of having a canopy bed. In former times, it was not only a symbol of wealth and nobility, it offered a degree of privacy—very desirable when many people had to live in the same room. Thick brocade curtains have now gone out of fashion, but a canopy bed still provides a feeling of safety and security, as well as a touch of old-fashioned romance.

Blankets and Throws

Whether you're hunkered down on the couch with a good book or spending a summer evening on the patio, there's nothing nicer than wrapping yourself up in a soft blanket or comfy throw.

For cool summer evenings or during late spring or early fall, there's nothing cozier than a pure wool blanket. And a throw is just right for grabbing and tossing around your shoulders or draping over your knees when you're feeling chilly.

WOOL BLANKETS

▶ The traditional **wool blanket** still has a place in many households. Made of pure sheep's wool, it is wrinkle- and odor-resistant.

▶ **Merino wool, lambswool, camel hair, alpaca,** or **cashmere blankets** are of especially high quality and can't be beat when it comes to keeping you warm and comforable.

▶ **Don't wash** wool blankets—or at least, wash them rarely. Instead, air them out regularly, and occasionally brush them out.

▶ Blankets made of **polyester** or **fleece** have been slowly edging wool out due to their lower price points, but real wool still offers the most warmth.

▶ Buy **cotton blankets** for a solution that is easy to care for, durable, and affordable, even on a small budget. As light blankets, they're suitable for every season of the year. And they are easy as pie to care for: just toss them in the washer, then put them in the dryer. Done.

THROWS

A throw is a medium-sized decorative blanket that's usually on the bed or the couch. Here's what you need to know about choosing the right one:

▶ Throws can be made from a **variety of materials** and may come in **different sizes.**

▶ A **two-sided, patterned** or **colored throw** on the couch lets you change the look of the living room with a flick of the wrist. A larger throw on your bed does the same for your bedroom.

▶ **Plain-colored** blankets, or two-sided throws with a plain side, can have a balancing effect on colorfully-patterned sofas. Just lay the throw onto the couch with the plain side up.

▶ An attractive throw keeps does more than keep your bed clean. When supplemented with the right **pillows**, a tasteful throw can turn a bed into a comfortable place to sit.

▶ Throws need to be laundered frequently—make sure you choose one that is **machine-washable**. Of course, one that you can tumble dry as well is probably the best way to go, especially during winter months when you can't use your outdoor clothesline.

There's no better accessory for a short break on the sofa than a cozy throw.

Books

Books make wonderful companions; they enthrall, educate, and comfort us. For that reason alone, every book collection should be lovingly cared for and organized. An efficient ordering system will make it easier to find specific titles. Survey your books and root out those you no longer reach for.

Keeping books well-organized and dust-free will go a long way to increasing their life and ensuring that you can enjoy reading them for years to come.

STORING BOOKS PROPERLY

▶ Choose bookcases with **glass doors** if you want to keep your books from getting dusty. **Home-sewn book covers** serve nicely if a glass-fronted bookcase isn't in the cards.

▶ Display multi-volume **dictionaries** or **antique books** along walls with open shelves, so that they are easy to access.

▶ Try to install your bookshelves in a **dry room** or use a **dehumidifier** in damper climates or rooms. Moisture is no friend to your tomes.

▶ Make sure there is about 1 in. (2.5 cm) of **space** between the top edges of the books and the bottom edge of the shelf above. This makes it much easier to slide out books you want to read.

▶ Arrange books according to **authors, themes,** or **special subject areas**. This makes it easier to find what you're looking for and easy to reshelf books.

▶ Store **heavy volumes** on the **bottom shelf.** This will make your bookcase considerably more stable.

▶ Leave plenty of **room between subject areas** so you can add new books without having to reorganize the entire bookshelf.

▶ Don't pack your books too tightly on the shelves, especially over a **heating unit**; it will cause the glue in the bindings to become brittle.

Books can be quickly vacuumed with the book brush attachment of a vacuum cleaner.

Candles

Candles, along with oil and tallow lamps, were an important light source before the advent of the lightbulb. Today we use their warm, soft light more as a decorative element or for creating an intimate atmosphere than for illuminating our nighttime reading or workspaces.

One of the oldest candles is the beeswax taper, but the humble candle has evolved. Today, you can get candles of beeswax or tallow, as well as gel candles or those made from soy.

MATERIAL

▶ Candles made from **beeswax** are of high quality but relatively expensive. Real beeswax candles give off a sweet fragrance when they burn.

▶ Petroleum-based **paraffin** is the most frequently used material in the manufacture of candles today. Paraffin candles are an affordable option.

▶ **Soy wax** is made from hydrogenated soybean oil. As a natural substance, soy wax is a much more environmentally-conscious choice than paraffin. Soy candles are also less sooty when they burn.

▶ **Stearin**, or stearic acid, is made from vegetable and animal fats. Adding **stearin** to paraffin candles makes them easier to manipulate during production. The candles also burn more slowly.

CREATIVE CANDLESTICKS

Yes, a nice meal demands some chic silver or crystal candlesticks. But what about a cozy evening by the fire, or a romantic getaway at the cottage? Here are some time-honored solutions for when the crystal just doesn't fit.

▶ Use an old **wine bottle** with a raffia-wrapped bottom, or any nicely-shaped bottle. Just insert a candle in the top; the wax flowing down the side will give the bottle a vintage look. Use a **coaster** to avoid staining the table under it.

▶ You can also **paint** bottles, cover them with **decoupage** or fill them with **colored sand** or **ornamental stones.**

▶ Make candle holders by hollowing out a space for votive candles in **apples** or **pumpkins**, like you might have already done for Halloween.

▶ For a pretty dining-room table centerpiece, create a **floral arrangement** in a pot with **floral foam** and **seasonal blooms**, then tape **toothpicks** to the ends of your candles and insert them in the center.

LANTERNS

Candles add a warm glow to a nice supper, but sometimes a lantern works better—outdoors, for instance; candles can be too unstable or easily blown out by an errant gust. Here are some ways to make lanterns work for you:

▶ Candles in **jars** can look like twinkling fairy lights on the patio. Use large-bellied jars decorated with sand, stones, or seashells.

▶ Use **glass-frosting spray** on jars containing candles to create a nice, soft light.

▶ Drop **tea lights** into well-cleaned **baby food jars** and arrange them in small clusters on the table and sideboard. They'll look fabulous.

▶ Make **tin cans** into lanterns by punching holes in a pattern with a **hammer** and **nail.** To avoid denting the can, first fill it with water and freeze it for several hours.

CAREFUL, COMBUSTIBLE!

Candles are useful, warm, old-fashioned, romantic...and can be dangerous. Stay safe with these simple rules:

▶ Never leave candles **unattended**—not even for a short time, and not even if they are tea lights or lanterns.

▶ Always use a container in which the candle **stands up straight**.

▶ **Trim the wick** down to about 1/2 in. (1 cm).

This arrangement of candles of differing heights has a simple beauty. The stones combine nicely with the shape and material of the dish.

Carpets and Runners

Carpets and runners are good for decorating floors, keeping your feet warm, and reducing noise. Depending on where in the house a carpet or runner will lie, it may be subject to a lot of wear and tear, so it's best to consider the demands a carpet has to meet before selecting one for your home.

There's an enormous selection of carpets and runners out there. To make the right choice, decide how the carpet is going to be used, how the room is furnished, what the floor currently looks like, and how much you're willing to pay for the carpet.

THE RIGHT CHOICE

▶ On **wood, laminate,** or **stone floors**, a rug's primary function is to create an accent, so the design is extremely important.

▶ A rug in the **kids' room** should be easy to clean and care for. Choose one that hides stains or makes it easy to remove them.

▶ In an **office area** with rolling desk chairs, carpets have to be durable.

▶ Different kinds of certificates provide helpful information when purchasing a carpet. The **GoodWeave** program, for example, fights illegal child labor in the carpet industries of India, Pakistan, and Nepal. A regular component of their program is on-the-spot surprise inspections of workshops.

TYPES OF CARPETS

Just as not all carpet shapes and colors go with every decor, not all carpet types are created equal; you wouldn't want a luscious, deep-pile carpet in your mud room any more than you'd put AstroTurf in your living room. Here are some things to bear in mind when choosing a carpet for your home.

▶ **Sturdy** carpets have short, tough fibers. They are often made wholly or at least largely from **synthetic fibers**.

▶ Carpets of higher quality are usually made from **natural fibers** with **deep pile**. They're softer, but also get dirty more easily and require more maintenance.

▶ With **loop-pile carpets**, the threads of the pile, whether they are made of wool, synthetics, or mixed fibers, are sewn into the basic weave. Since loop-pile carpets are relatively impervious to stains, they're a good choice for rooms with more traffic.

A carpet on a stone floor creates a welcoming and cozy ambience.

good to know

CARPET QUALITY
The main indicators of carpet quality are its density (how closely the individual strands are packed together), its twist (how many times the carpet's fibers have been spun) and its pile height (how far the fibers extend from the backing). To check a carpet's quality, bend it backward. The less backing you can see, the higher the density and the better the carpet. Look for individual carpet fibers that are tight and neat; loose or flared strands indicate substandard quality. And finally, as a rule of thumb, the higher the pile, the better the carpet will wear.

▶ **Velour** or **plush carpets** are cut-pile carpets in which the loop pile is sheared off for a softer texture. Because of its velvety surface, this type of carpet works well for bedrooms or living rooms. A plush carpet in which the threads have been twisted double under heat is particularly sturdy.

▶ **Needlefelt carpets** are high-tech and durable. They're produced by electrostatic attraction of individual fibers, which results in a highly-resistant carpet. Hotels and businesses often have needlefelt carpet installed but, for most homeowners, this ultra-sturdy carpet is overkill.

a play carpet for the children's room

one Get a low-pile, square carpet remnant from the carpet store and have the edges bound.

two With tailor's chalk, draw the playing area for a board game—Parcheesi or chess, for example—or a roadway scene for toy cars.

three Trace and fill in the chalk drawing to the carpet with fabric paints.

four You can make play figures or tokens from old plastic bottles or fabrics.

TIPS FOR CARPETS AND RUNNERS

Here are some things to keep in mind when it comes to the safety, maintenance, and finishing of any carpet, runner, or rug you may decide to buy and lay in your home:

▶ Look seriously at **carpet tiles**. They're a savvy option for high-traffic areas of the home. You can replace dirty squares without replacing the entire carpet—and that means your floor covering lasts longer, which also means that you save money.

▶ Install **wood trim** along the border instead of carpeting. Wood doesn't get nearly as dusty, and it's far easier to clean than most carpeting.

▶ The turned-up corners of a **runner** can become dangerous obstacles for the unwary. To solve the issue, use **cornstarch paste** to stick the corners down. When the paste dries, iron the corners flat (put a piece of wrapping paper between the iron and the rug just in case). Then remove the remnants of the cornstarch with a small **nail brush**.

▶ A **runner** should occasionally be **turned 180°** to prevent excessive wear on one side, especially if that side is near the front door or another busy part of the house.

▶ Avoid **compression marks** in **deep-pile carpets** by slightly changing the position of the couch, coffee table, and other moveable pieces of furniture from time to time.

▶ Choose **dry** carpet cleaning products rather than **carpet foam** for cleaning deep-pile carpets; it can take quite a long time for a damp deep-pile carpet to dry.

▶ Rent a **carpet steamer** or **cleaning machine** from your local supermarket or home-improvement store. They work very well for a once-yearly mega-cleaning of your carpets.

▶ Protect carpets and runners against **moths** and eliminate **unpleasant smells** by sprinkling them occasionally with a little **lavender oil.**

▶ Renew **faded colors** by wiping down the carpet with a solution of **water** and **vinegar**, mixed in a 10:1 proportion. Just be sure to test an inconspicuous area of the rug for color fastness before you start in on the rest of the carpet.

▶ Deal with bothersome stains that won't come out by creating a **carpet of many colors**. First, punch out the dirty spots with a metal hole punch. Then, acquire some discontinued carpet patterns (inexpensive) or samples (free) from a carpet store. Punch out shapes to insert into the carpet's holes. Do it right, and you will have a creative design.

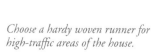

Choose a hardy woven runner for high-traffic areas of the house.

Clocks

Few things remind us of the comforts of grandma's house more than the regular ticking of an old-time clock. This household item from days gone by is also a striking element in today's home decor.

Most longcase clocks chime the time—on each hour and fraction of an hour.

The earliest mechanical clocks ticked away in cloisters back in the Middle Ages, while pendulum clocks have been around since the 17th century. Since then, timepieces have become increasingly precise and compact, and the advent of the digital clock has completely changed the way we look at timekeeping. But many people continue to take pleasure in the steady rhythm of old-fashioned analog clocks.

ANTIQUE CLOCKS

▶ A **grandfather clock** is a classic weight-driven **pendulum clock**. If you're lucky you'll find one at a flea market or online; you'll pay a lot more at an antique store.

▶ **Wall clocks** are smaller and easier to integrate into a space than a huge grandfather clock. Popular finds include quirky **cuckoo clocks** and pendulum clocks with a wooden case and glass on three sides.

▶ **Mantel clocks** come in many different forms. Some are protected by a glass cover, while others have wooden cases with a glass front.

▶ *Bakelite,* and other art deco clocks from the 1930s, will be tomorrow's sought after collectibles. Look for them at flea markets or garage sales.

WINDING YOUR CLOCK

Mechanical clocks need to be wound regularly; most have an eight-day cycle. Choose a day and time to wind your antique clock. Consistency is important for maintenance.

▶ Wind a **weight drive** before the weights reach the bottom. When you're resetting the weights, lift them slightly to protect the bearings (and oil them sparingly on occasion).

▶ Winding a **spring drive** calls for particular care; count the turns so you don't twist the key too far.

CLOCK MAINTENANCE

Here are some other points to bear in mind when keeping your antique clock in good running order.

▶ Never move the hands on antique clocks **backward**. You risk damaging the mechanism.

▶ Carefully treat the varnished case surfaces with **cleaning polish** and then seal them with a good **antique wax**.

▶ Remove the pendulum and immobilize the pendulum arm when **transporting** a pendulum clock. For short moves, hold the case in such a way that the pendulum can lean against the mechanism.

▶ Learn to live with a little **imprecision** if you're the owner of an antique clock. If you're continually adjusting the time, there's a chance that you will damage the clock.

good to know

A RADIO-CONTROLLED CLOCK

People who shy away from the maintenance requirements of an antique clock will appreciate the advantages of a radio-controlled model. This ingenious invention independently registers the signal beamed from a long-wave radio time signal broadcaster or the global positioning system (GPS). This way, it always displays the correct time and never needs to be adjusted by hand. These clocks also take care of the change from standard to daylight savings time automatically.

Colors

The colors you surround yourself with at home can influence your mood and sense of well-being. In general, the function of a particular room determines whether you choose warm or cold, dark or light, and strong or subdued colors.

This color chart contains cold colors (green to purple) at the top and warm colors (pink to yellow) below.

Different colors have different characteristics. Choose the right colors to match the mood of each room, entrance, and hallway.

THE ABCS OF COLORS

▸ **Bright colors**—that is, vibrant shades of green and blue, yellow, and orange—provide an expansive feeling. These are friendly, happy colors that encourage communication and are therefore especially welcome in the **dining area** and **kitchen**.

▸ **Dark colors**, such as red, purple, blue, and dark shades of green, can have a constricting and gloomy effect. But when applied in the right place or as accent elements, they can help convey **comfort** and **security**.

▸ **Warm colors**—orange and yellow hues, for example—raise the perceived **temperature** of a room. For that reason, they're best used in rooms that face north. Because they inspire activity, avoid them in rooms meant for relaxation, like the **bedroom**.

▸ **Cold colors**, such as icy blues and green, have a **calming effect**. They are especially well-suited for **bedrooms**; they help you to go to bed relaxed in the evening and wake up refreshed the next morning.

▸ **Navy blue** inhibits people's willingness to communicate; do not use it in **living** and **dining areas**.

▸ **Red** raises the energy level of a room, but it may also make people more irritable and hostile—so it's not a good choice for a **child's room**. Use it as an **accent** rather than a base room color.

▸ **Gray** should be avoided for the dining area and kitchen—unless you want to dampen your appetite.

HOW COLORS WORK IN A ROOM

The right choice of color can make a room appear bigger or smaller and make ceilings look higher or lower. This visual effect can actually compensate for some of a room's flaws.

▸ Use **bright** colors for **small rooms**; they will make a room appear more spacious.

▸ Choose **warm, dark** colors for **large rooms** to make them look cozier. A good example is deep hues of **red**.

▸ Go **light** for low ceilings: the ceiling appears **higher** when painted in a lighter shade than the walls.

▸ Go **dark** for high ceilings. If you want to visually **reduce the height** of a room, opt for a dark-colored ceiling. The ceiling will also appear lower if you paint the bottom area of the wall in a lighter shade that gradually darkens as it rises toward the ceiling. If, on the other hand, the color becomes lighter going from bottom to top, the ceiling will appear higher.

▸ Opt for lively hues for **narrower** rooms; **bright** colors on the walls make a room appear wider to the eye.

▸ Darken **wide rooms**; if you paint two walls opposite each other in a **darker** shade, a wide room will look cozier and less cavernous.

The red couch in this living room provides a strong accent. The pillows reflect the basic green of the wall.

THE RIGHT COLOR STRATEGY

The hues chosen for a room's walls and ceiling aren't the only factor in determining whether your interior design is a hit or miss. You'll need to come up with an attractive color combination for furniture, home fabrics, and accessories.

▶ First, choose a **basic color** that you like and make sure it conforms to the use of the room. Use this basic color for the walls, rugs, and curtains; perhaps in varying intensities.

▶ Choose a consistent **secondary color** for furniture and accessories. For a unified look, choose a **complementary color**, or design the room in color coordinates (for example, different shades of the same color). You can also choose **two secondary colors**, but in that case, the colors should appear next to each other in the color spectrum.

▶ Be careful when combining two colors of different intensities. For example, placing **strong colors** next to **pastel shades** forces the eye to jump back and forth between light and dark. This can create a visually-disturbing effect and affect the room's atmosphere.

▶ Pair neutral colors like **white** or **taupe** with some **fresh accents** in the form of cushions, artwork, accessories, and throws in colors like red, green, blue, and even pink.

▶ If you're uncertain about what color to choose and want to avoid a room that is either too boring and restrained or too jangly and colorful, get advice from a **local paint store** or **interior designer**.

INJECT A LITTLE COLOR

Want to make seasonal changes to liven up your room? Here are three easy do-it-yourself projects:

▶ Re-cover a **lampshade**. Trace and cut out the shape of your shade with **wallpaper**. Glue the ends with wallpaper paste for a slipcover. Summer calls for a fresh lime green against neutral furnishings. Winter? Switch it up with a rich brown or red.

▶ Create a **fabric wall hanging.** Sew a hem across the top and bottom of a one-of-a-kind piece of fabric and insert a wooden dowel at each end.

▶ Paint the back wall of your bookcase an **accent hue** that coordinates with your room.

good to know

THE COLOR WHEEL

The primary colors (red, blue, and yellow) form the basis of the color wheel. Secondary colors are the colors formed by mixing the primary colors (green, orange, and purple). Tertiary colors are the different hues formed by mixing a secondary color with a primary color (yellow-orange, red-orange, and red-purple). Complementary colors appear opposite each other on the color wheel. Although they are the strongest contrasting colors, they go together well. The colors that appear next to each other on the wheel (analogous colors) are also considered harmonious. Finally, colors that appear together in nature generally go well together regardless of where they appear on the color wheel.

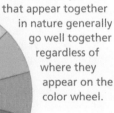

Decks and Balconies

Too small, too large, too narrow, too shady, too hot—the size and position of a patio, deck, or balcony are often beyond your control. But with a little effort, you can turn any outdoor space into a relaxing oasis.

When thinking about how to best utilize your deck or balcony space, choose appropriately-sized outdoor furniture, consider how to best protect yourself from the sun, and try creating an outdoor room.

OUTDOOR FURNITURE

▶ For small balconies or decks, it's a good idea to look at space-saving furniture. A good example is a **wall-mounted folding table** with a swivel-out table leg to stabilize it.

▶ **Stackable stools** and **folding balcony chairs** fit into a limited space, which makes them convenient to store. This is especially important for houses with tight balconies or tight storage spaces.

▶ On a small balcony, **chairs with adjustable backrests** are more practical than lounge chairs.

▶ Multi-functional furniture makes maximum use of your space: **watertight chests** make convenient seats as well as **storage** for chair cushions and pillows, for example.

▶ A **canopied beach chair** makes the most of a long, narrow balcony; set up lengthwise, it makes a cozy seating area as well as a windscreen. Protect it against rain and weather with a robust, weather-proof tarp.

▶ **Weather-resistant deck furniture** is a good option for those who aren't eager to carry heavy balcony and deck furniture inside every time it rains. Garden furniture made of **woven synthetic fibers** looks like wicker furniture, but resists inclement weather and UV rays.

▶ **Hammocks or hanging chairs** are more appropriate for larger patios—you need room to swing and a stand or solid beam to hang them from.

▶ Big balconies or decks are ideal for **sun loungers**, **deck chairs**, and **clusters of sofas** around an outdoor table.

An adjustable table that can be shortened or lengthened when needed is ideal for the balcony or deck.

Lushly planted pots and planters beautify any outdoor space.

▶ Large outdoor spaces can be structured into **"rooms"** with plant pots, folding screens, raised flower beds, canvas curtains, and outdoor furniture.

SUN PROTECTION

Most balconies, patios, and decks could use some protection against sun and glare in the form of a parasol, shade sail, awning, or trellis covered in greenery. Here are a few of the more common choices availabe today:

▶ **Parasols** come in many sizes, shapes, patterns, and materials—you'll get the best deals if you look for them in the fall. A parasol usually stands on a pedestal, but you can get space-saving brackets that screw onto the railing, or fixtures for the wall or ceiling, that work better for small balconies.

▶ **Retractable awnings** are fabric or vinyl shades on a permanently-mounted frame. With the help of a crank or a motor, they can be fully or partly extended, depending on your preference and the location of the sun. Installing an awning can be difficult because the frames tend to be heavy, and they must be firmly mounted. When in doubt, turn the job over to a professional.

▶ **Shade sails** are made of a tough, sturdy cloth and secured to fastening points with cords or snap hooks. They come in standard shapes such as triangles or squares, but if you can't find the perfect one for your yard, have one custom-made to suit your needs.

▶ **Plants** create shade as well. Tall tub plants, such as quick-growing **bamboo**, are a good choice. You can also plant **grapevines** and other greenery to climb a **lattice frame** or **trellis,** or train **climbing plants** up a **pergola**.

CREATE AN OUTDOOR ROOM

Just like your home's interior, your outdoor space needs to be well-decorated if you want it to feel cozy and finished. Small accessories can play a big role here, by helping to create a maritime flair with colors or lanterns, for example.

▶ If you want to create a Mediterranean mood, use **terra-cotta pots**, ancient-looking **sculptures**, or **wrought-iron furniture.**

▶ A **small pond** with **water lilies** or a **basin** with **floating candles** contribute to a tranquil, relaxed ambience. The gentle splash of a fountain or small water-fall can have the same effect as well.

▶ Bright, colorful **seat cushions** and **incense sticks** evoke Asia, as will red and gold accents—and, of course, a bamboo plant or two.

Original accessories such as this lantern provide a unique flair.

Decorating

Spring, summer, fall, and winter—each season has a special charm that should be reflected in your home and garden. Bring the rhythms of nature into your house by choosing seasonal fabrics, table decorations, flower arrangements, and embellishments.

SPRING

Emphasize Easter by going with colors like pale purple, pastel yellow, pink and eggshell blue. A few other springtime choices:

▶ Decorate the windowsill with early-blooming flowers like **crocuses, tulips,** and **daffodils** in small terra-cotta pots.

▶ Opt for **sheer curtains, tablecloths,** and **pillows** that lighten up the look of a room. Look for plain, embroidered, or printed sheer designs that complement your interiors.

▶ **Rework** your accessories. Clean winter dust off the shelves. Bring out floral china or clear glass, and switch out dark-colored couch cushions for more cheerful tones.

▶ Reorient furniture that centers on the fireplace towards a view of the **garden** instead. Change the focal point or rearrange the conversation grouping to take advantage of the garden scene outside.

In the summertime, colorful and lush arrangements of cut flowers and plants are a winner.

SUMMER

Summer is a time for rich and variegated colors that express the fullness of the season. To create a few nice summertime touches:

▶ Laying a **white linen slipcover** over the **couch** will create a summery mood, especially if you use colorful cushions as accents.

▶ Counteract summer's heat with cool hues: outdoor tables draped with **blue** and **white** are like a cool breeze in the garden.

▶ Create a **maritime** flair by simply filling glass tubes with **sand** of different colors and grain sizes, and setting them out on the balcony or patio.

▶ Change your **heavy oriental carpet** for a light and natural **sisal rug**.

▶ Replace your fireplace logs with **white candles** of different heights and sizes.

▶ Arrange **sunflowers** in glass vases and light them up with **lanterns** at dusk to add a warm, decorative element to garden parties or barbecues on the deck.

In March and April, no home should be without harbingers of spring like daffodils and tulips.

FALL

Fall is characterized by nature's rich harvests. With no effort at all, you can decorate your house or apartment with foliage and fruit from field and forest—think pumpkins, squash, ruddy leaves, and pinecones. Here are a few good ideas for decorating to suit this dynamic, changing season:

► Echo the changing colors of the leaves with accents in warm shades of **orange** and **red**. **Dark green** and **harvest gold** are also the perfect match for warm autumnal hues.

► Let fall usher in soft, textured fabrics like **suede, velvet,** and **felt**. **Satin** in fall colors adds glitz to table decorations.

► Place decorative elements such as fresh or dried **leaves, chestnuts, acorns,** or **beechnuts** in plain bowls to lend a little beauty to tables, sideboards, and windowsills.

► Create autumnal table decorations from **pumpkins, dried wheat stalks, corncobs** and **gourds**: simply spread them out on the table.

► Looking to create an edible fall accent piece? One easy concept is to place **vibrant red apples** and **juicy pears** into a large glass bowl to turn it into an ornamental arrangement.

WINTER

Even though it may be cold outside, you can create a cozy atmosphere in your home. Turn up the heat with these tips for sprucing up your home for winter.

► Bring ice and snow to mind with **white, turquoise,** and **bluish-green**. Of course, the true color of winter is **snow white,** which can be beautifully combined with other seasonal colors.

► Alternatively, chase the winter chill out of your home with rich shades of **purple, gold,** and **red**.

► Use winter decor fabrics like **soft wool, luxurious satin, chenille,** and **lambswool**. Incorporate them via pillows, throws, and drapes.

► Add warmth to a room (literally and figuratively) by swapping sheer curtains for **heavy draperies**.

► Use **carpet tiles** for a quick and inexpensive way to warm up the floors of your living room or bedroom.

► Make a colorful and cozy winter **bolster pillow** by sewing two **scarves** together lengthwise, stuffing them with batting, and securing the ends with ribbons.

► Grab attention with decorative glassware like **vases** or **lanterns**. They contrast pleasantly with rustic-looking decorations made of wood.

► Opt for a vase full of **winterberries** or **evergreen twigs,** or a bowl filled with glittering **Christmas ball decorations, apples,** or **oranges** for a nice winter touch.

Jack-o-lanterns with candles inside are a must for Halloween.

Candles bring a cozy glow to your home in the wintertime.

Displays

Almost everyone has a collection of cherished objects to display, whether it's porcelain, coins, or trophies. When displayed in a glass cabinet or display case with the proper lighting, collectibles can greatly contribute to your home decor.

A tasteful glass cabinet with a well-arranged display quickly becomes the focal point of any living room.

a money-saving *hint*

You can still find nice glass cabinets at flea markets, secondhand stores, and garage sales.

- Shadow boxes turn collectibles into art for the walls.
- A secretary's desk makes a fine display case in a living room, family room, or study.
- A corner cabinet gives you a place to display collections and makes good use of what might have been wasted space.
- Add cohesiveness to your exhibit by lining the shelves of your display case with materials that fit the flavor of the collection, such as bandanas for southwestern objects or lace for Victoriana.
- Dust your collectibles regularly. For small pieces, use an anti-static brush.
- Display valuable individual pieces in small cabinets or table boxes. These can be custom-made to fit your showpiece.

There are three fundamental factors to consider when it comes to displays: the case, glass, and lighting.

DISPLAY CASES

You can easily create display cases of comic figures or cars for a child or adolescent's room—or your own.

▶ Looking to display miniature items? With a bit of luck, you might find an original **typesetter drawer** or **case** (originally used to store printer's letters) at the flea market or on the Internet. Just Google the name of the item or look for it on eBay.

▶ Keep in mind that presenting objects in **open display cases** has one major disadvantage: since the items are exposed to the air, they can easily become **dusty**. That means more work for you, and it could even damage the objects.

▶ Keep valuable collector's items **behind glass**. In the old days, almost every living room had a glass cabinet for displaying precious crystal, porcelain figurines, coins, or pewter. These cabinets still work fine today, and make for an interesting design element in themselves because they are so rare and have a certain nostalgic appeal.

LIGHTING

The way you light up your treasured knickknacks can play a big role in how attractive the display is. In fact, it can be worthwhile to install a special lighting system to properly offset your treasured collectibles. Here are a few pointers for showing off your knicknacks in the best light possible:

▶ A **lighted glass cabinet** displays objects in the right light. You may also choose to highlight special pieces with small **halogen spotlights.**

▶ A light shining directly from above can be harsh and unappealing—ideally light should be projected at a **60° angle**.

▶ Before choosing a lighting system, check that the display objects can tolerate the light without **damage**. Not all lights run cool enough for use in a display case, and some collectibles are sensitive to **temperature** and **light**.

Door Wreaths

Door wreaths are a unique and friendly way to welcome guests to your home. Choose the basic components of a wreath according to the season and occasion—during the Christmas season, for example, decorate wreaths with pinecones and ribbons to spread yuletide cheer.

The proper wreath can set the right mood for any get-together—simply fasten decorations to suit the occasion. Every season brings with it a new collection of flora that would go well in a wreath.

AS THE SEASONS CHANGE

▶ A simple wreath made with **willow twigs** can be a lovely harbinger of spring.

▶ Decorative **grasses** and **hay**, as well as **flowers**, make nice components for a summertime wreath.

▶ In the fall use tendrils of **wild vine, ivy,** or **grape leaves**. **Berries, gourds,** and **Indian corn** are heralds of **Thanksgiving**.

▶ In December, wreaths of entwined **evergreen branches** are a reminder that Christmas is coming.

Incorporate dried fruit into a festive Christmas wreath.

SPECIAL OCCASIONS

▶ Use Santa Clauses and chubby-faced angels, and wooden toys, or colorful Easter eggs and bunnies, to herald **Christmas** and **Easter**.

▶ Explore the **shape** possibilities. Door wreathes don't have to be round; other basic shapes include **hearts** and **ovals**—or any other shape.

▶ Create unique designs with figurines, hearts, and twinkling lights. For example, for a **wedding**, weave a little bridal couple into the wreath.

▶ **Dried flowers** give wreaths a floral touch. But they tend to be fragile, so don't use them on doors that get opened and closed a lot.

▶ **Ribbons, strings of pearls**, and **dried flowers** add a wonderful romantic touch. To create a cheerful mood for a party, choose a variety of bright and colorful ribbons.

▶ If you intend to keep your wreath up for a long time, incorporate your **address** in the design. This way, it makes a good substitute for a door plate.

▶ Display the birthday boy or girl's age in the center of the wreath using small brightly-colored flowers or dried corn kernels for an extra special **birthday** celebration.

▶ Make a clever wreath with little cars or traffic signs for a teen who has just passed his or her **driver's license test**.

▶ Fragrant decorations such as **herbs** and **spices** look lovely and smell even better when incorporated into a wreath.

an autumn door wreath

one Deck a Styrofoam wreath with twigs, ivy tendrils, or other greenery. Wrap it in place with florist's wire.

two Add decorations such as flowers, fruit, and other embellishments. Attach items that lack a stem with florist's wire.

three As a final touch, decorate the wreath with colorful ribbons.

Fireplaces and Woodstoves

Fireplaces and woodstoves are great for anyone who likes the sound, smell, and warmth of a crackling fire. They can really help keep heating costs down as well, by lessening your dependence on oil or electrical heating.

a money-saving *hint*

Throw dried flowers or berries into the fire shortly before it burns out. They'll reduce the unpleasant smell of smoke and you won't have to spray the room with a deodorizer.

But keep in mind that conventional wood-burning fireplaces actually suck heat out of your home through the chimney, as well as releasing emissions into the environment. If you've already got an old wood-burner, you might consider putting in a fireplace insert or replacing your current stove with a newer, high-efficiency one. Most fireplaces in newly-built homes actually run on gas. No matter what kind of fireplace you have, though, it is a possible safety hazard, so make sure you observe the appropriate safety regulations.

OPEN FIREPLACE

A built-in fireplace can be a source of cozy warmth. But you'll need to take into account certain factors to keep it safe:

▶ Use a **fireplace screen** to prevent sparks from flying out.

▶ Install a special **fireproof glass panel** in front of the fireplace for safety and an unobstructed view of the fire without fear of sparks.

▶ Make sure you have the right fireplace tools—**bellows** and **tongs** aid in stoking the fire.

A gas fireplace is a great way to warm up a room without the ash and grime associated with wood.

There is room for a wood-burning stove even in smaller homes, and it can be an important heat contributor.

▶ If you're looking for something a little more traditional, opt for a favorite among wood-burners: a **cast-iron stove**.

▶ Look at the **efficiency factor** of a stove. It informs you how much energy is actually transferred to the surrounding air in a room.

GAS FIREPLACES AND FIREPLACE INSERTS

Gas fireplaces and fireplace inserts give you the look and warmth of a wood fire, but with the added efficiency and ease-of-use of modern convenience: you can turn them on or off with the touch of a remote control button or wall switch.

▶ Choose a gas fireplace to fit the decor of your home. A **two-sided gas fireplace** makes a lovely **room divider**, for example. But if you're fond of your antique mantel, you can buy an **insert** to fit your fireplace rather than replacing the whole thing.

▶ Find a **certified inspector** to check your fireplace periodically for **carbon monoxide** and **leaks**. Many municipal governments recommend or require annual inspections. Many utility companies provide a yearly safety inspection service for furnaces and water heaters—ask if they'll include your fireplace.

▶ Check the chimney flue for **blockages** such as bird nests and leaves before lighting your first fire in the fall. Remove anything within reach or call a **chimney sweep** to get rid of obstructions that are beyond your reach.

▶ Gas fireplaces don't produce smoke and other by-products that can be hard on people with **asthma** or **allergies**. In addition, they're easy to maintain and don't require you to sweep up ashes or deal with the ocassional runaway spark or ember.

WOODSTOVES AND FIREPLACE INSERTS

The contemporary variants of the open fireplace are woodstoves and fireplace inserts. In both cases, the fire burns in a closed chamber and is visible through a glass panel. You get all the appeal of a wood-burning fire with none of the hassle, smell, or soot. A few things to consider:

▶ You can place a woodstove virtually **wherever you wish.** Today's models come in a range of colors including **ivory** and **crimson red**, so you can find one to fit any decor.

▶ Install a **wood-burning fireplace insert**. It can help you maintain a traditional look by turning an inefficient masonry fireplace into a wood burner with an efficiency rating of about 70 percent. However, one disadvantage of woodstoves and inserts is that dust particles from the air land on the stove and burn up there—making the air very dry, even though the fire itself is closed off.

▶ Wipe the glass panel regularly with **window cleaner**, because you just can't prevent the glass panel from collecting soot. Just remember to spray the window cleaner on a cloth rather than directly on the panel.

good to know

THE RIGHT FUEL
Modern woodstoves burn logs, wood briquettes, and wood pellets. Around 1,500 lb. (700 kg) of dry, seasoned firewood can replace the energy from about 55 gallons (210 liters) of fuel or 7,063 ft.³ (200 m³) of natural gas. Ashes of a light gray to gray color are a sign of efficient combustion, containing no carbon remnants—you can even use them in the garden as fertilizer. Another tip: start a fire using dried lemon peels. They burn well and give off a pleasant aroma.

Floral Decorations

A bouquet of flowers isn't just for young lovers or weddings—the right floral decoration can really bring a room to life. Summer's a great season for taking advantage of your garden's bounty by using fresh-cut flowers; in winter, dried flowers and arrangements add a nice touch.

Flowers are a welcome addition to any room. Whether they are tucked in a corner or used as a centerpiece, flowers add colors and rich scents that everyone can enjoy.

CUT FLOWERS

A nice bouquet of cut flowers is great, but try to prolong your enjoyment of them for as long as possible.

▶ Gather cut flowers only during **dry weather**. Snip off blooming flowers in the morning and those that haven't yet bloomed in the evening.

▶ Cut the stem **on a slant** so they can absorb as much water as possible. This will help them last longer.

▶ Put flowers into **lukewarm water** right up to the bloom immediately after picking, preferably in a bucket. Before you arrange them in a vase, cut the stems again.

▶ Spray cut flowers with **water** occasionally to keep them fresh in the heat of summer.

▶ Lengthen the life of flowers with a milky sap (like poinsettias and poppies) by dipping the stems in **boiling water** for 10 seconds to cauterize the stalk.

▶ Gently remove **lower leaves** from the stem so there will be none in the vase water.

▶ When flowers begin to wilt, **shorten the stems** by about 1–1.5 in. (2.5–4 cm) and put them in **hot water** for a while, using a paper towel to protect the blooms from the steam. Then move them to **deep, cold water** for one hour before arranging them again in the vase.

▶ Give extra support to the stem of a bent flower using **wire** or **tape**.

DRYING FLOWERS

▶ Hang freshly-cut flowers (tied together in small bouquets) **upside-down** in a **dry, well-ventilated room**. The stems will thin as they dry, so you may have to tighten the strings holding the bouquets together. After about three weeks, you can use the flowers for a wreath or other arrangement.

▶ Dry flowers with **glycerin** (available at any craft shop) to preserve their shape and suppleness, although most of the time their color will change. **Berries, periwinkle, roses,** and **anemones** are good candidates. Pour one part glycerin and two parts boiling water into a tall, narrow container. Cut the flowers on an angle and place them 3–4 in. (8–10 cm) deep in the hot solution. Store the container in a cool place until you notice little glycerin drops appearing on the leaves.

▶ Dry flowers such as **French marigolds, peonies,** and **carnations** with **silica gel crystals** from a craft store. Shorten the stems to about 2 in. (5 cm) and stick them

This arrangement in shades of cream, rose, and lavender lends a light and breezy atmosphere to the room.

To create a pretty package, wrap flowerpots with satin ribbon to match the color of the blossoms.

try to distribute the filler flowers evenly.

▶ Add a little more visual interest with some **trailing greenery** that droops over the edge of your vase or container.

▶ Use **moss** with fresh flower arrangements, since you'll need to moisten it regularly.

▶ **Pebbles** or **marbles** can add a decorative touch to an arrangement in a tall glass.

VASES AND VESSELS

When you're adding flower displays to your home decor, the flowers themselves are a major part of the equation when it comes to a successful arrangement. But another aspect to consider is the vessel in which you are placing your blooms. The vase you choose will depend largely on context.

▶ **Pewter vessels** harmonize nicely with peach-colored blossoms.

▶ Use an attractive **bottle** for a single, tall flower.

▶ A **wooden frame** turns into a living picture if you drill holes in the bottom for test tubes and fill the tubes with a continually-replenished display of fresh flowers.

▶ **Woven baskets** are well-suited for wildflowers and cornflowers. To keep the flowers from wilting after you pick them, immediately insert the stems into **plastic bags filled with water** and tie them up carefully.

▶ **Terra-cotta pots** make rustic, but pretty, containers for many types of flowers, including branches from **berry bushes** and **evergreens**. They also go extremely well with balconies and sunrooms. Just make sure they're lined, so that moisture doesn't leach from the soil.

creating floral arrangements

one Get some floral foam from your local florist and water it thoroughly.

two Cover it with moss and wrap tightly with wire.

three Attach decorative elements such as Easter eggs, berries, or fruit with florist's wire or toothpicks.

four Beginning at the center, carefully insert the selected flowers. As a rule, flowers that appear together in nature tend to harmonize in floral arrangements as well.

onto a **blunt wire**. Then spread the silica gel on the bottom of an airtight container of appropriate size. Lay the blossoms on top and cover them with about 1 in. (2–3 cm) of silica gel crystals. Place the closed container in a warm place for two days.

▶ Use **quartz sand** to preserve the shape and color of **pansies, larkspur, forget-me-nots,** and **orchids**. Place the flowers in a tightly-sealed container with a 2 in. (5 cm) layer of quartz sand. Take care that the flowers don't touch each other—once dry, they can't be separated. Close the container tightly, taping it shut, and set it aside for about 10 days. You can reuse the quartz sand as long as you let it dry at moderate heat (about 210–250°F/100–120°C) in the oven.

FLORAL ARRANGEMENTS AND AIDS

Beautiful floral arrangements can be fashioned out of both fresh and dried flowers. Here's what to take into account:

▶ Never combine more than **five different types** of flowers.

▶ Add the **greenery** first, then add the **tallest flowers** (for structure), which generally occupy the center of the arrangement.

▶ Next, add the **filler flowers** (shorter blooms). Opt for a simple dome-shaped arrangement, (which will look beautiful from all sides), and

Fragrances

Many of our fondest childhood memories are associated with certain smells: the fragrance of cookies baking, flower blossoms, or lavender in a closet. Bring back treasured memories—and create new ones—with flowers, herbs, potpourris, or fragrance sachets.

You don't need artificial products like room deodorizers or fragrance oils to produce pleasant home scents. There are many natural solutions if you're willing to explore a little bit, and the rewards are sweet scents without harsh chemicals.

NATURAL FRAGRANCES

Remember the rule of thumb: don't overdo it. It's easy to become so accustomed to certain fragrances that you use too much of a good thing. Here are some tips and tricks:

▶ Place a big bouquet of fresh flowers, particularly **lilacs, roses,** or **lilies**, on a table in the corner. It will be enough to fill a living or dining room with a wonderful scent.

▶ Hang herbs such as **rosemary, thyme,** or **peppermint** to dry from a ceiling or balcony; they give off a pleasant aroma.

▶ Fill a nice bowl with fruit and spices, such as **oranges, limes, green apples, cinnamon,** and **cloves**. They will look decorative and fill the room with intriguing smells.

▶ Bring home a nice **potpourri** made of dried blossoms and leaves from aromatic plants. Rose blossoms, jasmine, lilies, lavender, rosemary, cinnamon sticks, and vanilla pods are wonderful additions. You can set out potpourris in open bowls or fill a sachet with them; just make sure all ingredients are thoroughly dried beforehand. To intensify the fragrance, add a drop or two of **essential oil.**

▶ Assemble your own **potpourris** from **dried fruit, herbs** and **spices**. A sachet or small cushion filled with them makes a special gift.

▶ In winter, place **orange** and **lemon slices** on the heater and let them dry there.

▶ Use **scented candles** to create a soft, warm, or romantic atmosphere. They don't have to smell of roses or vanilla—even plain old **beeswax** candles emit a distinctive fragrance.

▶ Investigate **incense**. Using smoke to send prayers to the gods is one of the oldest known forms of ceremony, used in everything from the censers of the Catholic church to pagan bonfire rituals. But incense sticks don't have to be about religion; they're just a good way to quickly spread scent through a room.

▶ Or opt for a **fragrance lamp.** They're available in every conceivable shape, but the principle is always the same. A candle is placed under a plate or small bowl, which is filled with water and few drops of essential oil. The flame underneath warms the water-oil mixture and spreads the fragrance throughout the room.

▶ Spread the scent of an **essential oil** throughout your house by simply sprinkling a few drops on the **vacuum cleaner bag** before cleaning.

▶ Make a **scent ball**: spread glue on a Styrofoam ball and fasten on dried blooms from a potpourri.

▶ Create your own simple **fragrance dispenser**: just fill a lidded jar with **rose blossoms** and sprinkle each layer with salt to prevent the blooms from rotting. When you wish to add fragrance to a room, simply unscrew the jar for a while.

Fill a fragrance lamp with water and any type of oil that suits your mood.

HOW FRAGRANCES WORK

The sense of smell is often dismissed as insignificant compared to eyesight or hearing, but it's more important than many most people realize. Advocates of aromatherapy believe the power of scent can directly affect our nervous systems and even have a healing effect. Here are some of the more common scents:

▶ **Eucalyptus** is a bright, fresh scent that most people find refreshing. It clears your sinuses when you have a slight cold, and some feel it even heightens concentration. Bonus: it can also repel certain species of insects.

▶ The bewitching fragrance of **lilac** is stimulating, but can be a little strong. For this reason, it's best to use it sparingly or in conjunction with other scents. In some cultures, lilac is a symbol of love.

▶ The fragrance of **honey** can help you relax and dispel nervousness. No wonder the ancient Maya considered the bee a sacred animal.

▶ **Lavender** not only banishes moths, it's thought to have a relaxing and refreshing effect and can act as a counterbalance to nervous tension and depression. For this reason, it is often found in balms and creams, as well as in its usual aromatherapy forms, like sachets and candles.

▶ The fragrance of **tangerines** and **oranges** awakens memories of summer and therefore has a well-deserved reputation for chasing away winter depression. This may be why, in western cultures, it is not unusual to find a few tangerines in one's Christmas stocking.

▶ When suffering from a cold, use the fragrance of **peppermint** to clear congestion. Its strong, exhilarating smell can also enhance your powers of concentration.

▶ The beguiling fragrance of **roses** has a practical role to play in reducing pain and producing euphoria. It can be helpful in stressful and hectic situations.

▶ Whereas ancient uses for **vanilla** included aphrodisiacs and fever reduction, recent research indicates that its smell can stem a ravenous appetite for sweets.

▶ The fragrance of **cinnamon** has a warming and relaxing effect on most people.

▶ **Cloves** smell spicy and sweet, and have a mildly sedative effect.

▶ **Patchouli** has a musky aroma and is known to have aphrodisiac qualities.

▶ **Sage** has a refreshing, calming odor.

▶ **Rosemary** is energizing and promotes creativity.

▶ **Cedar** has a warm, grounding aroma and is often used as an aid to meditation.

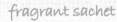

fragrant sachet

one To make a fragrance sachet, cut two pieces of cloth, each about 2 x 4 in. (5 x 10 cm). Sew them together, right sides in, along the length of two sides and the width of one. Linen, cotton, and cambric work well for sachets, but transparent fabrics like organza look particularly pretty when filled with some colorful blossoms.

two Turn your bag right-side out. Sew a seam around the open end of the sachet and pull a string through so that the sack can be closed nicely, or simply tie it closed with a ribbon after filling it.

three Fill the cloth bag with blooms or herbs and tie it off.

Fragrance bowls filled with potpourri can lend a gentle, natural scent to any area of your home.

Home Safety

By taking care and paying attention to simple common sense while planning a renovation or arranging furniture, you can both improve your quality of life and reduce the risk of accidents in your home.

Start with common sense when thinking about home safety. Remember that every room and area of the house has to be considered, including the bathroom, balcony, and even the yard.

USEFUL AIDS

▶ Place a **light switch** right next to the front door; you won't have to stumble around in a dark house.

▶ Opt for light switches and outlets that **contrast** with the **wallpaper** or **paint**. They'll be easier to spot, and will offer a little flair.

▶ Plug in a **small night-light** in the hall to ensure safe passage to the bathroom in the dark.

▶ Opt for **shatterproof glass patio doors** to prevent accidents. Use decorative aids, such as adhesive designs or stickers, to make the glass visible.

▶ Use noise-reducing measures like **sound-absorbent curtains** or **floors** to reduce echoes and other noise.

▶ Choose **dining-room chairs** with **armrests**, because they make it significantly easier to stand up after your meal.

▶ Choose **sofas and chairs** with **raised seats** to make sitting down and getting up easier. The same rule applies to your **bed** .

▶ Ensure you don't forget your **keys** and **cell phone** by designating a storage area next to the front door that is invisible from the outside.

▶ Install **electric blinds** and **motorized window shades** that open and close at certain times of the day to make your daily routines more convenient.

good to know

AVOID ACCIDENTS JUST WAITING TO HAPPEN
Most falls occur within your own four walls. Look for problem areas in your home: Are there obstructions such as raised thresholds? Or perhaps electrical cords you could trip over? Are there rugs or runners in the living room that could be potential stumbling blocks? Is the lighting in each room adequate?

BATHROOM AND KITCHEN

If there are rooms that offer more opportunities for disaster than the bathroom or kitchen, we don't know what they are—except for maybe a workshop. Here are some preventive secrets:

▶ Stick water-resistant, adhesive **bathtub decals** to the bottom of your tub. They offer better protection against slips and falls than does a bath mat.

▶ Buying a **shower** or **bathtub seat** is not only for seniors—it can really simplify bathing kids, too.

▶ Install sturdy **bathtub rails** to help you get in and out of the tub.

▶ Install a **single-handled faucet**. It is a safe and easy-to-operate fixture that allows even little ones to regulate water temperature, protecting against **scalding**.

▶ Take a look at a space-saving, **collapsible step ladder**. It will allow you to reach the uppermost cabinets in the kitchen without risk, and they can be stored away neatly.

A shower you can step into at floor level is convenient, and recessed shelving is both practical and easy to clean.

▶ **Repair uneven pathways** and keep them clear of leaves, broken branches, and overgrown plants.

▶ Illuminate the entranceway and all steps in the garden with **glare-free lights** to avoid stumbling in the dark.

▶ Install **motion detectors** on lights outside the house and in the garden so that when someone approaches—whether an invited or uninvited guest—the surroundings light up.

▶ Lay **non-slip doormats** that are flush with the floor to make entrance areas safer.

▶ Mount an easily-accessible **doorbell** and an illuminated, legible **address number** to help your guests find the right home.

▶ Your newspaper and mail carriers aren't the only ones who appreciate a **house number** that is clearly identifiable from the street and a large, visible **mailbox**.

▶ Weatherproofing devices like **non-skid stair mats** or an **awning** will make you and your guests thankful in nasty weather.

▶ Install a **pump** in your outdoor water feature. Keep water moving so mosquitoes can't breed in the standing water and spread the dreaded West Nile virus.

A tasteful outdoor wall light can bring a touch of class as well as security.

PATIO, BALCONY, AND DECK

A patio is a great place to unwind after a hard week. Just make sure that it's a safe place as well:

▶ **Flat thresholds** on patio doors reduce the risk of tripping. It might prove helpful to use wooden structures to raise the level of the balcony floor.

▶ A **windscreen** enables you to enjoy your outdoor space even on cooler days.

▶ Make sure the height of the **balustrade** on the balcony complies with building regulations.

▶ A **transparent balustrade** allows for a good view from the balcony even when you're seated, as well as curbing children's yearning to climb up and peek over.

YARD AND ENTRANCE

The steps from your patio to the yard are a good-looking and common device, but replacing the drop-down steps with ramps increases safety and makes it a lot easier to clean off the winter snow and ice, as well as autumn leaves. Here are a few other good ideas:

Stable hand rails provide security for staircases and contribute to the style of a room.

Interior Protection

Derive pleasure from your new furniture or freshly varnished hardwood floor by keeping it free of unattractive stains or scratches. And keep the couch protected and well-maintained without having to leave it encased in showroom plastic.

Slipcovers, armrest covers, throws, and furniture glides all work well to keep furniture and floors in our treasured homes damage-free.

SEATING

Your chairs and couch will go through a lot over the course of their lifetimes. A few well-chosen covers can really extend that time and keep you from repairing or replacing them sooner than you need to.

▸ **Slipcovers** prolong the life of upholstered furniture. They come as either custom-made or loosely

If you ask your guests to remove their shoes, provide slippers for them to wear.

draped coverings that protect your couch from small, sticky fingers and four-legged friends. When slipcovers get dirty, just remove them and wash.

▸ Slipcovers also serve a **decorative purpose**: they enhance seating arrangements and ensure different types of chairs are well-coordinated.

▸ The armrests of chairs and sofas wear out the quickest. Use an **armrest cover** to protect against abrasion and sweat.

▸ A **decorative blanket** draped over the seat of a chair or sofa can save seating from wear.

▸ **Throws** that cover an entire sofa have a modernizing effect on older or outdated furniture, giving the living room a new ambience.

▸ Removable covers can be **dyed** if you get tired of the hues.

▸ Protect your furniture from your beloved kitty by investing in a **scratching post** and placing it near where the cat sleeps or eats. You can also use a cat repellent (available at your local pet store) to keep cats away.

FLOOR

A brand-new floor delights the eyes. Although wear and tear may be unavoidable, you can postpone damage by taking a few simple precautions:

▸ Always put **felt glides** under tables and chairs. Self-adhesive glides often come loose, leaving ugly remnants of glue. Opt for more durable, screw-on felt glides instead.

▸ Put a **protective mat** under your desk chair. Even casters specifically made for hardwood floors can scratch them over time.

▸ Prevent dirt and stones from being tracked through the house by asking people to **remove their shoes** at the door. You can take the sting out of this rule by providing a few pairs of **warm slippers** or **wooly socks** for visitors to wear.

▸ Use **area rugs** to protect any area of the floor that might be susceptible to water leakage or spills.

If you can't get the stains out of your upholstered fabrics, opt for an elegant, custom-made slipcover which ties in with your decor.

Lighting

Lighting has an obvious function: it helps us see what we're doing, especially at night. But that doesn't mean that it's alright to just toss a lamp into the corner. Lighting a room properly does take care. Harsh, glaring lights in the den or office can give you a headache, while insufficient lighting in the kitchen or workshop can be downright dangerous.

To make sure that you and your family are safe, observe guidelines on hanging lamps, chandeliers, and wall lamps, and follow lighting tips for each room of the home.

BASIC LIGHTING

▶ The light source should illuminate the room **fully** and **evenly**.

▶ Light projected from the **ceiling** should not be so bright as to diminish the effect of nearby floor or table lamps.

HANGING LAMPS

A hanging light fixture is a common sight in any modern home, but not all are properly hung. Here are a couple of hints for hanging a pendant light:

▶ **Pendant lights** are perfect for casting light on **dining-room tables**. Hang them about 30–34 in. (76–86 cm) above the table (for an 8-ft./2.5 m ceiling) so that they provide enough light without disrupting sight lines or blinding your guests.

▶ If your **ceiling is higher** and you plan on using large, dramatic table centerpieces, you might want to hang your pendant light a little higher. You want your guests to see one another, after all.

This classic floor lamp is a winner; its fabric shade diffuses a soft light.

CHANDELIERS

The impressively glittering crystal chandelier is the most elegant form of the hanging lamp. Through the use of glass-like synthetic materials, such beauties have become much more affordable. That being said, your chandelier won't show your dining room to its best advantage if it's draped with cobwebs and a layer of dust, so make a habit of cleaning it regularly.

WALL LAMPS

Wall lamps supplement the main light source in your room and play an important role in mood lighting. Here are some hints for using them best:

▶ A beam of light shining up or down on the wall can visually separate **different areas of activity** in a room from each other.

▶ If you want wall lamps to help spread the light evenly in a room, make sure that more light is shining **upward** than **downward.**

FLOOR LAMPS

Looking to liven up the living room or den? Why not opt for a floor light or two? Here's what you need to bear in mind:

▶ Floor lamps create a cozy atmosphere, liven up dead corners, and provide **reading light** in a room.

▶ **Torchères** (lamps on tall stands) can add a striking accent and also be used as reading lamps.

This appealing dining room is stylishly illuminated and free from glare.

TABLE LAMPS

Table lamps make the perfect companion to a floor lamp. Here's what you need to know about them:

▶ Table lamps bring depth and visual interest to a space, serving a primarily **aesthetic** function.

▶ You can make an imaginative **lamp base** yourself from a clay pot, clear vase, or ceramic urn and a lamp kit from the hardware store. Be sure to only use materials that aren't combustible, as the lightbulb is bound to emit heat.

KITCHEN

Basic lighting is provided by a ceiling light. But halogen spotlights or fluorescent tubes installed under hanging cabinets can illuminate important working areas much better.

▶ **Recessed downlights** over the sink or stove can create good task lighting for cooking, baking, or scouring pots and pans.

▶ Kitchen islands and breakfast bars can be effectively highlighted and lit with a series of **pendant lights.**

▶ A **pendant** over the **kitchen table** provides lighting for doing homework, paying bills, or working on hobbies.

LIVING AREA

The living room is less about function and more about ambience—therefore tall torchère lamps can provide basic lighting. But torchères will reveal any bumps on the ceiling and walls, so place them carefully. Other things to think about:

▶ **Indirect lighting**—mounted, for example, under the sofa, in glass cabinets, or behind a curtain rod—can provide a pleasing lighting effect.

▶ Islands of light created by several small **table lamps** pointedly accentuate certain spaces.

▶ **Colored lights** can create fun and funky effects, depending on the hues and positions.

▶ To relieve eyestrain, illuminate the **wall behind the TV** with a soft light source.

DINING AREA

▶ Choose a **hanging lamp** with a pleasant and glare-free light to install over the dining table. A **dimmer switch** that allows you to adjust light conditions is ideal: turn the light up for a family dinner, and low for romantic moments.

BEDROOM

▶ A **ceiling light** that can be turned on and off at the door or from the bed generally provides the basic light source in a bedroom. However, it's also important to invest in a good **reading lamp** if you enjoy reading in bed.

BATHROOM

▶ In many bathrooms these days, **halogen lamps** or **fluorescent lights** provide basic lighting. For a more focused illumination of the vanity area, you may choose to install additional lights that don't cause glare or shadows on both sides of the **mirror.**

Lighting Conditions

Be environmentally friendly by making the most of natural light in your home and reduce electricity use during the day. Get a positive energy boost as you start your day by opening the curtains wide and letting the morning sun beam into your home.

It makes sense to situate the kitchen and living room where they get the maximum amount of daylight. But, unless you've designed the house yourself, that's not always possible. Even so, there are plenty of tricks to help you make a dark home (or an overly bright one) more appealing.

PROVIDING THE PROPER LIGHTING

▶ A dark and windowless **hallway** can create a gloomy first impression. Save such a hallway from desolation by illuminating it evenly, perhaps with **ceiling pot lights** along the length of the hall.

▶ If natural sunlight only penetrates the part of the room that is close to a window, you can capture that elusive light with a **mirror** and reflect it wherever you wish.

▶ **Light-colored** or **well-illuminated walls** give a room an expansive feeling because they appear to reflect the sunlight. They can make a room appear larger and friendlier.

▶ **Dark walls** absorb light and therefore seem visually closer to the observer—an optical trick that you can use for long, stretched-out rooms.

▶ To reduce **glare**, place the TV out of the path of direct sunlight and reflected light.

▶ By designing **windowsills** and **patios** to look like a continuation of the interior furnishings, you can cleverly enlarge a room; the natural light will evoke the same colors inside as well as outside.

PROTECTION FROM SUNLIGHT AND GLARE

Although bright, sunlit rooms are generally pleasant, too much sunlight can be stifling in the heat of summer. Here are some ways to cool things down:

▶ **Shutters** deflect sunlight when placed on the outsides of your windows.

▶ Equally important is protection from **glare**. Anti-glare devices like **louvered blinds** and **interior shutters** go on the inside of windows, and usually have adjustable wooden or plastic slats that direct the light up or down or otherwise control it.

▶ **Panel curtains** mute the direct light from the outside yet still allow light to enter, keeping all areas of the room free from glare.

▶ Anti-glare **screens** reduce eyestrain when using a computer monitor on a sunny day.

In order to prevent eye fatigue, the contrast between a computer monitor and the ambient light in a room should not be too strong.

Natural Materials

Go green when it comes to painting, decorating, and choosing home decor. Avoid chemicals and pollutants that take their toll on the planet. Natural, eco-friendly materials tend to be good for the environment, as well as for your health.

Floors

Beautiful, eco-friendly flooring is well within reach for anyone who is renovating their home or having a new house built.

- Cork flooring is warm and springy underfoot. You can even sand down a cork floor.

- Linoleum is also a natural product. Due to its noise-reducing, antibacterial, and antistatic qualities, it is undergoing a renaissance.

- Naturally-oiled wooden floors are an alternative to engineered hardwood, laminates, or glued parquet floors. You can sand off scratches and repair them with oil.

- In comparison to synthetic flooring, tile or stone floors are extremely long-lasting and free of toxic materials.

Walls

From plaster to paint, your home's walls play a huge role in the quality of your home's interior environment. It's not difficult to find materials that won't emit harmful fumes. Here are some of the choices open to you:

- Lime plaster (not to be confused with lime-based stucco) is made of finely-sifted sand and lime. It is good for controlling humidity and offers tremendous durability.

- Clay plaster has a similarly positive effect on the climate of a room. It can be used as a base, top coat, brush plaster, or textured exterior plaster.

- Clay paint consists of clay, chalk, water, and pigments. It is non-toxic and affordable.

- Whitewash is ideal because it resists mildew. It is best applied to lime and clay plaster, but will also stick to oil paint or wallpaper.

- Milk paints are good for allergy sufferers. Based on a centuries-old, non-toxic formula made from casein (a milk protein), water, limestone, clay, and natural pigments, they come as a fine powder that can be mixed at home. They stick only to unfinished, porous surfaces such as wood and plaster.

Furniture

Furniture made from natural substances, and finished with chemical-free stains or varnishes, not only looks beautiful—it's also non-toxic.

- Solid wood furniture is preferable to pieces made from particle board or veneer, which can emit formaldehyde. A bonus: by absorbing and releasing humidity, solid, oiled wood positively influences the climate of a room.

- Wicker furniture made of cane, bamboo, rattan, or willow provides a natural ambience. Just moisten the furniture with hot water to freshen it up.

- Wrought iron or stainless steel furniture is a good alternative, especially for allergy sufferers.

- When buying upholstered furniture, seek out pieces made with natural materials—soy or vegetable-blend cushions, for example, as well as cover fabrics such as hemp and organic cotton.

Beds

For maximum comfort and sound health, it's a good idea to stick to natural materials when it comes to your bed. A solid wood, wrought iron, or stainless steel bedframe is a good choice. Also:

- Opt for eco-friendly materials when buying a mattress. In terms of energy consumption, all-natural latex (free of synthetic latex) rates much better than synthetic latex made from petroleum, even when you factor in harvesting and transport.

- Check the stuffing of a potential new futon to see if it was enriched with breathable, warming, natural fibers such as horsehair, virgin wool, coconut fibers, and natural latex.

- Choose down, feathers, cotton, and linen for blankets and bedding. The exception: if you're an allergy sufferer, opt for blankets that can be washed in water up to 140°F (60°C)—or even in boiling water—and pillows that are made of synthetic fibers.

Household Fabrics

When choosing the fabrics and linens for your home, going green means looking a little more closely when you're buying—but it's not all that hard to do. Here are some ideas:

- Look for blankets made of wool or organic cotton.

- Make an inexpensive duvet cover from sewing together two linen tablecloths.

- Look at organic cotton, bamboo, and linen for bedding and sheets; the absorbency of the natural fibers contributes to a dry, warm sleep environment.

- Consider felt-backed bedroom curtains for smokers and allergy suffers. Not only does this have an insulating effect, but such curtains tend to absorb the vapors and scents in the air.

Parties

Create the perfect party space, whether it's for a family event, a simple barbecue with friends, or a child's birthday party. Part of the fun of hosting a party is the decorating beforehand.

Colorful flowers, candles, and party favors set a welcoming mood for this outdoor summer party.

There's always something to celebrate. Of course, different occasions dictate entirely different approaches. Before sending out the invitations, settle on the theme and style of the occasion: will it be an evening gala, a colorful and entertaining afternoon event, a drop-in tea party, a barbeque, or a casual brunch?

FAMILY PARTIES

▶ Send **invitations**. This is usually done in writing, although for a casual event you might send an e-mail. Make your invitation original, personal, and tailored to the occasion.

▶ Using **place cards**? Make sure they suit the context. Be imaginative: hand-lettered stones, homemade cupcakes, or little silhouettes in miniature picture frames can spell out where people are to sit, as will cardboard cards with ornamental calligraphy.

▶ Give your event a restaurant feel by posting the **menu** on a **blackboard** or printing it on **decorative paper,** then rolling and tying it with a ribbon and placing one on each guest's plate.

▶ Make the **floral decorations** suit the occasion: a bouquet of wildflowers works well for a barbecue, while a single amaryllis in a slim silver vase adds elegance to a dinner table.

OUTDOOR PARTIES

Tables set for summer need fresh flowers and lots of green. For example, a garland of ivy looks festive on a brightly-decorated table. But you can deck out the table any way you want. Just try to stick with one or two bright colors (say, a cool blue and white or sunflower yellow).

▶ Once your table decor is settled, you can add a playful touch to cocktails or ice cream sundaes with cheerful **paper umbrellas**. **Straw hats** with colorful **flower wreaths** hung about the terrace contribute to a rustic decor. Also, it's a good idea to make sure there are plenty of flickering **lanterns** spread along the tables at an evening barbecue, and **strings of light** are a must. **Torches** can create a romantic light in the yard and they work particularly well for a luau-themed party.

▶ But a well-decorated party space doesn't have to be just about looks; **scented candles** can do double-duty, contributing to the ambience as well as keeping the bugs away. The scents of carnations, mint, and eucalyptus work best.

The colors red, green, and white dominate this festive yuletide setting.

A CHILD'S BIRTHDAY

Kids look forward to their birthdays all year long. The good news: there are lots of simple yet splashy ways to get ready for their extra-special day.

▶ First, let the children make their own **party invitations**. They can pull together fanciful creations with stickers, crayons, and colored paper, or hone their design skills on the computer. It's fun for them and gives the invites a special, personalized touch.

▶ On the day, use **bright paper plates, napkins,** and **confetti** to add color to the table.

▶ Make the birthday girl or boy's seat of honor stand out from the rest: crown it with **streamers** and **garlands** or a **bouquet of balloons**.

▶ Use **plain paper tablecloths** and put a few cups of **crayons** on the table so your pint-sized guests can practice their artwork and be entertained while they wait for their food.

▶ Of course, blow up plenty of colorful **balloons**. They can serve double-duty as place cards if you write a child's name on each and tie it to his or her assigned chair.

▶ Finally, opt for a sweet and scrumptious **wreath** to make your party unique: use toothpicks to stick licorice, jelly candies, and candied fruits onto a Styrofoam form.

CHRISTMAS

No one wants to be miserly during the holiday season, but you really don't have to spend a fortune to come up with tasteful holiday decorations. In fact, traditional items like red velvet bows, nutcrackers, and handcrafted nativity scenes or angels can often decorate your home more festively than any life-sized Santa Claus climbing the wall, or rows and rows of lights flashing on the roof.

▶ Buying a real **tree**? If you have to trim off the lower branches, keep them to use for **wreaths, floral arrangements,** or **garlands**. Then, mirror the tree's festive green hue with **embroidered napkins, place mats,** or **tablecloths** and add a pop of red to set it off. Think ribbons and smaller accessories.

▶ Place nuts, pinecones, or glass marbles covered with **metallic paint** in a silver bowl and decorate it with ivy tendrils. Or create a pyramid of **oranges**, then tuck **whole walnuts, brazil nuts,** and **hazel nuts** into the crevices and place the pyramid on a bed of pine boughs. Presto! You've just made a beautiful, but edible, holiday centerpiece.

▶ Create an inviting Christmas atmosphere with **candles** in pretty candlesticks or lanterns spaced throughout the room. (Be sure that no candles are too close to the Christmas tree.) If you like, decorate the windows, terrace, balcony, and trees on your property with **strings of lights, lanterns,** or a variety of **glittery ornaments.**

Flying Balloons

Cups
Strings
(about 40 in./1 m long)
Balloons
(filled with helium)

Fill around 10 cups halfway with water. Dip the end of each string in a cup and put everything in the freezer. After freezing, tie the balloons to the strings and distribute the cups around the room. As soon as the ice melts, the balloons float up—one after the other. One warning, though: don't do this outside, as balloons represent a threat to birds and animals, which can swallow them once they've deflated.

Pictures

Draw special attention to oil paintings, family portraits, or photos from your last vacation, with a tasteful arrangement, the right lighting, and suitable frames.

This nearly square arrangement is cohesive and clear, thanks to the fact that it combines a number of same-sized pictures.

A little prep work will help ensure that your pictures are hung properly, arranged in a suitable fashion, and shown in the best lighting conditions.

ARRANGING PICTURES

The basic principle of arranging pictures is that you should line up the horizontal center of each picture or group of pictures at eye level on the wall. You can drop the centerline 1–2 ft. (30–60 cm) in areas where the admirers will mostly be seated, such as a living room. Beyond that, you are free to arrange them as you like, though it helps to observe certain ground rules.

▶ Hang pictures of the **same size** and **shape** next to or underneath each other in strict geometrical order.

▶ Create a harmonious arrangement by organizing **pictures of different sizes** according to imaginary lines that go through the middle and the lower or upper border of the specific picture.

▶ Be creative: arrange a **larger group** of pictures in a square, an oval, or a circle, or alternatively, orient them according to an imaginary cross in the middle of the arrangement.

PUTTING PICTURES IN THE BEST LIGHT

▶ In the limelight: even in a well-illuminated room, a **picture light** can accentuate a piece of art or group of photos.

▶ From **below or above**: well-placed lamps can cast a mellow light on pictures from below or above.

▶ From behind: to bring out the glow in a photo, illuminate it from **behind**. Press a photo to piece of plastic wrap, glue it onto **matte glass**, and install a light behind it so that it shines through the picture.

HANGING PICTURES PROPERLY

Besides the good old nail in the wall, there are many options for hanging pictures almost invisibly.

▶ Hang pictures using nearly invisible **nylon line** that matches the color of the ceiling from a rail or molding. You can move them back and forth and adjust them for height, too.

▶ Hang artwork on the wall over an **art shelf**, or set it directly onto the shelf.

▶ If your picture always hangs askew, simply glue a bit of **foam** behind the **corners** of the frame to hold it in place.

Pillows and Cushions

Pillows provide a fresh, creative, and inexpensive way to decorate—they come in a wide variety of shapes and sizes, colors and fabrics, textures and patterns. Colorful pillows and throw cushions enliven any room, create a stylish effect, or offer the perfect finishing touch.

One of a pillow or cushion's main jobs is to ensure good comfort and support at bedtime—or during any other time. Here is how to take full advantage.

PILLOWS AND CUSHIONS FOR EVERYDAY USE

▶ Choose a pillow or cushion **filled with down and/or feathers** if you prefer a soft, warm pillow or cushion.

▶ Take a look at **specialty pillows filled with buckwheat, spelt, or memory foam**, which offer better support for your neck.

▶ Suffer from neck pain? Take a look at a **neck roll pillow.** They can relieve neck strain. **Inflatable neck pillows** are ideal for travel and don't take up much room in luggage.

▶ For back pain, try adding a **relatively firm wedge cushion** to your chair. The tapered angle of the wedge encourages correct posture, providing relief for your spinal column.

▶ Why not get some **general-purpose seat cushions** for your hard-surfaced chairs, benches, or stools? The cushions will up the comfort factor.

▶ Choose the fabrics to **harmonize** with the rest of the decor.

▶ Floor cushions are both **portable and comfy**. They make wonderful spots for sleeping pets or napping children to curl up, while **beanbag chairs**—large fabric bags filled with Styrofoam or sand—provide remarkably comfortable moveable seats.

DECORATING WITH CUSHIONS

Comfort isn't the only task a cushion can fulfill. Well-chosen pillows can also play a central role in your home's decor.

▶ Deck out a sofa, armchair, futon, or bench with **accent cushions** that tie in with the overall design of the room.

▶ Use **matching cushions** to create a connection between different kinds of seating furniture, and complement your color scheme.

▶ You can also arrange **cushions of different shapes** and **fabrics** on a plain sofa. Vary patterns in the same color for a nice effect.

▶ Opt for **floral patterns, paisley,** or **brocade** for a country home design, while simple upholstered furniture and a contemporary ambience tend to call for cushions with **geometric patterns,** or **brightly-colored silk** and **velvet** fabrics.

Decorating Cushions

Cardboard stencil
Plain-colored cushion cover
Fabric paint

First, cut your stencil to the desired shape (or ready-made from a craft store) and stick it onto the fabric with tape. Apply the fabric paint over the stencil: only the cut-out pattern will be colored.

Clusters of cushions add a pop of color to a plain sofa.

Plants

Plants bring atmosphere into your home. Tall plants such as gum trees or palms act as accents, while smaller plants can decorate a windowsill. When choosing a plant, consider carefully where you're going to put it in order to enhance your decor and ensure its survival.

Armed with a few tips and patience, anyone can care for a variety of plants that will help enliven any living space. And remember that a room with plants is known to help pick up one's spirits.

A HEALTHY ROOM CLIMATE

Plants are not only beautiful, they increase the humidity level of a room. That's good for the overall climate and, ultimately, for your health. This is especially important in winter, when the heat is often on and can be very drying.

▶ Bear in mind that **big plants,** like gum trees, produce more **humidity** than smaller ones.

▶ Select plants that are particularly effective for **counteracting offgassed chemicals** and contributing to balanced internal humidity. Among those plants are: areca palms, dwarf date palms, Boston ferns, rubber plants, and peace lilies. Plants kept in **water** (such as bamboo), with no need for dirt, can increase this effect.

▶ Don't fill your **bedroom** with plants, as they use up oxygen and produce carbon dioxide at night.

WATERING PLANTS CORRECTLY

Many plants do well when simply watered from above—but there are, in fact, myriad factors that go into the seemingly simple process, depending on the size and species of plants involved. One general guideline to follow is that you should always use water at room temperature.

▶ Put **bulbs** and other plants with sensitive roots, such as **poinsettias** and **African violets**, on a saucer and water them from **below** to keep the bulbs or roots from rotting. Also, check planters about an hour after watering and drain off excess water.

▶ **Immersion** can be beneficial to many kinds of plants, including **cacti** and **citrus plants**. Immerse the whole root ball in a large container of water; you'll know the ball is fully saturated when no more air bubbles rise to the top.

▶ Keep **rainwater** and **stale mineral water** around; both are good for watering plants, as is water that has been used for boiling potatoes or eggs—just allow it to cool and make sure it's completely salt-free.

▶ Leave tap water to sit **overnight** before you water plants with it.

▶ **Spray** your plants on occasion. Use only **lime-free water** for spraying to keep ugly lime scale from building up. And pamper your plants (especially cacti and plants with large leaves) with a **cleansing shower** twice a year: either put them out in the rain or spray them with a shower head. Tip the pots of **cacti** to keep water from running directly into them.

REGULAR CARE

With a little TLC, your plants will reward you with healthy foliage and lush blooms. It's not hard to keep your plants healthy.

▶ Check new plants thoroughly for **pests** before buying. Indoor plants can be susceptible to spider mites, aphids, and other troublesome creatures that spread easily.

▶ Carefully **dust** your plants from time to time to let the leaves breathe.

▶ Wipe plants with larger leaves with **diluted beer** to make them shine.

▶ Immediately **remove wilted blooms** and **leaves** to keep them from attracting bugs.

When properly cultivated, orchids will bloom over and over again, for years to come.

Plants create a comfortable atmosphere and give rooms a pleasant feel.

▶ Prevent a harmful accumulation of water by occasionally **loosening the soil**. Repotting your plants? Make sure that the new pots' drain holes are clear. Line the bottoms with seashells or slightly curved shards from broken clay pots to keep the holes open to provide drainage, but keep the dirt from flowing out.

▶ Pay attention to your potting soil: a mixture of **strained compost, garden soil,** and **sand** is a good bet. Also, **egg shells** (for calcium), **coffee grounds,** and **black tea** make an excellent natural fertilizer. If you have some tea left in the pot, give a little to your plants.

▶ Avoid **moving** or **turning** your plants around: even a slight change in position causes many houseplants to shed their leaves.

▶ Leaving your plants directly exposed to either **heat** or **drafts** is the equivalent of leaving outdoor plants unprotected from the elements.

▶ Water plants more **sparingly** during the **cold months,** as winter is a time of rest for most plants. Also, keep them in rooms with cooler temperatures, if possible.

CUTTING BACK

Cutting plants back regularly is important for both controlling and encouraging growth. Careful pruning can help your plants grow strong, and it's a good way to shape certain plants.

▶ **Prune** plants once a year, but exactly when depends on the type of plant. Learn each of your plants' best pruning times first.

▶ Increase the number of shoots and blooms by **pruning the main shoot**. This will cause it to sprout new shoots.

▶ Make the **cut straight**, no matter why or where you prune.

▶ Cut plants that spend the summer on a balcony or patio **downward at a 45° angle** to allow rainwater to flow off.

Sprucing Up

You may love where you live, but even a carefully maintained home can use a little sprucing up over time. As earlier generations well know, often just changing a few small details, along with a bit of "spit and polish," can make a whole room look brand-new.

From Old to New

Sometimes replacing a few small details are the difference between a home that looks neglected and one that's simply beautiful. Here are a couple of examples:

- Bring new life to a room by adding wallpaper. Back in fashion today, wallpaper can help make a small room feel bigger or add some much needed style.

- Are your doors looking a little tired? You don't have to paint or replace them to give them a more updated appearance. Simply replacing the door handles or fittings may just do the trick.

Problem Floors

Carpeting and floors undergo a lot of abuse over a home's lifetime. Sometimes the only thing to do is rip the whole thing out and lay a new carpet or hardwood, but you'd be surprised at how often a few small tricks can put that drastic step off for a while, whether the problem is due to wear or changing tastes.

- Lay an inexpensive area rug over the worst spots to hide stains and damage on a carpet that needs replacing, if you just don't have the budget for a new one right now.

- If the floor has stains, make a virtue of necessity and cover them with a nice chest, big plant, area rug, or decorative floor vase.

- Detract from the brightness of a carpet by adding darker colors to the room—and vice versa if you want to create a lighter feel.

- Deal with truly hideous flooring in your laundry or kitchen by slapping on some peel-and-stick tiles. They're remarkably durable and can give the room a whole new look for a minimal investment.

- Hide unsightly patios or decks with modular carpet tiles, rugs made from recycled plastic, or stenciling. Combined with some elegant patio furniture and an outdoor fireplace, guests will feel as if they're stepping into a lovely outdoor room.

Beauty Treatment for the Bathroom

Old-fashioned fixtures make any bathroom look dated. Modern faucets and showerheads come in every price range, and it doesn't take a professional to replace them. For instance, a new mirror over the sink is a surefire way to give a bathroom new life.

- Clear off the bottles and tubes from the rim of the tub by storing these items on a shelf, or in a wicker basket or wooden bucket.

- If you can't change the bathroom tiles, change the accessories instead: a new rug, towels, and shower curtain will give the whole bathroom a new flair.

Decoration In Place of Paint

If you have neither the time nor the inclination to paint a room, you can still work with it in other ways:

- Apply photo wallpaper. It's simple, affordable, and usually means that you need only accentuate a single wall (or part of it) for a cool new look.

- Apply wall tattoos. They are easy to apply and come in all kinds of colors and designs, ranging from floral patterns to mottos and quotations.

- Conceal the hot water radiators in an old house with radiator covers for a whole new ambience.

Out of Sight

Even the tidiest homes have areas that aren't really for guests' eyes. Here are some ideas for keeping those areas private:

- An attractive room divider is a quick and easy way to hide certain areas from sight. For instance, it's easy to hide the chaos of a crowded shelf behind decorative blinds made of wood, fabric, or metal.

- Hang blinds from the ceiling or archway to block an open kitchen from view when you haven't had time to clean up between the food prep and the arrival of dinner-party guests.

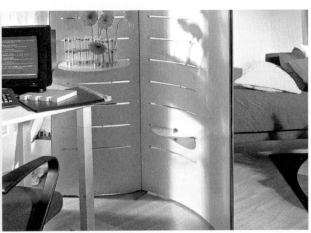

Storage

Closets, wardrobes, dressers, and shelves have long been used for storing our treasured belongings—but those storage spaces can easily become dusty and untidy. Organize your belongings in neat and decorative ways with functional furniture and organizing systems that can help you create order from chaos.

If your closet, dresser, chest, shelf, and cabinet are overstuffed disasters, just remember that in times past, people got by quite nicely with much less space. Granted, they had fewer belongings, but even today it's possible to organize your storage space to make better use of the available room.

Higher closet shelves, accessible only by stepladder, can still be used to store seldom-used items in decorative boxes.

do-it-yourself decorative boxes

If you need some boxes for storing small household items, you don't need to spend a bundle; shoeboxes can be smartened up nicely to do the trick, using nothing more than some inexpensive art supplies.

one Select a suitably-sized shoebox for the items to be stowed.

two Select a wrapping paper or wallpaper that matches the decor and cut is to size.

three Spread wallpaper paste on the box and glue on the decorative paper.

four Glue the paper to the box. When it's dry, stow your items.

A TIDY CLOSET

▶ Never **overload clothes hangers, shelves,** and **drawers**—clothing should be easy to remove and put back.

▶ Select **multi-armed hangers** for a smaller closet.

▶ Make the best use of space by installing **two clothing rods** in the closet—one for longer clothes such as dresses, and another for shorter ones such as shirts.

▶ Keep **accessories** such as scarves, ties, belts, stockings, and gloves in a **drawer**. Alternately, hang handbags and ties over from **hooks on the inside of your closet door**.

▶ Use **drawer inserts** for keeping items organized and accessible.

▶ When you pack away seasonal clothes, **dust your shelves**. Dust mites are bad for fabric and for people with allergies, and dust can make your clothing appear dirty.

▶ **Donate outgrown garments**. Let's face it: even if you do get back into them, chances are they'll be out of style.

DRESSERS

Drawers of different depths can be useful. Store undergarments in shallow drawers and sweaters in deeper ones, for example. But the following should be considered when looking at a new bureau:

▶ Check that the **drawers slide smoothly**.

▶ When stowing clothing in a drawer, leave about 1 in. (2.5 cm) of **clearance** between the top edge and the contents, so that the drawer can be opened and closed smoothly.

▶ **Arrange** the dresser so you have enough room to easily put items in and take them out.

▶ Avoid storing **heavy items** in your drawers; you risk breaking the bottoms.

SHELVES AND GLASS CABINETS

When it comes to storing and organizing, shelves and cabinets are a no-brainer. That's why they're ubiquitous. But one shelf doesn't necessarily fit all:

▶ You can use **open, decorative shelves** as excellent **room dividers**—to tastefully separate the dining area from the living room, for example—and use the shelves for storage.

▶ Opt for a **cabinet with a glass door** if you're not fond of the duster. Open shelves do need to be cleaned regularly.

▶ When buying shelves, make sure they can accommodate the **weight** of whatever you're planning to store. Lightweight shelves may buckle or even break under a heavy load of books or tools.

CHESTS, BUFFETS, AND SIDEBOARDS

Nice as they are, a shelving unit or glass cabinet won't fit in every room. Sometimes a sideboard or chest is the way to go:

▶ You can use a lovely old **chest,** with no partitions, to accommodate either large items of clothing or kids' toys.

▶ Put a **buffet** or **sideboard** in the dining room for a decorative storage place for dishes, glasses, and silverware, as well as offering extra space to lay out food and drinks during a dinner party. Don't have room for a massive old antique? There are plenty more streamlined models available today.

PRACTICAL AIDS

There are as many different storage solutions as there are objects to store, as long as you have a little creative flair.

▶ Use **decorative boxes** to store off-season clothing or footwear, as well as seasonal decorations. Store them inconspicuously on the top shelf of the closet, under the bed, or in the basement. By adding peepholes covered with plastic wrap or a photo of the contents, you can readily find what you need.

▶ **Wheeled carts** allow you to store diverse items in an organized manner. A classic here is the **tool cart** that can be rolled out of its niche as needed.

▶ **Magazine racks** are practical, too; just don't forget to empty them regularly.

▶ Put up a **peg board with hooks** to keep the workshop tools nicely organized. Traced and painted outlines of the tools make organizing easy.

▶ **Hooks** are great for kitchen utensils; **magnetic strips** work well for knives.

▶ Sturdy **plastic boxes** are good for storing general smaller household tools.

▶ **Paper** is a perpetual problem for most families—from bills to school notices and notes, it tends to clutter our counters. Solve the problem by keeping an **expandable file folder** in the kitchen, with a folder for significant categories. Then tuck it away out of sight when not in use.

▶ Store all your **instruction manuals** in one **binder** in the kitchen or pantry.

▶ Store toys in **see-through stackable containers** that are clearly labeled (e.g., dolls, trucks, or building blocks). That way, kids can easily put them away themselves and toys don't get buried at the bottom of a large toy box.

▶ Store kids' bath toys in a **mesh bag** and then hang it from the faucet or showerhead until it is fully drained.

A partitioned box with a transparent cover lets you see at a glance what's inside. Just shove it under the bed when you don't need it.

Storage Space

When the closets are bursting, bookshelves are overflowing, and your computer is sitting on the dining room table, it's time to create new storage space. Every home has a few empty nooks and corners that can be pressed into service.

So, you've decided that it's time to expand the storage capacity of your living space. Every area in the house has the potential for storage space, including the kitchen, dining room, bedrooms, hallways, and corridors, as well as added new closets. What next? Well, it's important to let the available space dictate how you will proceed.

ADDITIONAL CLOSETS AND SHELVES

▶ Turn a **nook into a closet** by installing a **rod** for clothing. The space between the clothes rod and the back wall should be the width of half a hanger. If there's no room for a door, install a **roller blind** or a **curtain**.

▶ Create additional storage space under a **pitched roof** or a **sloping staircase** by adding a **moveable wardrobe** on casters or a custom-built **closet door**. Or transform **windows** that don't offer a nice view and doors that are never opened into **shelves** with panels of wood or glass. Show them off with an artistic display of ornaments or collectibles.

STORAGE SPACE IN THE BEDROOM

Ah, the age-old problem of how to organize a bedroom. It can sometimes seem like there aren't enough closets in a house to deal with even just the bedroom's needs, but it's really not all that hard to organize. Here are a few ideas for how to make the best of the space in your home's bedrooms:

▶ Use the space **under the bed**. Tuck away extra blankets or pillows for guests in drawers, low chests, or sturdy boxes that are low enough to fit under your bed. A chest or drawer with casters and handles or loops is particularly easy to move in and out. Of course, this works best with a bed with a taller frame.

▶ No space left under the bed? Hang shelves **above it** instead. If you want to store important, but not particularly attractive, objects on open shelves, use a set of matching decorative boxes to hide them away in plain sight.

▶ If you have a high-ceilinged bedroom, consider installing a **platform** for the bed to turn it into a **loft-style bed**. You will have loads of extra storage space beneath it. What works best in this case will be a chest of drawers, a trunk, or a set of shelves covered with cabinet doors.

There is plenty of room beneath a loft-style bed for closets and shelves.

A wheeled cabinet, shelves, and fitted desktop turn this nook into a practical office space.

USING HALLWAYS AND CORRIDORS

Hallways and corridors can make up a large percentage of a home, yet they're rarely used as storage spaces. Why not put every nook and corner to work with custom-fitted shelves? Home-improvement stores offer modular, multi-use shelving systems that can stretch your available storage space to the max without stretching your budget. But there are all sorts of other solutions as well:

▶ Install a shelf or shelves over the **front door** or along one wall in the foyer, along with some well-placed **hooks**. This will make it easy to better organize coats, boots and shoes, scarves, and sporting equipment. You can use matching pull-out **baskets** to make everything look tidy and attractive. Or you might want to conceal it all behind a **curtain** or a **blind**.

▶ Or don't hide the shelf away, but showcase it instead. If you equip the shelf with **halogen spotlights**, it will create a welcoming island of light in the entryway.

▶ Another great idea is to build a small custom-made **office** or **chest of drawers** to go beneath a staircase in the hallway. A **desk** made exactly to fit and one or two shelves are perfect for using this potentially dead space.

STORAGE SPACE IN KITCHEN AND DINING ROOM

A cozy kitchen will quickly become the hub of the entire home, which is all the more reason to make sure there's enough storage space to keep it neat and uncluttered.

▶ Store larger items such as **pots, pans,** and **small appliances** in the kitchen's **bottom cabinets**. For up above, choose **overhanging cabinets** that are the right height. The topmost shelves, which you may only be able to reach with a stepladder, should contain **seldom-used appliances** like the fondue pot or the waffle-iron.

▶ Install tall cabinets with **vertical slide-out drawers** that are accessible from two sides. They are versatile space-savers, while a **corner cabinet** with a lazy Susan makes good use of a space that often goes to waste.

▶ Use a nook to hold a **garbage can** or a **kitchen towel rack**.

MORE SPACE IN THE KIDS' ROOM

Children's rooms simultaneously serve as the place where kids play, learn, and sleep, so they have to perform miracles when it comes to providing adequate storage space. Over time, most kids' bedrooms accumulate a mind-boggling assortment of toys, clothes, books, and crafts, all of which has to be stored somewhere.

▶ Consider putting a **loft bed** in a kid's room that has little space—it will have plenty of room underneath for a desk, seats, or storage unit.

▶ No shelf space ? Maybe hang a **bag** made from sturdy **material** or a **mesh net** from a ceiling hook for storing stuffed animals, balls, and other toys.

▶ Use colorful **baskets, boxes,** and **chests** to stash toys for the evening. Make it easy for kids to sort and put away their own toys by gluing a magazine picture of the contents (e.g., cars, blocks, doll clothes) on each container.

good to know

PROPER STORAGE

Pack articles of clothing in white tissue paper to protect them. A layer of blue tissue prevents white clothes from yellowing, and a lavender sachet or cedar chips between clothing help guard against moths. Vacuum-sealed bags with a vent make practical space-saving storage devices for bulky clothes and blankets; just put the items in the bag and suck out the air with a vacuum cleaner. Finally, store hats in hat boxes, and stuff leather handbags with tissue paper so they keep their shape.

Table and Kitchen Fabrics

The right choice of fabric and color goes a long way to setting the tone of your kitchen or dining room. Choose table linens, napkins, and dish towels that give personality to the room and offer a warm welcome to both family and guests.

When tablecloths, napkins, and dinnerware harmonize perfectly, they make for a beautiful table.

Choose your tablecloths and napkins according to the occasion—a formal celebration calls for a different table setting than a family dinner or a kid's birthday party.

BUY TABLE LINENS THAT MATCH THE COLOR OF THE DINNERWARE

▶ Go for the old tried-and-true **linen** or **cotton tablecloth**. It should be washable up to about 140°F (60°C) to ensure that the red wine stain from last night's fancy dinner will come out.

▶ Check that colored tablecloths are **colorfast**. Otherwise the colors will fade when washed.

▶ Make sure your new **lace tablecloth** is also washable up to about 140°F (60°C).

▶ Before adding **lace trim** to a tablecloth, preshrink the lace by washing it. Otherwise, you risk having to remove it and sew it on again.

▶ Think about a **plastic tablecloth.** They are extremely practical—and not only for an outdoor table. There are plenty of contemporary designs and colors that will do your kitchen proud.

▶ For a one-off, consider **paper**. Paper tablecloths come in any number of sizes, colors, and patterns, but they can be used only once.

▶ Use a **liner** to keep your tablecloth from slipping and to protect your table from heat and any spills that might happen.

▶ Or go for a **table runner** and **placemats** to protect the surface of the tablecloth. In a pinch, they can also be used to cover stains—but even so, keep a fresh tablecloth on hand as a replacement.

a money-saving *hint*

Sew kitchen towels from old cotton drapes and tablecloths and save yourself the expense of new ones.

▶ Place mats come in many different materials, but for households with kids, wipeable **plastic place mats** are ideal.

▶ You can lay a **table runner** across the table to add color and style, as well as to protect the table from scratches, scuff marks, and stains.

▶ Get some **small, crocheted trivets** so you can safely put pots directly on the table.

▶ Choose **cloth napkins** to bring a note of elegance to a dinner party. But for everyday use and less elegant occasions, choose **paper napkins,** which come in all shapes, colors, and patterns.

IN THE KITCHEN

In some ways, the humble dish towel is the unsung hero of the kitchen; you use them countless times every day, for drying dishes and handling pots. As well as soaking up water and spills, they also harbor bacteria and should be washed regularly. Nowadays you can buy them in a great variety of colors and fabrics, so that you can find a towel (or three) to fit in with virtually any decor, need, and taste. As with all things, the different fabrics used for dish towels have widely varying characteristics, and some work better than others.

▶ **Cotton** dish towels are the cheapest option, but they tend not to be the best choice. For one thing, they don't dry especially well, and they often start to smell after a while. Even several washings may not eliminate the odor, so consider the cotton dish towel a last choice.

▶ **Linen** or **half-linen** dish towels are absorbent, and they dry thoroughly without shedding lint onto your sparkling glasses. They tend to be very durable, although they need to be washed a few times before first use in order to work their best.

▶ **Microfiber** dish towels are a more modern solution that will absorb up to **five times as much water** as an ordinary dish towel. They also dry very rapidly after use. Microfiber is made from a blend of tiny nylon and polyester strands that are woven together.

▶ The only downside to microfiber: people with **very dry skin** or **eczema** might find that microfiber towels can be annoyingly clingy and irritating to their skin.

▶ Always wash dish towels in **200°F** (**90°C**) water before using them.

▶ Avoid chemical **fabric softeners**, since these leave a coating on the towel that keeps it from drying dishes properly. Trying using regular **white vinegar** as a softener instead. It has the additional advantage of eliminating unpleasant odors, even in cotton towels.

Old-fashioned, hand-crocheted pot holders are always in vogue.

folding napkins: the lily

one Fold a napkin into a triangle. Then turn the right and left corner up to the upper tip to form a square again.

two Now fold up two-thirds of the lower tip and then back down again to the bottom line. The top must not be longer than the bottom piece or else the folded napkin will be prone to tipping over.

three Finally, fold the napkin together by folding back the left and the right side to the rear, and tucking one tip into the fold of the other. Round out the shape by hand.

four Turn down both upper corners (the leaves of the lily).

Upholstered Furniture

Plush upholstered furniture adds romance and nostalgic appeal to your living room. Remember, though, that the most important qualities of upholstered furniture are hidden beneath the fabric covering.

When you're shopping for a sofa or an armchair, be aware that it will be used day in and day out, so it has to be sturdy—both in terms of its construction and the material of the fabric.

SELECTION CRITERIA

▶ For a piece in a lighter color, check whether it has **removable covers** that can be washed or dry-cleaned.

▶ See if the upholstery fabric has a **water- and stain-resistant Teflon coating.** This coating will keep your furniture looking like new.

▶ Consider an easy-to-clean **leather** model, particularly if you have kids who tend to spill things, or if your pet likes nothing better than to be curled up beside you on the sofa.

Upholstered furniture may look great in the showroom, but ask yourself if it will truly harmonize, in color and shape, with your furnishings at home.

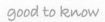

good to know

MODERN UPHOLSTERED FURNITURE
Today's armchairs and sofas consist of a basic frame, several layers of inner springs or foam, and soft padding. Look for frames made of hardwoods such as kiln-dried maple and oak, rather than pine. And opt for seats made with spring coils; webbing between the frame and the springs that is tightly woven and taut; and cushions with even stitching and seams. Loose threads can signal low-quality work. Microfiber, leather, and textured fabrics tend to last.

▶ Keep your new armchair or a sofa away from **direct sunlight** to prevent cover fabrics from bleaching out.

▶ Alternatively, use a cover fabric that may bleach out, but can be easily **stored** when guests arrive.

▶ You can buy high-quality upholstered furniture with different degrees of **firmness.** The heavier you are, the firmer the cushions should be, if you want to enjoy maximum comfort.

▶ Consider the **height** of the **seat** and **back rest** as well. It's easier to pull yourself up from the higher seats of taller furniture than from a low-slung couch.

▶ If you have weak legs, consider an armchair with **mechanical** or **electric power lift**. They help you stand by raising and tilting the seat in an ergonomically-appropriate way.

▶ **Measure it out**. You won't really know whether a couch is a good fit until you get it home, but you can get a sense of whether the size is right by taking the measurements of a potential purchase and then laying out squares of **newspaper** in that exact size in your living room.

▶ Give yourself plenty of time to **shop around**—after all, you need your sofa and chair to stay comfortable even after a long evening spent in front of the television.

▶ Stand about **3 ft. (1 m) back** from the sofa you're considering and look at it with a critical eye: does the pattern line up? Does the couch look symmetrical? Do the cushions fit together in a straight line? Does everything look right?

▶ Don't buy a sofa, chair, or loveseat without first sitting in it just **as you would do at home**—even if this includes lying down or slouching. Noticing the flaws in a piece of furniture only once you've got it home can be an expensive mistake.

Ventilation and Heating

Properly manage your home's heating and ventilation systems to save on energy costs, create a healthy interior climate, reduce greenhouse gas emissions, and banish mildew before it gets a chance to set in.

Most people feel comfortable in a room with an average temperature between 64–72°F (18–22°C). Different areas of every house require specific temperatures to ensure comfort and prevent mildew.

HEATING SENSIBLY

▶ A temperature of around 64–68°F (18–20° C) is usually sufficient in the **bedroom,** where you will mostly be snuggled under the blankets.

▶ Keep the **bathroom** well-heated. At least for mornings and evenings, the bathroom should be pleasantly warm; stepping out of the bathtub or shower, you might find temperatures around 64°F (18°C) a bit too cool.

▶ Never let rooms **cool off too much**: the energy expended to warm up cold walls again is comparatively high.

▶ **Floor heating** can offer an added element of comfort, while adequately heating the entire home.

▶ Save energy by keeping the doors that connect to **uninsulated rooms** (such as the garage or a cellar) closed.

THE RIGHT VENTILATION

▶ For quick air circulation, **open two windows** that face each other to create a draft.

▶ **Open your windows** three times a day for about 3–10 minutes for effective circulation, without cooling your home down excessively. Experts all recommend short, periodic bursts of ventilation to maintain air quality.

▶ **Air your house out** for longer periods during the warm seasons of the year. The exception: if you suffer from **hay fever**, you should stick with short periods of ventilating, even in the summer.

PREVENTING MILDEW

Too much moisture creates a breeding ground for mildew. In living areas you may find mildew on wood, carpets, wallpaper, drywall, or masonry. Improper ventilation is usually the cause.

▶ Air out the room immediately if steam rises while you're **cooking** or **bathing**. Just open a window or turn on a fan.

▶ **Keep doors closed** to prevent moist air from spreading to the other rooms.

▶ Open the windows when **drying laundry inside** your house, to allow damp air to escape.

▶ Leave about **1–2 in. (2–5 cm) clearance**, if possible, between **big wardrobes** and **outer walls**. Mildew can easily develop behind the wardrobe without being noticed.

▶ Regular ventilation is especially important if you have newer **insulated glass windows**—these are so airtight that fresh air can hardly enter the home through the frames or windows.

A ceiling fan keeps air moving during hot and cold months.

Adequate ventilation provides the right humidity level—generally about 50% relative humidity.

Wallpaper

Wallpaper is making a comeback. Not only can it look richer than paint, it gives rooms more dimension, and can even mask a wall that is in bad shape. Whether you prefer a muted color or opt for colorful patterns is a matter of taste. The key here is that whatever wallpaper you choose should create a unified look with the fabrics and the style of your furnishings, without overwhelming the space.

Wallpapering is easier that you think. A few tips, some basic instructions, and a little imagination are all you need to subtly or radically change the atmosphere of a room.

THE EFFECT ON A ROOM

Wallpaper has a significant impact on a room. It can subdivide and structure a room, as well as make it appear larger. The trend these days is to wallpaper only one or two walls rather than the entire space.

▶ **Large patterns** tend to dominate a room, making it ideal in a big room; in a small room or one full of nooks and crannies it can be overwhelming.

▶ Cover small rooms with a **bright, monochromatic color** or **small patterns.**

▶ For a striking wallpaper pattern to show itself off to best advantage, the style of the furnishings should be **low-key**.

▶ **Vertical lines** on the wall make low ceilings appear higher—particularly if the ceiling remains white.

▶ Before you start, get an idea of how your chosen wallpaper will look by holding a large piece of it **against the wall.**

▶ **Textured wallpaper** effectively covers up small holes or lumps.

▶ Make a note of the **serial** or **model number** of the wallpaper you're buying so you can find it again if you need more.

▶ Another good idea is to grab an **extra roll or two** when buying.

The color of this wallpaper harmonizes perfectly with the sofa and the accessories.

THE RIGHT CHOICE

Which wallpaper is right for you will depend on your personal preference and where you'll be using it, as well as on the skill of the installer.

▶ **Vinyl wallpaper** is the type most commonly found in paint, hardware, and home improvement stores. It's easy to handle and stands up to scrubbing and moisture fairly well, so it can be used in bathrooms, kitchens, and children's bedrooms.

▶ **Flocked wallpaper** has raised "velvet" patterns and works well for creating decorative highlights and for formal areas such as dining rooms. Although it's washable, it can be damaged by rubbing and scrubbing.

▶ **Grasscloth** is made from a weave of grasses. It's better suited to areas that sustain very little wear and tear.

▶ **Fabric wallpaper** is made of cloth, sometimes laminated to regular paper. It's not the easiest to keep clean and it's fairly difficult to work with.

▶ **Foil wallpaper** is made of patterned metal foil. It can add an interesting touch, but it can be unforgiving if it gets wrinkled or folded and has a tendency to reveal any defects in the wall behind it.

WALLPAPERING MADE EASY

Once you've selected the wallpaper for your room, it's time to roll up your sleeves and get to work. Here are some ways to make that work go as smoothly as possible.

▶ To remove old wallpaper, pierce it with a **scoring tool** and moisten it with **water**. A little **white vinegar** added to the water acts as a glue solvent.

▶ **Turn off the electricity** at the fuse box or breakers before moistening your wallpaper—otherwise electrical outlets and light switches can pose a danger while you're applying it.

▶ Fill in holes and cracks in the walls with **drywall compound** and **sand** them until they're smooth.

Thanks to new styles and designs, wallpaper use is again on the rise.

▶ Check the **undercoat** for the wallpaper by sticking a piece of **tape** onto the wall and pulling it off with a jerk; if the paint remains on the wall, the wallpaper will stick, too.

▶ **Sand down** painted walls to help make the glue stick better and eliminate any unsightly bumps.

▶ Lay a coat of **primer** on drywall before beginning in order for wallpaper to stick.

▶ Repaint the room's **trim and ceilings** before you begin wallpapering, and protect furniture and rugs with **drop cloths** to ward off drips.

▶ Always begin wallpapering at the edge of a **window**.

▶ Using a **level** or **plumb line**, draw a vertical line from floor to ceiling as a guide to keep your paper straight. Repeat for each strip.

▶ Cut **lengths of wallpaper** that are about 4 in. (10 cm) **longer** than the wall from ceiling to baseboard.

▶ Fill a tray with **lukewarm water** and dip each strip of your prepasted wallpaper for 30 seconds or more. Change the water in the tray every 6–8 strips.

▶ Match the edge of your first strip to the plumb line you've drawn on the wall, leaving 2 in. (5 cm) of **extra paper** at the top of the ceiling.

▶ Be especially thorough when gluing down the **edges** and **corners** of wallpaper seams.

▶ **Trim excess paper** at the top and bottom of the wall with a **utility knife** and **ruler**.

▶ Wipe wallpaper and baseboards with a **damp sponge** to remove excess glue. Rinse the sponge well, or streaks will appear as the paper dries.

make your own fabric wall panels

By creating fabric panels for your walls, you get all the drama of wallpaper but can easily change the patterns and colors.

one Pick up wood frames for stretching canvas from your local craft store (they can be different or uniform sizes) and cut your fabric so it's slightly bigger than the frames.

two Iron the fabric, position it on the frame, and tack down the fabric on one long edge with a staple gun.

three Stretch the fabric taut over the frame and staple the opposite long edge, followed by the short sides.

four Finish the corners by folding down the fabric as if wrapping a present, then staple it down. Presto! You've got a dramatic wall treatment for very little money and effort.

Walls

Colorful and creatively decorated walls accentuate your home's uniqueness and create a cheerful mood. There are numerous possibilities for adding a special touch to your walls—you can use templates, sponges, wall stamps, or other decorative elements to achieve the look you want.

Stenciling, cork tiles, moldings, embellishments, and wall treatments are some of the easiest ways to make a huge impact on any room.

PAINTING WITH STENCILS

Many historic buildings have splendid patterns that were created using stencils. To this day, painting with stencils continues to be a way to give interior walls a one-of-a-kind design.

▶ You can buy **prefabricated stencils** at craft stores. If you can't find the stencil you want, make it yourself by tracing shapes onto **poster board** or **stencil plastic**, then cutting them out. This way you can create any image you desire.

▶ Limit yourself to **two** or **three colors** and opt for **simple patterns** if you don't have much experience using a paintbrush.

▶ Use a **stiff, dry brush** to ensure that the pattern shows up; the smoother the base coat, the easier it is to apply the pattern. But even materials such as **textured** or **grained wallpaper** can be beautified.

A small paint roller make prep work for stamping a breeze.

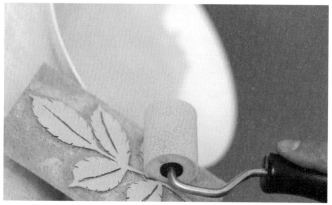

▶ You can use any **fairly thick paint,** or you can opt for the **special stencil paints** that are available at local dealers. Either will likely work fine.

▶ Use stenciling to beautify **furniture, doors,** and **fabrics** (with fabric paint), as well as walls. Using the same stencil on everything helps unify the look of a room.

INNOVATIVE WALL TREATMENTS

Sometimes a great wall treatment is all you need to take your room from so-so to super. And really, wall treatments have come a long way since the clumsy wall-sponging so popular in the '80s.

▶ To get the look of the new high-end wallpapers without the price tag, create it yourself. Paint the wall with a **dark-colored base coat,** for example, and stencil or stamp the **design** in a lighter paint.

Light floral stamping adds pizzazz to any room.

Stencils can be used to decorate stairs as well as walls.

You can get **wallpaper stencils** in small or large sheets, so you just roll the pattern and repeat. The best part? You can easily paint over it when you're ready for a change.

▶ **Beadboard wainscoting** can lend a charming, slightly old-fashioned appeal to walls. You can buy **pre-fab panels** that are simple to install. Just run them halfway up the wall and top them off with some complementary trim.

▶ Paint one wall with **chalkboard paint** for a dramatic and interactive finish.

▶ Paint stripes either in **contrasting colors** or **two shades of the same color**. They're easy to manage: paint a base coat of colour, then apply masking tape the width of your stripes, and paint your second color between the strips.

▶ Use **wall stickers** to easily decorate a child's room. They can be easily removed when your toddler outgrows his current passion. Similarly, **wall decals** cost little and can add a note of drama.

CORK TILES AND WALLPAPER

Cork can add a warm and pleasant atmosphere. The bonus: it's a sturdy, water-resistant material that is immune to the effects of temperature.

▶ You can apply **cork tiles** to all stable surfaces, provided they're firm, clean, and dry. First, thoroughly remove old paint and smooth out imperfections on the wall with **spackling compound.**

▶ Take the cork tiles out of their packaging **two days** before installing them, and stack them in piles of no more than five pieces in the room where you will be installing them. This will prevent the tiles from contracting or expanding on the wall.

▶ **Cork wallpaper** can be combined with normal fabric wallpaper, so it's a perfect choice for creating room accents.

▶ Let cork wallpaper **soften** for a short time after putting it up. Use a special **seam roller** to press down the seams.

MOLDINGS AND EMBELLISHMENTS

Decorative elements allow you to create stylish, classical, or avant-garde designs—there need be no limit to your creativity.

▶ Use **moldings** to embellish junctures where walls meet the ceiling or the floor: off-the-rack **crown moldings** from your local home-improvement store can give ho-hum walls a note of grace and elegance. They'll also cover up imperfections at the edges of the wallpaper, hide cables, and offset plain curtain rods. What's more, they're inexpensive to install—particularly if you do it yourself.

▶ Install **decorative trims**, **cornices**, and **baseboard moldings** to cover up bumps and small tears in the plaster, and to hide small pipes.

▶ Opt for a ceiling **rosette** or **medallion** for a special flair in an older home with high ceilings. You can buy them in many different shapes and designs.

▶ Use these decorative elements to help **visually correct** and **even out** a room.

good to know

SMOKE-STAINED WALLS
You can't simply paint over walls that are heavily yellowed by cigarette smoke—the nicotine absorbed into the plaster will seep through again. When painting nicotine-stained walls, always wash them thoroughly first and remove smoke-stained wallpaper completely. If you move into a home that has been inhabited by a heavy smoker, you might even have to chip off the plaster.

Windows

Curtains, drapes, blinds, and accessories should be coordinated with the overall decor and proportions of a specific room. Choose your window fabrics and decorative elements only after you've decided on the overall feel you want.

Window coverings aren't only about design—they have to be functional as well. After all, they protect your home from drafts, heat, and bright light, as well as from prying eyes.

CURTAINS FOR EVERY STYLE

There are several different kinds of window dressings, each with certain advantages over the others.

▶ **Sheer curtains** should limit your view outside as little as possible, but at the same time, they should assure at least a modicum of **privacy**.

▶ **Drapes** can keep out blinding light and act as a **privacy screen**.

▶ **Blinds** often take the place of **sheers** in contemporary-style homes.

▶ For a classic contemporary look, use **distinct shapes, geometrical patterns,** and **bright colors**.

▶ To create a luxurious effect, combine light sheer curtains with drapes of **silk, cotton,** or **damask**.

▶ **Damask panels** are perfect for giving rooms an early 19th-century flair.

▶ Heavy **valences** of **tufted cord, brocade,** or **velvet** look sumptuous. They can be combined with curtains of **tulle** and **gauze**. But this striking combination can look stifling in the wrong room; it requires a room with high ceilings.

▶ **Pleated pull-up sheers** or **drapes** made from light fabrics with flowery patterns set a romantic and playful theme.

SHORT OR FLOOR-LENGTH?

▶ **Short curtains** look rustic and are well-suited for short and square or wide, low windows. They stop just short of the windowsill or a little below it.

▶ **Arched sheer curtains** are a good choice for windows with flowerpots or windowboxes, because they put the fruits of your green thumb in full view.

▶ **Floor-length curtains** enhance the high, narrow windows often found in many older apartments and houses. They should reach to about 2 in. (5 cm) above the floor so that you can easily vacuum underneath.

THE EFFECT ON A ROOM

▶ Choose **floor-length** curtains to make a room's windows look longer and the ceiling look higher.

▶ Install the curtain rod a little **higher than the frame** to make the window look taller.

▶ Use **wide curtains** to make a narrow, high window look broader.

▶ Create **uniformity** between windows of differing heights by hanging all curtains **at the same height**.

Blinds are adjustable and infinitely variable—if you put a pretty bouquet of flowers on the windowsill, you can simply leave the blind halfway down.

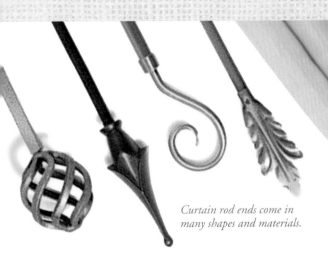

Curtain rod ends come in many shapes and materials.

CURTAIN RODS

These days, many windows are covered by venetian blinds or roll-up panels of paper or reeds, but the good old curtain and rod still has its place in a great many homes. Of course, hanging curtains isn't quite as simple as hanging the blinds that cover so many windows but, if done right, they can bring a comfortable, old-world allure to any room. Here are some pointers for doing it right:

▶ Display window treatments to their best advantage by installing curtain rods not less than **6 in. (15 cm) above the window frame**, and at least the same distance beyond the sides of the window.

▶ If a windowsill sticks out a lot further than the wall, it's a good idea to install **wood molding** on the wall around the window first. Then, mount the brackets for the curtain rod on the molding.

▶ Install the rod so that it is **almost touching the ceiling** if you want the ceilings to appear higher.

DECORATION

Window shades, blinds, and curtains aren't the only way to dress up a window. With a little creativity and thought, you can use all sorts of items to bring visual interest to your windows.

▶ Install **stained glass windows** to give a room a unique appearance and shield you from prying eyes outside, too.

▶ Use the **windowsill** as a ready-made shelf for blooming or green plants. Or, add accessories such as pretty stones, elegant vases, knickknacks, or artistic flower arrangements.

▶ Install a **glass shelf** across the center of the window, then place plants on the shelf. This is especially good for bringing a touch of green to the **kitchen** or any area that doesn't require the same level of privacy as, say, the bedroom. Just make sure that the plants are not too heavy.

Above right: a heavy, luxurious curtain, held in place with an ornate tie-back, clearly creates an elegant effect.

Window treatments allow your creativity free reign, as this arrangement with dried flowers shows.

The Traditional
Garden

Discover the wisdom of gardeners past to create

a beautiful and more productive garden today.

Unlock their secrets of growing bigger blooms,

sturdy shrubs, and delicious fruits and vegetables—

all without using harsh chemicals.

Berry Bushes

Small berry bushes have a place in every garden. Berries are chock-full of vitamins and antioxidants, and they don't require a whole lot of care. They thrive best in a partly sunny yard sheltered from the wind.

Berry plants prefer deep, rich soils without too much moisture. In heavy, clay soils, they tend to age quickly and bear less fruit.

REQUIREMENTS FOR A GOOD START

▶ Plant **bare-root berry bushes** (blueberries, raspberries, etc., with roots not in soil) as soon as you can work the ground in spring so that the plants are well-established before hot weather arrives. Plant on a cloudy day or late in the afternoon.

▶ Plant **potted berry plants** any time, as long as you can work the soil; however, bushes root better when they're planted in the fall or spring.

▶ Buy varieties of blackberries, currants, and gooseberries without **thorns**, so that even kids can pick their fill.

▶ Beautify an arbor or trellis with **thorn-free, climbing blackberry** varieties.

▶ Plant the **root ball of a currant bush** around 3 in. (7–8 cm) below the surface of the ground to encourage strong growth at the base of the plant.

▶ Add a little **rock dust** along with **compost** in the hole for a red currant bush. The sprigs should be bare of leaves to a height of about 6 in. (15 cm) above the surface of the ground.

▶ Form a **depression** around the base of berry plants to capture the water.

Currants are an excellent source of vitamin C.

▶ Leave enough **space between plants** to assure that they'll thrive without competition. This also prevents **gray mold** during rainy summers.

▶ When planting **raspberries,** don't choose a location where raspberries have been grown in the preceding five years.

▶ Incorporate **organic matter** into the soil before planting **blueberries** to make them grow better. Good options include peat moss, well-rotted manure, straw, compost, or aged sawdust. If possible, use only **rainwater** for watering.

PRUNING BUSHES

Prune berry bushes before the onset of winter or right after the harvest. Raspberry bushes bear on one-year-old shoots; gooseberries and red currants on one-to-two-year-old shoots; and blueberries after three to eight years. A good harvest requires proper pruning to provide the bush with light and air. Remove damaged canes or shoots, as well as sick shoots lying on the ground.

▶ After planting, **cut raspberry shoots back** to about 2 in. (5 cm) above the ground.

▶ With **blackberries,** cut off **brown, dead shoots** right down to the soil and remove them from the bush in spring.

▶ With **currants,** cut back the previous year's main shoot by about a third. Currants need a total of eight strong base shoots: two each of one-, two-, three-, and four-year-old shoots.

▶ Make sure that the oldest shoots on **black raspberry bushes** are only three years old.

planting berry bushes

one Dig a hole for the plant about 20 in. (50 cm) deep and as wide as the root ball. Loosen up the soil thoroughly to prevent any waterlogging.

two Add a little rotted compost to the hole, then carefully insert the very well-watered bush.

three Fill in the hole with dirt and compost, tamp down carefully, and be sure to water thoroughly.

▶ Keep **gooseberry** bushes from having more than five strong shoots at the base—otherwise it's difficult for them to develop new shoots. Cut shoots back by about a third, and ensure that no shoots are more than six years old.

PROPER CARE

▶ Since most berry bushes are shallow-rooting plants, **hoe them carefully** and **close to the surface,** if at all, to avoid damaging the roots.

▶ Plant a **common wormwood** next to a **currant** bush to prevent stem rust and aphids.

▶ Plant **garlic, lily-of-the-valley,** and **yarrow** next to **gooseberries** to keep the bushes healthy and increase their yield.

▶ Plant **bear's garlic, marigold,** and **forget-me-nots** beneath **raspberries** to keep pests away.

▶ Help many varieties of berry bushes with a layer of **mulch** consisting of dried **grass cuttings, straw,** or **leaves**. It keeps weeds from growing, and the soil remains fine, crumbly, and damp. If the berry varieties in your garden are not mildew-resistant, a layer of **bark mulch** will help.

▶ Don't expose **gooseberry** bushes to **direct sunlight**. Berries can get sunburned, especially when they're ripening.

Raspberry varieties that bear fruit on two-year-old shoots in early summer and on one-year-old shoots in late summer provide a good harvest.

AT HARVEST TIME

▶ **Blueberry rakes** aren't a good idea for harvesting, as they tear off the leaves of your plants; it may be a little bit more time-consuming, but handpick blueberries instead.

▶ **Gather berries** in fairly small containers to prevent them from being crushed under their own weight. You can harvest with both hands if you hang a container with a handle over your arm. Line the containers with **paper towels** to pick up any stains.

▶ If the **gooseberry** harvest looks promising, **pick some of the fruit green** and preserve them; as a result, the remaining berries will grow bigger and better.

▶ Protect the harvest from **birds** by hanging **nets** above the bushes—but make sure that they're high enough that you can easily walk beneath them.

After the harvest, cut raspberry canes off close to the ground so the plant can conserve its strength.

Bulb Plants

Tulips and daffodils are some of the first messengers of spring, whereas other bulb types, like dahlias, gladioli, or autumn crocuses, bloom into late fall. These plants don't require a lot of care and can even be grown in pots on the balcony or deck.

The saying "the bigger, the better" really applies to flowering bulbs, because the biggest bulbs are generally healthier and bloom better.

MAKING THE RIGHT SELECTION

▶ Buy bulbs with an **undamaged outer skin** and a **firm core**. If they are sprouting or exhibit decay, toss them out.

▶ Store bulbs that you can't plant immediately after purchasing in a **cool, dark,** and **airy** place. Store rare and valuable varieties in the **crisper drawer** of your refrigerator, and leave undisturbed until they are ready to be planted.

▶ Plant lilies, lilies-of-the-valley, or glories-of-the-snow in **shady areas;** wood anemones and wild daffodils flourish in **full shade.**

PROPER PLANTING

▶ Bulb plants grow best in **loose, porous soil.** If the soil is on the heavy side, fill the trench with a layer of sand about ½–1 in. (1–2.5 cm) deep. This layer keeps the bulbs from rotting during the wet and cold seasons of the year.

▶ Remember that the depth for planting should always be at least twice the **diameter of the bulb.**

▶ When in doubt, follow the instructions on the package of **lily bulbs,** as there are many considerations concerning how deep lilies should be planted.

▶ Plant bulbs at **different depths** to get a nice, thick blooming. This produces better results, especially in restricted spaces such as a clay pot.

▶ Lightly water **daffodils** and **checkered lilies** after planting. Their roots will grow quicker in moist soil.

▶ Plant bulbs in **plastic baskets, nets,** or **wire mesh** if you plan to take them out later. They'll be easier to remove and will also be protected from rodents.

▶ Plant summer bloomers such as **dahlias, gladiolus,** or **crocosmia (falling stars)** in well-loosened and aerated soil.

CULTIVATING BULB PLANTS

Most bulb plants flourish beautifully without special care. And they barely need watering, which makes them ideal for areas with less rainfall or gardeners who are tight on time.

▶ Put a stake in the ground at the same time as you plant **tall-growing plants,** such as **gladiolus**

Plant spring bloomers, such as irises, crocuses, grape hyacinths, or tulips, in the fall.

or **dahlias**, that will need support later on. If you wait until the root system is already developed before driving a stake in, you risk damaging the plant.

▶ In damp regions, remove **tulip bulbs** after their leaves have wilted and store them until the fall in a bed of sand, peat moss, or saw dust, in a dark place.

▶ Snip off the **blooms** of bulbs after they wilt in order to save them the energy needed to form seeds. Don't touch the leaves, though—the plant needs them to store nutrients for the winter.

▶ Always plant **bulbs** and **tubers** in different places to avoid diseases caused by fungi or bacteria.

PROPAGATING BULBS AND TUBERS

The propagation of bulb plants is very easy. Many form small bulbs or sprout tubers by themselves. These simply have to be detached from the parent plant and stored in a cool and sheltered place over the winter.

▶ Dig up the **bearded iris rhizome** every two to three years after it has finished blooming, divide it into several pieces, and trim the leaves. Dispose of the oldest part of the plant.

A multi-layered effect is created by planting low-blooming bulb plants in front of high-stemmed lilies, narcissuses, or tulips.

▶ Divide **dahlia tubers** with a knife before planting them in the spring. Each division should have a budding sprout.

PROPAGATING LILIES THROUGH BULB SCALES

▶ Dig up the bulbs in the fall and gently pull off four to six of the fleshy outer **scales**. Then dust the wound of the parent plant with **charcoal powder** for protection and replant the bulbs.

▶ Place the scales to half their depth in a mixture of **potting soil** and **sand**. Keep them moist at room temperature by covering them with plastic wrap. Don't expose them to direct sunlight.

▶ When **small bulbs** with **delicate roots** form (within about eight weeks), plant them individually in little pots so that only the uppermost tips poke out of the soil. Store them in a dry and dark place at about 40°F (5°C).

▶ Carefully plant bulbs as soon as the first delicate **leaves** sprout in the spring—just choose a day when it's not too cold.

Early-blooming hyacinths and daffodils are among the first harbingers of spring.

a money-saving *hint*

Buying flower bulbs instead of plants can save you a hefty sum. In addition, there is a much greater choice of early-blooming bulbs, and more unique varieties often aren't even sold as plants.

289

Climbing Plants

Climbing plants can beautify an arbor, unattractive shed, wind barrier, or old wire fence. Even a humble lamppost can look great with the help of a few strategically placed climbing plants.

Depending on the species, climbing plants prefer different locations. They should be situated a certain distance from walls or climbing aids and provided with organic material to help them grow.

WHERE AND HOW TO PLANT

▶ **Evergreen plants** like shady or partly-shaded north or northeast walls; these include ivy, evergreen honeysuckle, and winter jasmine. This is also a very comfortable spot for climbing hydrangea.

▶ **Deciduous climbers** such as clematis, Dutchman's pipe, and trumpet flower thrive along sunny southwestern or southeastern walls.

▶ Plant climbing plants in **spring** so that they can become well-established before fall.

▶ Cover the **root balls** of the plants with at least 2 in. (3–5 cm) of dirt.

▶ Put a layer of **coarse gravel** over the planting site to keep the wall of the house from getting dirty when the plants are watered or when it rains hard. It also protects the soil against excessive drying out. Before adding the layer of gravel, wait until the dirt has compacted from repeated rainfall or waterings.

Annual climbing plants such as the black-eyed Susan can be raised in a pot.

Remove wilted flowers in order to ensure your plants continue blooming for a long time.

▶ Remember that, like other climbing plants, **clematis** likes to keep its feet cool—in other words, it likes a base in the shade. Since it also needs sun, however, shade only the base with mulch, a circle of stone, a brick, or even a low plant.

SUPPORT FOR CLIMBERS

Climbing plants hold onto their supports in various ways; some, like ivy and Virginia creeper, can cling by themselves without too much trouble. But others, like clematis and wisteria, need a climbing aid. When choosing a climbing aid, consider the characteristics of the plant you'll be tying to it.

▶ Use **vertical climbing aids** such as trellises for climbing roses and winter jasmine. Roses can also use their thorns to get a grip.

▶ Use either **vertical** or **horizontal** climbing aids for clematis and vetch.

▶ **Hang** climbing aids from hooks on a wall. This makes it easy to take them off once the plants have been trained.

▶ Make **wooden supports** and **trellises** yourself. When choosing and working with wood, remember that the plants will add weight to the structure. Snow will provide an additional load and wind will tug at the vines, so plan for stability.

▶ **Tie individual shoots** to the climbing aid carefully and fairly loosely with **soft string.** They must be able to move in the wind and increase in diameter as they grow.

CUTTING CLIMBING PLANTS

If you regularly cut back climbing plants, be fore-warned that they will become stronger and send out new shoots. Once the climbers have reached the desired height, simply prune them lightly every month. Shorten the tips of the shoots by a third so that they branch anew.

▶ Cut back **early-blooming clematis** immediately after it flowers. If you have a late-flowering variety, cut back the shoots from the previous year to two buds above the base.

▶ **Prune** wild clematis, ivy, Virginia creeper, and climbing hydrangea only **every couple of years**.

▶ Cut back the **shoots** of climbing plants that are several years old significantly in spring.

▶ Cut back **older plants** radically once they've stopped sending out shoots the way they should. This sometimes works wonders.

▶ Protect bricks and gutters by keeping a close eye on powerful climbers such as **fallopia** and **wisteria**; cut them back as required, otherwise serious damage to the wall or gutters can result.

Climbing roses need sun and can grow up to 30 ft. (5 m) high.

CLEVER COMBINATIONS

▶ Plant some undemanding, **shallow-rooting perennials** around the roots of climbing plants to keep the ground below them from ap-pearing too bare.

▶ Use a **tree** as a climbing aid: place a climber near the trunk of a tree with a narrow crown. For a tree with an expansive crown, plant the climber un-der the edge of the crown and allow it to climb up a rope to a sturdy branch.

▶ Combine two varieties of **clematis** that bloom at different times, or an **early-flowering clematis** and a **climbing rose** for an attrac-tive two-tone effect.

▶ Plant alternating varieties of climbers on the **posts** of a **balcony railing.**

Mandev-illa likes a bright, warm location, but not direct sunlight.

Companion Planting

For hundreds or even thousands of years, gardeners have used companion planting to repel insect pests. Aromatic plants such as garlic, marigolds, and peppermint are all reputed to send a signal to bugs to go elsewhere. So take a tip from grandpa and try companion planting your prized vegetables.

Plant broccoli and French marigold together; the root excretions from the French marigold help keep ravenous pests away.

Companion planting is a kind of botanical buddy system. It works on the principle that plants that grow together interact and influence each other. Apart from removing certain nutrients from the soil, individual plants give off substances and fragrances that can be good or bad for their botanical neighbors.

WHERE AND WHEN TO START COMPANION PLANTING

▶ Implement companion planting starting in the **center of the bed**; harmonious partners generally have similar seeding or planting times.

good to know

HARMONIOUS PARTNERS
When implementing companion planting, take into account whether plant varieties tolerate one another. Tomatoes go well with lettuce, cabbage, carrots, radishes, red beets, celery, spinach, and parsley—but not with potatoes, cucumbers, fennel, and peas. Potatoes go well with nasturtium, many types of cabbage, caraway, horseradish, peppermint, and spinach, but not with sunflower, pumpkin, cucumber, or celery.

ADVANTAGES OF COMPANION PLANTING

▶ Companion planting uses **far less water.** Since the companion plants grow close together and shade the ground more effectively, less moisture evaporates.

▶ **Because the plants are closer together**, you get a higher yield per surface area.

▶ Companion planting tends to require **less fertilizer.** Why? Because the plants absorb different nutrients from different soil depths, as well as excreting beneficial elements into the soil.

▶ Many plants enhance their neighbor's **flavor.** **Caraway** and **cilantro** improve the taste of early **potatoes**, and **dill** intensifies the taste of **carrots**.

▶ **Pests** are less drawn to gardens where companion planting is employed because some plants form a type of protective shield for others by means of their excretions.

▶ **Garlic** can prevent mildew and kills many fungi when planted near **fruit trees**; in addition, it fortifies the defenses of **strawberries** and keeps **gray mold** away.

▶ **Nematodes** can't stand the root excretions from **lilies** or **marigolds**, while **tomatoes** and **celery** drive away **white cabbage butterflies.**

▶ With **carrots** and **onions** you can literally kill two flies with one blow: they protect one another from carrot-fly infestation and onion-fly infestation.

▶ Choose the right companion plants to reduce, if not eliminate, the need for **pesticides.**

▶ Eliminating pests will result in **higher yields.**

Compost

The simplest and least expensive fertilizer is compost from your own garden. A backyard compost is the perfect spot for disposing of organic kitchen and garden waste. When well-mixed over the course of a year, your kitchen waste turns into nutrient-rich humus, which is one of the best fertilizers you can find.

With a compost pile, you're basically putting the cycle of nature to good use. The greater the variety of materials used, the richer the subsequent compost dirt. After as little as three to four months you will have raw or fresh compost, which is best for mulching or fall fertilizing of the vegetable patch. Compost needs about a year to ripen fully; you'll know when it's ready because it becomes fine, crumbly, and dark, like fresh soil.

MATERIALS FOR THE COMPOST PILE

All healthy, organic materials that rot within a year can be added to the compost pile, including:

▶ **Kitchen waste** such as vegetable and fruit peelings and cores (as long as they haven't been sprayed with pesticides); spoiled, dried-out foods; coffee grounds and tea leaves; paper filters; and eggshells.

▶ **Paper** from napkins, paper towels, uncoated paper, and paper bags for disposing of biodegradable waste.

▶ **Garden waste** such as shredded tree, hedge, and shrub cuttings; residue from flowers and perennials; leaves (but, because of the high tannic acid content, no leaves from **nut trees** and **oaks**); roots; and weeds without seeds.

▶ **Grass cuttings** can be added in thin layers, preferably mixed with coarser material so that enough air still gets into the compost pile.

▶ **Potting soil**; cut flowers, and potted plants with soil; and small pieces of untreated **scrap wood.**

SPECIAL CONSIDERATIONS

▶ A **partially-shaded location** is ideal for a compost pile. In bright sunlight, the compost will dry out quickly, and in the shade it may rot.

▶ Compost needs a certain amount of **moisture** and should feel like a sponge that has been squeezed out. A **grayish-white coating** or lots of **ants** mean that the compost material is too dry and must be watered.

Keep animals out of the compost by securing the opening with chicken wire.

► **Good ventilation** is also crucial. Use a pole to poke ventilation holes down to ground level.

► **Elder** and **hazelnut trees** are good choices for planting near compost piles as their leaves and roots aid in decomposition. They shouldn't be too close, though, as the compost has to remain accessible and you need to be able to manipulate a shovel and a digging fork easily when you occasionally turn the pile over.

► Surround a fairly small compost pile with a **trellis,** on which nasturtium, vetches, or other climbers can grow. **Sunflowers** are also good for concealing a compost pile.

► **Fragrant plants** can be used to combat the smell of rot; but they're often unnecessary. Compost usually smells like fresh forest soil.

The material in your compost pile keeps compacting toward the bottom. Temperatures can be as high as 140°F (60°C) during the rotting process.

MAKING THE COMPOST PILE

► The compost pile should be formed right on the top of the soil, never on stones or concrete. It needs contact with the earth so creatures that contribute to rotting can get in without hindrance and the resulting seepage can run off easily.

► Use the **three-pile method** for large gardens: use the first pile for garden waste. In the winter it can be moved into a second pile, which can be left to ripen undisturbed. By the following winter, the ripe compost can be sifted and moved to the third pile for use in the garden.

► A composter with **sliding panels** at the bottom enables you to remove compost from the base.

► A **wire-bin composter** with a hinged front provides easy access.

► Lay **coarse wood cuttings** to make up the bottommost layer of the compost. Place a little dirt on top, then pile on the compost material to a depth of about 3 ft. (1 m).

► Add a judicious sprinkle of **lime sand** or **rock flour** on each layer to provide the compost with important minerals and trace elements.

► Collect **leaves** separately in a covered circle made of wire mesh. They'll decompose quickly, and their acidic qualities will promote the growth of **blackberries, raspberries,** and **rhododendron.**

ENCOURAGING THE COMPOSTING PROCESS

A few shovelfuls of garden soil or an herbal slurry can be used to speed up the rotting process.

► Occasionally spray the compost with an undiluted **slurry** made from **dandelion** or **stinging nettle,** or a thinned-down **borage extract.**

► The allantoin contained in **comfrey** encourages the rotting of straw, as well as other plant remains that contain cellulose.

It's important that your compost be easily accessible—you will need to turn the pile over every once in a while and must keep it very well-ventilated.

Crop Rotation

Farmers have known the benefits of three-field crop rotation for centuries. Use the rotation principle in your own vegetable and fruit garden and you'll get a higher yield. In addition, you won't have to fertilize as much, and it helps to prevent garden pests and fungal diseases.

In comparison, if you plant the same varieties in the same spots every year, you'll deplete the soil because the plants will always remove the same nutrients. Sooner or later, those nutrients will run out, and your plants will cease to thrive.

FORTIFYING REST

Cycling plantings gives soil a well-needed rest so it can regenerate.

▶ The more time that passes before you put the same plant in the same location the better: a **four-year cycle** is ideal.

▶ Crop rotation often does away with the need for **fertilizing**, as some plants replace nutrients in the soil that other plants need. The roots of **bean** and **pea plants** release plenty of nitrogen when they rot, for example, which encourages growth in **cabbage plants** in the following year.

▶ Rotating crops also prevents **pests** and **fungal diseases** that spread in the soil. Why? Because the fungus spores and insect larvae can't locate the proper host plants, they die. For that reason, return **cucumbers, tomatoes,** and **peas** to the same spots only after two years or more, and **onions** after three years.

▶ If a variety of **cabbage** is afflicted with **clubroot**, wait seven to eight years before replanting cabbages in the same bed.

▶ You can even rotate crops in a small gardens with just one vegetable bed; simply rotate the plant varieties by **rows** in subsequent years.

PLANNING CROP ROTATION

When planning for crop rotation, take into consideration the nutrient requirements of each plant. Some crops grow abundantly and quickly and use up plenty of nutrients; these plants need strong fertilizer. Other plants require fewer nutrients, grow more slowly, and need more moderate fertilizing. Plants with a low nutrient requirement just need a little compost.

▶ In a vegetable bed, follow a plant that uses **lots of nutrients** by a **moderate** nutrient consumer, and finally by a plant with **low nutritional needs** in the third year.

▶ Use a **journal** to plan crop rotation, noting precisely what, when, and where plantings were done.

▶ For a well-planned crop rotation sequence, begin planting with vegetables in the **cabbage** family, followed by **legumes**, **tubers** and **nightshade** plants, and finally by **bulb** plants.

Cabbages benefit from the extra nitrogen available in the soil where leafy greens grew the previous year.

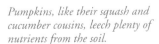

Pumpkins, like their squash and cucumber cousins, leech plenty of nutrients from the soil.

Diseases in the Garden

Until a few years ago, most of us still turned to chemicals to combat plant diseases. But many gardeners have come full circle, opting for tried-and-true organic methods to counteract pests and keep plants healthy.

Apply herbal sprays for diseases in the evening or on overcast days so that the wet leaves won't burn.

Some jurisdictions have even banned chemical fertilizers and pest controls, which makes it mandatory to adopt more environmentally-friendly solutions. There are many garden diseases, each with its own unique problems and cures.

CAUSES AND PREVENTION

Fungus in garden plants is usually weather-related; either very damp or very dry weather can encourage fungal growth. In addition, viruses and, much less frequently, bacteria, nutrient deficiency, or overabundance can also cause health issues for plants.

▶ Prevent disease by considering **location** and observing the rules of **mixed cultivation** and **crop rotation**.

▶ Avoid overfertilizing plants; instead, fortify them with **broths** and **slurries.**

CHLOROSIS

This metabolic disorder is also known by the term jaundice. The plant doesn't produce enough chlorophyll, so the leaves turn yellow. This occurs as a result of too much lime in the soil, excessively dense soil, or waterlogging, especially with raspberries, hydrangeas, pelargoniums, rhododendrons, and roses. Individual leaves, plant parts, or even the entire plant turns yellow, and the flowers become pale. Only the veins of the leaves retain their green. The plant withers. For prevention:

▶ Water your plants with **soft rainwater,** or douse them occasionally with a **stinging nettle slurry.**

▶ If chlorosis is already present, **loosen up the soil** and improve it by working in some **humus**.

BOTRYTIS BLIGHT

This fungal disease, also known as gray mold, frequently attacks fruits and vegetables, especially strawberries, bell peppers, lettuce, tomatoes, and grapevines. Ornamental plants can also be affected.

▶ Afflicted produce develops a **grayish-white fungus**, and may rot and die.

▶ **Space** plants out well and **prune** to ensure good air circulation as prevention.

▶ Place **straw** underneath **strawberry plants** to keep the fruit from lying on the ground.

▶ If botrytis bunch rot has already gained a foothold, **remove all diseased plants.** Burn or bury them to prevent further spread.

MILDEW

This dread fungal disease is one of the oldest on record. Mildew can be subdivided into two basic kinds: powdery mildew and downy mildew. In both cases, the infection is characterized by a white or gray fungal growth.

▶ **Powdery mildew** is a threat to apples, apricots, peas, strawberries, cucumbers, peaches, delphiniums, roses, gooseberries, and grapevines.

▶ **Downy mildew** is more apt to attack peas, strawberries, lamb's lettuce, cabbages, lettuce, horseradish, radish, black salsify, spinach, and onions.

The grape leaf (far left) shows typical characteristics of chlorosis. The raspberry and blackberry leaves (middle and right) are afflicted with rust fungus.

▶ Powdery mildew usually appears on **dry days** as a **whitish, floury layer** on the tops of leaves and flowers, stems, and fruit.

▶ Prevent both by purchasing **mildew-resistant strains**. Choose a sunny location to grow them and space the plants out well. Plant **garlic** between them and fortify the plants with **horsetail broth**.

▶ For a powdery mildew infestation, **cut off sick leaves**, **shoots**, and **branch tips**; they can be composted.

▶ **Downy mildew** sets in during damp weather or in a moist greenhouse, and it spreads very quickly. You'll recognize it by the **light spots** on the top of the leaves and the **grayish coating** on the underside.

▶ To prevent downy mildew, **buy resistant varieties** and avoid planting too close together. Avoid getting water on the **leaves**. In spring and summer, spray every two to three weeks with **horsetail** or **rhubarb broth.** Their high silicic acid content will help combat fungal infestations.

▶ If plant parts are already affected, remove the **entire plant** immediately.

BROWN ROT

This fungal disease takes hold on trees and wood, as well as on stone fruit, especially peaches and plums. Infections on wood and blossoms tend to occur when there is prolonged wet weather during blossoming time. Fruit rot generally occurs when the skin of the fruit is damaged.

▶ **Blossom and twig blight** occurs frequently with apricots, cherries, peaches, and plums. The blossoms wither and the shoots die from the tip back. Affected leaves don't fall off.

▶ **Fruit rot** is characterized by small, squishy brown spots that rapidly grow in size until the whole fruit is rotten. It especially affects the fruits of apple, cherry, and plum trees. The fruits don't always fall off.

▶ To prevent the blight, **prune** endangered trees, open them up, and provide good **ventilation**. Fortify them by applying a tea made from **horseradish leaves and roots;** or try a broth made from **horsetail reeds** and **garlic tea**.

▶ If brown rot is already present, immediately **discard all diseased fruit** on both the tree and the ground. When blossom and twig blight are present, **cut back diseased branches** to the healthy wood. Both fruit and branches can go into the compost, where the heat will kill the fungus.

RUST FUNGUS

Rust is a fungal infection that appears on the leaves and stems of plants. Rust fungi are the most diverse group of fungal plant pathogens in the world, containing more than 7,000 species. Rust species tend to be specific to the host plants they infect (e.g., mallow or snapdragon, beans, leek, and asparagus), although some do change host plants. They spread by tiny spores and grow best in humid, moist environments.

▶ You will recognize the disease by the **orange** or **red pustules** on the underside of leaves, as well as the **yellowish-red** spots visible on the tops of leaves.

▶ For prevention, plant in a **sunny, well-ventilated area** and loosen the soil frequently. **Horsetail broth** may help fortify the plants.

▶ **Remove diseased leaves** immediately. Add them to the compost pile as the heat generated will kill the fungus.

Moss Extract

About 2 oz. (50 g) dried moss
1 quart/liter water

Mince the moss and soak in the water for 24 hours. Then strain it and put the solution in a spray bottle. Spray every couple of weeks to prevent powdery mildew; in case of infection, spray every couple of days. Peat moss, liverwort, and bryophytes are the most effective mosses to use.

Fertilizing and Revitalizing

For centuries, gardeners relied on natural nutrient sources such as cow manure. Several decades ago, chemical fertilizers became popular because they were inexpensive and easy to handle, contributing to today's environmental problems. It's time to go back to organic methods to improve the soil and grow lush, healthy plants.

Green fertilizing involves improving soil by planting specific crops whose roots penetrate the soil, providing thorough aeration. Generally, they are dug into the soil before blooming to enrich it. The results may not be immediate, but in the long run, you'll be rewarded with a healthier garden and know that you're helping the environment.

Thoroughly mix fertilizers such as compost and cow manure into new garden beds with a garden fork.

GREEN MANURE

▶ Leave small quantities of **grass clippings and leaves** spread out across your garden and lawn to decompose and enrich the soil.

▶ Use green fertilization for empty areas and areas with some permanent crops such as **strawberries, rhubarb, roses, and asparagus.**

▶ Green-fertilizing plants that are sown in the **spring** should be mowed shortly before they bloom, then chopped up and raked under to enrich the soil with their nutrients.

▶ Leave green manure plants sown in the **fall** to stand through the winter and then mow them in the spring.

▶ **Prevent diseases** by ensuring that green-fertilizing plants belong to a different plant family than that of the subsequent vegetable crop.

▶ Plant **phacelia** in light to heavy soils in spring and summer. It grows quickly, is easy to care for, and attracts bees.

▶ Opt for **black medic** and **hairy vetch**. They're winter-hardy; they're also a good bet for medium-heavy to heavy, or light to medium-light soils.

▶ Plant **lupine** from spring to the start of fall to enrich sandy to loamy soils with nitrogen.

▶ Use **forage radish** for medium-heavy soils; but don't plant any vegetables from the **cabbage** family in that soil from then on.

NATURAL FERTILIZERS

Organic fertilizers spread easily, and they keep working for a long time.

▶ Use **compost**, which consists of waste from the garden and kitchen. It's a good source of nitrogen for the soil when added to the garden in the spring. Work it in to a depth of 1 in. (2.5 cm).

▶ **Cow manure** has to be aged or composted; otherwise it will burn the plants. If you buy it fresh, first pile it in a heap, water it thoroughly, and cover it with a sheet of plastic so that it stays moist and rots. Spread cow manure in the fall and work it into the soil well. You can plant **cabbages, lettuces, and pumpkins** immediately; but wait a year before planting **beans, peas, carrots, and radishes.**

▶ Spread commercially-available **dried cow manure** on the beds or use it as a very effective composting accelerator.

▶ Spread **bone** and **blood meal** in springtime; they mainly contain phosphorus and calcium. Mix bone meal into the soil to encourage healthy growth in young **shrubs**, and dose your **potted plants** on occasion, too.

▶ **Hoof** and **horn meal** is easily absorbed by the soil and offers a quick supply of nitrogen, phosphorus, and potassium. It can be spread throughout the year, especially before sowing or planting. Use 2–3 oz. per 10 ft² (60–90 g per m²).

▶ Fertilize potatoes, carrots, tomatoes, celery, and roses with **wood ash.** In springtime, spread the fine powder thinly in planting furrows or holes and then lightly work it into the soil.

▶ Plop **coffee grounds** right onto the flower bed to fertilize plants and keep **snails** away. Since you're not likely to generate enough to take care of all your fertilization needs, you'll probably have to use other fertilizers as well.

▶ An occasional **milk fertilization** benefits ferns, roses, and tomatoes. Mix **milk** or **whey** with water

Carefully spread compost among the plants and then work it into the soil with a rake.

in a 1:3 ratio. The plant roots will drink up the amino acids from the milk. The solution helps prevent mildew, too.

▶ **Sandy soil** needs **fertilizer** and added **nitrogen**, as rain sweeps away many of its nutrients.

▶ **Crushed eggshells** are a good source of **calcium**, and they're especially useful in acidic soil—they raise the pH level. Another benefit: if you scatter them around tender young plants, their jagged edges discourage **slugs** and other pests.

FEED YOUR GARDEN
A BROTH, SLURRY, OR TEA

Use various herbal preparations to fortify your plants against pests, diseases, and fungus. Make sure to prepare or dilute your concoctions with rainwater, or tap water that has been allowed to sit so that the chlorine and fluoride can dissipate.

▶ Create an **extract** or **infusion** by putting about 2 lb. (1 kg) of herbs into 10 quarts/liters of cold

water for up to 24 hours. You can then strain the infusion and use it in its diluted form. A **stinging nettle extract** keeps pests away; a **garlic extract** with a little added **liquid soap** can combat aphids and prevent fungal diseases.

▶ Make an **herbal broth** with equal parts of the extract and cold water. After letting the mixture sit for about a day, boil it gently for about 30 minutes.

▶ Spray **common horsetail infusion** to ward off many diseases, including leaf drop disease in berries, leaf spot disease, peach leaf curl, powdery mildew, brown rot, rust, bottom rot in lettuce, marssonina leaf spot, and scab. Mixed with a little soft soap, it's also effective against **aphids** and **spider mites.**

▶ Combat snails by spraying an infusion made from **bracken fern, fir cones,** or **strong coffee**.

▶ **Basil tea** (8 tsp./40 mL of dried leaves in 1 quart/liter of water) is an excellent spray weapon against **leaf lice** and **spider mites**.

▶ To make a **tea**, snip off fresh herbs, and place them in a bowl or large cup. Pour boiling water over the herbs and let the liquid steep for about 10 minutes.

▶ Make an **herbal slurry** by soaking about 2 lb. (1 kg) of fresh or about 5 oz. (150 g) of dried herbs in 1 quart/liter of water and let it ferment for 10–20 days, stirring daily. Use herbal slurries only in highly diluted form.

▶ Use a **birch leaf slurry** with fresh leaves as preventative medicine for fungus on leaves and fruits; a **dandelion slurry** promotes a better-quality yield from most berry and fruit trees.

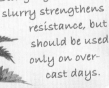

Stinging Nettle Slurry

About 2 lb. (1 kg) fresh or 5 oz. (150 g) dried stinging nettle
10 quarts/liters water

Crush stinging nettle in a bowl. Add water and thoroughly immerse the plants. Cover with plastic wrap or a lid and let ferment for three weeks, stirring daily; strain. Stinging nettle slurry strengthens resistance, but should be used only on overcast days.

Flower Beds and Borders

When planning and planting a flower bed, the soil conditions and position of the bed each play an important role. Ideally, you should choose a variety of flowers that bloom at different times to ensure that your garden always looks colorful and fresh.

Small annuals work nicely at the front of the flower bed. An uneven number is usually more attractive.

If you select your plants carefully, there can almost always be blooms in the garden, whether in sun or shade, through spring, summer, and fall—and even winter, in warmer climes.

THE RIGHT PLANTS

▶ Make a **seasonal bed** that contains early-blooming onion plants next to colorful perennials. Geranium, threadleaf coreopsis (tickseed), pansy, and French marigold all bloom for a very long time.

▶ **Shade-loving plants** include cyclamen, anemone, bishop's hat, lady's mantle, mimulus (monkey flower), St. John's wort, and lungwort.

▶ **Damp shade-tolerant blooms** include Christmas rose, foxglove, hosta, and lily-of-the-valley, plus primrose and snowdrop.

▶ Plant some poppy, lupine, and delphinium for an **early summer flower bed**. Threadleaf coreopsis and multicolored hollyhock are also good choices.

▶ In the summer, plant **ornamental grasses** to make an attractive visual island in a flower bed. These grasses are eye-catchers until late fall and will add a uniquely romantic note to summer flower bouquets.

▶ Keep flower beds from being appearing totally bald even in the winter, by including **ornamental grasses, evergreens,** and perhaps some **stone garden ornaments.**

▶ Create **flower bed variety** with some plants with attractive leaf shapes, or low shrubs with colorful bark or fruit.

▶ Look for **lots of buds, good branching,** and a **well-developed, moist root ball** when you're choosing plants to buy.

A set of miniature tools comes in handy for smaller jobs in the flower bed.

Draw the buildings, patios, shrubs, and beds in your gardening plan to scale, as well as the intended plantings.

PLANNING THE LAYOUT OF THE FLOWER BED

Use a detailed plan to make your work much easier. It will save you cash as well, because you end up getting the right plants in the right quantities. If you're a beginner at gardening, start with a few fairly easy-to-care-for varieties.

▶ First prepare a sketch complete with a **planting diagram.** Take into account the size of the plants when grown and sunny or shady areas.

▶ Bear in mind that flower beds should never be too **narrow.** Many plants like to spread out, so leave enough space between them.

▶ Use a **vertical planting scheme** for a tiered effect: set out taller plants in the center of the garden or at the back edge; place the medium-sized plants in front of them; and put the lowest plants in front.

EDGING AND MAINTAINING THE BED

A flower bed doesn't have to be angular. You can create precise outlines in other shapes, too.

▶ Map out **straight edges** by driving two stakes into the planned ends and stretching a string between them.

▶ Lay out **round, oval,** and **elliptical beds** by using a **garden hose** as a guide.

▶ Create **irregularly-shaped** flower borders by outlining them in **sand** or **stones.**

▶ Use **stepping stones** to make it easier to access hard-to-reach spots in your garden without trampling the plants. They also keep the soil looser as you won't compact it by walking on it.

▶ Lay a layer of **mulch** between plants to keep soil damp and hold weeds at bay.

▶ For a more formal or Asian-style flower bed, use **white gravel** or **ballast stones** for the same purpose.

PROBLEM LOCATIONS

Use a little forethought and effort to establish flower beds in some of the problem areas of the yard.

▶ Protect new plants from sliding down a hill in the rain by embedding **plastic netting** in the soil.

▶ Put plants that tolerate more moisture at the **foot of a hill** where runoff accumulates.

▶ Situate plants that like dry soil **in front of a wall.** The soil there warms up more, especially if it receives plenty of direct sun.

▶ Lay **dry-soil plants** at the corners of a garden, because the corners often dry out quickly.

▶ Create shade for sensitive plants in **very sunny gardens** by using **shrubs** and **small trees.**

Fruit Trees

Fruit trees are a good choice not only as the centerpiece of a nicely laid-out backyard, but also as a means of feeding a family. They need plenty of sun and dry soil in order to produce abundant fruit.

Always consider tree maintenance before planting. If space is limited, an espalier tree may be a good choice. Placing any type of tree in a protected location helps reduce the chance of damage from frost.

CONSIDERATIONS BEFORE AND DURING PLANTING

When choosing a fruit tree, look for a straight trunk, strong, well-distributed side branches, and strong roots. Fruit trees prefer permeable soil; the roots can't survive heavy, damp soils.

▶ During transport and up to the time of planting, **keep the roots moist.** It's a good idea to wrap the root ball in a sheet of plastic.

▶ Water **bare-root plants** about fours hours before planting. Then remove any rotten or damaged root parts. **Cut the roots** a little bit so they draw water better after planting.

▶ When planting in **rocky ground**, dig a larger hole and give the seedling an ample amount of good earth and compost.

▶ Give a tree the right support and a good foothold; drive a **stake** into the soil on the **west** side of the tree. It should reach into the crown. Pantyhose are great for tying the tree up; they stretch easily and are soft enough that they won't harm the tree.

▶ Wrap the trunks of young trees with **straw, reeds,** or **jute strips** to prevent drying out and cracking due to sun or frost.

FRUIT TREE MAINTENANCE

▶ Even resistant fruit tree varieties must continually be checked for **pests.** For the first couple of years, keep the ground around a young tree free from plants right out to the drip line of the crown. That way its roots won't have to compete for nutrients.

▶ Keep about a 6 in. (16 cm) **weed-free ring** around the trunk of all fruit trees in order to prevent **crown rot.** In the winter, cover the trunk on the southern and south-western sides with **boards** or **gunny sacks** to protect it. A thick covering of **horse manure** around the trunk helps keep the roots warm and prevents them from drying out.

Fruit trees should be held as straight as possible when being transplanted to help ensure even spacing.

Pomes (pears, apples, and quince) and stone fruits can be raised using an espalier system.

fruit in a limited space. In addition to one- and two-armed trees growing flat against a wall, the U-shape is a very traditional espalier configuration.

▶ Espalier trees are very high-maintenance; in the summer they must be **continually trimmed** and tied up.

▶ Brace **wood** or **metal** espaliers about 8–12 in. (20–30 cm) away from the house wall so that the branches open and no heat can build up.

▶ An espalier tree should have **paired side branches** off the main shoot. It's easier to shape a tree when the branches are bent early.

▶ Shorten the shoots that develop from **side buds** some time in late spring, and bend the main shoots in the desired direction 4–8 in. (10–20 cm) before the tips.

▶ **Cut** repeatedly and **prune** continually until you achieve the right growth direction.

Use clean tools to prune fruit trees to avoid spreading diseases and pests.

Tree Paint

5½ lbs. (2.5 kg) fresh horsetail
10 quarts/liters water

Steep the chopped herbs in water for 24 hours, then boil for about one hour and let cool. Brush down the trunk and branches with this broth, then stir clay into the rest of the broth to produce a thin mush. Let stand for two hours and apply with a coarse brush.

▶ On sunny, frost-free days in late fall and midwinter, apply a coat of **tree paint** made from **horsetail broth** to prevent frost cracks. Repeat the process in spring to keep animals from gnawing the tree. The only caveat: the trunk and branches should be **dry** before you paint.

▶ Break off the **blossoms** in the first year to encourage shoots to grow.

▶ **Prune** fruit trees on sunny, frost-free days, starting when temperatures rise above about 23°F (-5° C). Your growing zone will determine exactly when you should begin.

▶ **Cut off diseased and damaged parts**, as well as all branches that are growing toward the inside or straight up.

ESPALIER TREES

Espalier is the art of training trees to branch in formal patterns, usually along a wall or on a trellis. It's a technique that first became popular several hundred years ago in Europe's medieval gardens. Espalier trees make it possible to raise and harvest

Furniture

A well-designed and well-furnished backyard can be a pleasant warm-weather extension of your house. It's important to bear in mind the garden's layout and climate when choosing your outdoor furniture—after all, it has to fit the available space and be able to withstand your region's harshest weather.

Unlike stone furniture, outdoor furniture made from wood is rarely weather-resistant. But wood furniture, if properly treated and cared for, can enjoy a relatively long life, even in areas with extreme weather.

Thoroughly waterproofing wood furnishings will protect them from moisture, but you'll still have to store the furniture during the winter until warmer days return.

cleaning wicker furniture

one If possible, place the wicker items in the bathtub. Larger items may have to be cleaned outdoors.

two Rinse furniture thoroughly with the showerhead or garden hose, then scrub it with a brush, soap, and washing soda. Allow to dry thoroughly, but not in the sun.

three Treat stains with a soft cloth moistened with peppermint oil.

Varnish or seal wooden outdoor furniture regularly with an environmentally friendly product.

WOOD AND STONE

▶ Don't store wooden furniture in a **heated** space or in **direct sunlight**. The wood may become brittle and split, and stained wood will begin to fade, eventually losing its color.

▶ Choose woods that contain **lots of oil**, such as acacia, larch, honey locust, and teak, because they can help keep moisture and rot at bay. To keep them from turning gray too quickly, rub in some oil every spring.

▶ Give a new stone bench the **patina of old stone** by painting it with water and plain yogurt in a 10:1 ratio.

WICKER, PLASTIC, OR METAL?

▶ Don't have a lot of space? Choose light, stackable items made from **wicker, plastic,** or **metal. Wrought iron** looks great, but it's bulky and heavy.

▶ Add a romantic feel to your garden with wicker furnishings made from **bamboo, cane,** or **rattan.** Since they're sensitive to moisture, don't leave them outdoors during the winter; they'll eventually decay and get moldy.

▶ Choose high-quality **plastic furnishings** that can withstand temperature fluctuations, rain, and sun. They are easy to care for. The caveat: they need protection from frost, which causes small cracks where dirt can collect. Put plastic furnishing in storage in late fall.

▶ Leave **aluminum** and **steel furniture** outdoors all winter, if you want—both can withstand all kinds of weather conditions.

▶ Select good-quality **wrought iron furnishings**. They are coated with clear or colored sealer, so in theory they are weatherproof. But before the onset of winter, you should still check the sealer for small cracks where rust can get a foothold. If you find them, either store the furniture away from moisture or restore the finish.

Garden Birds

It's hard to imagine a garden without the morning and evening serenade of birds. These enchanting singers keep garden pests in check, and some spend the whole year in your garden. In the summertime they are joined by migratory birds, who will nest and raise their families.

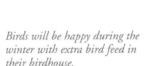

Birds will be happy during the winter with extra bird feed in their birdhouse.

Many birds, like this cardinal, nest in the same place for years.

If you offer birds favorable conditions—a place to sleep, nest, and feel protected—you will soon enjoy many different sights and sounds in your garden.

FAVORABLE CONDITIONS

▶ Plant as many **shrubs** and **hedges** as possible; they offer our useful fine-feathered friends a place to nest, as well as providing materials for nest building, secure places to sleep, and, above all, shelter from wind and weather.

▶ Plant **climbing plants**, too. Climbers are an ideal habitat for birds, especially when grown along masonry, walls, or fences.

▶ Know that flycatchers, redstarts, and wrens love small **hollows** in old trees.

▶ Plant **berry bushes**. Blooming shrubs and trees that bear berries in the fall supply birds with sufficient nourishment before winter. They especially enjoy the fruits from blackberry, rosehips, and blackthorn, or from hedge plants such as barberry, elderberry, dogwood, and hawthorn.

▶ Plant the beautiful blooming **honeysuckle.** It offers birds an excellent place to nest. Its berries, however, are poisonous for humans. The same goes for the spindle tree.

HOSPITALITY

▶ Build a birdhouse or nesting box by using **rough pine** or **spruce boards** about 1 in. (2.5 cm) thick. Remember to leave a fairly wide exit so birds can still get out easily.

▶ Hang a **nesting box** in a sheltered and not-too-sunny place, at least 10 ft. (3 m) high to give the nesting birds security, and locate the entrance hole so that it faces southeast.

▶ Place a **bird bath** on a **stone pedestal** that cats can't climb. Keep it filled with fresh water.

▶ Put a generous layer of **wood chips** or **shavings** in the box.

▶ In the winter, turn over the top layer of the **compost heap**; birds will find plenty of insects on its underside.

Bird Feed

9 oz. (275 g) unsalted suet (or unhydrogenated coconut oil)

18 oz. (500 g) seeds, raisins, and oat flakes.

Cut the fat into little pieces and melt it in a pan. Stir in seeds, raisins, and oats until a doughy mass forms. Let cool, shape into little dumplings, and hang them up.

Gardening Tools

You don't have to spend a fortune filling your toolshed with every gardening gadget on the market, but you'll need some basic gardening equipment to keep your garden looking its best.

Avoid damage to your gardening tools by cleaning them thoroughly, then drying the metal and wood parts.

Folk wisdom contends that "you get what you pay for," and you will indeed pay a premium for high-quality gardening tools. But well-made, sturdy tools—a shovel, rake, watering can, garden hose, shears, and trowel—will last a long time, so it's worth it in the long run.

LOOKING FOR QUALITY

▶ Opt for **spades** and **digging forks** made from **stainless** or **chrome-plated steel**. They are expensive, but they're the most durable and don't rust.

▶ Choose small garden tools in **bright neon colors**—they'll be easier to find in the grass or beneath weeds. The handles themselves can also be painted.

▶ Avoid buying gardening tools from a **catalog** or **on-line**; you have to know what they feel like in your hand and don't want them to be too heavy.

▶ Where possible or appropriate, select tools that have **extendable handles** to make garden work much easier on the back.

CARE EXTENDS THE SERVICE LIFE

▶ Remove **soil, grass cuttings,** or **dirt** immediately after using a gardening tool.

▶ Clean stubborn dirt from the cutting edges of garden clippers with **rubbing alcohol**.

▶ Prevent **rust** on metal surfaces by wiping them with an **oil-moistened rag** after use.

▶ Wrap **uncomfortable handles** with a little **foam material** for extra cushioning.

▶ No room in the toolshed for a **wheelbarrow?** Stand it upright with the handles against a wall—that way it won't collect water or rust.

▶ Use a **medium wire brush** to remove encrusted grass clippings under your lawn mower.

PREPARATION FOR WINTER STORAGE

▶ Sharpen the large blades of scythes or sickles with a **whetstone** and smaller blades with a **file.** Store indoors, safe from rain or snow.

▶ Oil wooden handles and shafts with **linseed oil** to keep them smooth.

▶ Clean metal parts with **fine steel wool**. Remove a light coat of rust by sanding it with **80-grit sandpaper.**

▶ Don't keep metal tools on the **floor**; it's the kiss of death. To prevent them from becoming damp and rusting or help them escape a possible flood, place them on a raised shelf or hang from hooks screwed to the wall. Store the lawn mower on a wooden plank.

▶ Do not leave any wood or metal tools in the yard over the winter months. Bring everything **indoors** for protection against the weather.

Coat moveable metal parts regularly with lubricating oil.

Greenhouses

A greenhouse extends the growing season so you can start vegetable and fruit seeds in spring. Unless it's well-heated, bring tender plants inside for winter.

Establishing a greenhouse is an investment. Having one built will set you back a little, and if you choose to build it yourself, you must consider the time and labor involved. The savings that will result in the long run, however, will eventually pay off all initial costs, and you will always be able to enjoy the sanctuary of the greenhouse.

LIGHT AND AIR

▶ Make a greenhouse as bright and as large as possible to allow **air** to circulate.

▶ Orient the greenhouse in an **east-west** direction so that it gets adequate **light** in the winter.

▶ Know that plants have varying light requirements: **delicate, soft-leaved plants** need to be close to the glass.

▶ Tight space? Put plants with **tough leaves** under the plant racks.

▶ Keep the plants at a safe distance when using **cleaning agents** on the glass panes. Alternately, you can cover them temporarily with **sheet plastic.**

▶ In spring, paint the outside of the greenhouse with a **whitewash** to keep it from getting too hot in the summer sun, then wash it off in the fall.

▶ Ensure **good ventilation** since you cannot always open windows. It's also important to create **shady** areas or cover up on particularly hot summer days.

▶ On hot summer days, **spray** the inside of the greenhouse with **water** to keep it moist.

The greenhouse is a good place to get an early start on spring seeding.

Lobelias are ready to transplant after they sprout in plant trays.

Racks and shelves create space but, when watering, take care that no drain water drips onto the plants below.

Hedges

Thick-growing hedges are a good substitute for a garden fence, especially if you choose evergreen plants. They provide privacy, wind protection, and a habitat for birds and other useful creatures.

The first task is to dig a planting trench for your hedge that is the proper length and width. The exact dimensions will depend on the purpose of the hedge, where it will be located, and the type of foliage you've chosen. A general rule of thumb: the trench should be at least 1 ft. (30 cm) wider than the plant's root ball and of equal depth.

Lilacs bloom in spring.

Keep a row of hedges straight; map out the bed with stakes and twine.

PLANNING THE HEDGE LAYOUT

▶ Position 1–2 plants every 3 ft. (1 m) for a **less dense hedge;** for a **dense hedge,** place 2–5 plants in the same space.

▶ Stagger individual plants in a **double-row hedge** so they can spread out better.

▶ Plant **mixed hedges** with different colored leaves or needles for a very attractive effect. You might combine a few varieties of **yews** or **arborvitae** with **copper beech.**

▶ Choose **yew, basswood,** or **elm** if the hedge is to serve as a **windbreak; cherry laurel** is a particularly good choice for **noise protection.**

▶ Plant **barberry, holly, hawthorn,** or **firethorn** to preserve **privacy** and keep out intruders.

PLANTING THE HEDGE

▶ Hedge plants grow in a very narrow space, so it's essential that the soil be **loose** and enhanced with **compost.** For heavy soil, mix in some sand or clay granulate for maximum effect.

▶ Put **plastic sheeting** over the bed and slit a hole for each of the plants; the plastic will help keep the weeds down, reduce evaporation in the summer, and protect the roots from frost in the winter. You can also spread **mulch** between the plants.

▶ Distribute the plants so that the **side shoots** just touch one another. If you put them too close together, you'll restrict their growth.

▶ Avoid **hollow spaces** by jiggling the plants thoroughly so that the dirt gets between the roots.

TRIMMING THE HEDGE

Your hedge's first "haircut" should take place shortly after planting: cut back deciduous bushes by half, since they grow very quickly. Trim plants with needles to a consistent height.

▶ Once a deciduous hedge is well-established, always **prune** back the new wood in the **summer** to encourage branching. In the **winter,** on the other hand, cut back into the **old wood** to encourage the formation of new, strong shoots.

► Trim **evergreen hedges** regularly, but avoid cutting into the old wood, or the branches will often remain bald.

► **Shaped hedges** should be trimmed three times in the course of the spring and summer.

► Trim the **sides of hedges** at an **angle** (e.g., less on the bottom than the top) to make them especially bushy and thick.

► Spread a **sheet of plastic** or a **tarp** at the foot of the hedge to make it easier to pick up the trimmings.

HEDGE MAINTENANCE

Hedges are realtively easy to maintain; prepare the ground well at planting so that you won't likely need to fertilize any more.

► Fertilize **evergreen hedges** in the spring with **hoof and horn meal**; otherwise, all you have to keep the soil loose.

► Keep the hedge **watered**, especially during dry periods—both winter and summer. **Evergreen** hedges need less water than **deciduous** or **flowering** hedges.

► In late fall, remove **dead wood** and **weeds** and, if necessary, restore the **mulch** layer around your hedge.

► Cover up **bald spots** in a hedge by planting a **flowering climber**. Train the shoots over the empty spots.

To keep the top of the hedge straight, stretch a string across at the desired height.

Pure white blossoms of bridal wreath are borne on branches that arch gracefully.

good to know

A FRAGRANT HEDGE
Fragrant hedges of garland spirea, lilac, or butterfly bush awaken memories of days gone by. These hedges are low-maintenance; they don't need yearly trimming, and they attract desirable guests such as bees, butterflies, and birds.

Heirloom Fruits and Vegetables

Heirloom fruits and vegetables are a tasty choice. Choose to grow them organically, without chemical treatments and fertilizers, and you'll reap a healthy reward. It's no wonder gourmets are rediscovering these oldies but goodies.

Many heirloom vegetables work well for smaller gardens, adding visual interest with their colors and leaf shapes. They also score high at the table for their great taste.

GOODS FROM THE VEGETABLE PATCH

▶ **Amaranth** has been cultivated for 5,000 years for its leaves. It's prepared like spinach but has a milder taste. This seed plant needs a sunny location and lots of moisture, but don't overwater.

▶ **Dandelion** has tender leaves that make a tasty salad. It's best grown from root cuttings. Old leaves have a bitter taste.

▶ Winter-hardy **sugar beet** sprouts forth every spring and after every harvest, and can be harvested from May to October.

▶ **Swiss chard** has long stems that can be cooked like asparagus.

▶ **Parsnips** tangy, spicy flavor makes it the perfect base for clear broths.

▶ **Common purslane** or **pigweed** is gaining popularity because the vitamin-rich vegetable is tasty in salads, and can be easily grown in most sunny locations that are protected from the wind.

▶ **Arugula** is a delicious salad green that fetches top dollar at the supermarket. But you can grow it for pennies at home. It thrives in cool weather, becoming peppery and bitter when weather turns hot. Full heads mature in five to six weeks but you can harvest baby greens after only three weeks of growth, depending on your gardening zone.

Both Swiss chard and black salsify are tasty and chock-full of nutrients.

▶ **Rapini** is an undemanding stem vegetable that prefers moderately coarse, fairly sandy soils. Sow thickly and harvest four to six weeks after planting. Prepare the young, pleasantly bitter leaf stalks like spinach or chard.

▶ **Jerusalem artichoke** is a winter-hardy tuber that should be planted about 6 in. (15 cm) deep in the spring. Cut the stalks back to about 5 ft. (1.5 m) in the fall to allow the tubers to ripen and harvest as needed.

▶ **Kale** provides more nutritional value for fewer calories than almost any other food around. This leafy green vegetable belongs to the *Brassica* family (which includes cabbage, collards, and brussels sprouts), noted for their health-promoting phytonutrients. It's easy to grow, even in colder temperatures.

HEIRLOOM APPLES

In the early 19th century, as many as 6,650 apple varieties flourished in North America. Fast-forward to today, and only a handful of them survive in large numbers. Here are some choices:

▶ Many **old apple varieties** place no great demands on the soil and thus are comparatively hardy. These include the Alexander, Baldwin, Ben Davis, Canada Red, Grimes Golden, Golden Russet, Jonathan, Northern Spy, Roxbury Russet, Scarlet Pippin, and Winesap.

Because of its tart-sweet flavor and lovely aroma, the Jonathan apple has long been considered one of the best-tasting American heirloom apples.

Fruit designated for storage should have no bruises. An apple picker prevents the fruits from falling onto the ground.

► Good varieties for **storage** are the Arkansas Black, Albemarle or Newtown Pippin, Granny Smith, Acey Mac, Honeycrisp, Empire, Virginia Beauty, Winesap, and York Imperial.

► **Early apple varieties** include the Pristine, Lodi, Jersey Mac, Earligold, Mollie's Delicious, Zestar, Red Melba, Red Astrachan (Red Lincoln, American Red), and Gala.

► Good varieties for **espalier growing** are the Gravenstein, Winesap, Northern Spy, McIntosh, Cortland, and Yellow Delicious.

► **Varieties for making cider** include the Russet, Baldwin, Winseap, and McIntosh.

► Good apples for **baking** and making **applesauce** and **baked apples** are the Cortland, Empire, Crispin (or Mutsu), Gala, Golden Delicious, Granny Smith, Honeycrisp, Ida Red, and Jonathan.

HEIRLOOM PEARS

Pears, which can be used for fresh desserts, cooking, or canning, are presumed to have originated in the Caucasus or Anatolia. Today, there are around 5,000 pear varieties worldwide. Here's a quick rundown of some of the more common heirloom pear varieties:

► **Hardy, undemanding varieties** include the Summercrisp, Bosc, Anjou, Bartlett, Early Golden Pear, Ure Pear, and Tyson.

► Pears that **store well** include the Anjou, Packham, and Asian pears such as the Kikusui, Hosui, and Chojuro.

► **Good cooking varieties** include the Anjou, Bosc, and Concorde.

HEIRLOOM STONE FRUITS

Cherries, plums, and damson plums are considered stone fruits. Here, too, the heirloom varieties generally make few soil demands and stack up well in terms of hardiness. Here's what you need to know:

► Good plums for **preserving** are the Damson, Marabella, Green Gage, Yellow Egg, and Black Prince.

► With some plum varieties, the **stone** is easier to remove; just use a teaspoon to pry the stone from a halved plum.

► **Cherries** with particularly **split-resistant skins** include the Sandra Rose, Silvia, Lapin, and North Star.

► Good cherry varieties for **preserving** are the Montmorency and Bing.

making a basic root cellar

one Dig a hole about 16 in. (40 cm) deep—length and width depends on available space and how much produce you plan to store. Line it with a fine-mesh screen to keep the mice out, then add a layer of sand and dried leaves.

two Immediately after harvest, layer the root crops in; twist the greens off first and lay straw between layers.

three Cover the last layer of straw with a layer of dirt 4 in. (10 cm) thick.

Parsnips, like other root vegetables, can be stored for up to six months in a root cellar.

Herb Gardens

An herb garden located close to the house gives you easy access to flavor-enhancing herbs, as well as many useful medicinal ingredients. An open window is all it takes to fill your home with the refreshing scent of growing herbs.

An herb garden needs a sunny area with loose, permanent soil. Raised spiral herb gardens, built up with rocks and soil, have been used for many generations to get maximum productivity out of small spaces. Two additional bonuses: they tend to suffer from significantly fewer pests, and the garden is accessible from all sides. The basic design calls for a spiral or knot of rocks, enclosing soil in which many species of herbs are planted. The rocks warm and humidify the soil, and the design allows for a wide variety of soil conditions.

ESTABLISHED HERB BEDS

▶ Plant an herb spiral in the spring or fall on a surface of at least 32 ft.² (3 m²). **Sketch out** the spiral shape in advance.

▶ Add a **small pool** about 32 in. (80 cm) deep at the beginning of the spiral; line it with pond film and reinforce with stones.

▶ Dig out the remainder of your herb bed to the depth of a shovel and fill it with a mixture of **sand** and **humus**. Create a small mound about 3 ft. (1 m) high in the center of the bed and reinforce it in a spiral shape with **stones**.

▶ Fill the upward-spiraling bed with different types of **soils** to create the following areas:

Plants find ideal conditions in the very small space of an herb spiral, which is less likely to attract pests than an ordinary garden bed.

▶ In and around the **pond** at the base of your spiral, the loamy soil should stay **moist**; watercress, brooklime, calamus, and water mint will thrive.

▶ The next level provides a **sunny, compost-rich moist zone;** plant chervil, garlic mustard, parsley, peppermint, sorrel, chives, garlic chives, wild arugula, and lemon balm.

▶ The **normal area** will be partly shaded, with rather dry **humus soil**, creating the best conditions for basil, dill, coriander, lovage, lemon balm, oregano, marigold, and hyssop.

▶ Plant herbs from warmer climates in the **dry zone** atop the spiral. The soil is permeable and water will drain naturally to the lower levels. This is where savory, lavender, marjoram, sage, and thyme grow best.

After harvesting, place the fresh herbs loosely in a basket lined with paper so they don't get crushed.

MAINTAINING THE HERB GARDEN

▶ Give herbs only a little **water;** they don't usually require very much.

▶ Make sure that the water is able to **run off** effectively, e.g., through a drainage layer of **gravel** or **topsoil.**

▶ Regularly **hoe the ground** between herbs to keep it loose and let the water run off without soaking in.

▶ Add **garden lime** to give herbs an additional source of calcium and magnesium; varieties that thrive with its help include savory, tarragon, caraway, marjoram, mint, parsley, rosemary, chives, and thyme.

▶ Plant a **hedge** of boxwood, lavender, or hyssop to protect your herbs from wind and winter frost.

Pick leaves and flowers by hand, but cut off tougher stems with sharp scissors.

▶ Cut back **bushy herbs** like lavender and thyme in the fall to prevent frost damage.

▶ Keep herbs from **spreading out** too much by cutting them regularly.

▶ Plant **mint** and **lemon balm** in clay pots to restrict their growth. They can form strong runners that quickly take over the entire bed.

▶ Seed annual herbs in a **different location** every year. This form of herbal crop rotation will help to keep the soil from becoming too depleted.

▶ Remember that many herbs need room: **lovage** can damage adjacent plants, and **dill** shouldn't be placed next to **fennel.**

HARVESTING HERBS AND SEEDS

▶ Gather herbs and seeds in **late morning** or at **midday** for best results. The only exception: gather **roots** in the **early morning**.

▶ Collect the seeds of **dill, fennel, coriander,** and **lovage** as soon as the flowers turn brown.

▶ Dig up **garlic** before the leaves dry up; that way the bulbs keep better.

▶ Harvest most herbs before they **bloom,** otherwise their flavor fades or (in the case of **sage**) disappears entirely. Only **lavender, thyme,** and **oregano** are harvested at flowering time.

▶ Pick **lemon balm** in the afternoon; that's when the leaves develop their greatest intensity, before or just after the flowers open.

Many herbs, such as parsley, tarragon, and chives, can spend the winter on the kitchen windowsill and provide fresh seasoning.

Kitchen Gardens

A kitchen garden is part of a long-standing tradition. Part of its charm is that it tends to combine the beauty of flowers with useful plants like herbs and vegetables, which you can pick fresh and enjoy while they're still bursting with flavor.

We can thank medieval monks for developing gardening culture. As they became aware of the benefits of mixed plantings for protecting gardens from pests, these monks increasingly grew medicinal plants and flowers along with their vegetables and fruits. As early as the 16th century, the rural population of Europe used these cloister gardens as a model for their own gardens.

THE STRUCTURE OF A KITCHEN GARDEN

▶ Ready to switch from a simple veggie patch to a full-on kitchen garden? Lay your kitchen garden on **flat ground** so that it is sheltered from the wind, but receives plenty of sun. If possible, the minimum size of a kitchen garden should be about 270 ft.² (25 m²).

▶ Choose your plantings carefully. Take into consideration the **height** and **width** of growth—will one fruit block the sun from another? Are some vegetables better suited to grow beside a particular pairing? (*See Companion Planting on page 292*). Make selections that will **ripen at different times** during the summer and fall; this will guarantee a continuous supply and variety of fresh produce.

▶ Make a **sketch** before you break soil. The sketch should show the locations of the beds, pathways, possible sitting areas, and desired plantings; this will make seeding and harvesting much easier.

▶ For a traditional kitchen garden, use a **four-square design**, based on the intersection of two major paths within a symmetrical, enclosed area. When laying out the pathways, take into account the width of the plants that will grow along its edges.

▶ Use **intersecting pathways** in your plan so you can easily reach garden beds to plant, care for, and harvest your fruits, veggies, and flowers.

▶ Delineate pathways with ease by lining them with **box hedges** that grow no taller than 20 in. (50 cm).

Trellis plants thrive against a south-facing wall, and wide paths make it easy to get from patch to patch.

Variety is key to any successful kitchen garden. Here, high and low perennials—either tone-on-tone or multicolored—thrive together.

▶ Save space in a smaller kitchen garden by edging individual beds with **marigolds, other perennials,** and even **chives.**

▶ Start laying out the kitchen garden in the **fall** by planting the **trees and shrubs,** keeping in mind their eventual height and the shade they'll create.

CENTER AND EDGING

▶ If you've got a fair bit of room, consider planting a **circular flower bed** in the center of your garden, potentially with a **fountain** or **standard rosebush** as a focal point.

▶ Place a **wooden** or **cement basin** in the center for collecting **rainwater**—you can easily disguise a less-attractive installation with climbing plants.

▶ Install a **small gazebo** or **bench** under an arch covered with climbing plants in the center of the garden.

▶ For larger properties, enclose your kitchen garden with a **hedge** or a **fence**. With fairly large gardens, plant **shrubs, hedges,** or **hawthorn**. The dark green brings a peaceful vibe into the multi-colored installation and keeps your kitchen garden from becoming too busy.

▶ Incorporate **trellis plants** or **hydrangeas** if the kitchen garden abuts a wall of the house.

PLANTS FOR A KITCHEN GARDEN

In a kitchen garden, plants are generally laid out close to one another in mixed plantings. The benefits: soil doesn't get depleted, vermin and diseases don't spread, you don't have to fertilize too much, and you get a large yield with very little effort. It's fairly easy to select your plants as well. Here are a few examples:

▶ Include **heirloom vegetable plants** such as parsnips, runner beans, and tomato varieties.

▶ Plant **medicinal** and **seasoning herbs** such as valerian, savory, dill, oregano, chamomile, garlic, basil, and peppermint between the veggies.

▶ Plant **heirloom aromatic plants.** Sweet pea, phlox, sage, and centifolia roses attract butterflies and bees, which are important for pollination.

▶ Ensure you always have a variety of plants by including **self-propagating perennials** such as columbine, fennel, foxglove, bellflower, and lupine.

▶ Plant **marigold**. It blooms abundantly from June to first frost. The flowers can be eaten or used as a **medicinal herb** to prevent infections. In addition, they help ward off aphids.

▶ Place tall perennials such as **delphinium** and **hollyhock** against a fence or hedge where their long stalks can get support.

A kitchen garden becomes beautiful, as well as functional, with the help of perennials such as bellflower, daisy, yarrow, and phlox.

315

Lawns

Whether it consists of decorative grass, a play area, or ground cover, the green surface of your yard needs to be laid out and maintained properly. For routine care, you'll need a lawnmower, rake, digging fork, hose, and lawn sprinkler.

Before seeding a new lawn, there are a few important considerations, including your yard's soil quality and what type of seed would grow best.

PLANNING A NEW LAWN

▶ Check the **soil quality.** Is it heavy, light, rocky, acidic, or alkaline? You'll need to know in order to prepare it properly.

▶ Choose your **sod** or **grass seed** according to how you plan to use your lawn. If children or animals are going to romp around on it, opt for a heavy-duty type.

PREPARING THE SOIL AND GETTING THE SEED

▶ Remove all **roots, rocks,** and any **construction waste,** and thoroughly dig up the ground about two weeks before sowing your lawn.

▶ If the soil is very heavy, mix in some **sand** for better ventilation and permeability. Enhance humus-poor soil with **peat, bark chips**, or **compost** until it turns dark in color.

▶ At the same time, level out uneven areas and, on fairly large surfaces, **pack it down** with a **lawn roller.** Then leave the dirt to settle.

▶ Sow in **spring** while the ground is damp (but not frozen) for best results.

▶ Spread the seeds evenly by first practicing with **sand**, or make a **spreader** by drilling small holes in the bottom of an old tin can.

▶ Choose a day with as little wind as possible. Spread half the seeds in **one direction** and the other half in the **opposite direction.**

▶ Sow by **sections** and, on larger surfaces, mark off individual sections with **string**. Sow more heavily at the edge so the lawn comes in thicker.

▶ **Rake the seeds** into the soil just a tiny bit so they don't blow away and can sprout properly. Pack down the seeds with the lawn roller or opt for a low-tech solution: footboards tied to the bottom of your shoes.

▶ Finally, sprinkle **water** on the seeds, but avoid washing them away. Don't apply **mineral fertilizer** during the first two weeks, since seeds and fertilizers are incompatible with one another.

Curved transitions between flower beds and the lawn provide variety and harmony in a decorative garden.

MOWING AND WATERING THE LAWN

How often your lawn requires mowing depends on the thickness of the turf. The cut grass should be no shorter than about ¾ in. (2 cm); shorter lawns burn easily in the summer.

▶ Mow a **new lawn** for the first time when the blades of grass are around 3 in. (7–9 cm) tall.

▶ Shorten the lawn by no more than about 2 in. (5 cm) per mowing. In the first mowing of the spring, remove only the **tips** of the grass.

▶ Leave the **cuttings** where they fall to provide nutrients to the soil and shade the lawn's roots.

▶ Water thoroughly **once a week** during summer dry spells. The soil should be moist down to about 6 in. (15 cm) so the grass can form deep roots.

▶ Minimize **evaporation** by watering in early morning or after 6:00 PM.

LAWN CARE

You can whip old lawns back into shape by de-thatching or aerating.

▶ **Dethatching** involves using a rake to pull the thick mat of dead grass and roots that accumulate under the living green blades of your lawn. Normally, you should dethatch the lawn in spring or early autumn, every one or two years.

▶ **Aeration** helps combat waterlogging. Poke holes about 3 in. (7–9 cm) deep with a digging fork and fill them with sand.

▶ Spread **fine sand** over the surface of the lawn to deal with minor waterlogging. Worms will bury it when it rains.

The more precise the delineation between lawn and flower bed, the easier it is to mow along the edge. But edge trimmers can help when the dividing line isn't clear.

▶ Use **nitrogen fertilizers** in the spring; in the fall, opt for a fertilizer that contains more **phosphate** to stimulate root formation. Apply fertilizers high in nitrogen only in wet weather.

▶ Keep off the grass in **frosty weather**, or the blades of grass could break and leave unappealing tracks.

▶ If a piece at the edge of the lawn is damaged, **cut it out** vertically and put it into the resulting hole upside down. Then even out the spot with a little dirt, sprinkle some seeds onto it, and carefully water the area.

patching bald spots on the lawn

one Dig up the area with a shovel and loosen the soil with a rake.

two Remove all weed roots and smooth out the surface.

three Add a mixture of sand and compost to the area and sow the grass seed. Compress and water.

Water can soak in more effectively through aeration holes poked into the lawn with a digging fork.

Organic Pest Control

Tired of reaching for noxious chemicals every time you see an aphid? Live in a region where chemical plant treatments are banned? Take heart, because there are gentle ways to deal with pests.

You can fight little nuisances—aphids, flea beetles, winter moths, potato beetles, cabbage white caterpillars, slugs, snails, spider mites, voles, and ants—with plant-based sprays, or use other plants to repel the unwanted invaders with their scent or excretions from their roots.

ANTS

▶ Sprinkle **ant trails** that lead toward the house or deck with the leaves of fragrant herbs such as **chervil, lavender, mint, thyme,** and **juniper**, or with spices such as **chili pepper** or **salt**. The pungency of the herbs not only repels the ants, it disrupts the scent trail that the scouts leave behind for other ants to follow.

▶ Plant **ferns, lamb's lettuce,** or **tansy** and ants will also make a major detour around your garden.

APHIDS

▶ Plant **anise** or **cilantro** between individual trunks to protect trees; for roses, you can plant **garlic, lavender,** or **French marigold**. Aphids particularly dislike **nasturtium**.

▶ If plants are already infested, spray them in the morning with a strong jet of **water** or a **mild detergent solution**. A spray made from **tansy** or **stinging nettle tea** will also help.

FLEA BEETLES

▶ Flea beetles like to take up residence in **planters**. But if you stick a few **matches** (the wooden variety is best) headfirst into the soil, they disappear—the sulfur dissolved by watering drives them away without harming the plant.

▶ Tuck one or two cloves of **garlic** in potting soil to get the same effect.

▶ Sprinkle **wood ashes** or **sawdust** in your pot or flower box in dry weather.

▶ Plant **peppermint, lettuce, wormwood,** and **onions** to make flea beetles avoid your garden.

WINTER MOTHS

The first winter moths arrived in North America from Europe in the 1930s, and the pest has been spreading rapidly ever since. The larvae of winter moths damage the leaves of woody plants and may even cause complete defoliation.

▶ Apply **insect glue bands** to tree trunks in early fall and leave them in place until late winter; females crawl rather than fly, so this is an effective control at egg-laying time.

▶ Use **birdhouses** and **birdbaths** to make sure that songbirds feel at home in your garden. They will eat the moths.

▶ Spray plants with **tansy tea** as leaves are falling.

POTATO BEETLES

This pest of Mexican origin eats the leaves of potato plants and other nightshades.

▶ Remove the **eggs** and gather up the **larvae** and **bugs** if the infestation isn't too severe.

▶ Then sprinkle the plant with **rock powder** (or **diatomaceous earth**) to kill the larvae.

▶ As a preventive measure, plant **caraway** between nightshade plants to repel potato beetles.

Be on the lookout for slugs after repeated rainfalls. Infestations increase in inclement weather.

Aphids are eaten by lady-bugs and pest larvae are eaten by hover flies, while spiders eliminate a variety of garden pests.

CABBAGE WHITE BUTTERFLIES

The larvae of the cabbage white butterfly are harmful to all types of cabbage and other plants in the mustard family, including horseradish, kale, and broccoli.

▶ Collect the **caterpillars** and kill them if the infestation is not too severe; the worst time for these pests is from May to September.

▶ Plant **mixed crops** including mugwort, peppermint, sage, celery, thyme, and tomatoes as a preventive measure, or protect vegetables with **netting**.

SLUGS AND SNAILS

In mild weather or damp heat, slugs and snails are a threat to all young plants and soft-leaved plants. They are best dealt with as soon as possible.

▶ **Handpick** them morning and evening and destroy them—if there aren't too many.

▶ Protect your plants with **companion plantings** of savory, chamomile, nasturtium, parsley, sage, and mustard.

▶ Pile **straw** around garden beds. This can be effective against slugs—they don't like to crawl over sharp edges.

▶ Use **rock powder** or **diatomaceous earth** for a similar effect; its sharp edges cut slugs on their soft underbellies, killing them. You'll have to reapply it after every rainfall.

▶ Spread **oak leaves** around your garden. They contain tannins that slugs and snails don't like.

SPIDER MITES

Fine gossamer on the underside of the leaves indicates an infestation of tiny-but-mighty red spider mites. They prefer to munch on the leaves of cucumbers and bean plants, as well as houseplants.

▶ Spray with **stinging nettle slurry** to help rid your plants of this pest.

▶ Use **beneficial predator mites,** available in well-stocked gardening centers. They'll search your plants for pest mites and kill them, then move on to spider mites elsewhere.

VOLES

▶ Woody plants, roses, perennials, onions, bulb plants, and root vegetables are susceptible to voles. Pour strong-smelling **slurries** made from **elder** or **walnut leaves, arborvitae branches,** or **fish heads** into their passageways.

▶ Keep voles away with **defensive plants** like mole plant, white sweet clover, garlic, narcissus, and crown imperial.

▶ **Get a cat**. Its mere presence may be more than enough to deter the pests.

The emissions from the roots and leaves of nasturtiums keep aphids away from ornamental and vegetable plants.

Ornamental Shrubs and Trees

Ornamental shrubs and trees are undemanding plants that add beauty and fragrance to your yard. They can provide a visual framework for the garden or draw the eye to significant spots when grown singly on the lawn. Their foliage, blossoms, and berries provide colorful accents to any home.

Take your yard's light and soil conditions into account when you're planning where to put trees and shrubs. After all, you don't want to be transplanting trees and shrubs year after year.

CHOICE AND LOCATION

▶ Ornamental shrubs and trees which offer a visual treat in all four seasons of the year are perfect for smaller gardens that lack space for a larger selection of plants. The **goldenrain tree** displays yellow blossoms in the summer, and yellow leaves and unique seedpods that look like little Chinese lanterns in fall. The **Amur maple** sprouts red shoots, has yellowish-white blooming stalks, reddish fruit, and red foliage in the fall.

▶ Plants that thrive in the **shade** are red-flowering currant, beech, yew, beautybush, dogwood, Oregon grape, daphne, wild black cherry, and witch hazel.

▶ For **damp locations,** select alder buckthorn, Japanese maple, purple willow, red osier dogwood, black alder, white willow, or hawthorn.

▶ Never plant birches, alders, willows, or flowering cherries next to **flower beds** or **vegetable plots,** since these are shallow-rooted plants that make it difficult to cultivate the soil.

▶ Shrubs and trees draw **water** and **nutrients** from the soil, so make sure neighboring plants can tolerate their proximity.

COLORFUL SHRUBS AND TREES FOR FALL AND WINTER

▶ Find pretty, red **berries,** even during the cold season, on the barberry bush, mountain ash, yew, staghorn sumac, cranberry bush, or hawthorn.

▶ Rich blue fruits adorn the **mahonia,** purplish-pink-colored fruits the **beautyberry.**

▶ The green and white striped bark of the **snakebark maple** is

Every spring, old magnolia trees like this splendid specimen bring delight with their lush, fragrant pink and white blossoms.

appealing in winter. The **winged spindle tree** has attractive green bark, and the **Chinese red birch** boasts orange-red bark.

PLANTING SHRUBS AND TREES

Spring and fall are the best times to plant shrubs and trees as they are either still in a state of rest or already preparing for winter after shedding their leaves.

▸ Loosen up **matted root balls** with a fork before pulling the roots apart.

▸ **Clip** the **roots and shoots** to promote the growth of new and healthy plant parts. To prune a tree, lay it across a pair of sawhorses.

▸ Erect the **supporting stake** into the planting hole before inserting the tree to avoid damaging the roots. It will also be much easier to handle and insert the supporting stake without the tree or shrub in the way.

▸ Use **pantyhose** to tie the tree to the stake. They're cheaper than store-bought ropes and cords for tying trees and, because of their softness and elasticity, they provide more protection, especially to younger trees.

PRUNING AND CULTIVATING SHRUBS AND TREES

Although they don't need too much care, ornamental trees and shrubs do need pruning to supply them with light and air.

Use figure-eight knots to tie a rope around a tree and its supporting stake.

▸ Prune in **early spring,** shortly before plants sprout. Don't prune during a severe frost, and avoid pruning the plants that bloom in **spring** and **summer** right after they've finish blossoming.

▸ Thoroughly thin out **flowering shrubs** that have become scrubby and have stopped producing blooming branches.

▸ Prune the bent branches of **barberry** and **forsythia** right behind the bend.

▸ **Do not regularly prune** evergreen shrubs and conifers, golden chain, dogwood, magnolia, or witch hazel; in fact, it can do them harm.

▸ Put layers of **mulch** around the base of shrubs and trees to keep the soil from drying out during the heat of summer and, at the same time, provide protection against **weeds.**

▸ Protect the trunks of young trees from damage with a slit **plastic bottle** or **chicken wire.**

▸ Try adding **hardwood ash** to the soil for a shrub that fails to bloom; there may not be enough **potash** in the soil.

The hole for planting ornamental shrubs and trees should be at least twice as big as the root ball of the plant.

Plant Propagation

Choose a method for propagating a plant based on the type of plant. Propagation has to take place at the right time, and the seeds or cuttings have to be planted in properly prepared soil.

You can sow seeds for lawn grass or sturdier plants outdoors in the springtime. Sensitive plants will likely need to be sown indoors or in a greenhouse.

Cuttings are shoots or parts of a shoot that have been cut off from the parent plant. You can place them in either water or soil to grow roots. A mixture of potting soil and coarse sand is ideal for cuttings.

sowing in a pot

one Place several seeds in a pot filled with potting soil. Insert a plastic stick that identifies the plant.

two Put a plastic bag over the pot. It will keep the soil moist and protect it against any draft.

PROPAGATION BY SEED

▶ Collect **mature seeds** during sunny weather and leave them to dry on paper towels where there is plenty of air—try to avoid direct sunlight.

▶ Store seeds in a cool, dry, and dark place. Use **labeled paper bags, envelopes,** or **plastic boxes** for storage.

▶ Test the **capacity of seeds** to **germinate**. Place several in a glass of water. Those capable of germinating will sink to the bottom.

▶ Sow seeds that germinate in the **dark,** such as beans, about 1 in. (2 cm) deep. Those that germinate in the **light** (such as basil and lobelia) should be strewn on fertilized soil, then lightly pressed down in firm contact with the earth. You can lightly sprinkle soil on top of them using a sieve.

AIDS FOR SOWING

▶ Make holes in the soil for sowing seeds with an old **pencil** or a **screwdriver**.

▶ Sow bigger seeds outdoors by putting them into a **plastic bottle**. Then drill a hole in the **cap**, screw it on, and insert a **drinking straw** in the hole for air. The seeds will come out one at a time.

▶ When sowing small seeds outdoors, keep them from falling too close together by mixing them with **sand** or by sprinkling them onto the garden bed with a **sieve**.

▶ Use an empty plastic **yogurt** or **margarine tub** as an economical alternative to commercial seed containers. Just wash thoroughly and punch drainage holes in them.

CARING FOR SEEDLINGS

▶ Keep seeds or young seedlings from being washed out of the soil by hydrating them with a **mister** or **spray bottle** instead of watering directly.

▶ Outdoors, protect seeds from being washed away by covering them with **burlap bags**. The sacks let light pass through, but soften the impact when the seeds are watered or pelted by rain.

▶ Ensure your seedlings get the light they need by placing the seeded pots on **aluminum foil** that reflects and intensifies the natural light.

▶ Transfer **small plants** outdoors in the evening or on overcast days. Once they're in the ground, water them carefully.

Once small perennials have been divided, plant them in clay pots so that they form stronger roots before being planted.

Make two or more divisions in the root ball with a sharp knife or spade to propagate a perennial.

DIVIDING PERENNIALS

▶ Divide all perennials, as long as they have **no taproots** and more than one **shoot.**

▶ Each divided portion should have enough **roots** and two or three vigorous **shoots.**

▶ Ornamental perennials, such as **irises** or **black-eyed Susans**, reach their peak after five to seven years, after which point they should be divided.

LAYERING PLANTS

▶ Bend down the shoots to the soil to form roots. Once they've rooted, they are **clipped** from the parent plant.

▶ Choose a one-year-old, flexible **shoot** that sits relatively close to the base of the parent plant.

▶ Layer many types of **berry bushes** and **climbing plants.**

▶ Put **plastic bottles** over young plants to protect them from snails, frost, or dehydration. Use a transparent **plastic sheet** to cover a larger number of plants lying next to each other.

CUTTINGS

▶ Prevent cuttings from drying out too quickly by placing them in a **plastic bag.**

▶ Ensure that **softwood cuttings** grow roots in a glass of water by holding them up with chicken wire or aluminum foil with holes poked in it and placed over the top of the glass. This will keep the cuttings from slipping too deep into the water.

▶ Promote the root growth of hardwood cuttings by adding some **rock flour** or a 5% solution of **brown algae** to the potting soil.

▶ Make a small incision at the bottom of **hardwood cuttings** and stick a **grain of rye** or **wheat** in the notch. The nutrients produced by the grain will also encourage the root growth of the cuttings.

Using sharp garden shears, clip softwood cuttings from fuschias and place them in water to grow roots.

Pot and Container Gardening

Some flowerpot plants can beautify a balcony, patio, or deck with colorful blooms for the whole year. But if you live in a region with a cold winter, most plants need to be taken indoors.

Plants will grow in anything that will hold dirt. Many flowers can even feel right at home in baskets, boxes, or half a small wine cask. You may need to make a few preparations in order to keep your plants happy.

To improve drainage in a planter, add some stones or clay shards in the bottom.

THE SELECTION

▶ Choose containers made from **fired clay**; they're permeable to water and air.

▶ Prevent the similar but much flimsier **plastic pots** from falling over in a strong wind by dropping a few **heavy rocks** in the bottom before adding potting soil.

▶ Use plastic pots to line metal and wood containers and prevent **rust** or **rot**. Alternatively, line the containers with plastic or aluminum foil.

PREPARING THE CONTAINERS

▶ Thoroughly **clean all containers**, including new ones, and completely rinse off any residue.

▶ Scrub off the unattractive **white lime deposits** on the outside of clay pots with vinegar and water, and feed plants with water that has aerated for 24 hours to prevent the deposits from returning.

▶ Use a hammer to carefully knock a **drain hole** in the bottom-center of a clay pot that doesn't already have drainage holes, or drill several small holes in the bottom.

▶ Keep dirt and nutrients from being washed away while watering by covering small drainage holes with a **seashell** or **bottle cap**. Try placing a coffee filter over larger drainage holes; it allows the water out, but keeps the dirt in.

▶ In large tubs, prevent **waterlogging** of the roots by filling the pot to about a quarter full with **coarse gravel** before adding the potting soil.

▶ Avoid **inexpensive potting soil**. It clumps together during watering and dries out quickly on hot days. The result: it becomes rock-hard, making it difficult for water to reach the roots, and your plant withers.

▶ Ensure that the area where planters are kept has good **water runoff**; if necessary, place the containers on large stones or logs.

▶ **Lift pots up** to protect the roots on **cold nights**, when the chill from the ground could do some serious damage.

Use a dolly to protect your back and move heavy potted plants more safely.

To keep tall plants such as this rose of Sharon from tipping over from the weight of the blooms or from a strong wind, support them with a wooden pole.

CARE AND WINTER PROTECTION

▸ Stick your finger a ½ in. (1 cm) into the soil to see whether a plant needs water. If the soil feels **dry**, water the plant.

▸ Loosen up crusty **topsoil** regularly to allow water to penetrate better.

▸ Use a little more **plant fertilizer** during the growing season on potted plants, as the soil contains fewer nutrients.

▸ Pour water used for cooking **vegetables** and **eggs,** and any **tea** remnants on your potted plants; they contain plenty of minerals which are good for your blooming beauties.

▸ Depending on the zone in which you live, plants that are not winter-hardy should be in their winter quarters before the **first night of frost**.

▸ Make sure that your plants' **winter quarters** are bright and cool; the optimal temperature is between 41–46°F (5–8°C).

▸ Wrap the containers of even winter-hardy potted plants in **burlap**, and place **fir-tree branches** around them, because they still need protection from frost. Tie up everything above the top edge of the pot.

▸ If you do water potted plants in the winter, make sure that it is on **frost-free days** because any cold winter winds will quickly dry out their roots.

good to know

THE FLEA MARKET: A PLACE OF DISCOVERY
You can find all kinds of things at flea markets that can be used as flowerpots: various colorful ceramics from other countries, tubs or pans, metal buckets, or an old basin. Flowers can even feel at home in discarded cooking pots.

PRACTICALLY EVERYTHING THRIVES IN A CONTAINER

In addition to boxwood and small conifers, weeping pussy willow, winter jasmine, and slow-growing ornamental bushes thrive all year long in plant containers.

▸ Provide a pop of color among winter-hardy evergreens with a frost-resistant **Christmas rose** or any other early-spring bloomer.

▸ **Climbing plants** such as passionflower, clematis, or a potted rose can live comfortably on a balcony or a deck and cover up unattractive concrete walls.

▸ Bothered by lots of **snails**? Grow dahlias, verbena, hydrangea, or marigold in tubs so that snails can't get to them.

▸ If your garden soil isn't hospitable for rhododendrons, azaleas, or other **acid-loving plants**, put them into the appropriate soil in tubs and place them in the flower beds.

▸ Choose boxwood, impatiens, fuchsia, heather, hydrangeas, lobelia, laurel, or palm ferns for **shady** or **partially shady** areas.

Flowerpots come in many sizes and shapes, but there should always be a little room around the root ball for soil.

Privacy

Your yard should be a refuge in which you can unwind. But in order to maintain such a private space, you'll need visual cover, whether it's a fence made of wood or an artfully placed planting. Visual cover can add beauty and practicality to your yard.

Apart from sheltering you from prying eyes, cover can be used to hide unattractive garbage cans or compost piles. Fences come in a variety of materials, styles, and colors. Planting hedges is a more permanent cover option, and using potted plants as visual cover allows you to maintain maximum flexibility in your space. By replacing plants and moving pots around, you can continually come up with new combinations and surprising accents.

FENCES

▶ Natural materials such as w**ood, willow,** or **bamboo** are fine for nearly every yard. Attach bamboo matting or visual screens made from woven willow to a newly-erected fence for added privacy.

▶ Green up an existing or a new wood fence with **climbing plants** and **hanging baskets.**

TALL POTTED PLANTS

Many plants grow well in planters, though they may not get as tall as in the garden.

▶ Opt for **hydrangea, cornelian cherry,** and **weigela**. They produce abundant flowers and have thick foliage.

▶ Plant **boxwood** or **arborvitae** in buckets for an evergreen visual cover.

▶ **Elevate** the plants by putting them onto a flat stone, a block of wood, or an old, low bench.

Fast-growing bamboo, even in tubs, helps create visual cover on a deck.

PLANTED TRELLISES

When planning visual cover in the form of a trellis, take into account the prevailing wind direction and angle of the sun; they will play a role in determining whether the climbing plants will thrive. Excessively tall trellises sometimes cast unwelcome shadows.

Trellises adorned with passion flower, runner beans, and firecracker vine provide warmth and privacy.

▶ Wooden trellises or pergolas should be made from **weatherproof, pressure-treated wood** so that you don't have to use toxic wood preservatives to maintain them.

▶ Annual **runner beans** grow especially quickly on trellises; in just a few weeks they produce a green wall with attractive red flowers. In the fall, you can eat the beans.

▶ Trellises provide perfect visual cover—even in the winter—with evergreen climbing plants such as **ivy** and some varieties of **honeysuckle**.

▶ Make a trellis out of **bamboo poles** for annual climbing plants that are not too heavy. Place the poles on top of one another in a grid pattern and tie them together at each intersection with garden wire, then attach your trellis to the wall.

▶ A trellis thick with **climbing roses** produces abundant blooms and, depending on the variety of rose, a wonderfully fragrant privacy screen.

▶ **Cut back** trellis plants regularly so they retain their shape and don't become too heavy—maybe even breaking the trellis with their weight.

▶ Fragrant plants, including **honeysuckle** and **jasmine,** can do double duty. When trained on a trellis around the compost pile or in front of a trash can, they can cover up the view and simultaneously mask the smell.

HEDGES

Hedges act as living fence to define a yard or plot of land and, depending on the plants chosen, can also provide visual cover.

▶ Plant a **flowering hedge** around a bench in the yard. Mix ornamental shrubs that bloom at different times, such as lilac, forsythia, rose of Sharon, seabuckthorn, and butterfly bush.

▶ Choose nearly impenetrable **shrubs** such as barberry, scarlet firethorn, blackthorn, holly, hawthorn, and wild roses for even more privacy. They all have **spines** or **thorns**.

▶ Provide **evergreen** visual cover with barberry, mountain pine, boxwood, yew, cherry laurel, privet, rhododendron, spreading cotoneaster, Hinoki false cypress, and arborvitae.

▶ Choose **fast-growing hedge plants** like hedge maple, cherry laurel, and privet. **Conifers** like Leyland cypress and Hinoki false cypress are also good choices.

▶ Use **tall bushes** or **sunflowers** for quick-growing visual cover. **Ferns** and **tall ornamental grass** varieties, such as giant Chinese silver grass, also achieve vertical height quickly.

▶ Consider **hardy evergreen bamboos** for a great privacy hedge; their dark emerald canes hold their color even in the darkest winter. They grow quickly and tall, and some varieties have especially thick foliage for providing visual cover. Use a combination of different-colored leaves or stems to provide visual interest.

▶ **Leaf hedges** consisting of **European hornbeam** or **copper beech** are an excellent choice. They don't lose all their leaves in the winter and they provide shelter for hedgehogs and other useful creatures. Birds are often drawn to **privet** and **barberry**.

Roses

The rose existed long before humankind. Today this queen of flowers, with its countless colors and shapes, evokes passion and romance more than any other blossom. One of the most fragrant flowers known, the rose has a place in any garden, trellis, or arbor.

Planting and caring for roses is not as difficult as it may seem. Armed with a sturdy pair of gardening gloves to protect you from the roses' sharp thorns, some garden shears, and patience, your garden can soon include a wide variety of roses that will delight any visitor.

good to know

COLOR RIGHT INTO WINTER
Regional climate permitting, in the fall a number of rose varieties, including *Rosa canina, Rosa rubiginosa,* and *Rosa rugosa* form large, shiny red rose hips, as long as the spring blooms aren't cut off. These fruits make excellent purées and fruit teas.

ROSE CULTIVATION

▶ The original species and natural rose hybrids **grow wild** in most northern, temperate countries.

▶ Gardeners have long cultivated the rose, developing the double flower and, eventually, modern hybrids with a **high, pointed center**, in which ancesteral floral characteristics are almost totally submerged.

PLANTING ROSES

Potted plants can be planted throughout the year, but roses may not always take root well.

▶ Be sure to plant **bare-root roses** after the last of the frosty days.

▶ Soak bare-root plants in a **bucket of water** for several hours before planting.

▶ **Cut back** your rose plants before putting them in the ground. Shorten fairly small thread roots by half, and larger roots by a third. In addition, cut back the branches to around 10 in. (25 cm).

▶ Make sure to plant your roses so that the **graft area** is just below the surface of the ground. Rose growers will argue endlessly about the exact correct planting depth, but it really depends on where you live. If you live in a colder area, it is best to plant a bit deeper.

▶ Pay attention to the **distance** between plants: it should usually be 16–18 in. (40–45 cm), but for **dwarf roses,** 8 in. (20 cm) is adequate. **Climbing roses** need at least 5 ft. (1.5 m).

▶ Provide your roses with at least one botanical buddy—fragrant flowers or herbs will definitely help keep many pests away. **Lavender, rosemary,** and **thyme** repel aphids; **French marigold** kills nematodes; **chives** prevent powdery mildew; and the sulfur in **garlic** and **onions** wards off fungus growth.

Prune climbing and rambling roses sparingly—even shoots that are several years old can bloom.

ROSE CARE

▸ Remove any **winter protection** from roses on a cloudy, overcast day; too much sun and warmth can give the plants a real shock after a long winter's rest.

▸ **Fertilize** your roses in early to mid-spring.

▸ Use **water-soluble fertilizers** only when the weather is damp.

▸ Nurture roses with **manure** and **water:** add 1 cup (250 mL) of dried cow manure to 8 quarts/ liters of water, and let soak for a couple of days. Dilute the liquid so it is the color of weak tea and pour on the root area.

▸ Rake finely-chopped **banana peels** into the soil to provide the plants with lime, magnesium, sulfur, nitrogen, potassium, phosphate, and silicic acid.

▸ Water your roses **thoroughly**, but **not daily**, during dry times. Depending on its size, during periods of drought a rose plant will need 10–20 quarts/liters of water per week to produce luxuriant blooms.

▸ Never water roses from **above**; this may produce fungal diseases.

▸ Prevent fungal diseases by spraying roses in the morning with a solution of 1 tsp. (5 mL) of **baking powder** in 4 quarts/liters of water. Adding 2–3 drops of **soap** blends the solution more effectively.

▸ Stop **fertilizing** roses at least one month before the first annual frost date. Fertilizing too long into autumn encourages roses to produce tender new growth that will get nipped by the cold.

▸ Keep bush roses from lifting in the winter by covering the root crown with **compost.** Tie large bush roses or climbing roses with string to keep them from breaking in the wind or under a heavy load of snow.

CUTTING ROSES

Cut roses properly to encourage growth and the formation of blossoms.

▸ Use special **gloves** and good **clippers;** it's particularly easy to injure yourself when cutting climbing or bush roses.

▸ Twist off **wild shoots** that sprout from the ground right at the base.

▸ Remove **prunings** immediately from the garden, as they can be a haven for insects and disease pathogens. Add this garden waste to the **household trash**, rather than the compost pile, since many disease pathogens can withstand even the high temperatures inside the compost.

▸ Cut back **bush roses** by about a third in the fall to produce bushier growth.

Maintenance involves regularly removing wilted blooms and dead plant parts.

Soil

A loose soil rich in humus and nutrients, with a slightly acidic to neutral pH value, is optimal for most garden plants. You'll rarely encounter such ideal conditions but, fortunately, you have centuries of garden wisdom to call on to help improve the soil in your garden.

Soils can be divided into light sandy soil, heavy clay soil, and medium loamy soil on the basis of their sand, clay, and loam content, plus lime and humus.

SOIL TYPES

▶ **Sandy soil** is easy to work and plant roots can spread out easily, but water and nutrients are poorly absorbed. Use **compost** to increase the amount of **humus,** and **mulching** to prevent rapid drying.

▶ **Clay soil** makes it difficult for roots to spread. The soil is so tightly-compacted that the roots of many plants can't penetrate it to reach water and nutrients; they quickly wilt. Loosen clay soil by adding **sand** and **compost.**

Sandy soil is dry, grainy, and crumbles easily; good loam soil first smears, and then crumbles after some time.

▶ **Loam soil** offers the best gardening conditions. This soil stores water and nutrients effectively, and the soil structure is loose enough for plants to root easily and reach the nutrients. By adding a little **compost** or **organic fertilizer**, you can ensure that the soil doesn't become depleted over time.

SOIL ANALYSIS

Determine soil types before you get started on your gardening to ensure you choose the right one.

▶ Take a **shovel sample** at several places in the garden. Dig to a depth of about 20 in. (50 cm) to get your samples; you should quickly be able to tell whether the soil is sandy or loamy, dry, rocky, or compacted.

▶ Alternatively, determine soil conditions by studying the **roots** of plants currently growing in the garden. A small root ball and crooked, intertwined root strands point to impenetrable soil.

▶ Look for **creepy-crawlies.** They may not look pretty, but the presence of many helpers such as woodlice, earthworms, and millipedes in the soil are signs of good soil quality.

NOTHING GETS BY PLANTS

So-called indicator plants prefer certain soils. Their appearance in your garden makes it possible to draw conclusions about the soil conditions.

▶ **Compacted, heavy clay soil** attracts creeping thistle, horsetail, lamb's foot, coltsfoot, fleece flower, mullein, and dandelion.

▶ On the other hand, **dry soil** is preferred by yellow chamomile, sickleweed, storksbill, plantain, and white campion.

▶ Soil with plenty of **humus** attracts nettle, dandelion, and chickweed.

▶ **High-nutrient soil** lures nettle, thistle, goosefoot, wild radish, shepherd's purse, coltsfoot,

Hydrangea blooms signal whether the soil is acidic or alkaline. In an acid soil they bloom blue; in alkaline, a pinkish purple.

determining pH value with a kit

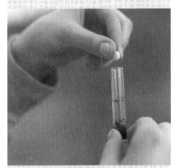

one Put a soil sample with some water into the glass container from the kit and add a tablet. Close the container and shake well.

two Determine the pH value by comparing the resulting color change in the liquid to the color chart on the kit.

saltbush, nightshade, round-leaved dock (bitter dock), and chickweed.

▶ Clear indicators of soil **low in nutrients** include daisy, heather, common sorrel, dog daisy, common wood sorrel, pansy, and white clover.

ACID AND LIME CONTENT

The health of your garden plants may well depend on the acid content of the soil. Some plants grow well in acidic or alkaline soils, while others don't.

▶ **Alkaline soils** are indicated by the presence of charlock, common wild oats, alfalfa, chicory, and meadow clary.

▶ **Acidic soils** make bracken fern, speedwell, daisy, haresfoot clover, common sorrel, common wood sorrel, holly, and purple pansy thrive.

▶ Soil with a **high lime content** is indicated by the presence of creeping bellflower, field bindweed, haresfoot clover, coltsfoot, field poppy, clover, liverwort, marigold, delphinium, storksbill, chicory, meadow clary, and spurge.

▶ A **vinegar test** also provides a clear indication of lime content. Spray a little vinegar onto a clump of dirt; the vinegar will bubble when it comes in contact with soil containing lime.

SOIL IMPROVEMENT

Add the right substances to improve most soils.

▶ Work **garden gravel** or **coarse sand** into heavy clay soils to a depth of about 12 in. (30 cm) to increase permeability.

▶ Add organic material such as **compost** or **cow manure** to sandy soil regularly. Plant **St. John's wort, ornamental grasses,** and **tamarisks** to help stabilize the soil.

▶ Dig **garden lime, chalk,** or **marl** into acidic soil in the fall. Acidic soil also needs the addition of **phosphate** and **potash** in the form of wood ashes.

▶ **Calcareous soil** can often be modified only through repeated additions of large quantities of **sulfur** or **peat.** It's better, however, to plant beech, box, forsythia, viburnum, beans, cabbage, or lettuce, which manage to grow well in the soil. Regular use of **organic fertilizers** can help calcareous soil store nutrients more effectively.

The Garden in Winter

Indigenous plants are normally winter-hardy, but they still need to be ready for the season. Prepare your garden well so that all the plants, including the more delicate ones, can survive the coldest winter.

Much can be done to help your garden better survive the ravages of winter, including tree trimming, a paint job, and even bringing part of the garden inside.

NATURAL PROTECTION

Opt for leaves, spruce and fir trimmings, straw, burlap, and jute when considering covering or wrapping plants.

▶ Consider **spruce trimmings** for optimal winter protection—they gradually lose their needles and let more light reach the plants. Arrange cuttings like a small roof over the plants, but make sure that air can get to them; otherwise, they may rot or become diseased.

In a hard frost, even winter-hardy potted plants need protection. Place them on pieces of wood or tilt them slightly so they don't freeze to the ground, then wrap them in blankets or plastic.

good to know

POTTED PLANTS

Potted plants are better off in the ground during winter. If at all possible, find a spot in your garden to either plant your potted beauties temporarily for the winter or bury them pot and all. Mulch with 2–4 in. (5–10 cm) of bark or leaves, once the soil has frozen.

▶ Check **leaves** for pests, fungus, and other diseases before deciding how to proceed with winterization.

▶ **Burlap** and **jute** are light and smooth, so they don't harm plants. For better protection, you can put **straw** between the plants and a jute wrap over them.

PROTECTION FROM THE COLD

Plants from warmer regions and newly-transplanted or young plants will make it through a tough winter only if they are well-wrapped in sturdy burlap or spruce trimmings.

▶ Give the trunks of **fruit trees** a coat of **white paint** or wrap them in **cardboard** to keep them from cracking due to major temperature changes or very cold nights.

▶ Protect delicate **perennials** and late-fall plantings with **dried leaves** or **straw**, and use **spruce cuttings** to protect evergreen varieties.

▶ Tie **tall ornamental grasses** together in bunches to protect them from frost and snow and to provide winter shelter for helpful creatures.

▶ **Press back down** any soil around perennials that may have that buckled due to frost. This will protect the roots.

▶ Tie the **branches of young evergreen trees** together with wide strips of **burlap** to mitigate snow buildup.

OTHER WINTER OPTIONS

▶ Find the room. If you have enough space inside, **bring potted plants indoors** for the winter. Their addition will bring color and extra oxygen to the home. Just remember to give them adequate **light** and **water,** and be careful not to place them too close to the cold of the window or any heat sources.

▶ Create a **windowsill herb garden.** Use several small terra-cotta pots and some enriched earth to plant basil, savory, rosemary, chives, parsley, and any other favorites. You will have fresh herbs all winter long.

Transplanting

Redesigning your garden may involve transplanting perennials, shrubs, or even trees. It's not a daunting task, but remember that timing is key because no plant should be kept out of the soil for too long.

The best time for transplanting is late summer or early fall. That gives plants the chance to put down roots and start growing before the onset of winter.

THE RIGHT TIMING

▶ Try to transplant during **wet** and **cool** weather to reduce stress on the plants.

▶ Transplant **evergreen trees** and **shrubs** in April or October, when the soil is moist and warm.

▶ Transplant shrubs that are sensitive to frost, such as mallow, hibiscus, or hydrangea, in **spring**.

To determine the right depth for a plant, put the plant into the hole and lay a stick across the hole. The location of the graft should lie inside the soil.

TRANSPLANTING LARGE TREES AND SHRUBS

Trees and older shrubs should be prepared before being relocated—otherwise they won't tolerate the change. It takes two to three seasons to fully root-prune a tree but, in the end, a compact, well-branched root system will greatly increase your tree's chance of survival once it is moved.

▶ In spring, dig a **furrow** (15 in./40 cm deep and 10 in./25 cm wide) one-third of the way around a tree, slightly closer to the trunk than you will eventually be digging when the tree is moved. By doing so, you can break long, unbranched roots, prompting the regrowth of new roots nearer the main trunk of the tree. **Cut off** the roots around the main shoots, at a slight angle toward the shrub or tree.

▶ Fill the trench with **fresh soil** and **compost** and keep watering the plant well to promote the growth of new fibrous roots. Don't transplant until the following year.

▶ **Prune the shoots** of the transplant by up to one-third of their length to prevent harmful effects from damaged roots.

▶ A handful of **bone meal** and some mature **compost** will give the tree or shrub a good start in its new hole.

▶ Keep transplants, whether perennials, shrubs, or trees, from dehydrating by spreading a thick layer of **mulch** on the ground around them.

TRANSPLANTING PERENNIALS

▶ Transplant **perennials** after they've finished flowering. If you transplant in the spring, don't expect the perennials to bloom that year.

▶ Transplant in **late fall** so you can save yourself the labor of extensive watering.

▶ Add **compost** or **humus** to the hole for perennial plants to help them sprout new shoots.

Vegetable and Lettuce Beds

Plant your greens in the sunniest and flattest part of the garden to ensure a bounty of vegetables all summer and fall. Plan your vegetable and lettuce beds well so that they're easy to maintain, accessible for weeding and watering, and protected against garden invaders.

Cardboard egg cartons are good for starting seedlings, but use them only once.

How you plan your beds will help you immensely in the long run. It will save you time and effort, ease retrieval, and likely prevent you from developing a sore back.

MAKING A NEW BED
Keep vegetable beds no wider than 4 ft. (1.2 m). To make sure they're accessible on all sides, don't place them right next to a wall or a hedge. The paths between individual beds should be about 12 in. (30 cm) wide.

▶ Lay simple **boards** on the paths to keep from sinking in the mud during rainy weather.

▶ Divide your vegetable bed into two: one with things you **harvest daily,** such as carrots, radishes, and lettuce, and the other with **permanent crops** such as herbs, horseradish, and cabbages.

▶ Use **berry** and **hazelnut bushes** to provide attractive protection against cold wind.

▶ Plant fighting veggies: **pumpkin** and **squash** restrict weeds; **potatoes** and **Jerusalem artichokes** loosen the soil.

▶ Add basic **fertilizer,** preferably with compost, about three weeks before the first planting.

▶ Plant **low-growing veggies** on the sunny side of taller ones so that they get adequate light.

▶ Allow for **varying ripening times** when laying out the bed so you can grow different plants close together.

This small vegetable bed is located right next to the compost pile, making it easy to fertilize.

SEED PROPAGATION INDOORS AND SOWING

▶ Use plastic **starter flats.** They're easy to clean, which makes it difficult for diseases to take hold.

▶ Don't forget to **label** individual starter flats with the name of the vegetable and the date of planting.

▶ Don't plant **too many seeds** in one container; the fewer seeds you plant in a container, the less work you'll have when it's time to thin out the plants.

▶ Sew **larger seeds** farther apart, singly, or in pairs (just in case one of them fails to sprout).

▶ Scatter **smaller seeds**—such as spinach and chard—directly onto the bed.

▶ Mix **very small seeds** with a little **sand** so they don't fall so close together and are easier to spread.

▶ Soak seeds from legumes or vegetables (like squash or tomatoes, which are really fruit) in a **milk marinade** for 24 hours—they'll sprout faster.

▶ You can do outdoor seeding earlier if the ground is covered with a **black tarp** or **black plastic sheet** a few days in advance to warm it up.

▶ Make optimal use of space by planting slow-growing vegetables such as **carrots** between fast-growing **lettuce.**

Sow seeds in straight rows by stretching a string between two stakes at either end of the row.

BED MAINTENANCE

▶ Dig **irrigation ditches** between rows to let the water soak in slowly and reach the roots—this works well for any vegetable that shouldn't be watered from above.

▶ Make sure the water is **warm to the touch**; otherwise your plants will get a real shock in hot weather.

▶ Dig **living mulch,** such as clover, alfalfa, and downy vetch, into the soil in the fall. This provides a natural source of nutrients.

▶ In late fall, enhance the soil in harvested beds by adding **mulch.**

▶ Plant **aromatic herbs** or **flowers** around the vegetable patch, such as dill, meadowfoam, and French marigold, to attract useful garden visitors such as **ladybugs** and **hoverflies.**

Weed your garden regularly to keep invaders from stealing space and strength from your veggies.

KEEPING OUT INVASIVE PESTS

▶ Pick off harmful pests such as **caterpillars** and **snails** individually. Snails tend to lurk in grass, so keep the lawn around the vegetable patch cut short.

▶ If bushes or hedges near the garden are infested with **aphids,** protect vegetables with transparent cloth or plastic sheeting.

▶ Install **chicken wire** over a freshly-sown bed to keep cats and birds at bay. Once the sprouts have emerged, use it to make a fence around the tender sprouts.

▶ Make a **scarecrow** by hanging shiny objects such as CDs or tin-foil pie plates from branches or from a forked pole stuck into the ground. They'll reflect the sunlight as they move in the wind, frightening away hungry birds.

An Herbal Extract for Seedlings

1³/₄ oz. (50 g) stinging nettle
1/3 oz. (10 g) sage
1/3 oz. (10 g) rue
1/3 oz. (10 g) wormwood
2/3 oz. (20 g) wood ferns
2/3 oz. (20 g) onion peels
10 quarts/liters water

Soak the herbs in water for 24 hours, then boil and strain. Dilute the completed slurry 10:1 and sprinkle on the seedlings to strengthen them. Repeat weekly.

Watering

Regular watering—not too much, not too little—is important for all plants. Collecting rainwater in a barrel or cistern for use during dry spells is an ancient practice that can be used by anyone today, even if you have only a small vegetable garden.

With fairly large new plantings, install a soaker or ooze hose to ensure a slow but steady release of water.

Collecting rainwater is not only an earth-friendly practice, it is better for your plants than using tap water, which main contain small traces of bleach.

WHO NEEDS HOW MUCH?

Look at a plant's leaves to see if it needs a lot of water or only a little.

▶ Small, leathery, thorny, shiny, or fleshy leaves indicate a **low need for water,** as do leaves with a **wax-like layer** on them. Plants in a **stone garden** or **Mediterranean** plants do fine without a lot of water, as do ivy, amaranth, nasturtium, sage, French marigold, and zinnia.

▶ Plants with soft, large, or thin leaves, on the other hand, tend to be **thirsty**, as do all blooming plants and those with solid root balls and shallow root systems.

WHEN AND HOW TO WATER

▶ Water hedges and plants in both the flower and vegetable gardens **before 9:30 AM.** The leaves will dry off quickly, reducing the risk of a fungal infection. If you water plants at night, the dirt surrounding them remains wet, potentially causing the roots to rot—plus, the moisture could attract **snails.**

▶ Water **infrequently, but thoroughly**. The pauses between watering leave time for a branching, deeper root system to form in the drier soil. Don't waterlog your plants in heavy soil.

▶ Make an **inexpensive soaker hose** at home from an old garden hose: drill some small holes into it, connect it to the main hose, and presto, you've got an effective, efficient watering system.

▶ Be particularly careful not to water the leaves of **melons, bell peppers,** and **tomatoes**. You might even shake rainwater from the leaves to ensure fungal diseases don't set in.

▶ Don't water **blooms**. In the sunlight, the little water droplets act like a magnifying glass, potentially burning the delicate blossoms.

▶ During **hot summer weather**, just spray the plants—but don't do it in bright sunshine.

▶ **Young sprouts** need more water than plants that are several years old with deep root systems.

Water young plants very carefully so that they don't lose their foothold.

a money-saving *hint*

A plastic bottle is a simple and economical watering device: cut off the bottom of the bottle and stick it top-down in the soil. When you fill up the bottle, it slowly releases the water through the neck and to the area of the plant's roots.

▶ Make sure the water is **lukewarm,** and let it stand before use.

▶ If you water intensively with a **watering can** every couple of days in the summer heat, **repeat** the process after about 30 minutes. The water will penetrate deeper into the soil.

▶ Using a **sprinkler?** Check how far down the soil is dry. If the first 1 in. (2.5 cm) of soil is dry, figure on watering for about **60 minutes,** and if the first 2 in. (5 cm) is dry, water for **90 minutes.**

▶ Water **bushes** and **shrubs** in the root area beneath the outer branches. During dry periods, large trees need plenty of water, especially **fruit trees** when they're blossoming or when fruit is ripening. Water for several hours.

COLLECTING RAINWATER

Most plants tolerate rainwater better than water from a spring or a tap—collected rainwater is usually warmer and free of fluoride, chlorine, and lime. Water that is high in lime leaves white spots on the leaves.

Newly planted bushes and shrubs need plenty of water. Make a depression for watering so that you can be sure to give them a good soaking.

▶ Keep water clear by occasionally adding a little **charcoal** or **activated carbon** (for use in aquariums) to the barrel.

▶ **Cover** rain barrels and above-ground cisterns so that small animals can't get in.

▶ In an **underground tank,** the water doesn't evaporate and no algae forms. But you do need a pump that connects to your garden hose in order to distribute the water.

OPTIMUM MOISTURE

▶ Rake the soil regularly, including in the furrows for the plants. **Loosening the soil** allows water easier access to a plant's roots.

▶ After a **heavy summer rain,** loosen up the soil only on the surface; otherwise the moisture in the soil will evaporate too quickly.

▶ Lay a layer of **mulch** to hold the moisture in the soil longer and prevent your plants from getting thirsty too quickly.

Connect your rain barrel directly to the downspout of the roof gutter. If the barrel is raised up, it's easy to fill the watering can.

watering aids

one Dig a hole about 6 in. (15 cm) deep next to a plant that needs lots of water.

two Place a flowerpot of the right size into the dug hole, drain hole downward, and cover it with a plate or piece of plastic.

three Fill with water at regular intervals. It will trickle slowly into the earth and reach the roots directly.

Weather Lore

Humans have been forecasting the weather for almost as long as we've been on earth, looking for signs in the wind and clouds, as well as animals and plants. Modern meteorologists acknowledge that many of the old weather rules actually hold up quite well when compared to science.

Colors in the Sky

Colors in the sky—red in the morning and evening, or rainbows—tell us different things about the weather. They're the result of water vapor in the lower layers of the atmosphere; the more water vapor there is, the stronger the colors. A colorful sunrise indicates rain, but in the evening it merely produces dew on the ground. Gardeners can rely on the following rules:

- Red sky at night, sailor's delight; red sky at morning, sailor take warning.

- Evening red and morning gray set the traveler on his way; but evening gray and morning red will bring rain down upon his head.

- Rainbow in the morning gives you fair warning. A rainbow to windward, rain ahead; a rainbow to leeward, rains end. A rainbow at noon, more rain soon.

- If there is enough blue sky to make a sailor a pair of pants, the weather will soon clear.

- When clouds look like black smoke, a wise man will put on his cloak.

Wind, Clouds, and Leaves

"A change in wind, a change in weather," goes the old farmers' lore, and in fact, a change in the weather does follow a rapid change in wind direction. The following sayings also apply to home gardeners:

- A wind from the south has rain in its mouth. A wind from the east is not good for man or beast.

- When smoke descends, good weather ends.

- A sunny shower won't last an hour.

- When leaves show their backs, it will rain.

Sun and Moon as Weather Breeders

Meteorologists call rings around the moon and sun halos. For ages, they have been used as predictors of changes in the weather. The following sayings about the sun and moon have been handed down for generations, and every gardener should be familiar with them.

- A halo around sun or moon means rain or snow very soon.

- Clear moon, frost soon.

- Pale moon rains, red moon blows, white moon neither rains nor snows.

- Plant your beans when the moon is light; you will find that this is right.

- Plant potatoes when the moon is dark, and to this line you'll always hark.

- If the moon lies on her back, she sucks the wet into her lap.

Animals Predict the Weather

Animals are rooted so firmly in nature and its events that they sense changes in the weather—their lives often depend on it. Gardeners should pay particular attention to birds:

- Swallows and bats fly close to the ground before a rain. Birds flying low, expect a blow.

- If the goose honks high, fair weather; if the goose honks low, foul weather. South or north, sally forth; west or east, travel least.

- Seagull, seagull, sit on the sand; it's a sign of rain when you are at hand.

Research has proven this lore to be true. Migratory birds do indeed instinctively sense when winter is coming. Also:

- If a rooster crows on going to bed, you may rise with rain on your head.

By observing the behavior of other animals, you can draw additional conclusions about the weather.

- When spiders' webs in air do fly, the spell soon will be very dry.

- If garden spiders forsake their webs, it means rain is coming.

- Cows lying down in a field before noon are a sign of rain.

- When a cow thumps her ribs with an angry tail, look for thunder, lightning, and hail.

- Cats scratch a post before wind; wash their face before rain; and sit with their back to the fire before snow.

- The louder the frog, the more the rain.

Flowers and Seasons

The flowers of certain plants indicate the seasons:

- Early spring: the start of snow-drop flowering

- Springtime: apple blossoms

- Early summer: elder blossoms

- High summer: full flowering of the small-leaf linden

- Late summer: start of the oat harvest

- Early fall: full blooming of autumn crocuses

- Fall: start of general leaf fall

Weeds

An ancient Chinese proverb wisely counsels, "The best shade in the garden is the gardener's own shadow." That's why our grandparents were out in the garden every day—pulling weeds. But if you're pressed for time, here are a few preventative measures that you can try to keep botanical invaders from setting in at all.

Weeds are sturdy plants that aren't welcome in the garden because they quickly edge out the more delicate flora. But they also have some positive aspects: they allow you to evaluate the composition of the dirt, and their roots ventilate the soil, enrich it with nutrients, and stem erosion. In addition, many weeds serve as the basic element in liquid fertilizers or compounds used to prevent and combat garden pests and diseases. Moreover, herbs such as common horsetail, coltsfoot, and many others enjoy an excellent reputation as medicinal herbs.

COMMON WEEDS

▶ **Creeping thistle** is not only tough, it also attracts pests. This root-spreading weed grows up to 4 ft. (1.2 m). Remove its blooms first, then dig up the plant, roots and all if possible. Don't dispose of its remnants on the compost heap, since the roots could multiply.

▶ **Common horsetail,** also called bottlebrush or cat's tail, has a far-spreading root system that is hard to pull out. The plant breeds by means of spores and roots. Since it likes moisture, you can effectively combat it only by draining the soil or through sporadic liming of the ground. Again, don't throw it on the compost heap; it will continue to multiply there.

Be especially careful when hoeing weeds among single plants in a vegetable bed.

▶ **Stinging nettles** are unassuming weeds that like nitrogen-rich soil. If they go unchecked, they grow rampant and form whole clusters. They are shallow-rooted plants that must either be mowed once a week—the roots will wither away within two years—or pulled out singly from the ground along with the roots.

▶ **Veronica,** or **speedwell,** thrives in loose, nitrogen-rich soil. This weed is spread by seeds and usually blooms between March and July. It has to be removed by hand.

▶ **Coltsfoot,** or **ribgrass,** grows even in the smallest cracks between flagstones or on house walls. Dig out each plant singly before it flowers. The weed, whose flowers resemble those of the **dandelion,** tends to grow in clusters. It propagates by seeds and can be composted.

Lady's mantle thrives even in shady spots, and its dense growth and broad leaves help banish weeds.

► **Chickweed** blooms from March till October, establishing itself not only on the lawn but also in vegetable patches or shrub beds. Before the seeds form, you can easily pull the plant out of the ground by hand.

► **Vetches** such as the **bush vetch** or **tufted vetch** are tough climbing plants whose shoots— which quickly grow long—are hard to control. They multiply through seeds and shoots that develop long taproots. Weed and hoe them regularly and, most importantly, remove their roots.

WEED REMOVAL

Make sure that weeds are pulled out regularly since they spread very quickly and rob other plants of nutrients.

► Weed on **dry days after a rain;** the soil is loose, allowing plants to be pulled easily.

► In dry weather, let the weeds **decompose** right where you pulled them.

► **Weed again** a few days after breaking up the soil of a bed; when you turn the soil, the seeds of weeds lying on the bottom may come to the top and start to sprout.

► Cut off **flower heads** or **seed pods** before weeding or hoeing to prevent the seeds from getting into the soil.

► Make short work of weeds growing in cracks and fissures between flagstones or on house walls by pouring **boiling water** on them.

► Pour **salt** on lawn weeds, or sprinkle them with a solution of one part **vinegar** and one part **water.**

PREVENTING WEEDS

Chemical substances run the risk of damaging the soil so much that the plants you've nurtured will die, too. Chemical weed controls are illegal in some jurisdictions anyway—but even in areas where they are allowed, chemical weed- and pest killers are a bad idea, especially since there are so many completely natural ways to control weeds.

► Plants that rob weeds of light and nutrients through their own growth are an environmentally-friendly way to control weeds. **Ground-covering plants** are especially useful.

► Use **dense-growing** ground cover plants, such as Japanese spurges, fairy wings, barren strawberry, and Himalayan fleeceflower, for **shady** areas.

► Prevent weeds in **sunny beds** by planting stonecrops and ground cover roses.

► Sow plants that **nourish** the soil. This also suppresses weeds and will later contribute to healthy growth in the flower bed.

► **Mulch between plants** to prevent unwanted weeds from coming to the surface. For mulch, use **freshly-cut grass** or **wood chips;** in stone gardens you can also use **gravel.**

► Lay out **black plastic mulch** over larger or inaccessible areas and **cut a cross** into the mulch where the plants are coming up.

The taproots of dandelions reach far into the ground. With a trowel you can dig deep and remove them completely.

Year-Round Gardening

There's a comforting, age-old rhythm to the cycle of the seasons and the corresponding work your garden needs. Depending on your location and climate, the chores may come a little sooner or a little later, but they won't change much. The reward for that year-round love and attention will be a horticultural haven of which you can be proud.

Late Spring:

Plant shrubs in the ornamental garden, prune early-blooming bushes after they've bloomed, tie up climbing roses, and move potted plants outdoors when the danger of frost is past. Plant two-year summer plants and early bloomers, as well as summer bulbs such as dahlias and gladiolus.

Add mulch or straw around strawberry plants. Thin out excess fruit on the trees and prop up branches overloaded with fruit using boards. Finally, water fruit trees well.

Plant tomatoes, peppers, and other tender veggies, as well as herbs like dill, oregano, and basil.

Harvest early beets, radishes, rhubarb, lettuce, and spinach, plus the first berries.

Spring:

In ornamental gardens, plant or cut back roses, bushes, and shrubs; divide and transplant existing perennials; and sow annual summer flowers such as pansies and snapdragons.

In the fruit garden, cut back berry bushes and grape vines. Plant delicate fruit varieties such as apricots and peaches and paint any frost cracks on tree bark.

Plant cold-hardy vegetables such as peas, spinach, asparagus, broccoli, cabbage, kale, broad beans, and onions.

When there's no danger of frost, plant carrots, beets, Swiss chard, cauliflower, potatoes, celery, and radishes.

Late Summer:

Trim evergreen hedges in the ornamental garden, tie up late-blooming perennials, and plant biennial summer flowers. Now you can plant the bulb plants for next spring and remove annual bloomers entirely.

Plant berries and hazelnut bushes in the garden; new blackberry shoots must be tied up. Fruit trees shouldn't be cut any further.

Plant green mature plants on fallow soil in the vegetable garden. To prevent potato blight in tomatoes, protect them with a cover of transparent plastic sheeting.

Harvest nature's bounty: apples, pears, blackberries, elderberries, hazelnuts, and walnuts are ripe, as are tomatoes, leeks, late potatoes, and late carrots.

Early Summer:

Trim deciduous hedges, remove wilted blooms, deadhead perennials, plant fall-blooming bulbs, and cut back to the ground the stalks of all early summer bloomers. In addition, divide iris and lily of the valley bulbs after they flower.

Support heavily-laden branches on fruit trees and, after the harvest, begin the first pruning and trimming to remove dead or diseased wood. Don't water fruit trees and shrubs after the end of August. Trim berry bushes after the harvest.

Plant pumpkin, squash, garlic, leeks, onions, beets, etc. in the vegetable garden so you'll still have fresh veggies in fall. Remove all the side shoots from tomato plants, and stop growth once about five fruit clusters have formed.

Harvest the first potatoes and tomatoes, in addition to lettuce and many vegetable varieties, and the last berries, early apples, and stone fruit.

Fall and Winter

Plant rose bushes in the flower garden and hill-up hybrid tea roses with soil, straw, or peat moss to prevent them from freezing.

Remove dahlias, gladiolus, tuberous begonias, and ranunculus from the ground after the first frost, and store in a cool location.

Prune ornamental shrubs, and cover perennial gardens and borders with compost, bark mulch, or leaf litter. Give evergreen bushes and shrubs a last good watering before the frost comes.

Plant fruit trees in the garden when there is no frost. Prune trees and remove dead or damaged wood on frost-free winter days.

Protect vegetable gardens from the first night frost. Cover any vegetables not yet harvested with transparent plastic to help them ripen faster.

glossary

Agrimony: a medicinal herb used for treating skin ailments, including athlete's foot. Available at health food stores.

Almond bran: ground almond skin that is rich in antioxidants. Available at health food stores.

Alum: a water-soluble, nontoxic chemical compound often used in pickling and preserving. Available at grocery stores.

Ammonia: a strong chemical used in a number of cleaning products. Available at hardware stores.

Arnica: a medicinal herb belonging to the sunflower family that is often used in tinctures or creams. Available at health food stores and some pharmacies.

Autogenic training: a meditative relaxation technique invented by German psychiatrist Johannes Heinrich Schultz in the 1930s that can be used to help relieve stress-induced disorders.

Bear's garlic: an edible, medicinal herb related to chives. Also called ramsons, buckrams, or wild garlic. Available at health food stores.

Bearberry:  the fruit of a small shrub found in northern climates that is usually used in medicinal tea to treat a number of ailments, including bladder infection, water retention, and diarrhea. Available at health food stores and some pharmacies.

Biotin/Vitamin B7: a B vitamin that is important for healthy hair and skin. It can be found in foods like egg yolk and nuts, or as a supplement available at health food stores and pharmacies.

Bloodroot: a flowering herb that can be used to flavor liqueurs. Note that it can be toxic. Available at health food stores.

Bonemeal: coarsely ground bones used as a natural fertilizer. Available at garden supply stores.

Brewer's yeast: an edible microorganism rich in B vitamins that is often used to make beer, but can also be used for skin care. Available at health food stores.

Bulgur: a cereal made from wheat, also known as bulghur or burghul. It is often used in Middle Eastern and Mediterranean cooking. Available at grocery stores.

Burdock root: the root of a thistle that can be used to treat a number of health problems, including hair and scalp problems and burns. Available at health food stores.

Calamus: a wetland plant whose leaves resemble that of the iris. Also known as sweet flag or flagroot, it can help with digestive problems. Available at health food stores.

Callus plane: a bladed device used to remove calluses or corns from feet. Available at pharmacies.

Camphor: a waxy tree extract with a cooling effect similar to menthol that can be used as a mild anesthetic or natural anti-itch product. Available at health food stores.

Castor oil: a vegetable oil extracted from the seeds of the castor plant, with many medicinal and household uses. Available at health food stores.

Chamois cloth: a cloth made from soft, porous leather that is useful for cleaning. Synthetic chamois cloths are made from microfiber or other materials. Available at hardware stores.

Cherry pit bags: a cloth bag filled with dried and cleaned cherry pits that can be heated and placed on sore body parts to ease pain. Easy to make yourself, or available at health food stores.

Chicory: a bushy herb often used medicinally or as a dietary supplement. Available at grocery or health food stores.

Clary sage: a medicinal herb used for digestive or premenstrual problems. Available at health food stores.

Cleaver, powdered: a medicinal herb used in a ground-up form to treat skin and urinary problems. Sometimes called cleavers. Available at health food stores.

Clove oil: an essential oil from the clove plant usually used to relieve toothache. Available at pharmacies or health food stores.

Coltsfoot: a flowering medicinal herb used to treat coughs and lung ailments. It should not be consumed by very young children. Available at health food stores.

Comfrey: a medicinal herb used on skin or to treat muscle pain. It should not be consumed. Available at health food stores.

Conjunctivitis: a contagious eye disease commonly known as pink eye that causes eyes to turn red and/or produce pus.

Dandelion: a weed used as a diuretic, digestion aid, and liver detoxifier. Available as an extract or in capsule form at health food stores.

Deadnettle: a medicinal plant that resembles stinging nettle and can be used to treat skin ailments or consumed as a tea. Available at health food stores.

Diuretic teas: natural herbal teas that encourage urination and help ease water retention.

Dyer's greenweed: a flowering herb used medicinally or to produce a yellowish natural dye. Available at health food stores.

Echinacea: a medicinal herb also known as purple coneflower that is used to boost the immune system and ward off colds. Available at pharmacies.

Elderberry: a dark berry that grows on elder trees or elderberry bushes and is rich in vitamin C. Available at health food stores.

Elderflower: the flower of the elder tree or elderberry bush. Used medicinally or in cooking. Available at health food stores.

Electrolytes: electrically-charged ions or salts that are important for staying hydrated and can be found in many natural foods or sports drinks.

Evening primrose: an edible and medicinal plant often used in skin care, sometimes in oil form. Available at pharmacies or health food stores.

Eyebright: a medicinal herb used to treat tired or irritated eyes. Available at health food stores.

Fennel seeds: the seeds of the herb fennel, which has a licorice-like taste. Can be used to treat indigestion. Available in the spice section at grocery stores.

Fern root: a medicinal root from several varieties of fern, notably the male fern. Available at health food stores.

Feverfew: a medicinal herb used to reduce fever, and treat migraines and arthritis. Available in supplement form at health food stores and some pharmacies. Feverfew can easily be grown in your garden or in a balcony pot.

Gentian root: the medicinal root of the gentian flower, used to treat digestive ailments. Available at health food stores.

Ginkgo: an ancient plant with broad leaves, also known as ginkgo biloba, which is thought to have a wide variety of medicinal uses, including memory enhancement. Available at health food stores.

Ginseng: an herb whose root is believed to boost energy and is used in traditional Chinese medicine. Available at health food stores and some pharmacies.

Goldenrod: a flowering plant used medicinally to treat wounds and as a diuretic. Available at health food stores.

Goldenseal: a medicinal herb, also known as orangeroot, which can be used as a natural antibiotic. Available at health food stores and some pharmacies.

Hawthorn: a thorny shrub of which the berries, leaves, and flowers can be used to treat some heart problems. Available at health food stores.

Hay flower: the flower of wild hay, used in baths, sitz baths, or compresses. Available at health food stores.

Healing earth: fine-grained clay, or loess, that is usually applied externally to treat skin problems, or can be taken internally in the form of capsules. Available at health food stores.

Heartsease: a wildflower, also known as pansy, which can be used to treat a variety of skin ailments, including eczema. Available at health food stores.

Henna: a flowering plant used to dye hair or paint designs on skin. Neutral and black henna are derived from other plants, but have similar applications. Available at health food stores.

Hops: the seed cones of the hop plant, used in the production of beer. It can also be used medicinally to treat sleeplessness or anxiety. Available at brewing stores or at some health food stores.

Horseradish: a pungent plant with antibacterial and diuretic uses. Available at some grocery stores.

Horsetail: a plant that can be used as a diuretic. It is not recommended for young children. Available at health food stores.

Horsetail broth: a liquid made from boiling horsetail in water.

Infrared: electromagnetic radiation that can be used in heat or light therapy.

Iris root: also known as orris root. Can be used medicinally and to make perfume. Available at health food stores.

Ivy leaves: the flat green leaves of the ivy plant, used medicinally to treat coughs and other ailments. Available at health food stores.

Jojoba: a shrub whose seeds are cultivated for their moisturizing oil, which can be used in perfume and cosmetics. Available at health food stores.

Juniper: a plant whose berries work medicinally as antiseptics or diuretics. Available at health food stores.

Kaolin: an absorbent clay taken internally to treat diarrhea. Available at most health food stores.

Kombucha: a fermented tea thought to have many health benefits, including antibiotic and antifungal uses. Available at health food stores.

Lady's mantle: a medicinal herb that can be used to treat excessive menstrual bleeding. Available at health food stores.

Lemon balm: a medicinal herb with a calming effect and citrus scent. Available at health food stores.

Linden: a tree whose flowers, leaves, and wood can be used medicinally to treat colds, high blood pressure, and infections. Available at health food stores.

Lovage: a tall plant whose leaves can be eaten or used to make tea. Available at health food stores.

Mallow: a family of plants whose leaves, roots, and flowers can be used medicinally to treat digestive ailments and coughs. Available at health food stores.

Marshmallow root: see mallow.

Meadowsweet: a multipurpose herb used to flavor alcohol, vinegar, jams, and jellies. Meadowsweet tea is known to alleviate the pain associated with earaches. Available at health food stores.

Millet: a small-seeded grain that can be eaten as a side dish, like rice, or in salads. Available at grocery stores and health food stores.

Mistletoe: a plant that usually grows attached to the branches of another bush or tree. The leaves are used to treat respiratory and circulatory ailments. Available at health food stores.

Monk's pepper: a medicinal herb used to treat premenstrual stress syndrome and other ailments related to both male and female reproductive systems. It is also known as chasteberry. Available at health food stores.

Monosodium glutamate: a flavor-enhancing food additive commonly known as MSG. Some people are sensitive to MSG and may experience headaches or other negative side effects as a result of consuming it.

Moor mud: a sticky, clay-like peat formed by decomposed plants that is used in skin care to detoxify and nourish skin. Available at health food stores.

Mugwort: a medicinal herb that can be used to aid digestion, as well as a seasoning for meat, fish, and rice. Available at health food stores and some pharmacies.

Mulberries: the fruit of numerous species of mulberry trees, used as a food dye or in tea form to treat a sore throat. Available at health food stores.

Mustard plaster: a poultice of crushed mustard seeds wrapped in a cloth and applied to skin—be sure that the mustard itself does not make skin contact. Used to treat pain and colds.

Mustard seeds: the small, round seeds of the mustard plant, used in cooking or to make mustard plasters. Available at grocery stores.

Naphtha: a highly flammable liquid used to make camp stove fuel and as a cleaner. Available at hardware stores.

Neem oil: a vegetable oil from the seeds of the neem, a type of evergreen tree. It can be used medicinally or as a natural pesticide. Available at health food stores and some gardening centers.

Neroli oil: the oil from the blossoms of the bitter orange tree, which is often used in fragrances. It is believed to have a soothing effect on the nervous system. Available at health food stores.

Neutral henna: an extract from the plant *cassia obovata* (not the henna plant used for hair dye). It does not color hair, but works well as a conditioner. Available at health food stores.

Organza: a sheer, thin fabric made from either silk or synthetic fibers. It is often used to make sheer curtains.

Paraffin: a solid, nontoxic waxy substance used to make candles or in home maintenance. Available at hardware stores.

Patchouli oil: an oil from a bushy herb, which is used in fragrances. Available at health food stores.

Peach pit oil: an oil extracted from the pit of a peach. Used in cosmetics and skin care. Available at health food stores.

Pearl-luster pigment: a pigment used to add subtle color and shine. Available at art supply stores.

Plantain (herb): an edible and medicinal herb that can be used in poultices and salves. Available at health food stores.

Pot marigold: a medicinal flower that can be used to treat menstrual pain, acne, and other ailments. Available at health food stores.

Potato wrap: warm, boiled potatoes wrapped in fabric that can be applied to sore muscles and joints to ease pain.

Poultice: soft, moist material spread on cloth and applied to an inflamed or aching body part to ease pain.

Powdered charcoal: a black, powdery substance made from burnt plants or vegetables that is used medicinally for detoxification and digestive problems. It is usually mixed with water and consumed. Available at health food stores.

Powdered yeast: powder made from microorganisms used in baking bread and the alcohol fermentation process. Available at grocery stores.

Probiotics: live microorganisms that aid in digestion and other bodily processes and can typically be found in foods like yogurt and cheese.

Propolis: resin collected by honeybees, used as a local antibiotic and antifungal. It can be used to help treat inflammation, burns, canker sores, and other ailments. Available at health food stores and some grocery stores.

Qigong: a variety of traditional Chinese practices and movements that can help manage arthritis, back pain, and stress.

Quinoa: a grain-like edible seed with a somewhat nutty taste, used in cooking. Available at grocery stores.

Rhassoul: a red Moroccan clay used in skin care. Also known as Ghassoul. Available at health food stores.

Rhatany: the medicinal root of the krameria plant. It can be used to treat toothaches when applied externally, and diarrhea when taken internally. Available at health food stores.

Rock powder: also known as diatomaceous earth. Used in gardening as a natural pesticide. Available at most home garden centers.

Rose hips: the vitamin C-rich fruits of the rose plant, with antioxidant and anti-inflammatory properties. Available at health food stores.

Rue: an evergreen shrub used medicinally to treat eyestrain and insomnia or as an insect repellent. Available at health food stores.

Saddle soap: a mixture containing soap and conditioners that is used to treat leather items such as shoes. Available at pharmacies and some cobblers.

Salvia miltiorrhiza: a medicinal herb also known as red sage or Chinese sage that can aid circulation. Available at some health food stores.

Sandalwood: a fragrant wood whose oil is often used in fragrances. Available at health food stores.

Seabuckthorn: a deciduous shrub native to mainland Asia used medicinally to treat coughs and indigestion. Seabuckthorn leaves and bark are believed to help treat some skin disorders and diarrhea. Available at health food stores.

Seabuckthorn oil: an oil made of the berries of the seabuckthorn shrub and vegetable oil. Available at health food stores.

Seborrhoea: a condition that comes about when skin's oil glands are overactive, producing greasy skin, usually on the face.

Senna: a flowering plant used medicinally as a laxative. A stimulant, senna should not be used by anyone suffering from high blood pressure and/or heart disease. Available at health food stores.

Shepherd's purse: a medicinal herb that can be used to slow down heavy menstrual periods. Available at most health food stores.

Silica gel crystals: small, round absorbent beads that can be used to dry flowers. Available at art supply stores.

Sitz bath: a bath where only the pelvic area is covered with water. Herbal sitz baths can be used to treat hemorrhoids, menstrual cramps, or anything else that affects this part of the body. You can make your own sitz bath using a plastic basin, warm water, and herbs available at health food stores.

Slurry: a mixture where solids are suspended in water, such as a slurry of fertilizer and water used in gardening.

Soap flakes: small, silky flakes of concentrated vegetable soap used as a natural cleaner. Available at health food stores.

Soapwort: an herb whose crushed leaves can be used as soap or shampoo. Available at health food stores.

Spelt: a species of wheat used for cooking. Available at grocery stores, usually as flour or pasta.

Spelt bag: a fabric bag filled with crushed spelt that can be heated and applied to sore body parts to ease pain. Available at health food stores.

St. John's wort: a flowering medicinal herb used to treat insomnia, depression, and anxiety. Available at pharmacies.

Stinging nettle: a plant whose leaves and stems cause rashes upon contact, but which can be used medicinally when cooked or soaked in water. Available at health food stores.

Stinging nettle slurry: an herbal slurry used in gardening to encourage beneficial insects.

Sulfur bath: a warm, therapeutic bath containing minerals.

Tai chi: a Chinese martial art whose practice can help increase circulation and flexibility, and decrease stress.

Tannins: a substance in tea and red wine that contributes to the taste and coloring of the beverage.

Thalassotherapy: therapeutic bathing in seawater.

Tincture: mix of alcohol (usually vodka), often with natural ingredients such as propolis or arnica.

Tree paint: a mixture of chopped horsetail, water, and clay applied to the bark of trees to protect them.

Turmeric: a strong-smelling, slightly bitter-tasting golden spice also known as curcuma, which is used in South Asian and Middle Eastern cuisine. Available at grocery stores.

Turpentine: a strong-smelling substance that comes from the resin of pine trees, used primarily as a solvent. Available at hardware stores.

Valerian: an herb whose roots can be used medicinally for pain relief and as a sedative. Available at health food stores.

Verbena: a flowering plant which can be used as an herbal tea or, as an essential oil, in fragrances. Available at health food stores.

Violet: a flower used in fragrances or herbal tea. Available at health food stores.

Wedge pillow: a fairly firm, wedge-shaped pillow that can be leaned against or lain on to improve posture, and relieve back pain and other discomforts. Available at some pharmacies.

Wheat germ: a protein- and vitamin-rich part of the wheat kernel used in healthy cooking. Available at health food stores and some grocery stores.

Wheatberries: whole wheat kernels, often used in healthy cooking. Available at health food stores.

Whey: the strained liquid from curdled milk. Whey protein powder is popular among weightlifters. Available at pharmacies and health food stores.

Willow bark: the bark of the willow tree. It can be used to treat headaches and other body pain. Available at health food stores.

Witch hazel: a plant whose bark and leaves can be used in skin care as an astringent. Available at health food stores.

Wood ferns: a plant whose roots can be used medicinally for various ailments. Available at some health food stores.

Wormwood: a bitter-tasting medicinal herb which can be used to treat digestive problems and other ailments. It is also used to produce vermouth. Available at health food stores.

Yarrow wrap: a wrap made with blooms from the yarrow plant to treat cuts and abrasions. Yarrow is available at health food stores or at nurseries.

Yellow sweet clover: a flowering plant that can be used to treat insomnia and fight hypertension. Available at health food stores and nurseries.

Ylang-ylang oil: a floral essential oil from a flowering tree of the same name, commonly used in fragrances. Available at health food stores.

index

Note: "(i)" after a page number indicates an illustration

photo credits

Credits are left to right, top to bottom:

Cover: Rosenfeld/Mauritius Images; RD; RD. **Back cover:** Tom Grill/Getty Images.

10 Masterfile (top); Alamy/Mauritius Images (2); 11 Lazi & Lazi/RD; 12 Yuri Arcurs/Fotalia; 13 David Sacks/Getty Images; Lazi & Lazi/RD (2); 14 Lazi & Lazi/RD (2); Corbis; 15 Tom Grill/Getty Images; West Studios/Mauritius Images; 16 RD/GID; 17 J. McCulloch/Parks Canada; RD/GID; Fotalia; 18 Photodisc; Roger Stowell/Getty Images; 19 Veronique Beranger/Getty Images; Dorling Kindersley/Getty Images; 20 André Pöhlman/Mauritius Images; 21 RD/GID; BAO/imagebroker/Mauritius Images; 22 Busse Yankushev/Mauritius Images; RD/GID; 23 Dorling Kindersley/Getty Images; age/Mauritius Images; 24 Dorling Kindersley/Getty Images; Alamy/Mauritius Images; RD/GID; 25 RD/GID; Alamy/Mauritius; Lazi & Lazi/RD; 26 Alamy/Mauritius Images; RD/GID; 27 RD/GID; Workbookstock/Mauritius Images; 28 Pierre Bourrier/Mauritius Images; RD/GID; Thinkstock; 30 RD/GID; Superstock; 31 RD/GID; Istock; 32 RD/GID; Lazi & Lazi/RD; 33 RD/GID; 34 RD/GID; Lazi & Lazi/RD; 35 Martin Ruegner/Getty Images; 36 Pacific Stock/Mauritius Images; RD/GID; 37 Julie Pigula/Getty Images; Istock; 38 Lazi & Lazi/RD (2); Stock Image/Mauritius Images (left center); 39 Lazi & Lazi/RD; Alamy/Mauritius Images; 40 Blickpunkte/Getty Images; Teubner/Getty Images; 41 BAO/imagebroker/Mauritius Images; Michael Brauner/Getty Images; 42 BAO/imagebroker/Mauritius Images; Brandon Harman/Photonica/Getty Images; 43 Frank Greenaway/Getty Images (2); Rosenfeld/Mauritius Images; 44 Botanica/Mauritius Images; Damir Begovic/Getty Images; 45 Candice Farmer/Getty Images; 46 Zia Soleil/Getty Images; Alamy/Mauritius Images; 47 Sean Justice/Corbis; RD/GID; 48 Photononstop/Mauritius Images; Lazi & Lazi/RD; 49 RD/GID; age/Mauritius Images; 50 Lazi & Lazi/RD; 51 H, Schwarz/Mauritius Images; 52 Lazi & Lazi/Mauritius Images; RD/GID; BAO/imagebroker/Mauritius Images; 53 Shutterstock; RD/GID; 54 BAO/imagebroker/Mauritius Images; Linda Whitwam/Getty Images; 55 Lazi & Lazi/RD; Fotalia; 56 RD/GID; Ulrich Kerth/Getty Images; 57 Rolf Bruderer/Corbis; Ulrich Kerth/Getty Images; 58 Superstock/Mauritius Images; Photodisc; 59 Alamy/Mauritiums Images; 60 Michael Rosenfeld/Getty Images; DreamPictures/Getty Images; 61 Altrendo/Getty Images; Peter von Felbert/Getty Images; BAO/imagebroker/Mauritius Images; 62 Food and Drink/Mauritius Images; 63 Milka/Corbis; RD/GID; Profimedia/Mauritius; 64 Phototake/Mauritius; Ypps/Mauritius Images; 65 Westend61/Mauritius Images; André Pöhlmann/Mauritius Images; 66 Andreas Schätzle/Mauritius Images; Michael Rosenfeld/Mauritius Images (bottom); 68 Istock; Erwin Rachbauer/Mauritius Images; 69 B.Boissonnet/BSIP//Corbis; Busse Yankushev/Mauritius Images; 70 Lazi & Lazi/RD; 71 Estelle Klawitter/Corbis; BAO/imagebroker/Mauritius Images; 72 Lazi &Lazi/RD; 74 Lifestock/Getty Images; 75 Phototake/ Mauritius Images; Urbanlip/Mauritius Images; 76 Pierre Bourrier/Mauritius; 77, 78 Lazi & Lazi/RD (2); 79 Anthony Marsland/Getty Images; 80-81 Lazi & Lazi/RD; 81 Mindbodysoul/Mauritius Images; Imagebroker/Maruitius; 82 Karin Skogstad/Mauritius Images; 83 Nikky/Mauritius Images; 84 Matthias Schlief/Mauritius Images; 84-85 Lazi & Lazi/RD; 85 RD/GID; 86 Dave King/Getty Images (background); PhotoAlto; A1Pix; 87 Lazi & Lazi/RD(2); 88 RD/GID; 88-89 Rosenfeld/Mauritius Images; 89 SELF/Mauritius Images; 90 Alamy/Mauritius; 90 Alamy/Mauritius Images; 91 Lazi & Lazi/RD; Alamy/Mauritius Images (background); RD/GID; 92 Lazi & Lazi/RD; 93 Alamy/Mauritius Images; Pierre Bourrier/Mauritius Images; 94 Baumann/Mauritius Images; 95 RD/GID (2); Alain Schroeder/Getty Images; 97 Garden Picture Library/Mauritius; Alexander Kupka/Mauritius Images; 98 RD/GID; Garcia/Corbis; Doug Sokell/Getty Images; 99 RD/GID; 100 Pierre Bourrier/Mauritius Images; Lew Robertson/Getty Images; 101 Alamy/Mauritius Images; Foodpix/Mauritius Images; 102 Inga Spence/Getty Images (top); Lazi & Lazi/RD; 103 Don Klump/Getty Images; PhotoAlto; 104 RD/GID (2); 105 Phovoir; Lazi & Lazi/RD; 106 Karayo/Mauritius Images; Lazi & Lazi/RD; 107 Istock; Shuji Kobayashi/Corbis; 108 Daniel Bosler/Getty Images; 109 Turner Forte/Botanica/Mauritius Images; Foodpix/Mauritius Images; 110 Alfred Saerchinger/Corbis; Nora Frei/Mauritius Images; 111 RD/GID; Lazi & Lazi/RD; 112 Nora Frei/Mauritius Images; age/Mauritius Images; 113 Lazi & Lazi/RD (right); Ralf Schultheiss/Getty Images; 114 Dorling Kindersley/Getty Images; 114-115 Michael Keller/Corbis; 115 John Curtis/Mauritius; 116-117 Masterfile; 118 Brad Simmons/Esto; 119 Lazi & Lazi/RD (2); 120 Elizabeth Whiting & Associates/Corbis; 121 Istock; Lazi & Lazi/RD; 122 Laurence Dutton/Getty Images; 123 Lazi & Lazi/Mauritius Images; Michael Jaeger/imagebroker/Mauritius; 124 Jonathan Knowles/Getty Images; Fancy; RD/GID; 126 Andrew Bordwin/Corbis; 127 pepperprint/Mauritius Images; RD/GID; 128 Chris Harvey/Getty Images;129 imagebroker/Mauritius Images; RD/GID; 130 Corbis; 131 Matthew Ward/Getty Images; Photo courtesy California Closet Company Inc.; 132 Westend61/Mauritius Images; 133 David Papazian/Corbis; Lazi & Lazi/RD(2); 134 Jochen Tack/imagebroker/Mauritius Images; 135 Photodisc; Busse Yankushev/Mauritius Images; 136 Turbo/Corbis (top); Ripp/Mauritius Images; 137 Marina Jefferson/Getty Images; Neo Vision/Getty Images; Masterfile; 138 Lazi & Lazi/RD; 139 Solus/Veer/Corbis; Roger Charity/Mauritius; 140 Lazi & Lazi/RD(top); Jamie Grill/Getty 141 Boris Kumicak/Mauritius Images; 141 Lazi & Lazi/RD; 142 Cristo Rich/Mauritius Images; 143 Lazi & Lazi/RD; 144 Haag & Kropp/Mauritius Images; Lazi & Lazi/RD; 144-145 123 Royalty Free; 146 Shutterstock; Britt Erlanson/Getty Images; 147 Shutterstock; Lazi & Lazi/RD; 148 Fotalia (top); Lazi & Lazi/RD; 149 Jesco Tscholitsch/Getty Images; Fernando Bengoechea/Corbis; 150 altrendo images/Getty Images (top); PhotoAlto; 151 PhotoAlto; Lazi & Lazi/RD; 152 Lazi & Lazi/RD; 153 Flora/Mauritius; 154 Andy Whale/Getty; 155 RD/GID; 156 Shinya Saskai/Getty Images; 157 Lazi & Lazi/RD; 158 Lazi & Lazi/RD; 159 Brigitte Protzel/Mauritius Images (background); Elizabeth Simpson/Mauritius Images; RD/GID(right); 160 James Mitchell/Corbis; 161 Corbis; 162 Lazi & Lazi/RD; Fancy; 163 IPS Co./Corbis; Hans-Peter Merten/Mauritius; 164 Lazi & Lazi/RD; 165 James Cotier/Getty Images; 166 Lazi & Lazi/RD; 166-167 Catherine Ledner/Getty Images; 167 Blend Images/Getty Images; 168 Roger Charity/Getty Images; 169 Shutterstock; Ulrich Kerth/Getty Images; 170-171 Getty Images; 172 Foodpix/Mauritius Images(top); RD/GID; 173 Michael Rosenfeld/Getty Images; Angie Norwood Browne/Getty Images; 174 Alamy/Mauritius; 175

GAP/Mauritius Images; 176 Hussenot/Corbis; Peter Rathman/Mauritius Images; 177 Lukas Creter/Getty Images; RD; 178 Tom Grill/Getty Images; Michael Rosenfeld/Getty Images; 179 RD; 180 Stock Food Canada/Maxx Images; Busse Yankushev/Mauritius Images (background) 181 RD; Stock Food Canada/Maxx Images; Dorling Kindersely/Getty Images; 182-183 age/Mauritius Images; 183 Pedro Perez/Mauritius Images; RD/GID; 184 Lazi & Lazi/RD; RD; Roulier Turiot/Corbis; 185 RD/GID; 186 Josef Kuchibauer/Mauitius Images; 187 Busse Yankushev/Mauritius Images; RD; 188 Westend61/Mauritius Images; 188-189 RD; 189-190 RD; 191 Dorling Kindersley/Getty Images; Johner/Getty Images (background); RD/GID; Fotalia; 192 Yellow Dog Productions/Getty Images; 192-193 PhotoAlto; 193 Chris Everard/Getty Images; Fred Hirschmann; Margaret Savino; 194 RD; Tom Grill/Getty Images; 195 RD; 196 Dorling Kindersley/Mauritius Images(background); Katsutoshi Hatsuzawa/Getty Images; 197 Dorling Kindersley/Getty Images; Göttfert Küchentechnik; 198 RD; 199 RD (2); Istock; 200, 214 RD/GID; 215 Michael Rosenfeld/Getty Images; RD(2); Johner/Getty Images(background); 216 Lew Robertson/Getty Images; Boris Kumicak/Mauritius Images; 217 RD/GID; Lazi & Lazi/RD; 218-219 RD; 220 RD; 220-221 Michael Rosenfeld/Getty Images; 221 Alexander Feig/Getty Images; Food and Drink/Mauritius Images; 222-223 Peter Oppenländer/Mauritius Images; 223 Manceau/photocuisine/Corbis; RD/GID (center); B.Norris/photocuisine/Corbis; 224 Fancy/Alamy; Lew Robertson/Getty Images; 225 Flora/Mauritius Images; Photodisc; 226 Y.Bagros/photocuisine/Corbis; Lazi & Lazi/RD; 227 Istock; Lazi & Lazi/RD (right); Alamy/Mauritius Images; 228-229 Datacraft/Getty Images; 230 Amanda Turner/Getty Images; 231 Matthew Ward/Getty Images; RD/GID (right); Istock; 232 AAGAMIA/Getty Images; 232-233 Biber Versand; 233 Veer/Corbis; 234 Gerhard Steiner/Corbis; 235 Lazi & Lazi/RD; 236 Alice Edward/Getty Images; 237 Quickimage/Mauritius Images; Stockphoto Pro; 238 Lazi & Lazi/RD; Tim Ridley/Getty Images; 239 Istock; 240 Andy Crawford/Getty Images (right); 240-241 William Geddes/Corbis; 242 Bieke Claessens/Getty Images; 243 altrendo travel/Getty Images; George B. Diebold/Corbis; 244 Maxx Images; Friedrich Strauss/Getty Images; 245 Flora/Mauritius Images; Gisela Caspersen/Brigitte/Picture Press; RD/GID/; 246 Bieke Claessens/Getty Images; 247 Flora/Mauritius Images; RD/GID; 248, 249 Lennox Hearth Products; 250 Neo Vision/Getty Images; Studio Tom Kinsbergen/Corbis; 251 Envison/Corbis; RD/GID; 252 Clay Perry/Corbis; Lazi & Lazi/RD; 253 Gregor Schuster/Corbis; RD/GID; 254 Angelika Klein/arturimages; 255 Maax Bath Inc.; Istock; 256 Fotalia; Abode/Corbis; 257 bildagentur-online; Istock; 258 Tips Images/f1online; 259 Firefly Productions/Corbis; 260 Richard Leo Johnson/Corbis; Rodney Hyett; Elizabeth Whiting & Associates/Corbis; 261 Steve Gorton/Getty Images; Mark Lund/Getty Images; Abode/Corbis 262 Busse Yankushev/Mauitius Images(background); Fotalia; 263 Istock; 264 Studio Tom Kinsbergen/Corbis; 265 Dreamstime/GetStock; Beautiful/Corbis; 266 Marie Krausova Mauritius Images; 267picture-alliance/Flora Press; Patrick Moynihan/Getty Images; 268 Lazi & Lazi/RD; redclover.com/Getty Images; Gabi Zimmermann/ Jahreszeiten Verlag; Helge Mundt/Jahreszeiten Verlag; 270 Stefan Thurmann/Picture Press; 271 Heinrich Heine GmbH; 272 Konstantin Eulenburg/Brigitte/Picture Press; 273 Heike Schroede/Schoener Wohnen/Picture Press; 274 Jeremy Samuleson/Getty Images; 275 Masterfile; RD; 276 Dana Hoff/Corbis; 277 Hunter Fan Company; Bloomimage/Corbis; 278 Jonas von der Hude/Living at Home/Picture Press; 279 Lazi & Lazi/RD; Chemistry/Getty Images; 280 Dorling Kindersley; 281 Russ Widstrand/Corner House Stock; 282 Ginette Chapman/Getty Images; 283 Friedrich Strauss; RD/GID; Karyn Millet/Getty Images (right); 284-285 Lee Avison/Getty Images; 286 Peter Anderson/Getty Images; RD/GID; Friedrich Strauss; 287 Klaus Hackenberg/Mauritius Images; Friedrich Strauss; Taurus/Mauritius Images (background); 288 Friedrich Strauss; 288-289 Reinhard-Tierfoto; 289 RD/GID; 290 Jeff O'Brien/Mauritius Images; Friedrich Strauss; 291 Friedrich Strauss; Massimo Listri/Corbis; 292 Friedrich Strauss; PhotoAlto; 293 RD/GID; Steven Wooster/Getty Images; 294 Friedrich Strauss; Photodisc; 295 Peter Anderson/Dorling Kindersley/Getty Images; RD/GID; 296 Turbo/Corbis; 297 Nigel Catlin/Getty Images; Alamy/Mauritius Images; Robert Knoll/Mauritius Images; Nigel Catlin/Getty Images; 298 Craig Knowles/Getty Images; Michael Peuker/Mauritius Images; H. Schwarz/Mauritius Image; 299 Friedrich Strauss; Rosenfeld/Mauritius Images; 300 Ephraim Ben-Shimon/Corbis; Boris Kumicak/Mauritius Images; 301 Lazi & Lazi/RD; 302 Bryan Mullennix/Getty Images; 302-303 Dorling Kindersley/Getty Images; 303 Hans Reinhard/Mauritius Images; 304 Thinkstock; Greg Ryan/Sally Beyer/Getty Images; 305 Photodisc (top); Friedrich Strauss; RD/GID; 306 Friedrich Strauss; 307 RD/GID (2); Friedrich Strauss; 308 Cash/Mauritius Images; RD/GID; 309 Jutta Klee/Getty Images; Janet Davis; 310 JIRI/Mauritius Images; Chrile/Mauritius Images; 311 Norman Jung/Corbis; Rosenfeld/Mauritius Images; 312 David Murray; 312-313 Rudolf Schmidt/Mauritius Images; 313 Friedrich Strauss; altrendo images/Getty Images; 314 Klaus Scholz/Mauritius Images; 315 Jeff O'Brien/Mauritius Images; Friedrich Strauss; 316 Friedrich Strauss; 317 Istock; Friedrich Strauss; 318 RD/GID; 319 RD/GID; Garden Picture Library/Mauritius Images; 320 Lazi & Lazi/RD; 321 Friedrich Strauss; 322 Dave King/Dorling Kindersley/Getty Images; Friedrich Strauss; 323 Friedrich Strauss; 324 RD/GID (2); Friedrich Strauss; / 325 Friedrich Strauss; Lazi & Lazi/RD; 326-327 Friedrich Strauss; 328 Hans Reinhard/Corbis; 328-329 Michael Boys/Corbis; 329 RD/GID; Peter Anderson/Dorling Kindersley/Getty Images; 330 Bob Rowan/Corbis; 330-331 Michael Melford/Getty Images; Lazi & Lazi/RD; 332 Lazi & Lazi/RD; 333 RD/GID; Friedrich Strauss; 334 Lazi & Lazi/RD; Mark Bolton/Corbis; 335 Dave King/Getty Images; Maxine Adcock/Getty Images; 336 DJV/Bildportal/Reinhard-Tierfoto; FhF Greenmedia/Getty Images; 338 Andy Sotiriou/Getty Images; Lester Lefkowitz/Getty Images; 339 Photo Researchers/Mauritius Images; Klaus Scholz; RD/GID; 340 FhF Greenmedia/Getty Images; 340-341 DJV/Bildportal/Reinhard-Tierfoto; 341 Busse Yankushev/Mauritius Images (right); Peter Anderson/Dorling Kindersley/Getty Images; 342 RD/GID (top); Friedrich Strauss; 343 Janet Davis; Friedrich Strauss;

Glossary: All photos are RD/GID, except: Almond Bran 344 Dreamstime/GetStock; Henna 345 Dreamstime/GetStock; Wedge pillow 347 courtesy Brookstone; Ylang-ylang 347 Dreamstime/GetStock;